The Lavender Scare

The Lavender Scare

*The Cold War Persecution of Gays
and Lesbians in the Federal Government*

David K. Johnson

The University of Chicago Press ★ *Chicago and London*

The University of Chicago Press, Chicago 60637
The University of Chicago Press, Ltd., London
© 2004 by David K. Johnson
All rights reserved. Published 2004
Paperback edition 2006
Printed in the United States of America

19 18 17 16 15 14 13 12 11 10   5 6 7 8 9

ISBN-13: 978-0-226-40481-3 (cloth)
ISBN-13: 978-0-226-40190-4 (paper)
ISBN-10: 0-226-40481-1 (cloth)
ISBN-10: 0-226-40190-1 (paper)

Frontispiece: Senator Kenneth Wherry (courtesy of the Senate Historical Office)

Portions of this book appeared previously as "'Homosexual Citizens': Washington's Gay Community Confronts the Civil Service," *Washington History* 6 (fall/winter 1994–95).

Library of Congress Cataloging-in-Publication Data

Johnson, David K.
    The lavender scare : the Cold War persecution of gays and lesbians in the
    federal government / David K. Johnson.
        p. cm.
    Includes bibliographical references and index.
    ISBN 0-226-40481-1 (alk. paper)
        1. Gays—Employment—United States.   2. Civil Service—Minority
    employment—United States.   3. Cold War.   I. Title
    JK723.H6 J64 2004
    352.6'086'640973—dc21
                                                                            2003009138

♾ The paper used in this publication meets the minimum requirements of the
American National Standard for Information Sciences—Permanence of Paper for
Printed Library Materials, ANSI Z39.48-1992.

To my parents, Kenneth and Julia Johnson

Contents

Acknowledgments

This project began over a decade ago in a dusty attic in Washington, D.C. As a historian working for History Associates, Inc., a public history consulting firm, I had volunteered to compile a history of the Gay and Lesbian Activists Alliance, a local civil rights organization, on the occasion of its twentieth anniversary. During my research, one of the group's founding members, Frank Kameny, ushered me up into his attic, where I discovered a cache of boxes filled with onionskin paper, mimeographed flyers, and yellowing newspaper clippings. This private collection documented an even older gay and lesbian rights organization that Kameny had founded in 1961, a few years after he was fired from the federal civil service because of his homosexuality. Kameny had saved copies of virtually every piece of correspondence of the Mattachine Society of Washington. On top of it all sat the simple, black-and-white, hand-lettered signs that a small group of Mattachine members had carried in front of the White House in 1965 to protest their exclusion from federal employment—one of the first gay pickets in U.S. history. Why had the federal government dismissed Kameny and thousands of other gay and lesbian civil servants as security risks?

How had they organized to oppose and ultimately overturn this policy? With my historical curiosity piqued, I began the research that ultimately resulted in *The Lavender Scare*. Above all, this project is indebted to Frank Kameny—to his tenacious activism and his profound appreciation for preserving the historical record.

With the support of the Gay and Lesbian Education Fund of Washington, D.C., I recorded a series of oral history interviews with Kameny and other early Mattachine members. I presented papers at the Washington, D.C., Historical Studies Conference and the Lesbian and Gay Studies Conference at Rutgers University. Mark Sullivan at the *Washington Blade* and Jane Levey, editor of *Washington History*, provided me with the opportunity to publish some of my early findings and taught me much about historical writing. With support and encouragement from historians Philip Cantelon, Jonathan D. Katz, Barbara Kraft, Jan Goldstein, and Kenneth Bowling, I received a University Fellowship from the Graduate School at Northwestern University.

As the project transformed from a community-based history project into a dissertation for Northwestern's Department of History, I benefited from the advice and support of numerous scholars. I am particularly indebted to Michael Sherry, my thesis advisor, who supported the project and pushed me to think about it in new ways. His help with issues intellectual and practical, as well as his wise and patient counsel, sustained me throughout the project. Nancy MacLean, Henry Binford, Lane Fenrich, and Alex Owen offered a helpful mix of encouragement and thoughtful criticism. George Chauncey and John D'Emilio provided not only the important example of their scholarship but also intellectual and professional support. Fellow Chicago-area graduate students Chad Heap, Wallace Best, Gabriel Gomez, Karen Leroux, Marisa Chappell, Charlotte Brooks, Brett Gadsden, and Mitchell Stevens gave me an intellectual home. Jeffrey Merrick, James Green, Marc Stein, Allida Black, Brett Beemyn, and other members of the Committee on Lesbian and Gay History provided opportunities to present my work and receive helpful feedback.

While researching and writing, I was fortunate to have the financial support of several scholarly institutions. Thanks to Harry Rubenstein and the Smithsonian Institution Predoctoral Fellowship Program, I spent six months at the Museum of American History and conducted research at the National Archives, Library of Congress, and other Washington research facilities. Given the political attacks on other federal agencies that supported projects with gay and lesbian content, this support was particularly courageous. The Lyndon Baines Johnson Foundation and the Harry S. Truman Library Institute funded crucial research trips to their respective presidential libraries. The Northwestern University Research Grants Committee supported a research trip to the Dwight D. Eisenhower Library. Generous support from the Social Science Research Council Sexuality Research Fellowship Program, funded by the Ford Foundation, gave me the opportunity to conduct research at collections focusing on the history of sexuality, including the Kinsey Institute, the New York Public Library, and the International Gay and Lesbian Archive in Los Angeles. The SSRC fellowship, coupled with a dissertation-year fellowship from the Graduate School at Northwestern University, allowed me time to write. While completing the final manuscript, I enjoyed the support of a CLAGS Fellowship from the Center for Lesbian and Gay Studies at the Graduate Center of the City University of New York.

The archivists and librarians at the many repositories where I conducted research provided invaluable assistance. Marty McGann and Kenneth Heger at the National Archives in College Park, Maryland, were particularly instrumental in helping me access federal government records, especially those of the U.S. State Department. Their expert knowledge and enthusiastic support enriched this project immeasurably. Rodd Ross at the Center for Legislative Archives provided important help with congressional records, including the previously unreleased files of the 1950 Hoey committee. I also want to thank John Haynes at the Library of Congress, Dennis Bilger at the Harry S. Truman Library, David Haight at the Dwight D. Eisenhower Library, Willie Walker and Susan Stryker at the Gay and Lesbian Historical Society of Northern California, Kath Pennavaria at the Kinsey Institute, and Matthew Gilmore, Roxanna Deane, and Peggy Appleman at the Washingtonian Division of the District of Columbia Public Library.

I owe a special debt to the men and women who shared with me their personal experiences of the Lavender Scare. Jack Nichols, Frank Kameny, Bruce Scott, and Madeleine Tress were particularly helpful in sharing their time, their private archival collections, and their friendship. I am also indebted to Chuck Bradshaw, Joan Cassidy, Jack Fry, Ramon G., David Jenkins, Peter Morris, Ted Richards, John Swanson, Lilli Vincenz, and many others I interviewed, some of whom chose to remain anonymous. Their courage and honesty is underscored by the reticence of many other men and women whom I contacted who experienced the Lavender Scare but chose not to share their stories. I thank Peter Schott, Elspeth Brown, Chad Heap, and the Metropolitan Retirees group for providing important leads in my search for men and women to interview about 1950s Washington.

Many historians and academic colleagues offered advice and support of various kinds as I completed this project. I particularly want to thank

Edward Alwood, Kenneth Bowling, Bob Bruegmann, Christopher Carrington, David DeLeon, James Green, Leonard Hirsch, Jonathan Katz, Barbara Kraft, Brian Martin, Dwight McBride, Margaret Rung, and Sara Vaux. My many friends in Washington, D.C., provided encouragement, diversion, and even lodging, especially Paul Albergo, Cris Arocho, David Bass, Jeff Coudriet, Robert Rokusek, Eric Salmon, and Paul Sliwka. Chris Bull and Hans Johnson provided the perfect setting for me to think about the relationship between the gay and lesbian community and American politics. The kindness of David Smith and Lenny Garcia-Duran allowed me to conduct research in Austin, Texas. In Chicago, I have depended on many friends and mentors, especially Steven Anderson, Craig Foley, Jim Beal, Steven Correll, Michael Baeur, Bob Cichocki, Chris DeChant, Allen Lungo, and Jay Pinkert. From my first days in the city, John Russell and Dan Nona have been the most supportive of friends. I might never have finished without the support of Toby Causby, Gabriel Gomez, Mark Peco, and Paul Shahbaz.

Special thanks go to Lane Fenrich, Gabriel Gomez, Barbara Kraft, Leisa Meyer, Jay Pinkert, and Geoffrey Smith for reading the entire manuscript and helping me shape it into a more successful book. Michael Sherry and Wallace Best provided crucial input on final drafts. Doug Mitchell, editor at the University of Chicago Press, was an indefatigable supporter of this project long before it took on the shape of a book. I am indebted to him and the entire team of professionals at the University of Chicago Press that shepherded the book through production, especially Tim McGovern, Christine Schwab, and Erin Hogan, and copyeditor Nick Murray.

My parents, Kenneth and Julia Johnson, have been continually supportive, even when they were not quite sure they understood what I hoped to accomplish. Finally, I thank Willard Dumas, who, more than anyone, has shared with me both the excitement and the traumas of bringing this book to completion. He has been a constant champion of the project and its importance to U.S. history. Our time together reminds me why it all matters.

Introduction

"Panic on the Potomac"

In February 1950, two statements by U.S. government officials concerning security risks in the State Department captured national attention. One has come to be seen as a pivotal moment in American history—the Wheeling, West Virginia, speech that catapulted Senator Joseph McCarthy (R–Wisconsin) into the national limelight and gave the era its name. In that speech McCarthy made the inflammatory claim that 205 card-carrying Communists were working for the State Department. The other statement, though in part a response to McCarthy's continuing charges about subversives in the State Department, has been all but forgotten. Appearing before a congressional committee, Deputy Undersecretary John Peurifoy denied that the department employed any actual Communists. At the same time, however, he revealed that a number of persons considered to be security risks had been forced out, and that among these were ninety-one homosexuals. Rather than see the revelation as evidence of an effective security system, many interpreted it as proof that the State Department—perhaps the entire government—was infiltrated with sexual perverts. Members of Congress demanded to know who hired the ninety-one, whether they found jobs in other government departments, and if there were any more. Seeming to confirm McCarthy's charges about subversives in the State Department, Peurifoy's revelation prompted concern and outrage throughout the nation, heated debates on the floors of Congress, congressional committee investigations, countless newspaper articles, and numerous White House meetings. It eventually led to the ouster of thousands of government employees. It marked the beginnings of a Lavender Scare.[1]

In 1950, many politicians, journalists, and citizens thought that homosexuals posed more of a threat to national security than Communists. One Pulitzer prize–winning columnist argued, "There is no record of comparable corruption in American history." In a national radio broadcast, liberal Elmer Davis noted, "It looks as if the enemies of the State Department, and of the administration generally, have gotten hold of a more profitable issue than communism." In one of many debates on the Senate floor that year, Senator Kenneth Wherry (R–Nebraska) asked his colleagues, "Can [you] think of a person who could be more dangerous to the United States of America than a pervert?" Three of President Harry Truman's top advisors wrote him a joint memorandum warning that "the country is more concerned about the charges of homosexuals in the Government than about Communists." Constituents writing to members of Congress confirmed this analysis. "Many of them tell me," Representative Clare Hoffman (R–Michigan) told his colleagues, "they are concerned before they get to the issue of communism or loyalty with this issue of morality and decency." By November, what some journalists derided as the "panic on the Potomac" and some politicians defended as the "purge of the perverts" resulted in the dismissal of nearly six hundred federal civil servants. In the State Department alone, security officials boasted that on average they were firing one homosexual per day, more than double the rate for those suspected of political disloyalty.[2]

Beyond McCarthy

Despite the concern, even hysteria, at the time, and the many people affected, historians of the McCarthy era have given stunningly little attention to the Lavender Scare. Political historians of McCarthyism, anticommunism, and the rise of the national security state emphasize the role of partisan politics and foreign policy, and minimize moral and cultural concerns. If they mention the Lavender Scare at all, they portray it as a minor byproduct of the Red Scare, one so seemingly natural and inevitable as to need no explanation.[3] Even the most recent studies of McCarthyism, both defenses from the Right and critiques from the Left, all but ignore how the

fears of Communists and homosexuals overlapped. In the 1950s many Mc-
Carthy supporters viewed the wholesale purge of homosexuals from the
State Department and other government agencies as McCarthy's vindicat-
ing legacy; with rare exceptions, however, neither new apologists for Mc-
Carthy nor those documenting the devastation he caused acknowledge the
Lavender Scare.[4] While the historical literature about the McCarthy era fo-
cuses on the hunt for Communists and headline-grabbing cases such as
those of Alger Hiss and Owen Lattimore, most of those fired as "security
risks" were not those named by Senator McCarthy as Communists. The
typical case involved a homosexual confronted with circumstantial evidence that he had associated with "known homosexuals" or been arrested
in a known gay cruising area. Almost all those accused quietly resigned
rather than risk further publicity.

The lack of attention in historical scholarship to the Lavender Scare—as
well as the lack of popular memory about it—cannot be attributed simply
to a lack of concern for homosexuals. Methodological and interpretive
problems have contributed to this oversight. Both the popular imagination
and the historiography of 1950s witch-hunting focus on the role of Senator
Joseph McCarthy. Even gay people who lived in D.C. in the 1950s and
watched the purges unfold attributed them to McCarthy, who was the first
major politician to publicly suggest that there were homosexuals in the
government and that they posed a risk to national security. His speeches often made passing references to "Communists and queers," and certainly
the political climate of fear and accusation he spawned fed these purges.
But McCarthy was not the principal backer of the homosexual purges. After his initial round of publicity in early 1950, he essentially dropped the
subject of homosexuals in the State Department. As one political commentator remarked, "When he started his probe he didn't know about the homosexual angle. Now, he's uncertain what to do about it." Despite pressure
from other Republican leaders who felt that such charges were creating
"more of a stir," McCarthy was not involved in any of the congressional investigations or hearings into homosexuals in government. Though he was
a member of the congressional committee that spent several months ex-
amining the homosexuals-in-government issue, McCarthy mysteriously
recused himself from those hearings. The press suggested he did not want
to be in the position of judging his own accusations. A knowledgeable observer at the time suggested that he did not pursue the "homosexual angle"
more aggressively because he was afraid of a boomerang. As an unmarried, middle-aged man, he was subject to gossip and rumor about his own
sexuality. So it fell to McCarthy's more senior colleagues such as Senators
Styles Bridges, Kenneth Wherry, and Clyde Hoey to press the issue more

aggressively. Whatever the reason for his reticence, turning the spotlight on McCarthy tends, paradoxically, to keep the antigay purges in the shadows.[5]

To attribute the purges to McCarthy serves to marginalize them historically. It suggests that they were the product of a uniquely unscrupulous demagogue, did not enjoy widespread support, and were not part of mainstream conservatism or the Republican Party. Much of the scholarship on McCarthy uses his attacks on homosexuals as evidence of his incompetence and lack of focus. This was a favorite tactic of the few 1950s journalists critical of McCarthy's methods. According to one of the more in-depth critiques, when things were not going well for him in early 1950, "McCarthy had an inspiration: sex was the answer to all his problems. Not plain, old-fashioned sex, of course, but homosexuality. If the facts about Communists were missing, why not substitute fairy tales?"[6] A critically acclaimed 1959 biography referred to the "bedlam quality" of McCarthy's speeches and pondered, "Could anything but sheer lunacy lead a man discussing eighty-one Communists to say that one of the Communists was an important example because he was not a Communist?" As McCarthy explained during that speech, the non-Communist was important precisely because he illustrated the "rather unusual mental aberrations" of State Department employees, aberrations that led to both sexual and political deviance. Historian Robert Griffith also used McCarthy's homosexual cases to discredit him, lumping them with cases where there was no evidence of misconduct, or ones which were skipped over, forgotten, or misnumbered. Although these commentators fault McCarthy for straying from the presumed central target of Communists, several of McCarthy's fellow Republicans urged him at the time to focus more on homosexuals and other "security risks," since they were more numerous and easier to uncover. For months during the Senate committee investigation into McCarthy's charges, a team of Republican leaders attempted to shift the focus from Communists to homosexuals, but such efforts are mostly overlooked in the extensive literature on McCarthy and his tactics.[7]

The association of the antigay purges with McCarthy not only serves to marginalize them but also suggests that they lasted only as long as McCarthy's tenure in the spotlight—from his Wheeling, West Virginia, speech in February 1950 until his censure by the Senate in December 1954. It ignores how the purges predated McCarthy, became institutionalized within the federal loyalty/security system, and continued to be standard government policy until the 1970s. Republican members of Congress began to express concerns about homosexuals in the State Department in 1947, at the very onset of the Cold War with the Soviet Union. With the rise of McCarthy in 1950, their concerns became public and sparked a moral panic within both popular and political discourse. After several congressional investigations, the homosexuals-in-government issue largely fell out of the headlines. Because opposition to the antigay campaigns was so limited, and because no fired gay employee stood up and challenged his dismissal until 1957, the press lost interest. There were no dramatic confrontations between congressional committees and accused homosexuals, as there were with accused Communists, to capture the nation's attention. Such encounters occurred not under the Klieg lights of a Capitol Hill hearing room, but in private, cramped, non-air-conditioned security interrogation rooms throughout Washington. While newsreels from the period capture members of Congress asking the famous question, "Are you now or have you ever been a member of the Communist Party?" another question was posed at least as frequently, if more discreetly: "Information has come to the attention of the Civil Service Commission that you are a homosexual. What comment do you care to make?" Though newspaper coverage diminished, the purges continued. The lessening of publicity after 1950 is not a testament to the lack of antigay efforts but to their routinization and institutionalization in the bureaucracy of the national security state.

The Euphemism "Security Risk"

The lack of attention to the antigay campaigns by historians cannot be attributed to a lack of public discussion at the time. There is a common assumption that sexual issues were not discussed in newspapers and other popular media outlets in the 1950s. Even knowledgeable people who lived through the McCarthy era claim that they never saw mention of homosexuality in their newspapers, suggesting that "the subject was still under wraps in those days."[8] Though some media outlets were reticent to discuss the topic directly and took refuge in euphemism and innuendo, the 1950s generally witnessed a tremendous upsurge in publicity about "sexual perverts." News coverage was particularly heavy in the spring of 1950, in the wake of the Peurifoy revelation, when homosexuality first became a national political issue and members of Congress were calling for investigations. Although the Washington, D.C., papers carried the most extensive coverage of the Lavender Scare, small-town newspapers carried it as well. When a Michigan congressman referred to homosexuals as "the unmentionables," a colleague asked, "Oh, you mean the people that Dr. Miller has talked about so much on the floor [of the House of Representatives]?" "Yes," the congressman replied, complaining about the effect such publicity was having on his reputation among his constituents. "When they begin to publish it in the newspapers, my folks want to know who I am associating with down here and how long they are going to keep those fellows on the payroll." The issue was so frequently discussed on the Senate and House floors that one congressman lamented, "I do not know what homosexuals are, but I never saw anybody get as much free advertising in the Congress of the United States in all my life." Columnist Robert C. Ruark considered the newspaper coverage so extensive as to constitute a watershed in the history of journalism. For the first time, he suggested, "it is possible to face the problem of homosexuality and perversion with the same honesty it took us so long to win in the case of venereal disease." In July 1950 *New York Post* columnist Max Lerner published a twelve-part series entitled "'Scandal' in the State Department." It remains the most extensive treatment of the Lavender Scare in print. Though reticence about sexual matters may have limited coverage in some situations, there is no dearth of materials from the 1950s detailing the issue of homosexuals in government.[9]

Although much newspaper coverage of the purges was explicit, some was cryptic, resorting to coded language that must be carefully interpreted by historians. One 1953 story from the *Buffalo Evening News*, for example, was devoted entirely to the perceived problem of homosexuals in the State Department yet never used the words "homosexual" or "sexual pervert"— the favored terms in the 1950s for men and women attracted to members of their own sex. It referred instead only to "men of unconventional morality" whose "habits make them especially vulnerable to blackmail." Citing Alfred Kinsey's studies, the article noted that men who have this "weakness" or exhibit these "peculiarities" constitute between 4 and 8 percent of the population. It even quoted testimony by a State Department undersecretary explaining to Congress why the foreign service was particularly attractive to "such individuals," referring vaguely to "morals problems." An informed reader in 1953, aware of the homosexual scandal in the department, would have known precisely what the article was about. Today, a reader unaware of this historical background might not be able to decipher its code.[10]

Often the explicitness of the homosexual references was determined less by the propriety or reticence of the publisher than by his political leanings. Conservative periodicals seeking to embarrass the Democratic administration delighted in raising the possibility that the federal civil service, which had ballooned during the Roosevelt and Truman administrations, was brimming with homosexuals. More liberal supporters of Truman often tried to downplay the Republican charges of perversion. This is most clear in the way in which the press covered Secretary of State Dean Acheson's defense of his department against Republican charges of both disloyalty and immorality in the ranks. In an often-quoted endorsement of his employees, Acheson characterized them as "honorable, loyal, and clean-living American men and women." Practically every historical survey of the McCarthy period includes Acheson's defense of his staff, but none bothers to explain why he felt compelled to defend their morality as well as their loyalty. Although Acheson's comments clearly addressed charges of both political and sexual deviance, his language was vague enough to allow for interpretation. The capital's leading daily newspaper, the *Washington Times-Herald*, controlled by arch conservative Robert R. McCormick of the *Chicago Tribune*, took the opportunity to remind its readers that the "clean-living" reference "apparently referred to charges the State Department is a hotbed of homosexuality." The more neutral *New York Times* provided context by citing Senator Karl E. Mundt's recollection about ninety-one employees "discharged as homosexuals." Liberal allies of the administration focused on the loyalty portion of the statement. The *Washington Daily News*, for example, ignored Acheson's reference to morality and noted only that he "rejected charges of communism in the State Department" and was confident about the "loyalty" and "qualifications" of his associates. Like other Truman allies, such papers preferred not to call attention to the homosexual charges. Although each newspaper put an interpretive spin on Acheson's statement—either by highlighting how it addressed the homosexual charges or by ignoring them—the conservative press more accurately reflected the dual nature of the secretary's defense and the close relationship in 1950s political culture between morality and loyalty. Much of the historiography of McCarthyism follows, wittingly or unwittingly, the more liberal stance of downplaying or ignoring the morality issue.[11]

The problem of vague language has complicated the issue of chronicling the Lavender Scare. When not referred to directly as homosexuals or sex perverts, such persons were often called "moral weaklings," "sexual misfits," "moral risks," "misfits," "undesirables," or persons with "unusual morals." But the most slippery and euphemistic term of all was "security risk." Although many people at the time and many historians since assumed that a security risk was simply a lesser version of a Communist—someone with Communist sympathies but no outright party connections—in official circles the two categories were quite distinct. Persons guilty of espionage or connections to allegedly subversive organizations like the Communist Party were guilty of disloyalty. Persons who might divulge secret information, because they were either careless or coerced, were labeled security risks. When defining the difference between a loyalty risk and a security risk, government officials typically explained that "loyalty" involved a current state of mind, a willful desire to betray secrets, while "security" involved behaviors or associations that might lead one inadvertently or unwillingly to betray secrets in the future.

When pressed to give an example of a security risk, government officials typically mentioned those who talked or drank too freely—or did both. As one government official explained, "a chronic alcoholic—he may be perfectly loyal to the United States but, under the influence of liquor, will talk and reveal classified information." It was the example of an alcoholic that Secretary of State Dean Acheson raised when asked to define the term during the same hearing when his assistant revealed that ninety-one homosexuals had been dismissed. One congressional leader referred to the alcoholic as the "classic Hollywood type of State Department story" whose weakness left him open to subversive infiltration. Despite the high profile given to alcoholism in public discourse surrounding security, few if any alcoholics were separated from the government as security risks. When questioned in 1951 by Congress, a State Department security officer responded, "I do not know of any cases that have been terminated as a security risk on account of alcoholism." By way of explanation he added, "We have not had any real complaints of alcoholism that would warrant our investigating them."[12]

In the troika of sinners routinely listed as security risks—the alcoholic, the loquacious, and the pervert—only the pervert was always a security risk. The other two categories involved qualifications—not all those who talk, but those who talk too much; not all those who drink, but those who drink too much. But even one homosexual encounter qualified someone as a security risk, making it perhaps the easiest such offense to prove. It was the only one of the three to be illegal, thereby automatically enlisting every police force in the nation in its enforcement. It was the only one that warranted a full-scale congressional investigation, the only one requiring specialized security officers, the only category about which government departments kept specific records. In most statistics about security risks, homosexuals composed the single largest contingent. Although "security risk" covered a variety of offenses, it often functioned as a euphemism for homosexual.

Even when used to describe alcoholics and the loquacious, the term "security risk" still invoked the specter of homosexuality. In 1950s public discourse, both alcoholism and loquaciousness were traits closely associated with same-sex desire. Government security officers routinely characterized homosexuals as so gregarious that they were unable to keep secrets. Their great desire to talk, officials asserted, meant they were quick to confess and name names. It was said that information passed through homosexual networks with astounding speed.[13] Though persons who threatened security with their "loose lips" were not all homosexual, the two categories were thought to overlap. Even closer was the link between drinking and homosexual activity. Both psychiatric literature and popular fiction of the period portrayed the alcoholic as a repressed homosexual who acted on his same-sex desires only while intoxicated. "Alcohol plays an important role in the problem of sexual deviations," *Time* magazine noted in April 1950, because it released repressed desires. If the psychiatric community already considered alcoholism a form of latent homosexuality, the connection was popularized by Charles Jackson's popular 1944 novel, *The Lost Weekend*, the basis for the film that won the academy award for best picture in 1945. The novel tells the story of an upper-class New York alcoholic and repressed homosexual whose binge drinking one weekend propels him into a number of gay milieus. When recognized there as a fellow homosexual, the protagonist claims he is merely "the potential confederate that was every alcoholic."[14]

As a term that invoked multiple dangers even in its official usage—and even more implications as used and misused by the general public—"security risk" was the ideal term for those who sought to portray the executive branch as riddled with subversives. Though it evoked danger, disloyalty, even espionage, it applied to a broad group of people considered potentially vulnerable to manipulation, homosexuals chief among them. A story from the December 1951 *New York Times* reveals how government officials often relied on coded language to mask how the security system targeted homosexuals. The story reported how the officials used lie-detector tests when investigating employees for "'security' but not 'loyalty'": "Persons who are indiscreet in talk about their work or in associations with disreputable people are subject to security charges," the newspaper explained. If the reader forged on, the newspaper revealed the meaning of the government's coded language: "It was understood that the few cases referred to were persons suspected of sexual perversion." Unless pressured, government officials often hid behind the generic term "security risk" when they were really talking about homosexuals.[15]

By looking beyond McCarthy and behind the ambiguous term "security risk," this study reveals that a Lavender Scare—a fear that homosexuals posed a threat to national security and needed to be systematically removed from the federal government—permeated 1950s political culture. Originating as a partisan political weapon in the halls of Congress, it sparked a moral panic within mainstream American culture and became the basis for a federal government policy that lasted nearly twenty-five years and affected innumerable people's lives. Though based on the flimsiest of evidence—no gay American was ever blackmailed into revealing state secrets—it prompted congressional hearings, presidential executive orders, and executive agency security briefings. Fed by postwar fears that America was in a state of moral decline, dominated by a new class of powerful government bureaucrats, and threatened by communism, the Lavender Scare was used to justify a vast expansion of the national security state. Ironically, its very success in eliminating thousands of suspected homosexuals from the government would also lead to its undoing, as gay men and lesbians began to organize politically to challenge what they came to see as an unjust government policy. It would provide much of the inspiration for the early gay rights movement.

New Sources

Integrating political, cultural, and social history, this book draws on a wide variety of primary sources. To uncover the thinking of politicians and security agents behind the purges, it makes extensive use of government documents such as congressional hearings, executive department records, and court cases, many only recently declassified and opened to historians. The records of the most extensive congressional investigation into the employment of homosexuals in government were only released in 2000, after being closed to the public for fifty years. This work also draws heavily on memoirs by and oral history interviews with gay and lesbian Americans who lived and worked in Washington, D.C., and experienced the purges first hand, whether as victims, survivors, or witnesses. One of those victims, Frank Kameny, provided unlimited access to his private papers and those of the Mattachine Society of Washington, the gay organization he founded in 1961 largely to fight for civil service reform. To uncover how the larger culture viewed homosexuals and Washington bureaucrats, I surveyed newspapers, magazines, novels, and films. Surprisingly, sensationalist tabloid publications often provided the most revealing accounts of the antigay purges and how they were perceived by average Americans. In 1965, *Confidential* reported that "a generation ago, Washington was the capital of Fairyland, U.S.A. More lavender lads and Lesbians worked there than anyplace on earth." But the McCarthy probes, the story continued, "resulted in the wholesale firings of thousands of government workers on grounds of 'moral turpitude.'" Although not entirely factual, this coverage managed to capture, even as it sensationalized, the magnitude of the historical change that occurred in Washington from 1945 to 1965.[16]

This study also relies on a wealth of previous scholarship by cultural historians and historians of sexuality. Recent work in cultural history, gender studies, and literary criticism highlights the importance of issues of gender and sexuality to Cold War political culture—how containment of sexuality was as central to 1950s America as containing communism. With the nation on "moral alert" because of the Cold War, stable, monogamous, heterosexual marriages were seen as a key weapon in the arsenal against degeneracy and internal Communist subversion.[17] In his groundbreaking study of the early gay rights movement, John D'Emilio provided the first scholarly treatment of what he called "the entanglement of homosexuality in the politics of anticommunism." Historians such as George Chauncey, Allan Bérubé, and Elizabeth Lapovsky Kennedy have documented the vibrancy and resilience of gay and lesbian communities in times and in places they were not thought to have existed.[18] Cultural theorists have studied how "moral panics" periodically sweep through American popular culture.[19] And very recently diplomatic historians have begun to examine how anxieties about gender and morality affected the formation of America's Cold War foreign policy.[20] Only by using the insights and methods of these scholars can the Lavender Scare be fully uncovered and understood.

J. Edgar Hoover's Dress

In the last ten years, popular perceptions of homosexuality in 1950s Washington have focused on celebrities. Since the 1993 publication of an exposé by British writer Anthony Summers, it has become an accepted fact in American culture that FBI director J. Edgar Hoover was a homosexual. Media outlets from PBS to *USA Today*, comedians like Jay Leno, and politicians from Bob Dole to Bill Clinton popularized the image conveyed in Summers's account of J. Edgar Hoover wearing a black negligee at a Plaza Hotel gay orgy. Summers's account of Hoover is more a reflection of Cold War political culture than an examination of it. It utilizes the kind of tactics Hoover and the security program he oversaw perfected—guilt by association, rumor, and unverified gossip. His psychoanalytic explanation of Hoover's sexuality—distant father, overbearing mother—is a vintage Cold War cliché. As historian and FBI expert Athan Theoharis points out, Summers's sources are highly suspect, and the evidence they present is highly implausible. As a former congressional investigator said of Susan Rosenstiel, the Mafia wife who claims to have seen Hoover in a negligee at the Plaza hotel, "She was a liar, a no-good bum. . . . I wouldn't believe her under oath if she were sworn in forty times." Journalist Ronald Kessler has since cast further doubt on Rosenstiel's veracity by revealing that she was paid for her story and once served jail time for perjury. Her description of Hoover in drag engaging in sex with young blond boys in leather while desecrating the Bible is clearly a homophobic fantasy. Even more implausible are the wealth of alleged public sightings of Hoover in compromising positions. Gay men who managed to hold onto government jobs in Cold War Washington did so largely through extreme discretion. Given the near hysteria in 1950s Washington about the threat posed to national security by homosexuals in high government office, the existence of so much evidence of Hoover's alleged homosexuality would have led to his ouster. Many civil servants lost jobs on the flimsiest of evidence—merely associating with a known homosexual was often sufficient cause. If Hoover's numerous enemies had photographs, arrest records, and eyewitness accounts of sexual activity, then not even Hoover's own secret files on the sex lives of politicians could have protected him. These stories only seem plausible because we have forgotten the vehemence with which the Lavender Scare held sway in 1950s America.[21]

The Lavender Scare did not just affect people who self-identified as "gay" or "lesbian." Because of the pervasiveness of the homophobia it unleashed, it affected the behavior of a wide segment of the population. "Male workers are known deliberately to avoid speaking to each other in places that might be considered secluded," a group of psychiatrists reported.[22] Many of those who engaged in homosexual behavior did not self-identify as homosexual persons. Like most men and women in 1950s America, Hoover saw homosexuality not as an inborn characteristic of a percentage of the population, but a sin or temptation to which anyone might succumb. It was precisely its insidious nature that made it seem such a threat to the nation. As Hoover himself suggested when discussing the case of a high government official caught propositioning male railroad porters, the problem was a lack of self-control. If Hoover did have same-sex yearnings, he undoubtedly sought to restrain them. Imposing present-day notions of sexuality—particularly the notion that persons are essentially born either heterosexual or homosexual—back onto this period further distorts our understanding.[23]

Women, too, were victims of the Lavender Scare, though not in equal measure. Much of the rhetoric of the purges stressed the threat from high-level bureaucrats or appointed officials, all of whom were assumed to be male. Of the initial ninety-one homosexuals fired from the State Department, for example, only two were women. Security officials seem to have targeted men more than women, even though women made up approximately 40 percent of the federal workforce. Since security officials relied heavily on arrest records in known gay male cruising areas, gay men were more likely to come to the attention of authorities than lesbians, who, as women, had more limited access to public space. As security officials tracked informal social networks within the gay community—either through names provided in confessions or simple "guilt by association"— their focus on gay men tended to perpetuate itself. Although not targeted equally, both gay men and lesbians were affected by the purges, thereby fostering a new bond between the two communities. Because gay men and lesbians in this period increasingly interacted, first to offer protective cover for one another and later to actively protest federal policies, I discuss both communities while acknowledging the limitations of this approach. As George Chauncey argued in his study of gay male life in the early part of the century, "The differences between men's and women's power and the qualities ascribed to them in a male-dominated culture were so significant that the social and spatial organization of gay male and lesbian life inevitably took very different forms." In some ways, the experience of lesbians was more similar to that of heterosexual women than to that of homosexual men. As Leisa Meyer suggests about the military in the 1940s, policies that affected lesbians were often not those specifically aimed at rooting out homosexuality but those which controlled and defined female sexuality in general. In the civil service, proscriptions against "immoral conduct" were used against heterosexual women as well as gay men and lesbians, but almost never against heterosexual men.[24]

★

The Lavender Scare is the story of how Washington, D.C., and the federal bureaucracy—synonymous in the national imagination—came to be thought of as havens for socialists, misfits, and perverts. But it is also the story of the effect the purges had on the local lesbian and gay population. It reveals both the vibrant lesbian and gay subculture that had developed in Washington as a result of the large influx of young people during the New Deal and World War II and the chilling effect the government witch hunts had on the community. It also chronicles the rise of an organized opposition to the federal government's antigay policies. Though intended to contain what was perceived as a growing homosexual menace, the Lavender Scare inspired not only the founding of the first sustained gay organization in the United States in southern California in 1951—an area heavily dependent on government-sponsored defense work—but also the later radicalization of the movement in 1960s Washington. Well before the 1969 Stonewall riots—commonly considered the start of the gay rights struggle—the movement had developed much of its organizational tactics and rhetoric and won significant legal victories. Responding to the perceived injustice of federal employment policies, activists fashioned a new movement. In addition to the story of the Cold War persecution of gays and lesbians, then, this is also the story of the Cold War origins of the gay rights movement.

1

Peurifoy's Revelation
The Politics of the Purges

If you had been in this work as long as we have been, you would realize that there is something wrong with each one of these individuals.
You will find that practically every active Communist is twisted mentally or physically in some way.

—*U.S. intelligence official, quoted by Joseph McCarthy*

Throughout the month of February 1950, the charges kept changing. In
Wheeling, West Virginia, Senator Joseph McCarthy first made national
headlines when he told a Republican women's group that the State Department harbored 205 "card-carrying Communists." In the next few days,
as journalists swarmed his office and the State Department issued denials,
he reduced their status to "bad risks" and the number to 57. Under mounting pressure to provide specifics, McCarthy stood in the well of the U.S.
Senate chamber on the evening of February 20 and gave the American public
detailed information about the subversives he alleged were still working in
the State Department. In what a reporter dubbed "one of the maddest spec-
tacles in the history of representative government," McCarthy presented a
case-by-case analysis lasting six hours of what he was then calling "81 loyalty risks." After numerous shouting matches over the conflicting figures
and statements made since the Wheeling speech, McCarthy led his Senate
colleagues through each case. In most he accused various officials of
"palling around with Communists," joining Communist-front organizations, reading their literature, or acting as Soviet agents. But two cases

stood out from the rest. They were not about individuals but groups, and they were less about political than sexual deviance. Case no. 14 involved a "flagrantly homosexual" translator who had been dismissed as a "bad security risk" but was later reinstated by a "high State Department official." The translator, McCarthy warned, had "extremely close connections with other individuals with the same tendencies," and therefore represented a larger problem. These "very unusual individuals," McCarthy explained, were not only homosexual but "active members of Communist-front organizations," including the Young Communist League. Some of them, McCarthy asserted, were "active Soviet agents." Case no. 62 was also unusual in that it involved a whole group of homosexual employees. "I think this will be of interest to the committee," McCarthy emphasized, "in that it gives a rather interesting picture of some rather unusual mental twists of these gentlemen who are tied up with some of the Communist organizations."

Although only two of his charges were homosexuals, McCarthy singled them out as illustrative of a larger truth. In the middle of reciting the details of both homosexual cases, McCarthy paused to relate a conversation he recently had with "one of our top intelligence men in Washington." Wondering why some people were so "fanatically Communist," McCarthy asked the official what was so attractive about the Communist philosophy. "If you had been in this work as long as we have been," the intelligence officer allegedly told McCarthy, "you would realize that there is something wrong with each one of these individuals. You will find," he asserted, "that practically every active Communist is twisted mentally or physically in some way." Historians of the McCarthy era often quote this twice-told tale to demonstrate how membership in the Communist Party was considered evidence of a psychological maladjustment in the 1950s. But the context of the story suggests that the claim was much more specific. Homosexuality, McCarthy asserted, was the psychological maladjustment that led people toward communism. The Red Scare now had a tinge of lavender.[1]

The State Department's responses to McCarthy's charges also changed, vacillating between clear denials and more vague pronouncements. They would eventually spark as much controversy as the charges themselves. John Peurifoy, head of the department's security program, quickly issued a press release denying that the State Department harbored any Communists. At the same time, the department admitted that it had dismissed 202 "security risks." At their first opportunity, members of Congress pressed department officials for clarification. On February 28, 1950, a week after McCarthy's speech to the Senate, Secretary of State Dean Acheson made his first public appearance on Capitol Hill since McCarthy had begun making headlines. Though the official purpose of the hearing was to review the department's appropriations for the next fiscal year, the furor over McCarthy's charges brought out the press and the news cameras. Senator Styles Bridges (R–New Hampshire), among the most powerful Republican senators, began the questioning. "Mr. Secretary, what do you consider a security risk?" Bridges inquired. Acheson carefully explained that under the State Department's security program, persons who engaged in espionage, divulged classified information, or joined Communist or Nazi organizations were all considered security risks. In addition to these specific examples, Acheson noted that the department considered other criteria when screening its employees—"whether the person has, as a matter of character, any defect which would lead him into any of these difficulties." Bridges sought clarification. "Such as homosexuality?" he wondered. "That would be included," Acheson conceded. Bridges, the ranking Republican on the committee, then asked about a provision the committee had added to the department's appropriations bills to facilitate removing such security risks. How many security risks, Bridges wanted to know, had been removed under this provision known as the "McCarran rider." When Acheson responded that only one person had been so removed, Bridges persisted. "Now, how many other people that have been under investigation by the department have resigned?" he asked. Jumping in for his boss, Deputy Undersecretary for Administration John Peurifoy offered to respond. "In this shady category that you referred to earlier, there are ninety-one cases, sir." Unsatisfied with this coy offering, Bridges pressed for clarification. "What do you mean by 'shady category'?" he intoned. Peurifoy, mindful of the presence of the press, tried another euphemism. "We are talking about people of moral weaknesses and so forth," he offered. At this point Chairman Patrick McCarran (D–Nevada) grew impatient. "Now, will you make your answer a little clearer, please," he insisted. Peurifoy was backed into a corner. "Most of these were homosexuals, Mr. Chairman," he finally conceded.[2]

Peurifoy was as reticent to utter the word "homosexuals" as his congressional interrogators were eager to hear it. No chance remark, this pivotal testimony was a political performance orchestrated by a congressional tag team intent on assisting Senator McCarthy and embarrassing Acheson's State Department and the entire Truman administration. For the last three years, Senator Bridges and his colleagues had been actively involved in establishing and monitoring the State Department's security program. As recently as a month earlier, their colleagues in the House had elicited nearly the same testimony from Peurifoy. But these previous oversight hearings had been held behind closed doors. With the rise of McCarthy and the new national spotlight on subversion in the State Department, Bridges and his colleagues decided it was time to reveal the results of what had been a quiet campaign to remove security risks from the State Department. It would strengthen McCarthy's position by lending credence to his charges. At the same time, it suggested that Communist infiltration was not the only threat facing the nation and that McCarthy might be more successful if he enlarged his campaign to include all those considered "security risks."[3]

Hoping to make headlines, Peurifoy's questioners were not disappointed. Like McCarthy's charges, the revelation that ninety-one homosexuals had been dismissed from the State Department unleashed a flurry of newspaper columns, constituent mail, public debate, and congressional investigations throughout 1950 about the presence of homosexuals in government and their connections to Communists. The revelation set in motion a chain of events that would have widespread repercussions for governmental security policies and the millions of people affected by them for the next twenty years. Within weeks, Guy Gabrielson, chairman of the Republican National Committee, observed that the revelation was "the talk of Washington and of the Washington correspondents corps." Writing to thousands of party workers, Gabrielson warned that "perhaps as dangerous as the actual Communists are the sexual perverts who have infiltrated our Government in recent years." Headlines warning of "Perverts Fleeing State Dept." peppered newspapers throughout the country. While members of Congress held hearings to determine how to "eradicate this menace," jokes circulated about the "lavender lads" in the State Department. The issue was so frequently discussed on the Senate and House floors that one congressman complained about all the attention given to homosexuals. With all the numbers being bandied about that spring, the number ninety-one became shorthand for the lavender menace threatening the nation. On the national radio program "Meet the Press" in April, guests discussed "the ninety-one" fired from the State Department as if the term needed no explanation. The issue of homosexuals in government, observed columnist John O'Donnell, constituted "a new type of political weapon—never used in this republic." He predicted it would destroy the confidence of the American people in the State Department and might "wreck the Administration." Seeing this as evidence of "depravity in the Roosevelt-Truman bureaucracy," Westbrook Pegler lamented, "[T]here is no record of comparable corruption in American history."[4]

Though politically motivated by congressional Republican leaders, the Peurifoy revelation soon became an issue well beyond the confines of Capitol Hill. Peurifoy's revelation seemed to substantiate McCarthy's charges and strengthen his public support. Letters poured into the White House, the State Department, Capitol Hill, and news outlets from outraged citizens. As one reporter wrote, "The unexpectedly large number of perverts dismissed from the State Department also worries the public, it appears from the mail which the lawmakers are receiving daily." A preliminary sampling of McCarthy's mail revealed that only a quarter of the twenty-five thousand writers expressed concern about "red infiltration." The other three-quarters, one newspaper reported, "are expressing their shocked indignation at the evidence of sex depravity." Another columnist noted that "the writers are less worried over the ideological tendencies of State Department officers who are involved then they are by their nasty moral habits." As one woman from Long Island wrote to the *New York Daily News*, "The homosexual situation in our State Department is no more shocking than your statement that 'they are uncertain what to do about it.' Let every American who loves this country get behind McCarthy or any committee which will thoroughly investigate and expose every one of these people. . . . This is no time for compromise. Democrats or Republicans— we must rid our Government of these creatures."[5]

News that the State Department had fired ninety-one homosexuals gave credibility to McCarthy's vague charges and enhanced his public standing. Though he was involved in neither their removal nor the revelation of their removal, McCarthy was soon given credit for both. "He has forced the State Department to fire 91 sex perverts," gushed conservative Representative Noah Mason (R–Illinois), praising McCarthy's alleged accomplishments in the two months since his Wheeling speech. Speaking of what he called "the popular side of his controversy with the State Department," Congressman Lawrence Smith from McCarthy's home state of Wisconsin echoed this praise. "Already his actions have flushed out homosexuals in that Department," Smith noted approvingly. Journalists also remarked on the close association in the public mind between McCarthy and the Peurifoy revelation. Trying to explain McCarthy's widespread public support despite press denunciations of his charges as reckless, irresponsible, and lacking proof, one commentator pointed to the Peurifoy revelation. "In the midst of all this, [the public's] confusion was increased and their resentment enhanced" by Peurifoy's statement, he explained. As the *Washington Star* reported, "Not much has been made of it in the press, but politicians generally agree that their constituencies have been more revolted at this voluntary disclosure than by anything else."[6]

In McCarthy's home state of Wisconsin, his attack on Truman's State Department reinvigorated what until then had seemed like a faltering political career. As historian Michael O'Brien noted, it transformed him "from a bumbling senator doomed to political oblivion into the idol of Wisconsin

Republicans." But here, too, it was the attacks on "sex perverts" that most concerned them. A columnist for the *Green Bay Press-Gazette* reported that rural politicians had learned that the Republican rank-and-file were most exercised about the homosexuals-in-government issue. At a meeting of Republican state party leaders to decide whether to back McCarthy, much of the discussion centered on "sex perverts" and the concern these charges raised with voters. One top Wisconsin Republican and McCarthy fund-raiser, Thomas Coleman, rallied national Republican leaders to McCarthy's cause by giving the homosexual charges equal billing with those against Communists. As he told a National Republican Strategy Committee in April, "Our party is finally on the attack and should stay there. And best of all, we may get rid of many Communist sympathizers and queers who now control policy."[7]

In 1950, Republicans were a desperate and frustrated party that had been out of power for eighteen years, since the 1932 defeat of President Herbert Hoover by a triumphant Franklin Roosevelt and his New Deal coalition. Not only had Roosevelt won an unprecedented four terms in office, through the Great Depression and World War II, but also his Democratic successor, Harry Truman, had come from behind to squelch what seemed like a certain Republican victory in 1948. That year Republicans were so certain of recapturing the White House that their presidential nominee, Thomas Dewey, barely campaigned and ignored the burgeoning issue of Communists in government. They would not let it happen again. But their lack of power was not the only thing that concerned Republicans. They were also concerned about the direction in which the country, indeed the world, seemed to be going. With the recent conviction of British atomic scientist Klaus Fuchs for espionage on the Manhattan Project and that of former State Department official Alger Hiss for perjury in denying he spied for the Soviet Union, McCarthy's charges, however vague, seemed plausible. How else, they reasoned, except through the infiltration of the U.S. government, could Communists have so quickly acquired the secrets of atomic weapons and taken over China. And now it seemed that Communists were not acting alone but had recruited homosexuals to help steal secrets.

Peurifoy Initiates the Purges

Though both McCarthy's charges and Peurifoy's revelation garnered considerable press coverage and public debate, neither was news to members of Congress. Both involved information accumulated from the State Department's security program over the past three years, repackaged for maximum partisan advantage. At the very beginning of the Cold War and the

heightened concern about internal security, the State Department had begun campaigns to rid the department of Communists and homosexuals. In
June 1947, the Senate Appropriations Committee warned Secretary of State
Marshall of "a deliberate, calculated program being carried out not only to
protect Communist personnel in high places, but to reduce security and intelligence protection to a nullity." This letter, historians of the Cold War
agree, was a pivotal moment in the growing anti-Communist campaigns
and the rise of an internal loyalty/security program. But those historians
have ignored the committee's warning that part of this subversive effort involved "the extensive employment in highly classified positions of admitted homosexuals, who are historically known to be security risks." To help
fight these subversive efforts, the committee attached the McCarran rider
to its appropriations bill, permitting the secretary of state to dismiss any
employee at his "absolute discretion" if he deemed such action advisable
in the interest of national security. The rider was intended for use against
both threats—Communists and homosexuals.[8]

Responding to congressional pressure, Secretary of State Marshall established a Personnel Security Board to draw up a set of "security principles" for the department. As reported on the front pages of most Washington papers, the security principles established a dual loyalty/security
test. Communists, their associates, and those guilty of espionage were considered disloyal under these principles. But a second group of individuals
who exhibited signs of character weakness were also to be excluded. Persons known for "habitual drunkenness, sexual perversion, moral turpitude, financial irresponsibility or criminal record" were to be denied employment. Although such people were not necessarily disloyal, the State
Department reasoned that "a person who has such basic weakness of character or lack of judgment" might be led into an association with a subversive individual or group. During the next three years, the State Department
instituted security checks on its employees using these principles, netting
thirty-one homosexuals in 1947, twenty-eight in 1948, and thirty-one in
1949. This dual loyalty/security system, with Communists and homosexuals as principal targets, would become the model for other government
agencies and the basis for a government-wide security program under the
Eisenhower administration. Clearly, concern about homosexuals as security risks was neither a creation of Senator McCarthy nor a minor byproduct of the Red Scare. The campaigns to remove Communists and homosexuals from the federal government began simultaneously in the State
Department in 1947.[9]

Overseeing this new State Department security program was John Peurifoy, assistant secretary for administration, whose reputation for straight-

forward honesty quickly won him praise on Capitol Hill. A self-described "farm boy" from South Carolina, Peurifoy had come to Washington in 1935 and worked as an elevator operator in the Senate Office Building before joining the department in 1938. He was credited with bringing efficiency and clear lines of authority to a department that had been considered a confederation of independent tribes. Unlike traditional diplomats, this ex-West Pointer eschewed formal "striped pants" for ordinary business suits and loud ties, drank bourbon and branch water, and had a reputation for speaking his mind. Even the many congressional critics of the State Department considered Peurifoy one of their own. "I don't like any of those bastards from the State Department," complained one senator. "They'll come up here and they lie and they hedge and they don't know what they're talking about. All except Jack Peurifoy." Gushing about his influence on the department, the conservative *Saturday Evening Post* claimed, "He's de-snobbing the State Department."[10]

The close, quiet cooperation between Peurifoy and members of the appropriations committee in removing homosexuals over the preceding three years changed after McCarthy put the spotlight on subversives in the department. The program was suddenly useful to both defenders and critics of the department. Senator Bridges wanted to publicize the number of homosexuals he had helped uncover to bolster McCarthy. Peurifoy, while reluctant to reveal the exact nature of the "security risk" firings, wanted to make it clear that they were not suspected Communists. Hoping to downplay McCarthy's charge, Peurifoy was forced to reveal the extent of the homosexual purges. As Richard Rovere explained to readers of the *New Yorker*, "Rather than let it be supposed that all the employees who had been dropped as poor security risks had Communist connections, the department released the information that ninety-one had been dismissed not on political grounds but because they were known to be homosexuals." Seeing it as an attempt to mollify Congress, some senators accused Peurifoy of trying to divert attention from the Communist issue by claiming half of the dismissals were merely sex perverts. But senators such as Bridges knew that the revelation would further incriminate the State Department and give credence to McCarthy's claims. "State would never forgive him," *Time* magazine said of Peurifoy, for having admitted in open session that ninety-one of its own had been ousted for homosexuality.[11]

Modifying McCarthy's Charges

Peurifoy might have refrained from uttering the word "homosexuals" had it not been for Senator Styles Bridges. While much of the public credited

McCarthy with uncovering homosexuals in the State Department, that honor belonged to Bridges. One of only two Republicans elected to the Senate in the Democratic landslide of 1936—ten years before McCarthy— Bridges quickly became a powerful behind-the-scenes leader of his party. A former New Hampshire governor, by 1952 he would become the president pro tem of the Senate, third in line of succession to the presidency, and chair of the influential appropriations committee. A profile of Bridges at the time commented, "It is somewhat surprising that a man so powerful should be almost an unknown." Among the first to blame the Truman Administration for "losing" China to the Communists, Bridges had long advocated a "housecleaning" in the State Department. But like many leaders in the Republican Party, Bridges knew that McCarthy's charges about Communist infiltration were based on outdated information. Appearing in McCarthy's home state of Wisconsin, Bridges delivered a remarkably candid speech in which he characterized the senator's charges about Communists as "too wild." "McCarthy will never prove that there are fifty-seven card-carrying Communists in the State Department," Bridges told his audience. "I've been investigating around Washington for a long time, and even I would find it difficult to prove there was one card-carrying Communist in the State Department." Bridges did not suggest that McCarthy abandon his campaign, but that he redirect it toward "bad security risks." "When they admit discharging ninety-one homosexuals, it doesn't look good," he told his audience. "A man doesn't have to be a spy or a Communist to be a bad security risk. He can be a drunkard or a criminal or a homosexual." These targets, Bridges implied, were more numerous, easier to catch, and just as dangerous. He was also critical of McCarthy's methods of public smears and name-calling, contrasting them to his committee's methods over the past three years. Its members had worked "quietly, almost secretly, without publicity," he noted, "and we got results." Indeed Bridges had been instrumental in the creation of the State Department's security program and its ouster of ninety-one homosexuals. But he was no longer working quietly.[12]

As Bridges knew, McCarthy's charges came entirely from a list developed by the staff of the House Appropriations Committee during a 1947 investigation of the State Department's security program. At that time subcommittee staffer Robert E. Lee assembled a team of investigators, mostly former FBI agents like himself, zealously concerned about the danger of Communist subversion. Given access to departmental personnel files, they compiled summaries of "derogatory information" on 108 employees, which they thought merited the attention of the committee. The result was the "Lee list" of 108 former, current, or prospective State Department employees with questionable security records. By the end of that congressional term, those on the list had either left the department or been exonerated, and the committee gave the State Department security system a clean bill of health. But the list continued to circulate among various congressional committees, wound up in the hands of McCarthy, and became the basis for his charges against the State Department in February 1950. Using the "Lee list," McCarthy stumbled upon the two cases of homosexuality he mentioned in his speech to the Senate.[13]

While criticizing McCarthy for his "reckless accusations" and the damage they had done to the nation's ability to conduct foreign policy, Bridges was also outspoken about the need to clean out the State Department. He called for an investigation into who put Alger Hiss in the State Department and "who put the 91 homosexuals in our State Department." These, Senator Bridges told his Senate colleagues, were "questions which are formed by the lips of the vast majority of the people of the United States." Calling Hiss and the homosexuals "foul enemies of our Republic," Bridges insisted that their presence in the State Department was no accident but part of a vast conspiracy. "They did not get there by osmosis, or by accident. They got there because Russia wanted them there," Bridges charged. He implored the Senate to "find the master spy, the servant of Russia," responsible for planting such people in the State Department. He suggested going back to 1933 and Roosevelt's decision to recognize the Soviet Union.[14]

Senator Bridges was not alone in his critique of McCarthy. Other Washington insiders suggested he shift his efforts from "card-carrying" Communists to security risks. "The Senator overstated whatever case he may have and called things by their wrong name," wrote Pulitzer prize-winning columnist Arthur Krock. "He made the important error of confusing security with loyalty." He would have made a better case, Krock advised, had he stuck to issues of security, such as "personal traits and behavior which lay the possessors open to blackmail." Attorney and former FBI agent Frederick Ayer, who turned down the role of aide to a Senate committee investigating McCarthy's charges, concurred. The real danger, he warned, stemmed not from Communists but from "plain carelessness, weakness of character, ignorance, and false idealism." He called for "character studies" of all job applicants and recommended that true security would only be achieved when anyone whose "personal behavior is embarrassing to our government" was dismissed from the federal payroll.[15]

Most important, the desire to refocus McCarthy's efforts was shared by the Republican Party leadership. When Guy Gabrielson, the chair of the Republican National Committee, appeared on "Meet the Press" in April, he refrained from endorsing McCarthy or his charges. But he repeatedly called for "cleaning up" the State Department. "I've just returned from a trip to the West," he told his national radio audience, "and I find people all over the country very much concerned with the type of people that are employed in the State Department." After three pointed references to the need for "cleaning up" the department—with no mention of Communist infiltration—a reporter asked what he meant. "Well, as I recall it, they admitted that they fired ninety-one individuals here within the last short while," Gabrielson responded. Did he think there were other "moral risks" in the department, the reporter continued. "I think the American people are entitled to know whether or not any more do exist there." Clearly the desire to widen the net from Communist to other security risks was not the plan of a few wild-eyed politicians. The Lavender Scare, even more than McCarthy's Red Scare, enjoyed the backing of the Republican Party leadership.[16]

Senator Tydings Investigates

The effort to shift McCarthy's efforts from Communists to "security risks" took its most public form during the Tydings investigation. Very quickly after McCarthy began to make headlines in February 1950, the Senate authorized the Foreign Relations Committee to conduct an investigation into McCarthy's charges. Casting a wide net, the Senate called for a full investigation into "whether persons who are disloyal to the United States are or have been employed by the Department of State." The resulting deliberations of the Tydings committee were among the most well-publicized hearings of 1950, dominating the headlines for much of March, April, and May, and considered "one of the most bitterly controversial investigations in the history of Congress." One of its principal fault lines became whether homosexuals fell within the scope of the investigation. It became a forum for Bridges and his Republican colleagues to try to refocus McCarthy's charges on homosexuals.

The chairman of the Foreign Relations Committee, Millard Tydings (D–Maryland), was a respected senior senator who provided the perfect foil for McCarthy. While McCarthy was a perpetually rumpled, poker-playing, former chicken farmer from small-town Wisconsin, Tydings was an intellectual patrician who wore tailored suits, lived on a secluded estate in Maryland, and was married to a wealthy socialite, Eleanor Davies, daughter of a former ambassador to the Soviet Union. While McCarthy was known as "Tail-gunner Joe" for his experience in the Marines, Tydings's critics called attention to his class privilege by mispronouncing his first name as "MiLord." Like Alger Hiss and Dean Acheson, Millard Tydings epitomized the Eastern establishment that McCarthy despised. A close ally of the Truman administration, Tydings boasted that the hearings would quickly destroy McCarthy's credibility. "Let me have him for three days in public hearings," Tydings predicted, "and he'll never show his face in the Senate again." On the first day of the hearings, before McCarthy could even read his prepared statement, Tydings went on the offensive. He demanded that McCarthy identify the man involved in case no. 14, the high State Department official who had reinstated a "flagrant homosexual," labeling it "the most important thing in the whole investigation." Tydings knew that the official, Joseph Anthony Panuch, was a McCarthy supporter singled out for praise in another case for his anti-Communist zeal. Revealing his identity would impugn McCarthy's credibility and show that his own camp protected homosexuals. McCarthy vehemently refused to answer the question and was allowed to proceed with his own presentation. McCarthy emerged looking like the victim of prosecutorial aggressiveness, and the issue of homosexuality in the State Department was again in the media spotlight.[17]

As the proceedings progressed into April, Republican senators launched a campaign on the floor of the Senate to pressure Tydings to delve into the homosexual charges. Tydings deflected these efforts, meeting each senator's argument with a counter-argument. Ralph Owen Brewster (R–Maine) opened the attack by asking, "Does the Senator consider that the cases testified to by Mr. Peurifoy, of ninety-one sexual pervert or moral degenerates, are bad security risks?" Conceding that they were security risks, Tydings noted that his committee was limited to investigating disloyalty. "Their loyalty might be subject to undue influence," Brewster insisted. Tydings agreed, but countered that a philandering heterosexual ran the same risk. Characterizing homosexuals as "collateral" to the Communists, Tydings promised to look into such cases if they came to the committee's attention. Senator Kenneth Wherry, the Republican floor leader, exclaimed that ninety-one homosexuals had *already* come to the committee's attention. Tydings responded that since they had already been fired, they were beyond the committee's jurisdiction. The committee was charged with investigating current and *former* employees, Wherry clarified. The ninety-one homosexuals should be brought before the committee, Wherry insisted, predicting they would provide "leads" to Tydings's main concern of disloyalty.[18]

The partisan wrangling over Communists and homosexuals escalated on the Senate floor the next day. With Tydings attacking McCarthy for the lack of specificity in his charges, McCarthy presented the case of a homosexual who left the State Department and joined the CIA. "I gave the complete police record of this man to the Senator from Maryland, this man who was a homosexual . . . [who] spent his time hanging around the men's room in Lafayette Park." Indeed, because the man had been arrested on a sex charge, this may have been McCarthy's best-documented "security risk" case. Tydings ignored the evidence and returned to the charges concerning card-carrying Communists. Frustrated by both sides, William E. Jenner (R–Indiana), one of McCarthy's closest supporters, pleaded for compromise. "If Senators can work out between them in the committee the question of Communists and of 'homos,' that is what the American people want done," Jenner advised.

Despite the pressure from a battery of Republican senators, Tydings stood his ground. His strategy was to recast the issue as a matter not of national security but mental health. "I know there is a great desire to shift from Communists to homos," Tydings proclaimed angrily. "I ask my colleagues to stop the continual heckling of the subcommittee about homosexuals and other matters of that kind." He assured his colleagues that he was pursing the homosexual employee McCarthy had presented, but argued that it did not involve national security. "Obviously, a man may have the terrible disease which has been referred to, and yet may not be a party to foreign espionage or may not be a party to deliberately being disloyal to his Government." Invoking a medical model of homosexuality, he characterized homosexuals in government as a low priority. "Of course it is a risk to have in the Government service persons who are afflicted with that disease," Tydings noted, but they were "incidental matters" compared to Communists and spies. For now, he assured his colleagues, "we are pursuing the Communist phase of this matter."[19] In a friendly conversation with Dean Acheson about his upcoming testimony before the committee, Tydings assured the secretary that the committee "is concerned only with loyalty and not with homogeneity [sic]." He made it clear that the testimony of Acheson or any other departmental officials "should steer clear of the latter." The strategy of framing the issue as one of mental health and not national security would be taken up and expanded by the Truman administration.[20]

The Tydings committee's final report, a harsh condemnation of McCarthy, labeled his charges "a fraud and a hoax." But it was widely faulted at the time as a partisan "whitewash" and as a result failed to squelch the hysteria McCarthy had unleashed. The investigation "utterly failed to convince the country that there are no skeletons in the State Department closets," noted the *Los Angeles Times*, using a euphemistic term clearly intended to include more than Communists. Indeed, the final report ignored the homosexual charges completely. It even omitted a list of questions submitted by the Republican minority, one of which called for an investigation into who hired the ninety-one "sexual perverts." To emphasize what was missing from the report, Republican senators labeled it a "perversion" of the truth. "I have never heard a more blasphemous perversion of the truth than the outburst of [Senator Tydings] yesterday giving a clean bill of health to the entire personnel of the State Department," proclaimed Senator Jenner. There was evidence, he pointed out, of an "army of sexual perverts who are engaged in the filthy immorality of blackmail and degradation." Tydings's decision to ignore such charges played a significant role in the perceived failure of his committee in stemming the rising tide of McCarthyism.[21]

Truman's "Fairy Deal" Administration

The mounting pressure from Congress, the press, and the public for an investigation of homosexuality had President Truman's advisors worried. As one senior White House aide warned in an internal memorandum, "The charges about homosexuality have struck home with far greater effect, in certain quarters, than the Communist allegations." The people most alarmed, according to White House aide David Lloyd, were the poor and working class, who were concerned less about any risk to national security than about the simple moral implications. "Intolerance of this kind of deviation increases substantially as you go down the income scale," Lloyd argued, though he offered no evidence for his claim. Since this was Truman's natural Democratic base, the homosexual investigation, Lloyd concluded, represented "a political problem of considerable magnitude." Aides feared the issue would be raised in the upcoming congressional elections, as well as in the 1952 presidential contest. Newspaper editorials were already suggesting that Republicans would be railing against "queer goings-on in the State Department" in the fall campaign. "If we were writing Republican campaign speeches," editorialized the *New York Daily News*, "we'd use the word 'queer' at every opportunity." Three aides wrote a joint memorandum to the president in which they highlighted the seriousness of the brewing homosexual scandal. "Although the matter is frequently discussed in whispers behind hands," they noted, "a number of responsible persons have advised that . . . the country is really much more disturbed over the picture which has been presented so far of the Government being loaded with homosexuals than it is over the clamor about Communists in the Government."[22]

Amid mounting pressure, President Truman asked the Federal Loyalty Review Board to look into the cases brought into the public spotlight by Senator McCarthy. Established in 1947 as part of Truman's loyalty program, the board had final jurisdiction over federal employees accused of disloy-

[handwritten margin notes: "gay scare hit harder than com", "c/a #'s divides"]

alty. But at a meeting in April 1950, the board rejected Truman's request and voted unanimously to limit its considerations to issues of *loyalty*, deciding that to pass judgment on broader issues of *security* was beyond its authority. The board did agree, however, that if it uncovered any "flagrant" security risks, such as alcoholics or homosexuals, it would forward the facts to the president. "The President himself," the board concluded, "could then decide whether such an employee was a security risk." Newspapers criticized the decision and called for an expansion of the loyalty program to give all agencies the power to remove persons for "habitual drunkenness or homosexuality." "What's there to hide?" cried one editorial, calling the lack of jurisdiction over such security risks "a serious loophole in the President's program." The pressure was growing to expand summary dismissal powers to ensure the removal of homosexuals from all agencies.[23]

When it became clear that neither the Tydings committee nor the Loyalty Board would delve into the homosexual allegations or squelch concerns about subversive infiltration, Truman administration officials and their allies proposed the establishment of a bipartisan presidential commission. In numerous discussions between May and July, White House aides insisted that it should have a broad mandate to include the homosexual scandal. Spingarn felt that a high-level commission would "take a lot of steam out of [Republican] charges." McCarthy supported the idea, as long as the commission had authority to examine civil servants' "personal habits" as well as their loyalty. But the administration delayed until after the November election, when Republicans in Congress effectively prevented it from functioning. Historian Robert Griffith wondered whether such a commission, if appointed earlier, would have prevented the rise of McCarthy.[24]

In April, House Republicans managed to bring the homosexuals-in-government issue to a vote. During debate on a foreign aid bill covering appropriations for the Economic Cooperation Administration (ECA), Representative Arthur Miller (R–Nebraska) introduced an amendment to bar the ECA from employing homosexuals. "They are not to be trusted, and when blackmail threatens they are a dangerous group," Miller warned his colleagues. Despite Miller's impassioned plea that "homosexuals have been used by the Communists," his amendment failed 67–77. Afterward, Miller used the vote to attack the Democrats. Claiming it was a "straight party vote" during which "administration forces were in control of the legislative situation at all times," Miller accused the Democratic majority in the House of "bring[ing] joy to the homosexuals now employed in Government work."[25]

Republicans capitalized on the administration's seeming reluctance to investigate the homosexuals-in-government issue, accusing Truman, his

Loyalty Board, Tydings, and the Democratic Party generally of coddling homosexuals. At a Republican fund-raiser at the Waldorf-Astoria in May, New York Governor Thomas Dewey attacked the Truman administration for tolerating spies, traitors, and sex offenders in government service. Columnist George Sokolsky conceded that "Certainly Harry Truman cannot like either Communists or homosexuals," but asked pointedly, "Why does he protect them? Why does he fight for them?" One newspaper cartoon depicted Truman as a ventriloquist, telling his puppet-like Loyalty Board, "Report to me on the traitors and queers in my administration, and I may or may not tell the people." Republicans emphasized Truman's refusal to release loyalty files to the Tydings committee, suggesting he was protecting someone. Calling on Truman to release the files, Wherry challenged, "[L]et the people decide who is harboring subversives and moral perverts in government." Summing up the association between the incumbents and homosexuality, Senator Jenner dismissed the previous eighteen years of Democratic administrations as the "New Deal and Fair Deal and *fairy* deal administrations" (italics added).[26]

The Truman administration was in a political bind. If it got rid of homosexuals in the executive branch, as it had begun to do quietly in the State Department in 1947, Congressmen wanted to know why they were there to begin with. If it did nothing, it was accused of harboring homosexuals. The Peurifoy revelation that ninety-one homosexuals had already been dismissed could have easily been interpreted as evidence of an effective government security program and might have reassured Americans. In less public settings, congressional leaders held up the State Department's security program as an example for other agencies to follow. But for widespread public consumption, they denounced it as a hotbed of homosexuality, cried for the need to "clean house," and turned the revelation into a political liability for the Truman administration. They manipulated a fairly routine reporting into a major political scandal. Summing up the administration's conundrum, the *Muncie (Indiana) Star* editorialized, "The people know that hundreds of Communists and sexual perverts have been kicked out of Federal jobs. They also know that these people were hired while President Truman and President Roosevelt were in office." The more subversives they removed, the more they would be tarred as the party of subversives.[27]

The "Homintern"

For much of 1950, the issue of homosexuals in government threatened to overtake that of Communists in government within public political discourse. What made the homosexual issue even more of a liability for the administration was how many Americans began to conflate homosexuals and Communists. The constant pairing of "Communists and queers" led many to see them as indistinguishable threats. Evidence that one group had infiltrated the government was seen as confirmation of charges that the other had as well. McCarthy had helped ensure this confusion by embellishing the details of the few homosexual cases he had raised during his presentation to the Senate. In borrowing the case of the "flagrantly homosexual" translator from the old Lee list, McCarthy added new details to make the case seem more sinister. He claimed the translator had friends with the same tendencies and that they were "Soviet agents." Unfamiliar with the subtleties of the term "security risk," and speaking extemporaneously, McCarthy fabricated connections between homosexuality and communism. McCarthy was not the only one confused. Much of the public misunderstood the distinction between loyalty and security. "I wish there was some way of clearing up in the minds of the public the security and loyalty question," commented Senator Margaret Chase Smith. "I think nine out of ten people think of one as the other." The *Washington Post*—an independent newspaper, but then only the city's third largest—tried to educate the public. In an editorial on "The Aberrants," the *Post* explained that the problem of Communist infiltration of the government and "the purported presence on the Government payrolls of a considerable number of persons of homosexual tendencies" should not be confused. "There is, as far as we know, no reason for supposing that a person of homosexual bias is psychologically any more predisposed to the Communist ideology than a heterosexual person," the editorial argued. But such careful distinctions were lost on many readers as well as many conservative newspapers, which saw clear connections between the two threats. Westbrook Pegler, in the more popular *Washington Times-Herald*, wrote, "Communist literature undertakes to justify degenerate acts on the grounds of personal liberty and preference." As a conservative Catholic newspaper argued emphatically, "[T]he time for being naïve about the substance of the McCarthy charges is long past. The presence of close to a hundred perverts in the State Department—even though Hiss has been forced out and convicted and the perverts fired—justify [*sic*] a complete and thorough search for further evidences of the Communist conspiracy within the departments of our government." Such news outlets assumed that homosexuals and Communists were working together to undermine the government.[28]

The individual in Cold War political culture who most embodied the association between communism and homosexuality was Whittaker Chambers. Appearing before the House Un-American Activities Committee in

1948, Chambers, an ex-member of the Communist Party, captured national attention when he accused several individuals of being Communists, including former State Department official Alger Hiss. The resulting series of charges, denials, and countercharges—including the dramatic finding of secret microfilmed documents inside a pumpkin on Chambers's Maryland farm—was by far the era's most contentious and high-profile case of alleged espionage. While Chambers claimed intimate knowledge of Hiss and his Georgetown townhouse from their common involvement in the Communist underground, Hiss at first denied knowing Chambers and then admitted becoming acquainted with him when Chambers worked as a journalist. An immaculately groomed, Harvard-trained lawyer, Hiss epitomized the New Deal insider, whereas Chambers was a rumpled, overweight, sometime journalist and admitted Soviet agent. Because of their disparate backgrounds and conflicting stories, the nature of their relationship became a key element of the hearings, and the likeliest explanations seemed to be communism, homosexuality, or both.[29]

Though Hiss could not be tried for espionage because the statute of limitations had expired, he was indicted on charges of perjury. During the two subsequent trials, rumors surfaced that the Chambers-Hiss relationship involved at least sexual jealousy if not behavior. "Freud's theory that paranoia is generally homosexual in origin," wrote one psychiatrist, was "hinted at recently in the Whittaker Chambers–Alger Hiss trial." Others argued that Chambers was romantically obsessed with Hiss and constructed a fantasy emotional relationship around what was a rather casual acquaintance. Although Hiss's friends sought to squelch rumors about an affair between the two men, the rumors sprung partly from the Hiss defense team, which had investigated Chambers's background in hope of using his homosexual past to discredit him. As reporter Murrey Marder, who covered the trial for the *Washington Post* remembered, "[W]e reporters thought the defense's first move would be to bring up Chambers's homosexuality." Fearful that such a revelation might backfire on their client and his family, the defense never raised the issue in court. Hiss's stepson Timothy had been discharged from the military for homosexuality and was also rumored to have had a sexual relationship with Chambers. Though never discussed explicitly in court, hints of homosexuality surrounded the trial.[30]

Fearing it would come out in the trial, Chambers provided a sealed envelope to the FBI containing a letter outlining his homosexual past. Chambers admitted that while in the Communist underground in the 1930s, he "engaged in numerous homosexual activities both in New York City and Washington, D.C." His cover as an underground courier gave him the opportunity to pursue a secret life of homosexual cruising, he explained, especially since his communications group was headquartered in New York's Greenwich Village. Chambers linked his involvements in the homosexual and Communist undergrounds, claiming to have broken away from both in 1938. That year, he told the FBI, marked "the advent of religion and God into my life." Though not publicly disclosed at the time, the rumor and innuendo surrounding the Hiss-Chambers controversy not only associated the State Department with homosexuality but linked communism and homosexuality in the minds of many public officials, security officials, and opinion leaders. As one journalist commenting on the Peurifoy revelation remembered, "[H]omosexuality has figured, off stage, in one of our traitorous operations."[31]

Whittaker Chambers's homosexual experience while in the Communist underground was merely one piece of evidence forging what many people in postwar America saw as an intrinsic link between homosexuals and Communists. Both groups seemed to comprise hidden subcultures, with their own meeting places, literature, cultural codes, and bonds of loyalty. As people feared Communist "cells" within the federal government, they feared "nests" of homosexuals. McCarthy's first mention of homosexuals referred not to individuals but to a collective, variously termed "these gentlemen," these "types," and "this group." Discussions about "the ninety-one" State Department dismissals expressed and reinforced this notion by lumping together disparate individuals fired over a three-year period. Critics referred to them as a "homosexual clique," wanted to know how they had come to "congregate" in the State Department, and assumed they had all been hired by one conspirator.[32] As one congressional report warned, "The homosexual tends to surround himself with other homosexuals, not only in his social, but in his business life." A postwar commentator on American sexual attitudes noted, "Part of our folklore about inversion is that all inverts belong to a sort of large, loosely-associated, secret organization."[33] Such assumptions about the bonds between homosexuals are typical of stereotypes applied to any demonized group seen as a threat to the nation. As Michael Paul Rogin has argued, "Discrete individuals and groups become, in the countersubversive imagination, members of a single political body directed by its head."[34]

Although indistinguishable from mainstream society, both groups were thought to be able to identify one another. As Arthur Schlesinger Jr. wrote in his influential work, *The Vital Center*, Communists could "identify each other (and be identified by their enemies) on casual meetings by the use of certain phrases, the names of certain friends, by certain enthusiasms and certain silences." He compared this mode of identification to that used by homosexual men, suggesting that it was "reminiscent of nothing so much as the famous scene in Proust where the Baron de Charlus and the tailor Jupien suddenly recognize their common corruption." One congressman explained to his colleagues how homosexuals had their own slang and "signs used on streetcars and in public places to call attention to others of like mind." Gay people acknowledged their ability to identify one another and used similar language to describe the phenomenon. As Gore Vidal noted in his 1948 novel *The City and the Pillar*, "Occasionally two homosexuals might meet in the great world. When they did, by a quick glance they acknowledged one another and, like amused conspirators, observed the effect each was having. It was a form of freemasonry."[35] *gays club*

Members of such subcultures were feared to have a loyalty to one another transcending that toward their class, race, or nation. In an influential 1952 article, read into the *Congressional Record*, preserved by State Department security officials, and reprinted and cited well into the 1960s, Countess R. G. Waldeck argued that "by the very nature of their vice," homosexuals "belong to a sinister, mysterious, and efficient international." Arguing that sexual promiscuity between the upper and lower classes characterized homosexual society, Waldeck suggested that taking on a Communist ideology "gave a respectable facade to that social promiscuity which is the secret element of their vice." The idea of a "classless society where everyone would be free" appealed to the homosexual's need to throw off "'bourgeois' constraint," she reasoned. Therefore, according to Waldeck, all homosexuals had a natural affinity not only for one another, regardless of class, but for Communist ideology as well.[36] Despite the many racial and class divisions within gay subculture, many gay people saw their position in a similarly utopian light. "The homosexual automatically finds himself a member of a world-wide freemasonry which cuts across educational and financial levels," wrote a contributor to the homosexual magazine *One*. This subculture, he argued, constituted "the only truly classless society." The very name of this premier 1950s gay magazine was derived from an aphorism of Victorian writer Thomas Carlyle: "A mystic bond of brotherhood makes all men one."[37] *Brotherhood*

Like the Comintern, or Communist International, homosexuals were thought to make up a worldwide network, or "homintern." First used around 1940 by Harold Norse and poet W. H. Auden, the word *homintern* conveyed the idea of a global homosexual community, particularly in the literary and artistic world. By the 1950s, fear that American culture was increasingly dominated by this community found expression in publications from highbrow journals like *American Mercury* to scandal tabloids like *Confidential*. Some feared homosexuals had a "stranglehold" on the theater, television, and radio. Some feared this "powerful coterie" of homosexuals and their sympathizers would "lead to a gradual corruption of all aspects of American culture." One commentator suggested that pro-homosexual propaganda was so pervasive that it "appears in comic strips, on the radio, TV and in movie scripts."[38]

While considered troubling in the cultural realm, cliques of homosexuals were thought to be especially dangerous in government. To highlight this threat, many pointed to the Eulenburg Affair, a scandal in Imperial Germany at the beginning of the century in which members of Kaiser Wilhelm II's entourage were accused of homosexuality, particularly his favorite, Count Philip Eulenburg. The widespread publicity over what was known as the Eulenburg Affair brought the word *homosexual* into popular European discourse and immediately associated it with a conspiratorial clique within governmental circles. "This condition among the men who manipulated the Kaiser was dangerous in Germany," wrote Westbrook Pegler soon after the Peurifoy revelation, and therefore should not be tolerated in the United States. "Homosexualism is worse than communism," Pegler's German informer assured him. "It changes the mentality, blurs morality and the outlook, not only on sex but upon life, ideals, principles and scruples. It is a cancer." By highlighting parallels with this earlier scandal in a Rightist monarchy, Pegler suggested that homosexuality and communism were parallel dangers, both representing a threat to the independence of any government.[39]

To McCarthy and many other Americans, not only did homosexuals and Communists form sinister social cliques, but also both groups were made up of individuals who were psychologically disturbed. In McCarthy's first speech to the Senate on subversives in the State Department, he explained the connection by suggesting that all Communists were "mentally twisted." Indeed, in 1950s culture, both communism and homosexuality were widely seen as the result of psychological maladjustment and early childhood development problems, particularly an overdependence on the mother. Many studies from the period of both Communist spies and homosexuals pointed to psychological causes such as a doting parent, a sheltered life, a sense of alienation from the norm, or other childhood traumas. This was not merely the thinking of psychologists and psychiatrists; it permeated the culture. When a Georgetown University professor was questioned by an FBI agent in a routine loyalty/security investigation about one of his students, he attributed both her lesbianism and her affinity for leftist ideology to her psychological problems. He told the security agent that she was "completely maladjusted psychologically, sexually and in every other way." Not only was she a homosexual "admittedly and known," but she was "resentful toward convention," and "very materialistic and sympathetic toward the Russian position." In his mind, these sexual, cultural, and political stances all emanated not from conviction and preference but from "a weakness in her character which I base on the need for love and affection." Since she had "sought and practiced extremes in all phases of her living," as shown in her "homosexual problem," the professor feared that she would make "excellent material for Communist front or Communist activity," and therefore he could not recommend her for a sensitive position in the government. Because homosexuals were psychically twisted, they were thought to be susceptible to influence by subversive groups.[40]

While McCarthy and others linked homosexuality and communism using the modern language of psychology, they more frequently invoked a traditional vocabulary of morality. In his famous Wheeling, West Virginia, speech, McCarthy argued that "the great difference between our Western Christian world and the atheistic Communist world is not political, ladies and gentlemen, it is moral." He identified the central problem with communism as its "immoralism." Many Americans thought Communists were hostile to the traditional family and advocated "free love." Stories circulated that after the Bolshevik Revolution women had been nationalized and forced to register at "bureaus of free love." Many saw the presence of strong professional women in the Soviet Union and their reliance on collective child-care as evidence of communism's antipathy to the patriarchal family. FBI agents routinely questioned civil servants about their views on marriage, because, as one agent noted, opposition to marriage was "one of the tenets of the Communist Party." As William Montgomery, president of Acacia Mutual Life Insurance, told an audience at Washington's Mayflower hotel, "The first thing Communists would do would be to destroy the family as a unit, because by destroying the family they destroy the basis of a free life." Some suggested that Communist societies were more tolerant of homosexuality than was the United States. As one congressman claimed in 1950, "It is a known fact that homosexuality goes back to the Orientals, long before the time of Confucius; that the Russians are strong believers in homosexuality," thus linking the two principal Communist countries with a history of homosexuality. Although in the Soviet Union homosexual acts were decriminalized in the immediate post-revolutionary period, this relatively tolerant climate changed with the rise of Stalin, who ordered mass arrests of homosexuals and viewed homosexuality as the product of bourgeois decadence.[41]

Many, including McCarthy, saw the struggle between the United States and the Soviet Union in apocalyptic terms, drawing parallels with the fall of the Roman Empire and warning that America was heading down the same path. "Once the people of a Nation become complacent about moral degeneracy in its leadership, then that nation has not long to live," McCarthy wrote. "For example, the great Roman Empire came to an end when the ruling class became morally perverted and degenerate."[42] Others echoed McCarthy's concerns that sexual perversion threatened the nation's survival. The American War Dads from Evansville, Indiana, wrote to inquire why such "vicious persons" were employed by the State Department and why no attempt was made to replace them with "young men and women of sound Christian families." The group lamented that "these sordid events and acts" had damaged our prestige "as a Christian Nation," and warned that "declining public morality in high official places leads to a breakdown in morality everywhere." Complaining of the "large congregation of degenerates" in the State Department, a Chicagoan wrote Truman that he feared official Washington was "intent on imitating the vices of Pagan Rome."[43]

In this Cold War view of a world divided into a Judeo-Christian West fighting atheistic communism, promoting immorality was seen as part of the Communist plot to hasten the moral degeneracy of America. "Communism actively promotes and supports sex deviation to sap the strength of the new generation and make the birth of another problematical," asserted tabloid journalists Jack Lait and Lee Mortimer in U.S.A. Confidential. In a series of articles in the tabloid magazine Vitalized Physical Culture, Arthur Guy Mathews advocated a "crusade" against homosexuality to save the nation from a Communist victory. He suggested that American newspapers run articles with the headline: "EXTRA, EXTRA! COMMUNISTS ARE NOW CONVERTING AMERICAN YOUTH TO HOMOSEXUALITY TO DEFEAT US FROM WITHIN!" Characterizing homosexuals as "pink pansies" who "shriek, scream, cry and break down into hysterical states of psychoses when they are called upon to carry arms to defend our shores from the enemy," Mathews accused Communists of encouraging homosexuality in the West to make us "physically weak." Homosexuality, Mathews argued, was "Stalin's Atom Bomb."[44]

Whether comparing their social habits, psyches, or morals, cold warriors drew many parallels between Communists and homosexuals, not all of which were consistent. Perhaps Senator Kenneth Wherry best captured both the ambiguity of the alleged connections and the certitude with which they were voiced. "You can't hardly separate homosexuals from subversives," he explained. "Mind you, I don't say every homosexual is a subversive, and I don't say every subversive is a homosexual. But a man of low morality is a menace in the government, whatever he is, and they are all tied up together."[45]

[handwritten: web of men of low morality]

★

With the Peurifoy revelation, the alleged danger posed by homosexuals in government emerged as a major political issue in American life. Though initially part of a partisan political strategy to embarrass the Truman administration, it was an issue that clearly resonated with the public. Many politicians saw it as a more potent political weapon than the Communists-in-government issue and pressed McCarthy and others to refocus their efforts. Much of the public, too, seemed more concerned about the charges that the government had been infiltrated with homosexuals. One reason the homosexuals-in-government issue had such political and cultural potency was the many ways in which homosexuals and Communists were imagined to pose similar threats. Both groups were perceived as alien subcultures that recruited the psychologically maladjusted to join in immoral behavior that threatened the nation's survival. Many claimed the two groups were working together. *[handwritten margin: made threats / parallel to / bolster one another]*

But the homosexuals-in-government issue caused even more concern because of significant differences between homosexuals and Communists. Unlike Communists, homosexuals themselves never entered into the debate in the 1950s. While their fate was debated in the nation's newspapers, on the floors of Congress, and even in the White House, the men and women themselves remained in the shadows. As journalist Max Lerner wrote, "This is a story in which only the accusers and the hunters—Senate probers, security officers, police officials—get their names in the papers. The hunted remain anonymous—unspecified, uncounted, nameless men." In an era known for the phenomenon of "naming names," the almost total anonymity of the thousands of gay men and lesbians touched by the purges is remarkable. This strategy of deliberate concealment served the purgers well. It allowed a fantastical image of sexual perverts to reign without the countervailing weight of any reference to reality. Gays, even more than Communists, were phantoms, ciphers upon whom could be projected fears about the declining state of America's moral fiber.[46] *[handwritten margin: anonymity of hunted]*

The two targets differed not only in their visibility but also in their numbers. By 1950, after many years of loyalty screenings and investigations by the House Committee on Un-American Activities, there were very few, if any, Communists in the federal government. That was one reason why the net kept widening to include Leftists and those thought to be at least sympathetic to the Communist cause. But the claims that the federal government contained many homosexuals and other security risks was true. "This used to be a very gay city," friends told Ramon G. when he moved to Washington in 1951. "People would practically carry on on park benches . . . the agencies here were filled with gays. Nobody bothered them, nobody cared," Ramon remembered hearing, "until this business with McCarthy started." After arriving in the city and finding a job with the Department of the Army, Ramon quickly came in contact with the devastating consequences of the purges, as he watched co-workers lose their jobs. But he also heard from many long-time Washington residents about an earlier, more liberal time. Although some individual cases of firings and harassment of gay people occurred, there was no systematic attempt to purge homosexuals. "If someone was fired they just went across the street to another agency," Ramon explained, "and they were glad to have them." His lover, "Patrick," had heard the same stories. "The government used to be quite gay," he noted, "before McCarthy."[47]

2

"This Used to Be a Very Gay City"
Lafayette Park and the Sex Crime Panic

In 1933 in the midst of the Great Depression, "Ladd Forrester" learned that his parents could no longer afford to send him to college. A young gay man, Forrester was looking for a way to escape his small, southern Mississippi River town when he heard of an acquaintance who had gotten a job in Washington, D.C., in one of the New Deal agencies. "I found a car of three people driving to Washington and joined in as the fourth paying passenger," Forrester remembered of that fateful trip. Through the intervention of his representative in Congress, Forrester soon found a job as a file clerk at the Reconstruction Finance Corporation and a place to stay in a room not far from the White House. Like many of his fellow entry-level federal workers, he enrolled in classes at nearby George Washington University. "While standing in line to sign up, I got into a conversation with Ronald, a most attractive junior classman," Forrester recalled. Ronald invited him to a dance that night, held in a former stable behind two Victorian townhouses on P Street. When he arrived, he heard a three-piece orchestra playing "Shine On Harvest Moon" and saw "young men like myself" dancing together "cheek to cheek." There were women dancing together too, but Forrester was more captivated by the many brunette men with their hair swept up and tinted with gold. It was "a party the likes of which I could never have imagined possible," Forrester remembered years later. "As I stood there, I suddenly thought: here I am, twenty years old, I have a job in the capital of the United States, a place to live that's my own . . . and a new friend who has brought me to this glamorous party. . . . I could not hold back tears." Soon after, Forrester attended a lesbian wedding at the home of a minister from one of the city's more "prominent congregations." The traditional wedding cake was topped with two female dolls holding hands. Like Forrester, the two brides had come to Washington to work in the new government agencies. For all of them, the New Deal meant more than economic opportunity during hard times. It meant a new way of life.[1]

The story of "Ladd Forrester" and his migration to Washington is representative of the stories of many gays and lesbians who forged Washington's gay subculture in the 1930s and 1940s. Forrester came to Washington to work in one of the myriad of federal agencies established in response to the Great Depression. He had no particular ideological commitment to the Democratic Party and its social welfare programs; he simply needed a job in a more tolerant location than his small hometown. Thousands of young men and women came to the nation's capital in search of both work and social acceptance. As the Depression and the New Deal transformed the relationship of American citizens to the federal government—creating the expectation that government should solve problems like unemployment, poverty, and labor unrest—it also transformed the city of Washington. This process of urbanization created the kind of social and economic base that is crucial to the development of gay and lesbian subcultures. Washington in the 1930s and 1940s was not unlike New York and Chicago in the 1920s— a time and place when persons attracted to members of their own sex were able to construct vibrant and visible communities in both their home and work environments. Though Forrester's recollection may have romanticized gay Washington, it confirms patterns historians of sexuality have discovered in other American cities. It suggests the need to reassess the still common assumption that gay men and lesbians led isolated, lonely lives prior to World War II or even prior to the 1960s. It also suggests one of the underlying targets of the Lavender Scare. By the 1950s the extent and the openness of this subculture in the nation's capital attracted the attention of Congressmen like McCarthy, Wherry, Bridges, and Miller. Their charges that the bureaucracy was honeycombed with homosexuals were not without merit. As the Depression drew large numbers of people into the Communist Party, so the New Deal drew many young men and women, including many homosexuals, into the civil service. What one former Communist party member said of their resulting vulnerability in the postwar era was also true of homosexuals: "We were sitting ducks."[2]

"Number One Boom Town"

In 1950, when senators sought an explanation for how homosexuals had infiltrated the State Department and other agencies, they imagined the work of an unseen "master spy." But the real reasons were economic. Washington in the 1930s and 1940s, under the New Deal and then World War II, was a boomtown. The total population of the metropolitan area doubled—from approximately 700,000 in 1930 to 1.4 million in 1950—while the number of federal workers in the city increased fourfold—from 70,000 in 1930 to a peak of 270,000 by 1942. During the war years, 5,000 new government workers arrived each month, creating an unprecedented housing shortage. Many of the new arrivals were young, single people looking for entry-level clerical positions. As one government economist recalled, "The New Deal was a young man's world. Young people, if they showed any ability, got an opportunity." Another writer recalled that one of the principal impressions of Washington was "youth, chiefly feminine youth, issuing in a surging late-afternoon tide from some great Government building." No longer a small southern town, Washington, D.C., was becoming a major city—the nation's ninth largest by 1940—and increasingly one of young, single men and women. In the 1930s, while the rest of the country experienced Depression and every major city except Los Angeles lost population, Washington's increased 36 percent. By 1940 it was being called the nation's "Number One Boom Town."[3]

Not only was the supply of jobs high in the nation's capital, but also the type of work available appealed to men and women who lived outside of traditional societal norms. The federal civil service, because of its neutral examination process, was more hospitable to women and others who had difficulty breaking into the "old-boy" network pervasive in the business world. Since passage of the Pendleton Act in 1883, all positions classified within the civil service were filled by competitive examination, held by the Civil Service Commission, which forwarded the names of the three top performers to individual agencies for consideration. This merit-based system was not absolute. Many positions remained outside of it and therefore subject to patronage hiring; consideration was given to geographical representation from all the states; and agencies could specifically request male or female applicants. Most significantly, the Wilson-era requirement that photographs be appended to CSC applications facilitated rampant racial discrimination. Although not a pure meritocracy, the civil service offered many white applicants who might be denied employment in other environments significant employment opportunities.[4]

For single, middle-class women in particular, the federal government offered unprecedented opportunities for making an independent living. The federal government had long been a pioneer in providing white-collar jobs to women. When the Treasury Department hired its first female clerks in 1861—for lack of available men during the Civil War—the idea was "not only avant-garde, but bordering upon scandalous" because it brought women into an all-male environment and violated the common ideology that women should remain in a female sphere isolated from public life. According to historian Cindy Aron, the federal government was "decades ahead" of the private sector in bringing women into its white-collar occupations. By the end of the nineteenth century, the civil service had become the "first large, sexually integrated, white-collar bureaucracy in America." Most of the female positions were clerical. By the 1920s, clerical work in both the government and private sector had been largely feminized. According to historian Margery Davies, it was the availability of cheap female labor which led to the routinization of clerical work. Between 1934 and 1944, the percentage of women in the federal workforce more than doubled, increasing from 15 percent to more than 37 percent. In Washington, with its high concentration of clerical work, nearly 60 percent of the federal workforce was female. As Mary Anderson, head of the Women's Bureau said, "Nowhere perhaps has the advance of women with any employer been more dramatic than with Uncle Sam." By the 1940s, with the huge influx of "government girls," or "G-girls," who came to work in the wartime agencies, the District of Columbia was home to more than 150,000 women on the government payroll. Washington quickly acquired a reputation as a city populated by more women than men. While they may not have been a majority, women in Washington had more opportunities than in other cities to earn their own livings. The Classification Act of 1923 even mandated equal pay for equal work within the civil service, though it lacked any means of enforcement. As one tabloid journalist wrote about the "dames" in the city, "[M]ost of them are government employees, and thus have better security than is provided by a husband." Although derided as a "femmocracy" because of the number and independence of its women, Washington offered unique opportunities for women looking to live outside of a traditional marriage.[5]

The large number of clerical jobs in Washington also attracted gay men. Research on other cities indicates that clerical environments, because they were increasingly feminized, often attracted young, openly gay men. In a University of Chicago sociological study in the 1930s, half of the gay men interviewed worked as office clerks, stenographers, or other clerical help. Known as "fairies," these men marked their sexuality through distinctive clothing styles and mannerisms, and were therefore unwelcome in either traditional working-class environments or middle-class professional settings. But the feminized worlds of retail and office work provided an environment where they could feel comfortable and not have to hide their identities. Jack Benny's popular radio comedy program reflected this stereotype by depicting "sissy" characters who were either retail clerks or secretaries. "Oh, she's his private secretary. I'm right out in the open," quipped one of Benny's characters, alluding to his homosexuality. By World War II, the military's job classification process institutionalized the notion that gay men made good secretaries. According to historian Allan Bérubé, a wartime military study of homosexual men concluded that they had "considerable talent in stenographic, musical, clerical, and special service activities." Although the military attributed a particular predilection for clerical work to gay men, an alternative explanation is that in these jobs they felt comfortable and could find others like themselves.[6]   *feminization of workpla-*

[This combination of neutral civil service entrance examinations and a *makes* feminized work culture made government offices in Washington prior to *gay* the 1950s hospitable to gays and lesbians.] Jeb Alexander, a gay man and *friendly* native Washingtonian, began working for the federal government in the 1920s. The extensive diary he kept from the 1910s to the 1950s is one of the most important windows into gay life in Washington during this period. He describes a work environment within the federal bureaucracy overwhelmingly populated with women—both gay and straight—and gay men. One of his co-workers, Mr. Brown, he describes as "a tall, diffident man about thirty-five, with the gentleness and shy loveableness of an in- *ME* vert." Throughout the rest of his long career in the federal service, most of Alexander's colleagues and supervisors were women. Many of Alexander's gay friends and acquaintances, including many he considered more "obvious types" than himself, also held low-level federal positions. "John Edward Collins," another gay man who left behind a first person account of his time in Washington, worked in a Washington office after being drafted into the military. Of his civilian supervisor, Collins noted, "as luck would have it, he was an invert." When he dated one of his female colleagues in a vain attempt to assume a heterosexual identity, she turned out to be a lesbian. "I marveled at the number of government employees who were inverts," Collins proclaimed. He was not alone in his assessment. Another gay man wrote from Washington in 1955, "I believe two-thirds of the population here are homosexual."[7]

Whether or not the nation's capital or the federal government actually had a higher percentage of gay men and lesbians than other cities or employers is impossible to determine.[8] But comments about the large number of gay federal employees speak as much to their openness as to their numbers. Those who worked for the government in this early period do not seem to have been particularly secretive or fearful for their jobs if their homosexuality were revealed. Jeb Alexander's co-workers knew of his sexuality and teased him about it, even though he did not talk about it openly. Alexander's self-presentation was distinctive enough that strangers would often identify him on the street as a "fairy." His gay friends, whom he described as more "flamboyant" and "obvious," visited him at work and encountered his co-workers at random events throughout the city. Miss Contadeluci, a co-worker with whom Alexander often sparred, called him "Old Lady" and teased him about his gay friends. "I've been told that Bolling has turned out to be a 'fine sister,'" she said of a mutual acquaintance, using a slang term many gay men used to refer to one another. When Alexander refused to respond she continued, "Well—does he have sissified ways?" Perhaps more telling of the politics of homosexuality within his office was the "insinuating" gift he received at an office Christmas party—a box of chocolate cigarettes or "fags." Co-workers openly teased him about his sexuality but without malicious intent or any threat of job loss. No doubt some persons who exhibited signs of an unconventional sexuality lost their government jobs, since civil service regulations disqualified anyone guilty of "immoral conduct." But the regulation was not rigorously or systematically enforced. As a congressional committee found in 1950, prior to the Peurifoy revelation and the resulting hysteria about the alleged threat homosexuals posed to national security, most government agencies practiced a "head-in-the-sand attitude toward the problem of homosexuality." Most officials assumed that what a government employee did outside of the office on his own time "was his own business." The few homosexuals who were quietly removed, the committee noted, could "promptly obtain employment in another public agency."[9]

Cruising Lafayette Park and Beyond

Many men and women migrated to Washington not only for its economic opportunities but for its sexual ones. For many, government work represented not an end in itself but a means to participate in Washington's vibrant gay subculture. Jeb Alexander, an aspiring novelist, considered his job "drudgery." He began as an editorial clerk and did not rise much beyond this initial station. "To hell with the government!" he proclaimed once in frustration, "Life begins at 4:30 for me," referring to the standard quitting time for federal workers before World War II. Similarly, Edward Collins disliked his boss and found little enjoyment in his work. "I was able to struggle through my working hours only because of the anticipation of the evening's pleasures," he commented, echoing Alexander's sentiments. For these young gay men, the real focus of their energies was not the civil service but Washington's increasingly active gay social world.[10]

The epicenter of Washington's gay male world in the first half of the twentieth century was Lafayette Park, one square block directly across Pennsylvania Avenue from the White House. References to Lafayette Park as a center for gay cruising and socializing go back to the late nineteenth century. A Georgetown professor of nervous diseases related in an academic paper in 1892 stories he had heard of men caught in the park *"in flagrante delicto"* by the police—who often called upon him for medical advice. Among gay men, the park had a venerable reputation. One man in the 1920s said he had heard of it "all the way down in the Virgin Islands." Gay novels published in the 1930s made reference to the park as a meeting place for homosexuals. Jeb Alexander visited what he called "the old Square" so frequently he had names for different benches and those who frequented them—including the "Wishing," "Nighthawk," "Magnolia," and "Nigger's" benches. A best-selling exposé of Washington, D.C., from 1951 called it "the chief meeting-place" for "fairies." The authors alleged that the number of gay men who congregated in this "garden of pansies" created "a constant soprano symphony of homosexual twittering," and therefore dubbed it "one of the most sordid spots in the world." Law enforcement authorities were also aware of the place the square held in gay male life. By at least the 1920s, a plainclothes police officer regularly patrolled the park. Alexander referred to him as "the Sneak," commenting that with his obvious surveillance technique he "might as well wear a uniform."[11]

Although sexual encounters occasionally took place in the park, the more common pattern was for men to meet one another there and then move on to a more private location. While Alexander described once seeing "two fellows furtively engaged in mutual masturbation" near the Von Steuben statue,[12] he also recalls meeting and socializing with friends. On a Saturday night in June 1923, Alexander, then twenty-three years old, "was determined to squeeze an adventure out of the old Square." He ran into a friend, who gave him tips on how to cruise the park more aggressively. "I've been observing your methods," the friend confessed. "You sit waiting for someone to start something. Well, you can sit *a while*. Then if nothing happens, make a tour of the park. Find one who appeals to you. Then *you* sit down with *him*." Alexander did make many acquaintances in the park with men who became friends or lovers. One night while sitting under a beech tree on "the best bench in the park," he met Randall Hare, who discussed his desire to become a diplomat and his interest in music. Before long they sought out more privacy in "the moon-misted lawns near the [Washington] Monument." As Alexander recalled that romantic night, "Nothing disturbed us, and we lay in each other's arms, my love and I, while the moon beamed from a spacious sky and the cool breeze rustled our hair." Although Alexander was anxious they would be discovered, Hare assured him, "We are safe."[13]

Using public spaces such as parks and streets for meeting, socializing, and having sex was common earlier in the century, before the rise of mass suburbanization. As George Chauncey explains about the situation in New York, urban streets and parks had long been a site of socializing, particularly for young and working-class men. For people crowded into small tenements and rooming houses, Chauncey argued, "privacy could only be had in public." At mid-century, Washington's downtown was much more heavily residential than it is today. Given the housing shortage that developed by the 1940s, people in the apartments and rooming houses of the District would naturally use the parks of the city to relax and socialize. Not only was the population of the city more dense, so was the foliage in the parks. Lafayette Park and sections of the Mall were heavily wooded, providing ample opportunity for privacy. Thus Washington's parks provided the setting for many romantic and sexual encounters—both heterosexual and homosexual. In the late nineteenth century, the British ambassador and the wife of the Spanish ambassador used to have clandestine rendezvous in Lafayette Park and, according to legend, got trapped inside one night after the iron fence then surrounding the park was locked. In the 1950s, one Washington newspaper discussed the advantages and disadvantages of certain park benches for romantic trysts. The writer lamented that Washington officials were not following the lead of Los Angeles, which, "mindful of the needs of lovers," was installing benches built just for two.[14]

More than venues for cruising, the parks and open spaces along the Mall were also sites of general socializing among gay men and lesbians. Ladd Forrester remembers that on warm evenings as many as two hundred gay men and lesbians would gather on the north side of the reflecting pool in front of the Lincoln Memorial to roller-skate. "We would skate holding hands, and the Park Police never interfered," Forrester remembered. Regular Sunday picnics at the Botanic Conservatory on Capitol Hill lasted all day. The gays and lesbians who gathered there would take photographs standing before the larger-than-life nudes on the monument to General George Gordon Meade, which then occupied the conservatory grounds.[15] Such openness was not unusual. One day as Alexander and Hare took the streetcar back from Hare's parents' home in Georgetown, Hare placed his hand on Alexander's. When a woman across the aisle "made an audible remark about it to her companions," Hare refused to move his hand, commenting defiantly, "There was no reason boys should not be demonstrative toward one another, as girls and Frenchmen were." Evincing a political consciousness not often associated with gay men in the 1920s, Hare remarked to Alexander, "Be glad she noticed, so she won't be shocked the next time she sees it." Such open displays of homosexual desire in 1920s Washington may not have gone unnoticed, but they had no serious consequences.[16]

The neighborhood around Lafayette Park featured a number of rooming houses, restaurants, and cultural institutions that became centers of gay social life in the nation's capital. As in many American cities, the Young Men's Christian Association (YMCA) on G Street, just west of the White House, became such a meeting place. Although nineteenth-century moral reformers founded the YMCA to provide wholesome activities and lodgings for young, single men adrift in the city, by the early twentieth century its cheap, all-male accommodations had developed reputations in many east coast cities as gay social centers. When Alexander moved to the YMCA at the request of his parents, who were renting out their house for the summer, he quickly discovered a circle of gay friends. The YMCA replaced Lafayette Park as the center of his social world. There he and his friends socialized in the hallways and held parties in each other's rooms. When he or any of this friends moved out, they frequently moved into a nearby rooming house or apartment building, often one in which other gay men had already set up house, establishing a migration pattern not unlike that of immigrant groups. Some who were too blatant in their behavior or disrespectful of the rule against overnight guests were asked to leave. Most remained within walking distance of one another and Lafayette Park. Many of the cheap cafeterias in the neighborhood, such as Childs and the Allies Inn, became frequent haunts of the gay men who lived in the YMCA or the nearby rooming houses. Alexander describes meeting friends for breakfast, lunch, and dinner at such commercial venues on a daily basis. Not only were these places convenient and inexpensive, but the staff was sympathetic. He used to dine with his friend Dash so frequently at the Allies Inn that the Italian waitress there once asked him, as he dined alone, "Where is the rest of the family?" When he replied that Dash was out of town, she inquired, "Miss him?" suggesting she was aware of their special bond. Although this downtown neighborhood had no name, it was compared by some gay men to neighborhoods in other cities which were known to be centers of a gay subculture, such as New York's Greenwich Village or Chicago's Towertown. As one gay man who moved from Chicago to Washington noted, "I lived in an area comparable to the Near North side, right near the White House, right off of Pennsylvania Avenue."[17]

Soon after the inauguration of Franklin Roosevelt came the end of prohibition and the reopening of legitimate bars. Among these were a number that catered to a largely gay and lesbian clientele.[18] Through much of the 1930s, Washington supported at least three such drinking establishments. One of the first to become popular was the Horseshoe, also known as "Margaret's" or "Maggie's," after the Italian woman who owned and operated it. It was located in a basement on Seventeenth Street behind the Mayflower Hotel, whose gentlemen's bar also became known as a gathering spot for gay men. A pianist named Howard entertained patrons on the weekends. On Sunday the bar sponsored a popular "Shrimp and Poetry Feast," an all-you-could-eat shrimp dinner followed by a poetry hour. The patron who received the most applause for his or her poetry reading got the meal free. Many of the selections spoke poignantly to the situation of gay men and lesbians, such as Oscar Wilde's "Ballad of Reading Gaol" or excerpts from A. E. Houseman's "A Shropshire Lad."[19]

The Showboat at Thirteenth and H Streets had both a gay male and lesbian following. Located in the basement of an all-night cafeteria, the Showboat was said to have "the dingy charm of a 1920's New York Childs' Restaurant." "About 75% of my customers are what are known as 'Queer,'" owner George Sachlis told the Army's regional headquarters in 1936. "We seat them all together on the other side of a dividing rail in the middle of the taproom," he explained, while on the other side of the partition sat soldiers and sailors, who would frequently jeer and insult the queers. Because of the disturbance to his business—and loss of the lucrative gay clientele—Sachlis appealed to the army to place his establishment off-limits to servicemen. Like most bars of the period the Showboat offered entertainment—a pianist named Chloe and a butch lesbian singer named "Lover Boy." Because regulars knew that the two entertainers were lovers, Lover Boy's heartfelt rendition of the popular love song "Chloe" would bring the house down.[20]

The third bar, Carroll's, was somewhat less genteel than the others, attracting "rough trade"—men, many of them in the military, who would have sex with men but did not consider themselves gay. As one patron put it, Carroll's "catered to a particular gay taste for sailors, soldiers, and marines, and to the armed services' fancy for a free weekend of entertainment." While the two other bars were located near the White House and Lafayette Square, Carroll's was on Ninth Street, then a notorious strip of burlesque houses, bars, and tattoo parlors. It was presided over by an elderly bartender and two waitresses who kept a careful watch over their customers. Rose and Betty acted as "affectionate intermediaries" between the gay men and the military types, recalled Haviland Ferris. "Any marine they knew to have robbed or beaten up on the gays was soon effectively ostracized." The waitresses also had "solid relations" with the uniformed Shore Patrol, who made nightly visits to the bar merely "to see and be seen."[21]

Gay men and lesbians in the nation's capital in the 1930s and 1940s enjoyed a comfortable working environment in the federal government and a vibrant social life in a fast-growing city. The networks of friends and acquaintances that formed around Lafayette Park, the YMCA, and Washington's gay bars engendered a strong sense of community. "To assume for those of us in the Thirties a dreary and repressed social life hardly fits the facts," wrote gay Washingtonian and poet Haviland Ferris. "The problem of personal acceptance of oneself as gay seems a greater problem now than it used to be." Of the notion of hiding in the "closet," he noted, "I can honestly say that I never knew what it was, for there was never a time when I or my friends were not out of it." Gay Washingtonians experienced not only a sense of openness and community, but also one of pride. Alexander shared books on homosexuality with his friends—such as English essayist John Addington Symonds's work on ancient Greek culture, the first to use the term "homosexual" in English. Describing one of his "beautiful books of life and love," Alexander proclaimed, "I am one of Symonds's fellow Catamites and I am proud of it." He also invoked Walt Whitman's "manly love of comrades" as a model and justification for his own interest in other men. Reading a bootlegged copy of Radclyffe Hall's lesbian novel *The Well of Loneliness* in 1929, despite the ban on its sale in the United States, Alexander was filled with "a deep melancholy and yet a sense of pride." Although this sense of community was circumscribed by racial and class division—Washington's public accommodations remained segregated until 1953—it demonstrates that notions of gay pride are not recent developments but have a rich history.[22]

World War II—The More the Merrier

If the influx of people into Washington during the New Deal created the urban and professional environments that allowed a gay and lesbian subculture to flourish, World War II accelerated the process. Because it provided opportunities for men and women to leave home, live and work in same-sex environments, and discover other people like themselves, historian Allan Bérubé has described World War II as "something of a nationwide coming out experience" for gay men and lesbians. World War II brought hundreds of thousands of men and women streaming through Washington, filling up its bars and cruising areas. "Swarming with sailors and soldiers," the nation's capital was the preferred stomping ground for men stationed at the myriad of nearby military facilities. The war increased access to Washington's gay subculture and created more opportunities for same-sex sexual encounters.[23]

The wartime atmosphere in Washington fostered a tolerant attitude toward sexual experimentation of many kinds. With thousands of young men and women arriving every day, housing was scarce, creating some very intimate sleeping arrangements. As horror stories circulated of six or more strangers having to share a single bedroom, the Defense Housing Coordinator considered constructing residence halls for unmarried government workers. In *The More the Merrier*, Hollywood highlighted the heterosexual possibilities such tight quarters made available, but that was only part of the story. David Brinkley, then a junior reporter, found shelter in the spare bedroom in the Georgetown apartment of one his NBC colleagues. "That was fine, I thought, until he insisted on climbing into bed with me. I asked him to get out. His response was that if he had to get out of my bed I had to get out of his apartment. I got out, while continuing with some awkwardness to write news scripts for him to read on the air." Dismissing this as a mere "inconvenience," Brinkley chalked the experience up to the war. "We consoled ourselves and romanticized it all by telling ourselves, 'Well, what do you expect? This is war.'" Observing the cramped living conditions in wartime Washington, John Dos Passos wondered if the city would become a center of alternative lifestyles and radical politics. "It might be in Washington that the Greenwich Village of this war would come into being." Noting that young men and women from small-town America had migrated to "sleazy lodgings" in the slums of downtown New York after the last war, he wondered if "maybe Washington was the new metropolis in the making."[24]

Not only did the war provide more opportunities for sexual encounters and an "anything goes" mentality, it also provided a new medical discovery. Gore Vidal attributed the heightened sexuality during World War II not only to men being removed from home and women, but to the recent discovery of penicillin, which significantly lessened the consequences of venereal disease. "We were enjoying perhaps the freest sexuality that Americans would ever know," he wrote of the winter of 1945–46. Indeed the demands of war had accelerated the normal time involved in testing a new medicine like penicillin. First brought to the attention of the Public Health Service (PHS) in 1943, penicillin had by the end of the decade dramatically reduced the number of cases of gonorrhea and syphilis. In 1949 one PHS researcher wrote that "gonorrhea has almost passed from the scene as an important clinical and public entity." Rates of cure for syphilis surpassed 90 percent. But in contrast to Vidal, some moralists feared the impact the discovery of this "silver bullet" could have on the nation's morals. One leading venereal disease specialist warned it might "inaugurate a world of accepted, universalized, safeguarded promiscuity."[25]

After the war, many gay men and women who had been stationed in and around American cities and tasted the freedom they offered decided to stay. Though historians usually attribute this migration pattern to port cities like New York and San Francisco, through which millions of veterans returned, it was also true of Washington, with its large numbers of military installations. The GI Bill brought even more veterans to the area to attend the large number of colleges and universities located in the city. With five major universities—American, Catholic, Georgetown, George Washington, and Howard—and many more colleges in the metropolitan area, Washington's second largest industry after the federal government became education, attracting thousands of young people. Madeleine Tress, for example, originally came to Washington to attend George Washington University, but ended up working for the federal government. Peter Morris and Jack Frey, a gay couple who met at a D.C. gay bar, were both students at Catholic University. Frank Kameny, who would later be fired from the federal government for his homosexuality and launch the first legal challenge to the federal government's antigay policies, originally emigrated to Washington to teach at Georgetown and only later transferred to the federal government. Of the over five hundred men detained in Lafayette Park in 1947–48, 92 were students—the single largest professional category.[26]

By 1948, with all the changes brought about by the New Deal and World War II, many Americans had a growing sense that the country's moral codes were loosening and that homosexuality was becoming more prevalent, or at least more visible. That year an obscure Indiana University professor confirmed their fears. With the publication of *Sexual Behavior in the Human Male*, Dr. Alfred Kinsey revealed the findings of the most comprehensive scientific survey of American sexual behavior ever conducted. Rarely has such a dense, scientific tome received such widespread readership. Though the *New York Times* would initially neither review nor advertise the eight-hundred-page book, it remained on the newspaper's bestseller list for six months. Readers discovered that the actual behavior of Americans was greatly at odds with prevailing sexual mores. In addition to discovering high rates of masturbation and adultery among white men, Kinsey found that 37 percent of those surveyed had engaged in at least one homosexual act to the point of orgasm since the onset of adolescence. "This is more than one male in three of the persons that one may meet as he passes along a city street," Kinsey dramatically noted. He found that 4 percent of the men interviewed were exclusively homosexual throughout their lives. Kinsey and his team of researchers confessed to being "totally unprepared" for such findings. They retested their data and found that no matter the geographical setting, the data on homosexuality were more or less the same. "In view of the data," Kinsey summarized, "it is difficult to maintain the view that psychosexual reactions between individuals of the same sex are rare and therefore abnormal or unnatural."[27]

Many saw the Kinsey report as a sign of declining American morals. As psychiatrist Edmund Bergler warned, "If these figures are only approximately correct then 'the homosexual outlet' is the *predominant national disease*, overshadowing in number cancer, tuberculosis, heart failure, and infantile paralysis." He feared that Kinsey's figures would be used in the international propaganda war between the United States and its Communist enemies, "stigmatizing the nation as a whole in a whisper campaign." Kinsey's revelation of a high incidence of homosexuality caused many parents to look for signs of homosexuality in their children and seek advice from professionals on how to ensure that their offspring grew up to be healthy heterosexuals. Psychiatrists and other medical professionals advised mothers to be affectionate with their male children to establish pleasant memories about intimacy with women. They also encouraged the presence of a male role model so the child could identify with "masculine attitudes," particularly "responsibility and home formation." This advice underscored how homosexuality was perceived as a danger not only to the individual but also to the creation of a responsible generation concerned with establishing families and rearing the next generation.[28]

For men and women attracted to members of their own sex, the publication of Kinsey's first report represented a watershed moment. "It simply blasted this damn country wide open," observed Samuel Stewart, a gay man from Chicago who had been interviewed by Kinsey. "There wasn't a radio stand-up comic, or a television comic, or a nightclub comic who didn't have a thousand jokes to make of it. His name was a household word. . . . Even the dumbest guy on the street had heard of Kinsey." For Stewart, publication of the report represented a transition for homosexuals from invisibility to a central place in the nation's consciousness. "He was our Stonewall. . . . After that everybody began to know and would look at the straightest guy in the street and say, are you gay?" Harry Hay carried a copy of the Kinsey report around "as though it were a Bible." It made him imagine how powerful homosexuals might be if they organized, something he began to do in his native Southern California several years later. If the numbers gave Hay hope, they gave others a cold chill. Kinsey's findings seemed to quantify signs that the war had loosened America's moral conduct.[29]

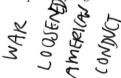

WAR LOOSENED AMERICAN CONDUCT

For those who may not have experienced World War II as a time of sexual experimentation and "coming out," a spate of postwar novels brought the phenomenon home to millions of readers. With authors like Truman Capote, Tennessee Williams, John Horne Burns, Charles Jackson, and Ward Thomas all publishing novels exploring gay desire, Gore Vidal called the postwar era a "golden age" for the genre. John Horne Burns, author of the critically acclaimed *The Gallery*, set in war-time Italy, self-mockingly dubbed the group "a pleiad of pederasts." Vidal's own *The City and the Pillar* was the most provocative of all. The story of two high school friends separated by the war, it broke, according to one literary critic, a one-hundred-year-old national taboo by depicting seemingly normal, middle-class men taking off their clothes and kissing one another. So many novels with gay characters appeared in the postwar era that critics and reviewers began to complain. One writer called *The City and the Pillar* "perhaps the least badly written of the post-Kinsey homosexual novels, most of which are mere peep-show exhibitionism." Another critic derided the story line of James Barr's 1950 novel *Quatrefoil*—"the latent homosexual and his struggle to find happiness in a hostile world"—as a "too-familiar theme." The *New York Times* dismissed the entire burgeoning genre as a "groaning shelf" of self-indulgent fiction.[30]

With so much attention being given to the issue of homosexuality in the postwar era, author John Cheever termed 1948 "the year everybody in the United States was worried about homosexuality." As he later wrote,

> They were worried about other things, too, but their other anxieties were published, discussed, and ventilated, while their anxieties about homosexuality remained in the dark: remained unspoken. Is he? Was he? Did they? Am I? Could I? seemed to be at the back of everyone's mind. A great emphasis, by way of defense, was put upon manliness, athletics, hunting, fishing, and conservative clothing, but the lonely wife wondered, glancingly, about her husband at his hunting camp, and the husband himself wondered with whom he shared a rude bed of pines. Was he? Had he? Did he want to? Had he ever?[31]

Postwar Sex Crime Panic

The anxieties that Cheever and others observed did not remain "unspoken" for long. In postwar Washington, as in the country at large, stories of sex crimes began to fill the newspapers. "The sexually aberrant male has become a problem in Washington," warned U.S. Attorney George Morris

Fay in 1948, as he announced that each day in the nation's capital two men were arraigned on sex charges. What had begun as sensational press coverage of a small number of particularly brutal sex crimes against children was becoming a moral panic. "The sex offender has replaced the kidnapper as a threat to the peace of mind of the parents of America," charged FBI director J. Edgar Hoover, who called for tougher legislation to prosecute sex offenders. Alleging an increase in sex crimes—as much an indicator of increased law enforcement as increased crime—Hoover blamed the problem on "the social and family upheavals" of World War II. "The wartime spirit of abandon and 'anything goes' led to a decline of morals among people of all ages," he wrote in the *American Magazine*. "Sex deviation" became a staple of public discourse in the late 1940s and early 1950s as fifteen states established commissions to study the problem. The media fueled the growing panic by highlighting sex crimes even in their routine crime reports. In the *Washington Star*, for example, a typical 1950 story announcing indictments handed down by a local grand jury featured the sex crimes—both in the headlines and the body of the article—while barely noting robberies or even murders.[32]

When George Morris Fay became U.S. Attorney for the District of Columbia in 1946, he launched a crackdown on sex crimes. "We saw the parade of sex offenses coming in—and nothing could be done," he complained. "There is no law." Fay discovered that most sexual offenses such as molestation, solicitation, or homosexuality resulted in a charge of "disorderly conduct"—a misdemeanor often punished by a light fine. Fay proposed a revision to the law to make a "sex perversion offense" involving a juvenile a felony and to commit habitual offenders to a mental hospital. The District Bar Association, the District Social Hygiene Society, the Metropolitan Police, the American Business Association, and many other civic, professional, and medical organizations came out in support of Fay's proposal. Most important, the *Washington Star* launched a campaign to enlist public support for tightening sexual offense laws. In a relentless round of articles and editorials, the newspaper contrasted the District's lack of a concrete sexual offense statute to the situation in other jurisdictions. "Unlike forty-seven states, the District has no statute on the books to assure full prosecution of degenerates who molest children," the newspaper warned. The *Washington Post* concurred, arguing that because of the weakness of current statues "Washington has become more or less a haven for sexual perverts and degenerates."[33]

"Sexual psychopath" was an ambiguous term, but one that frequently was conflated with "homosexual," since most observers assumed that homosexuals were sick, could not control themselves, and needed to recruit new members to their ranks. "The fags, fairies, pansies and other sex perverts hang around in the park areas usually looking for some boys upon whom they can foist their attention," warned one congressional aide. "Parents may think their boys are safe from being molested as long as they stay away from certain parks and restaurants where perverts are known to loiter," one Washington police officer explained, clearly implicating gay bars and cruising areas. "But the real danger may be in a boy's own neighborhood," he warned, suggesting that the sexual menace was spreading beyond its usual haunts. Another proponent of the law warned parents that "you may have a son in his teens who suddenly becomes quite affluent. . . . Under questioning, he finally confesses that he is receiving money from some man for permitting acts of perversion." Although working-class youth had engaged in this sort of "rough trade" for decades as a way of supplementing their income, proponents of the law argued that such behavior would lead them into a life of perversion. Police cautioned that homosexuality was a learned behavior, easily acquired by malleable children. "This form of depravity is developed by association of children with perverts, rather than being born with the defect, as it is popularly supposed," one officer argued.[34]

In February 1948, Congress held hearings on the need for a sexual psychopath law in Washington and looked at the experiences of other states as models. What they found made it clear that homosexuals were primary targets of the proposed legislation. Freshmen Congressman George MacKinnon (R–Minnesota) introduced correspondence from a Minnesota judge explaining how such a law helped local officials deal with a "type of screwball . . . who has no moral standards" but could not be prosecuted under existing criminal laws and could not be ruled insane. The judge offered only one concrete example. "Prior to the enactment of this law, we had the case of a high school boy who said he loved men and bragged about it," the judge explained. "We could not find him insane, he was a bright pupil, and we had to let him go. I think there should be a protection to society against people like this." Dr. Benjamin Karpman, senior psychiatrist at St. Elizabeth's Hospital, Washington's facility for the mentally ill, offered a conflicting viewpoint, but was quickly shouted down. Karpman cautioned that a large portion of the American population might be classified as sexual psychopaths under such a law. When he recommended that Washington follow the example of Europe and decriminalize private homosexual acts, Congressman MacKinnon objected. "If there is anything I consider to be despicable, it is where a [homosexual] is left to prey on society." Calling homosexuals "a constant menace," MacKinnon drew upon his own experience in the Navy during World War II to argue that homosexual acts were often not consensual. "They go around and they may not use actual force, but they intimidate by superior rank," he noted. Beyond policing behavior, such government officials wanted to contain what they saw as the increasing openness, even arrogance, of homosexuals.[35]

Hollywood helped seal the connection in the popular imagination between homosexuality and crime with the 1948 release of *Rope*. Loosely based on the sensational 1924 Chicago murder of Bobby Franks by Richard Leopold and Nathan Loeb, the film depicts the brutal murder of a young man by two homosexuals. Although the Motion Picture Production Code did not permit the portrayal of openly gay characters, director Alfred Hitchcock left obvious clues. Philip and Brandon live together in a fashionable New York apartment, with Philip playing the role of the weaker, younger wife, and Brandon that of the dominant husband. A pianist by profession, Philip is "artistic," an old code word for homosexual. In the opening murder scene, Philip and Brandon are shown together in a darkened room struggling and breathing heavily. When their task is completed, they rest together in the dark, and Philip lights a cigarette, further eroticizing their crime. A Warner Brothers promotional poster, which did not have to pass censors, touted *Rope* as "the most excitement-filled love story ever told." However tasteful and coded, the film suggested to millions of viewers how even middle-class homosexuals, believing that they were outside traditional moral constraints, could become criminal sexual psychopaths.[36]

In June 1948, President Truman signed what became known as the Miller Sexual Psychopath Law—named for its principal sponsor, Congressman Arthur Miller (R–Nebraska). The act substantially increased the penalty for sexual crimes in the District of Columbia involving children. It also codified for the first time the common-law notion of sodomy—defined as any penetration "however slight" of the mouth or anus of one person with the sexual organs of another. Such activity would be punishable by a fine of up to one thousand dollars or twenty years in prison. A recidivist would be examined by a team of psychiatrists to determine if he were a sexual psychopath—"a person, not insane, who by a course of repeated misconduct in sexual matters has evidenced such lack of power to control his sexual impulses as to be dangerous to other persons." Anyone determined to be a sexual psychopath would be indefinitely committed to St. Elizabeth's Hospital until the superintendent determined that he was "sufficiently recovered" so as no longer to pose a threat to the public.[37]

Propaganda about the Miller Sexual Psychopath law continually invoked the dangers posed to children; once passed, however, it was used to further criminalize consensual sex between adult homosexuals—both men and women. Soon after the law was passed, Fay announced that it might have to be invoked to combat the "recognized problem" of sexual perversion. Indeed, the first two arrests under the new sodomy statute were of a thirty-year-old African American man and an eighteen-year-old white sailor who were apprehended on the Mall in an apparently consensual encounter. They were held on a one-thousand-dollar bond. Prior to the passage of the Miller Act, such persons would have been charged with disorderly conduct, required to post a twenty-five-dollar bond, and released. Although the focus was mainly on the threat posed by men, women were also occasionally charged with sodomy. At a downtown hotel in 1949, a twenty-nine-year-old D.C. woman and a twenty-seven-year-old Baltimore woman were charged with sodomy and placed under a five-hundred-dollar bond. The risks of engaging in homosexual sex in the District of Columbia had significantly increased.[38]

Elimination campaign

The "Pervert Elimination Campaign"

While the media and legislative campaign to pass a harsh sexual psychopath statute in the nation's capital permeated the headlines in 1947, the U.S. government quietly launched its own campaign to combat homosexual activity. On October 1, the U.S. Park Police, which had jurisdiction over most of the parkland in the District of Columbia, inaugurated what it called a "Pervert Elimination Campaign"—an unprecedented federal program that mandated the harassment and arrest of men in known gay cruising areas. Under this program, involving increased patrols in Lafayette and nearby Franklin Park, hundreds of men were arrested and charged with disorderly conduct, loitering, indecency, or some other violation. More ominously, approximately four times as many men were apprehended, questioned, and released without arrest. Because "the evidence against them was not sufficient to warrant the commencement of criminal proceedings," the Park Police could not bring them before a judge. Instead, they held them in custody just long enough to fingerprint, photograph, and record the names and occupations of these men. This information was entered into a "pervert file."[39] *mass info recording*

The men arrested under the Pervert Elimination Campaign represented a complete cross-section of American society. While most of those detained were residents of the District of Columbia or surrounding communities, some were from as far away as Chicago, London, and Miami. There were college professors and students, accountants and real estate agents, truck drivers and elevator operators, stenographers and clerks. All ages and degrees of sexual experience were also represented. One thirteen-year-old, a ninth-grader from Jefferson Junior High School, was stopped on what was apparently his first foray into Lafayette Park. Having once fondled a man at a Ninth Street movie house, he had come to Lafayette Park to "to see what would develop." Notified by the police, the boy's father took him home and "guaranteed that the boy would receive medical attention immediately." The police also nabbed a sixty-year-old, white Georgetown professor and a sixty-five-year-old African American houseman who admitted "being a pervert since boyhood and being locked up several times." By February 1950, the Park Police had arrested two hundred men under this campaign. During the same period, another five hundred were apprehended and released without arrest. The typical detainee was a twenty-five-year-old government clerk.[40]

When Bruce Scott moved to Washington in the fall of 1947, he quickly became a part of the city's vibrant gay subculture. A native of Chicago, Scott, like many young gay men, had begun working for the federal government during the New Deal. After the passage of the Fair Labor Standards Act of 1938, Scott took the federal civil service exam and became one of the first wage and hour inspectors in Chicago. After serving in the military during World War II, Scott transferred to New York City and then, in 1947, to Washington. Scott had enjoyed an active gay social life ever since discovering Chicago's gay bars in the 1930s while a student at the University of Chicago. In Washington he discovered the Chicken Hut, one of the new gay bars that had opened up since the war. There he met Gordon Fahey, and together the two rented a place in Georgetown, increasingly known as a haven for bohemians, homosexuals, and other nonconformists. The capital's oldest neighborhood, Georgetown had been a largely poor, African American district until the large influx of young people to the city during the New Deal. Becoming part of this ongoing process of gentrification, Scott rented a quaint, two-story townhouse, part of a row of four nearly identical houses at the corner of Thirty-third and Q Streets. He was pleased to find that three of these four households were gay. A lesbian couple lived on one side, while on the other lived "Mr. Peters," who later lost his State Department job in the antigay purges. Both neighbors rented rooms out to single gay men. On Thirty-third Street Scott had found a small community of gays and lesbians with whom to socialize in Washington and take day trips to the beaches in Maryland and Delaware.[41]

Within months of moving to Washington, Scott also encountered the police crackdown on Lafayette Park. On a Saturday night in October 1947 Scott had dinner at the S&W Cafeteria and then walked back to his house in Georgetown. Along the way, he stopped in the Lafayette Park men's room, where he encountered a man leaning against the wall above the urinal in an awkward position. The situation made him uncomfortable, so he left the men's room and waited on the sidewalk outside for the other man to leave. Seeing a U.S. Park Police officer drive up, Scott realized he should leave to avoid any problems, but he said to himself, "Why should I run? I am doing nothing wrong. I have a right to stand here." He stood there for several minutes as the police officer observed him from his patrol car. After this situation also became uncomfortable, Scott returned to the men's room to try again to urinate. The police officer entered the men's room, announced he wanted to talk with him, and led him into a separate room from which the police could monitor the urinals. When asked why he had been standing on the sidewalk, Scott claimed he was feeling ill, not wanting to draw attention to the man in the men's room, who Scott did not realize was probably an undercover police officer. The officer questioned him about his sex life, threatening Scott with arrest unless he answered frankly. Frustrated by Scott's refusal to cooperate, the officer called the Metropolitan Police and had Scott arrested for loitering. He posted five dollars collateral and walked home to Georgetown. Scott had become one of the first victims of the Park Service's Pervert Elimination Campaign.[42]

For men such as Scott, the Pervert Elimination Campaign represented a systematic campaign of harassment and intimidation. Often the mere presence of a man in a known gay cruising area subjected him to being stopped, questioned, and having his identity recorded by federal police. Park Police records indicate that many men were simply "observed in Lafayette Park" or "observed in comfort station under suspicious circumstances." Two twenty-nine-year-old white men in an automobile were charged with disorderly conduct simply because, according to the police, "from all appearances, an act of perversion *had* taken place." A theater usher and a file clerk for Virginia Electric were arrested for kissing and charged with disorderly conduct. As M. H. Raspberry, Captain of the U.S. Park Police, told a congressional committee, if they observe "individuals generally known to the police, but who are not committing any act which could necessarily result in an arrest of the individual, they keep them under observation." The officers might also stop them for questioning. "We take it upon ourselves to record them even to the point of fingerprinting them and photographing them. We now have a file which is getting rather extensive," Raspberry boasted to the committee.[43]   medical power to police

Functioning as amateur psychiatrists, Park Police interrogated suspects not only about their behavior the night of their apprehension but about whether they were, in Captain Raspberry's words, "perversion minded." Authorities did not consider all those arrested or questioned to be "homosexual" or "perverts"; they made distinctions between physical acts and psychic identities. Even those seen engaging in a homosexual act were not presumed to be gay. Officials noted that a thirty-eight-year-old African

American clerk was "observed engaged in an act of perversion with another man," but also felt it necessary to record that he was "believed to be homosexual," as if the two statements had little to do with one another. Although park officials sometimes used such terms as "bi-sexual" and "dual sexual," the crucial variable was the amount of time someone had engaged in this behavior. Some perverts were considered "well-known," while others were "amateur . . . just learning the ropes." Some admitted homosexual tendencies, but were "trying to overcome them." One twenty-two-year-old white student at George Washington University who was stopped in November 1947 admitted to "being in the park to pick up a queer but denies being one." A thirty-one-year-old newspaper messenger denied being a "pervert" but admitted "he associates with known perverts and allows them to perform indecent acts upon him." Park police suggested such people should seek psychiatric treatment.[44]

The U.S. Park Police system of interrogation and classification reflected the common belief of many medical and legal authorities that homosexuality was a learned behavior that could be cured or resisted. One of the more overlooked aspects of Kinsey's study is that it did not divide men into heterosexual and homosexual identities, but classified them according to the extent of their homosexual activities at different points in their lives. While Kinsey found that 10 percent of white males were almost exclusively homosexual for at least three years, he found that 18 percent had as much heterosexual contact as homosexual contact during a similar period. Thirty-seven percent had had at least one homosexual experience in their adult lives. Kinsey's figures suggested that men might engage in homosexual behavior more frequently during certain periods than others. "Knowledge that men move into and out of the practice points to saner policing and to hopeful curing practice [sic]," commented one law professor on the Kinsey data, suggesting the need to distinguish between "the occasional and the habitual" offender. Emphasizing not how many engaged in homosexual activity but how many tried it without becoming habitual offenders, he interpreted the findings as a sign that such temptations could be resisted. "One out of three of all the rest of us have met and solved the problem," he noted. The goal of both the sexual psychopath law and the Pervert Elimination Campaign was to steer men away from homosexual activity, to prevent them from moving up Kinsey's scale to becoming habitual offenders.[45]

The desire to clean up Lafayette Park of sexual perverts soon became more than an effort to protect children or help people resist homosexual temptations. By April 1950, with charges flying about homosexuals infiltrating the federal government and acting as Soviet agents, the men cruising Lafayette Park seemed to threaten the nation's survival, particularly since one out of four worked for the federal government. The names and statistics of men arrested in Lafayette Park quickly came to be seen as a matter of national security. Both local and federal law enforcement agencies began providing reports of such arrests to government agencies, congressional committees, and the White House. As a draft of a congressional report noted, although such criminal behavior was usually the concern of local police, "sexual deviations have come to have a more dangerous significance when [they are] found in high places in the government or in positions which are security sensitive." By 1950 Congressman Miller, author of the District's sexual psychopath law, worried that gay bars and other meeting places were attracting foreign agents. "It is a well-known fact that several restaurants, clubs, and other establishments get most of their support from these sexual perverts," Congressman Miller noted. "How many secrets of the Government are spilled," he wondered, because "perverts and bottle clubs are tolerated in the District of Columbia?"[46]

By 1950 the nation and the District of Columbia in particular had an intricate and effective system of laws, tactics, and personnel to uncover homosexuals that would become enforcement mechanisms during the Lavender Scare. While catching Communists and other alleged disloyal citizens was difficult, as Senator Bridges told McCarthy's Wisconsin supporters, evidence of an arrest on a sex charge made homosexuality much easier to prove. When he came under attack for the lack of specificity in his charges about subversion in the State Department, McCarthy presented the police record and photograph of a man who "spent his time hanging around the men's room in Lafayette Park." Politicians and security officials needed to look no further than their evening newspapers to uncover homosexual government employees. "State Department Officer Forfeits $250 in Sex Case," reported the *Washington Star* in November 1947 regarding the Lafayette Park arrest of Merle Wood, a forty-nine-year-old administrative officer of Near Eastern and African Affairs. And when they wanted expertise on identifying and removing homosexuals, security officials turned to local law enforcement. After arresting hundreds of men in the Park Police's Pervert Elimination Campaign, Private Fred Traband became "special agent in charge of sexual deviation investigations" for the U.S. State Department.[47]

★

The crackdown on gay sociability in postwar Washington was a reaction to an earlier period of relative toleration and openness for homosexuals. The

New Deal and World War II allowed Washington's gay subculture to flourish. During the 1930s and 1940s, white, middle-class, gay civil servants in Washington like Jeb Alexander gave scant concern to the disclosure of their sexuality. They arrived in Washington full of hope as they built a community of others like themselves. They met and socialized in public spaces, restaurants, and other venues around Lafayette Park. Their "flamboyant" gay friends and heterosexual co-workers interacted without incident. Though Lafayette Park was patrolled by a police officer, he was seen as more of a nuisance than a real threat. They held hands on the trolleys and made love on the Washington Monument grounds. The war in particular was a period of sexual experimentation and loosening of societal norms. But it was this very openness and visibility which led to such a powerful cultural backlash. What made that later oppression particularly brutal was that it coincided with the advent of the Cold War, the fear of internal Communist subversion, and the rise of the apparatus of the national security state. Soon homosexuals were being removed not only from Lafayette Park, but from the State Department, and eventually from the entire federal government.[48]

3

"Cookie Pushers in Striped Pants"
The Lavender Lads in the State Department

How could [Truman] help it if par-
    ties both unusual and queer
Got into the State Department
    which true patriots hold dear?
To hear the dastards tell it
    they are true to Uncle Joey
And call each other female
    names like Bessie, Maud and Chloe.
And write each other poetry
    and confidential notes so tender
Like they was not he-men at all
    but belonged to the opposing gender.

—*Westbrook Pegler, 1950*

When Sumner Welles arrived at the Old State Department building next to the White House each morning, the chauffer of his Rolls Royce would hand his briefcase to a State Department usher. Undersecretary of state for Franklin Roosevelt, Welles was one of the most powerful and wealthy men in New Deal Washington. After attending Groton and Harvard, he had joined the State Department, and by 1940 he was at the pinnacle of his career in the diplomatic service. Roosevelt first appointed Welles to be assistant secretary of state for Latin America, but soon gave him many special assignments and eventually the second most powerful position in the department. He would later be called "the most influential under secretary of state of the twentieth century" and FDR's "global strategist." His influence stemmed not only from his expertise as a career foreign service officer and accomplished linguist, but from the social connections of his wealthy Eastern family—as a boy he held the train of Eleanor Roosevelt's wedding dress as Theodore Roosevelt walked her down the aisle. As an intimate of FDR and an expert on foreign affairs, Welles served as the *de facto* head of the department, with more influence over foreign policy than Secretary of State Cordell Hull, whom FDR had chosen for his political connections within the Southern wing of the Democratic Party. Hull's long absences due to chronic illness—he suffered from tuberculosis—exacerbated this unorthodox power dynamic. So did Welles's extreme wealth, much of it acquired in his second marriage to Mathilde Townsend, whose opulent Massachusetts Avenue mansion was patterned after Versailles's Petit Trianon.

Welles had caused a scandal when he divorced his first wife and married Townsend, who was rumored to have been his mistress. Welles's wealth, power, and profligate lifestyle earned him the enmity of many diplomats and politicians. According to writer Irwin Gellman, Hull "genuinely hated Welles" and conspired to oust him from the department. An incident on a train in 1940 gave Hull the leverage he needed. In the midst of the 1940 presidential campaign, with Roosevelt seeking an unprecedented third term, Speaker of the House William Bankhead suddenly died of a stomach hemorrhage. Wanting to shore up his support in the South, a key component of his New Deal coalition, Roosevelt ordered his entire cabinet to accompany him to the Speaker's funeral in Jasper, Alabama. But with the ailing Hull unable to travel, it was Welles who traveled on one of the two special trains that transported the presidential party and a congressional delegation to Alabama. On the trip back to Washington, Welles reportedly drank heavily at dinner. After finally retiring to his compartment late that night, Welles rang for assistance. When an African American railroad porter responded, Welles sexually propositioned him and several other porters who responded to subsequent calls. The administration tried to hush up the incident, giving one of the porters a job at the White House and eliciting Senator Harry Truman's help in squelching a threatened investigation in the Senate. Rumor of the incident quickly spread in Washington and caught the attention of Welles's enemies, principally Secretary Hull and William Bullitt, FDR's ambassador to France, who had also come to resent Welles's influence. They both urged Roosevelt to fire Welles, claiming that news of this incident could both embarrass the administration and be used by foreign countries against the United States. Roosevelt resisted firing Welles for three years, until Hull finally gave the president an ultimatum—Welles or he had to go. As Hull told Welles in their last conversation, "Your continuation in office would be, for the president and State Department, the greatest national scandal since the existence of the

United States." The press reported Welles's resignation as the result of a power struggle with Secretary Hull—which was only half the story.[1]

Though not reported in the press, the story circulated widely in Washington. Hull and Bullitt had approached Senator Styles Bridges about opening a congressional hearing into the matter and asked the publisher of the conservative *Washington Times-Herald* to print the story, all in vain. So in February 1950, when the scandal erupted about homosexuals in the State Department, many pointed to Sumner Welles as the source of the problem. "Blame is on the permission of one man to rig a whole hierarchy of misfits in the State Department," suggested syndicated columnist Robert Ruark, "and on our failure to recognize the rottenness and cut it out after the big sinner was caught and fired by President Roosevelt." Ruark claimed this unnamed official had "crowded the lists with so many homosexuals" that the ninety-one firings were the inevitable result. Another columnist wondered whether "an old family friend of Roosevelt's whose reputation, rightly or wrongly, became notorious" was among the ninety-one. The figure of Sumner Welles, the wealthy diplomat and member of the "Eastern establishment," was precisely the type of man born with a silver spoon in his mouth that McCarthy attacked in his Wheeling, West Virginia, speech. The Welles incident allowed critics to link the presence of homosexuals in the State Department directly to their chief villain, Franklin Roosevelt.[2] It helped seal the association between the department and homosexuality and formed a backdrop that seemed to confirm the charge that the department was honeycombed with—possibly even controlled by—homosexuals. It was the grain of truth around which was built the notion that powerful homosexual diplomats controlled foreign policy and could, by their scandalous behavior, expose themselves to blackmail.

"I Want It Understood I Was Fired for Disloyalty"

Though the Welles incident seemed to foreshadow the later State Department scandal, there was one significant difference. While the Welles scandal was kept out of the papers, the postwar ouster of "the ninety-one" made headlines. Indeed, in the spring and summer of 1950, allegations of sexual perversion in the State Department reached such a widespread audience that the oldest and most prestigious department in the executive branch became a dirty joke. The mere mention of the name suggested moral deviance. When a *Washington Post* reporter asked a man standing in line for concert tickets where he worked, and the man sheepishly replied "the State Department," those standing in line "burst into sniggering laughter." A newspaper column on "The Best Laughs of 1950" included several zingers about "the pansy tint in the State Dept." With both "pink" and "lavender" diplomats being ousted, one former employee reportedly remarked, "I want it understood I was fired for disloyalty." Another gag involved a mother answering her child's request for a fairy tale with the opening, "Once upon a time, in the State Dept." Some were quite explicit. One joke that circulated in Washington around this time posed the question, "Have you heard about the two State Department employees?" The answer was simply two names, "John Fitzpatrick and Patrick Fitzjohn." Although avoiding any obscenities and with a remarkable economy of language, the joke managed to conjure up the image of anal intercourse within the foreign service. Because they assumed knowledge about the charges of sexual immorality in the State Department, these jokes reflect the pervasiveness of those charges in American culture. When that proverbial measure of the zeitgeist, a taxi driver, was requested to go to Foggy Bottom, home of the new State Department headquarters, he reportedly turned around and, summing up the situation, exclaimed, "Fruits, the whole place is fulla fruits."[3]

With the image of the State Department so tainted by homosexuality, employees and officials became defensive. Male diplomats became self-conscious about any appearance of impropriety and were reluctant to be seen together in pairs. Some foreign service officers felt compelled to publicly demonstrate their heterosexuality. One such man would introduce himself at parties by announcing, "Hi, I'm so-and-so, I work for the State Department. I'm married and I have three children." As a lesbian friend of his explained, "He felt it was necessary to do that. He did it in a joking way, but . . . he didn't want anyone to think he was gay. The State Department was a major joke in the area." Even department officials had to acknowledge they had an image problem. Testifying before a congressional committee, Deputy Undersecretary of State Carlisle Humelsine admitted that "in the public mind, [homosexuality] seems to be a psychological illness or sickness generally associated with the Foreign Service and the Department of State."[4]

The most unrelenting attacks on "depravity" in the State Department came from Pulitzer prize–winning columnist Westbrook Pegler. Notorious for his vitriolic attacks on big government and its liberal supporters, particularly Franklin Roosevelt ("Mama's Boy") and Eleanor Roosevelt ("The Empress"), Pegler was widely considered a spokesman for the common man. His often-satiric column appeared in more than 140 newspapers around the country. In the spring of 1950, five of these columns focused solely on the discovery of "ninety-one peculiars" in the State Department. One took the form of an open letter to Dean Acheson, offering suggestions for changes to make the department reflect "the distinctive spirit and character of so many of the personnel." He suggested Acheson rename the street adjoining departmental headquarters Grimm Street after the author of the fairy tales; that he rename the smoking room the "fag room"; and that he replace the standard handshake greeting with a curtsy and the standard mode of address from "your excellency" to "precious." Courses in interior decorating, he mused, might provide better preparation for entry into the foreign service than history or political science.[5]

Homosexuals in the State Department even became fodder for potboiler mystery novels. Edward S. Aarons used the ongoing Washington sex scandal to add intrigue to one of his early novels. In *State Department Murders*, Barney Cornell, an American diplomat working on top-secret nuclear assignment "Project Cirrus," is accused of revealing secrets to the U.S.S.R. But this false accusation is quickly overshadowed by Cornell's own suspicions that his supervisor, Paul Evarts, is a homosexual. He first becomes anxious when they meet at a "peculiar" restaurant where his boss is overly familiar with the waiters and other patrons. "Nothing but the food in the cafe was normal. . . . Even the waiters wore their hair too long. . . . There wasn't a face that would be found at the ball park or football stadium." Noticing his boss's blond hair and his "long and white and graceful" hands, Cornell remembers that "he had heard rumors of trouble in the State Department with abnormal personnel who were open to morality charges." When a prominent American industrialist, Jason Stone—known to control the levers of power in Washington through a coterie of blackmail victims—is murdered by "a man dressed as a woman," suspicion soon falls on Evarts. The whodunit ends with Evarts confessing to killing Stone, to murdering another man long ago in a gay love triangle, and to passing Project Cirrus secrets to the Soviets. Communists barely make an appearance in this Cold War–era political intrigue, where the real villain turns out to be the homosexual. As the narrator explains, "There are [*sic*] a certain percentage of misfits in every ordinary group and walk of life; more than most people suspect. But you and I know how vulnerable these people are to outside pressure. Fear of disgrace and publicity makes them ready subject [*sic*] for blackmail."[6]

"Cookie Pushers"

Such popular satires on the foreign service drew on familiar notions that equated homosexuality with gender inversion and weakness. They also drew on long-standing rumors that the diplomatic corps was a haven for effete intellectuals. With a natural inclination toward negotiation and appeasement rather than action and war, diplomats were seen as ineffectual and unmanly. Because entertaining foreign dignitaries was one of their principal duties, foreign service officers were dismissed as "cookie pushers in striped pants." As early as 1942, Philip Wylie, a popular magazine writer, warned of a "sisterhood in our State Department." In *Generation of Vipers*, a critique of American society that became one of the best selling books of its time, Wylie claimed that "in American statecraft, where you need desperately a man of iron, you often get a nance." These "sissies" and "fake Englishmen," according to Wylie, were more interested in proper diplomatic protocol than managing foreign affairs. They made up a "covey of career boys who have been taught to toy with international affairs but not to direct them in any way."[7] Critics feared that after years of living abroad, such diplomats had come to identify with foreign powers more than grassroots America. Some said they formed a "freemasonry of European professionals." One journalist labeled them adherents of an "Internationale des Salonnards" or an "Internationale of the People-you-meet-at-parties" comprising "dukes, bankers, bishops, wealthy and pretty hostesses." Like the critical language applied to Communists and homosexuals, such terms implied an international, alien clique with its own language, culture, and bonds of loyalties.[8]

Portraying State Department diplomats, particularly Secretary of State Dean Acheson, as weak and effeminate was part of a larger critique of Truman's foreign policy. Conservative critics wanted the United States to take a tougher stance against the Soviet Union and were frustrated over what they termed Acheson's "powder puff diplomats." They wanted to combat, not simply contain, communism. One angry veteran wrote his senator calling for the removal of "that despicable and very treacherous Acheson . . . and his whole rotten gang, including his Russian-loving pansies."[9] McCarthy and other critics of the State Department called for Acheson's resignation and a whole new approach to the Soviet Union. As McCarthy's "Wisconsin lieutenant," Urban P. Van Susteren, explained it, "Joe would sit down with Stalin in a closed room. First thing he'd tell a couple dirty jokes. Then he'd look Stalin right in the eye and say 'Joe, what do you want?' And Stalin would tell him. The two would talk man to man, not like a lot of pansy diplomats." McCarthy, Susteren insisted, would not be afraid to back up his threats. "They'd find out what each other wanted and settle their differences. But when Joe left, he'd tell Stalin, 'The first time I catch you breaking this agreement, I'll blow you and your whole goddamn country off the map.'"[10]

Though many critics portrayed the alleged homosexuals in the State Department as weak when it came to defending the nation, they paradoxically portrayed them as very powerful within the organization. Ineffective in negotiating with the Soviets, they had somehow risen to control American foreign policy. Writing for the *New York Daily News*, John O'Donnell charged that "the foreign policy of the U.S., even before World War II, was dominated by an all-powerful, supersecret inner circle of highly educated, socially highly placed sexual misfits in the State Department, all easy to blackmail." McCarthy's Wisconsin patron, Tom Coleman, had told his fellow Republican leaders that queers "control foreign policy."[11] While the conservatives behind the homosexual purges portrayed their targets as high-powered State Department officials, like Welles, who were in a position to influence foreign policy and give away highly classified information, the people affected were more like Ladd Forrester and Jeb Alexander—secretaries and low-level clerks. The fragmentary evidence that exists about the original ninety-one suggests that most held positions as clerks, telegraph operators, or clerk-typists.[12]

Acheson's Vigorous Men

Of all cabinet-level departments, the State Department was uniquely defenseless against such attacks. While business supported the efforts of the Commerce Department, union interests identified with the Labor Department, and farmers could be counted on to defend the Agriculture Department, State had no natural base of support. But the attacks on it were so insistent that Dean Acheson had to respond. He needed to refute the charges that the department was filled with homosexuals without calling further attention to the scandal. He did not want to repeat Peurifoy's mistake of highlighting the large number of homosexuals already discharged. In April 1950, Acheson chose a speaking engagement before a group of newspaper editors to criticize the "filthy business" of McCarthy and his allies. In an often-quoted defense of State Department employees, Acheson characterized them as "honorable, loyal, and clean-living American men and women." In profiling the "top command" of the department, he tried to dispel the notion that they were all effete members of the East Coast establishment by highlighting their military and athletic prowess. Peurifoy had attended West Point, he reminded his audience, while another official, Adrian Fisher, had been a bomber navigator and captain of the Princeton football team. "We have men as distinguished, as able, as powerful, and as vigorous as any of my great predecessors," Acheson concluded. Acheson was clearly refuting not only the charges of Communist infiltration but of immoral conduct, giving his conservative critics the opportunity to remind the public of both charges. The *Washington Times-Herald*, for example, interpreted Acheson's comment by noting that "the latter remark apparently referred to charges the State Department is a hotbed of homosexuality." The next day, one Republican congressman paraphrased the secretary's remarks in more colloquial terms. "Acheson told the editors that now the State Department is pure as the driven snow," he summarized. "No Communists and no perverts." Senator Karl Mundt (R–South Dakota) complained that Acheson had taken in "too much territory" in defending departmental personnel in light of the removal of ninety-one "sex perverts and moral degenerates" from the department. Despite the criticism, Acheson repeated his defense of the department in June before the Conference of Governors, where he called State a "good, clean, loyal outfit," and his staff "courageous and vigorous men."[13]

The State Department viewed the charges against its employees as a public relations crisis with both the American people and Congress. In an effort to win over legislators, the department organized a series of informal gatherings of departmental personnel and members of Congress at Prospect House in Georgetown. Although the setting was typical for diplomatic entertaining, these "congressional smokers" were characterized by those in attendance as more reminiscent of "stag parties," featuring copious amounts of scotch and bourbon, and smiling women "whose identity remained undisclosed." As one senator remarked, "It reminded me somewhat of the fraternity rushing season at college." Dean Acheson tried to appear as "one of the boys," slapping senators on the back. A journalist reported that "his hair was rumpled, his tie awry. The stiff and precise manner and speech which have antagonized many of us had disappeared. He even seemed to have removed the wax from his mustache." But the effort was transparent. One newspaper attributed the "'he-man' atmosphere" to the department's sensitivity about "recent revelations of homosexuality among its members." The department continued public relations efforts to demonstrate the "'grass roots' quality" of its employees, such as awards ceremonies for employees who were veterans of World War II. As one memo explained, such ceremonies would help "dispel the myths that State Department employees are pinks, snobs, and worse." Later President Eisenhower would dedicate a plaque to foreign service officers killed in the line of duty, a gesture one historian noted was designed "to dispel the popular image of an effeminate diplomatic corps."[14]

A New "Homosexual System"

Beyond these public relations efforts, the State Department responded to the public perception that it was a haven for sexual deviants by strengthening its internal security system, particularly against homosexuals. Every applicant was checked against the State Department's master list of alleged homosexuals, a list which included anyone ever implicated in any interrogation or investigation of homosexuality—whether American citizen or foreign national, government employee or private citizen—numbering some three thousand names by 1950. All male applicants were subject to a personal interview by security personnel who specialized in uncovering homosexuals. If suspicions were raised, the applicant would be given a lie detector test. Security officials, for example, suspected an applicant in 1947 of homosexuality because of his "mannerisms and appearance (use of perfume, etc.)." He was subsequently given a polygraph exam, confessed to homosexual activity, and was rejected. A 1952 procedures manual for security officers contained a nine-page section devoted entirely to homosexuality, the only type of security offense singled out for such coverage. It indicated that although no "well-established pattern of appearance, behavior, education, position, etc." could be outlined to help them detect homosexuals in their personal interviews, they should obtain information regarding "hobbies, associates, means of diversion, places of amusement, etc." and report any "unusual traits of speech, appearance, or personality." They were instructed not only to check police records but to establish a "close working relationship" with the vice squad in their area and to be aware that in some jurisdictions acts of sex perversion might only be prosecuted as "disorderly conduct."[15]

Two investigators on the security division staff devoted all their time to the detection of homosexuals and "the study of the problem." If they received information suggesting an employee was homosexual, they opened an investigation, inquiring at all former schools, places of employment, and residences. The investigators checked credit and police records, and interviewed character references. Invoking the characteristic "guilt by association technique," the investigators checked whether any of the employee's friends or associates were homosexual. According to the department, they "rarely live with anyone other than another homosexual." If suspicions were high but evidence lacking, those suspected might be placed under surveillance to determine whether they frequented "known homosexual places or associated with other known homosexuals." For every homosexual caught through a standard background check of police records, the security division uncovered five more through its own investigation. As a result of such intensive investigative work, according to the head of Security and Consular Affairs, more than 80 percent of those confronted with evidence against them confessed. Many implicated others as well. One applicant for a college summer job remembered being closely questioned about his sexual habits as well as those of his roommate. Once he began work as a file clerk in the passport office, he found "huge files detailing the personal sexual histories" of both applicants and employees.[16]

Self-conscious about its public standing, the State Department undertook an internal audit to determine if the department was a haven for sexual deviants and why homosexuals might be especially drawn to the department—questions in which "we have been profoundly interested," one official noted. Security experts speculated that homosexuals were attracted to the "cultural atmosphere and attainments" available in the department. The opportunity to leave one's home and family and live overseas was thought to attract homosexuals. "Many of them have told our investigators that they believe the chances of detection in a foreign country are far less than in this country." The department also conducted a review of the records of all persons dismissed for homosexuality in the previous three years, including the infamous ninety-one, to see if any pattern could be determined, particularly in hiring and promotion. They found no evidence of conspiracy—no "'nest' of homosexuals"—but did conclude that given the "chronic nature" of the problem, it would be with them for a long time.[17]

In its internal study of the problem of homosexuality, the department articulated several rationales for removing homosexuals, none of which involved the threat of blackmail or any other link to national security. Instead, the department feared that homosexuals created a "morale problem" because most "normal" men did not want to work or associate with them. Sexual perversion was unacceptable in the department because it was "repugnant to the folkways and mores of our American society." In addition to upsetting their colleagues, homosexuals made poor employees because they were lonely, promiscuous, and "emotionally unstable." According to this study they lived "in a world all to themselves" where they sought "sexual gratification from one person one night and from another the next in a paltry and endless gesture at a happiness they never realize." The department never resorted to security regulations to remove homosexuals from its ranks, relying instead on older, well-established civil service regulations against immoral conduct. As one official commented, the removal of homosexuals was "always an administrative decision" that was only occasionally related to security.[18]

What the State Department and other federal agencies most feared was publicity about their homosexual employees. Security officials were protecting their agencies' reputations as much as or more than national security. When the acting officer-in-charge of Caribbean Affairs at the State Department was arrested on a homosexual charge in the fall of 1950, the security officers who interrogated him not only tried to force him to resign, but tried to postdate his letter of resignation so that he would not technically have been a State Department official at the time of the arrest. "They intimated to me that the publicity might be coming out on the case that very day," the diplomat remembered, "that there had been a great many accusations leveled against the State Department on the alleged ground that homosexuals were employed [there]; . . . that the very fact of my arrest under those circumstances placed the Department in a difficult position." When the official requested an opportunity to consult with his attorney, the security officers protested and threatened to immediately institute dismissal proceedings. But the employee held his ground, and the feared headlines appeared in Washington newspapers: "State Dept. Man Faces Sex Charge." Reprinted in the *Congressional Record*, the news story was cited by at least one member of Congress as proof that homosexuals and sex perverts were still working in the department, still posing "a menace to our security."[19]

The vehemence of the State Department's antigay campaign can hardly be overstated. The chief of every mission received a memorandum underscoring the need to eliminate the homosexual problem. Inspectors sent to every embassy, consulate, and mission were given special training sessions on "methods used in uncovering homosexuals," instructed to be "continually on the alert" to discover homosexuals, and asked to brief others on the topic during their tours of inspection. Recruiters in the Office of Personnel were given similar briefings and cautioned to "do everything possible to ferret out individuals with homosexual tendencies before final selection."[20] Testifying before Congress at the very beginning of the Eisenhower administration, Carlisle Humelsine, the State Department security officer, defended his department's antigay campaign. "It is quite clear to me," Humelsine testified, "that these homosexuals are sick people, and they just don't know what they are doing, they do some of the most foolish things, which lead to the compromising of our particular type of work." As he concluded, this was not mere talk. "We have to get rid of them and we have a program to do that." Although publicly the department had a loyalty/security system, in fact it had two systems—one for political deviants and one for sexual deviants. Such a bifurcated system was manifest in the special way homosexuality was treated in almost all memoranda, manuals, and statistics regarding the State Department's loyalty/security system. Homosexuals were not simply one of many types of security risks officials tracked. They were given unprecedented attention, equal to or surpassing that for Communists and the politically disloyal. In an unguarded internal memorandum, one official made the point quite explicit by referring to the department's "loyalty system" and its "homosexual system."[21]

The State Department's own statistics on employee dismissals confirm the inordinate attention paid to homosexuality. Peter Szluk, a State Department security officer from the late 1940s to 1962, admitted in an interview that of all the people forced out of the department during his tenure, "the gay was a pretty large percentage of them." As this self-described "hatchet man for the State Department" conceded, "To this day, nobody knows who some of the people were that I got rid of because they were sodomites. I would protect [that information], particularly because so many of them had families." Although the exact number may never be known, because of all the publicity surrounding the presence of homosexuals in its ranks, the State Department had an incentive to keep careful records of the numbers of homosexuals purged. Testifying before Congress in early 1951, Carlisle Humelsine indicated that since the inception of the department's loyalty/security program in 1947, 14 individuals had been separated as security risks, while 144 had been separated for homosexuality. Two years later he testified that of the 654 dismissals or forced resignations for security/loyalty grounds, 402 were for homosexuality. Over the course of the 1950s and 1960s, approximately 1,000 persons were dismissed from the Department of State for alleged homosexuality. The highest-profile cases may have involved suspicion of communism, but the majority of those separated were alleged homosexuals.[22]

The taint of homosexuality followed the department for years. In 1953, Secretary of State John Foster Dulles testified before a House Ways and Means Committee. Just as he had finished answering questions and was dismissed to go back to Foggy Bottom, the chairman commented, "It must be terrible to have to work among all those homosexuals." Secretary Dulles did not respond. Ten years later, when John Reilly, deputy assistant secretary for security, testified before a House appropriations subcommittee, he was asked why work in his department appealed to homosexuals. Reilly speculated that "they seem to be drawn to the attractiveness of overseas life. . . . Perhaps they feel life is a little freer there." One of the most authoritative studies of the loyalty/security program commented that it was "common opinion" that the State Department "has for some reason attracted colonies of homosexuals." By the early 1960s, with the proliferation of books describing the homosexual subculture, one study suggested that "the State Department has become identified with homosexuality to such a remarkable extent that the two are regarded by many persons as being virtual synonyms." Through the late 1960s, as State Department officials made their annual appearance before congressional appropriations committees, they were forced to reveal the number of homosexuals fired in the previous year. The practice became so ritualized that one gay activist dubbed it a "fertility rite." "The ancient Aztecs or Mayas used to sacrifice virgins, annually, to propitiate the gods and to gain favors from them," he wrote the *Washington Post* in 1968. "The State Department sacrifices homosexuals, annually, to propitiate the House Appropriations Committee, and to gain money from them."[23]

4

"Fairies and Fair Dealers"
The Immoral Bureaucracy

Despite all the misbehavior in the capital, I feel certain that the government will continue weeding out the perverts and security risks. Washington will not remain the Platonic and Socratic homosexual playground that it is for long.

—*Arthur Guy Mathews*

Within a month of the revelation that ninety-one homosexuals had been dismissed from the State Department, news from another congressional committee shocked the nation. Appearing under subpoena in March, 1950, Lieutenant Roy Blick of the Washington, D.C., vice squad testified that the nation's capital was home to 5,000 homosexuals. He estimated that three-quarters of them—3,750—worked for the federal government. Though Blick's testimony was taken behind locked doors, and all in attendance had been sworn to secrecy, the testimony became an Associated Press story within days. It set off a new round of press stories, columns, and editorials on the homosexual menace, dwarfing the publicity that followed Peurifoy's revelation. Reporters highlighted the accuracy of the figures, noting that they were given "under oath" and were based on extensive confidential files. Washington's largest-circulation newspaper reported, "Metropolitan police files indexed by name, age, address, and occupation upwards of 5,000 suspected sex perverts, nearly 4,000 of whom are federally employed here." *Newsweek* called Blick's testimony a "new shocker" and suggested that concern about "the 91" was now overshadowed by what it termed "the

3,750." Perhaps dazzled by all the numbers, it dubbed the story "Homosexuals Unlimited."[1]

Blick's testimony was part of a special, two-man investigation launched by Senator Kenneth Wherry (R–Nebraska) into "the infiltration of subversives and moral perverts into the executive branch of the United States Government." Though appalled by the situation recently revealed in the State Department, Wherry found that "there is much more to the sordid situation that will shock the American people when they are given the facts." He predicted it would prove "more sensational than the McCarthy spy charges." Wherry learned that "the crime of homosexualism" had grown tremendously in Washington, despite harsher penalties passed by Congress in 1947. According to Wherry, "an emergency condition" threatened the nation's capital. The Russians had acquired a list of homosexuals throughout the world that had been compiled by Hitler as an espionage tool. Using this list, Russians were prying secrets out of government employees. Even worse, Soviet agents were targeting heterosexual female civil servants, controlling them by "enticing them into a life of Lesbianism." Wherry warned that the conspiracy between Communists and homosexuals raised the potential for "sabotage" of "seaports and major cities" in the United States. He recommended that a Senate committee strengthen the D.C. vice squad, pass tighter sanctions against sex offenders, and establish liaisons among the various government agencies. Something had to be done, Wherry warned, "to eradicate this menace."[2]

Wherry's investigation represented a widening of the Lavender Scare. Though originally focused on the State Department and associated with McCarthy's charges against it, the fear of homosexual infiltration spread to other federal agencies and eventually the entire federal government. Led by a number of senior members of Congress, both Republicans and Democrats, the Lavender Scare became part of larger concerns about the makeup and function of the federal government. Long antagonistic to the bureaucracy that had grown up during eighteen years of Democratic control during the New Deal and World War II, these powerful members of the Senate and House appropriations committees now suggested that Washington and the federal government were teeming with sexual deviance. By thus expanding the Lavender Scare, enemies of the Roosevelt and Truman administrations found a new, more effective way to cast aspersions on the goings-on in Washington. To such conservatives, Moscow ran only barely ahead of Washington as the city they most despised. Wherry's investigation helped associate the nation's capital in the public mind with sexual perversion and thus brought the Lavender Scare into this larger cultural battle over the character and role of the Washington bureaucrat.

Expanding the Purges

Even before Peurifoy's revelation had hit the newspapers, there were signs that the Lavender Scare would expand beyond the State Department. Senators immediately began asking where the dismissed employees had gone and if any had sought refuge in other agencies. McCarthy fueled these suspicions when he highlighted the case of a homosexual who, after resigning from the State Department, was hired by the Central Intelligence Agency. Members of Congress soon began pressuring Harry B. Mitchell, chair of the Civil Service Commission (CSC), to determine how many others had slipped through the cracks. Mitchell confirmed their worst fears: twenty-two of the ninety-one had indeed found employment in other branches of the federal government. The CSC quickly initiated investigations and obtained resignations in all but one case. Pleased with Mitchell's results, members of Congress pressed for a new policy to prevent the situation from reoccurring. As a result, the CSC issued a circular to all government agencies, instructing them to report to the commission the specific reason for dismissals resulting from "suitability" charges. This would prevent "unsuitable employees" from reentering federal service after their removal. This action, Mitchell promised, would close the loophole that allowed one agency to unwittingly hire a homosexual fired from another. In their periodic inspection of agency personnel records, CSC auditors monitored compliance. When questioned later in the year, Commissioner Frances Perkins assured Congress that since issuance of the directive, "there has been a very vigorous conformity with it." The ability of fired gay civil servants to easily find employment in another agency, common in the 1930s and 1940s, was coming to an end.[3]

Tightened procedures at the Civil Service Commission were only the beginning of an effort to expand the antigay campaigns from the State Department to all federal agencies. Around the time Senator Bridges questioned John Peurifoy about his department's efforts to remove homosexuals, other appropriations subcommittees were pressuring the departments over which they had jurisdiction to implement similar programs. At the end of February 1950 Bernard L. Gladieux, executive assistant to the Secretary of Commerce, appeared before a House appropriations subcommittee during a routine budget hearing to report on the department's security program. Chairman John J. Rooney (D–New York) took the opportunity to grill Gladieux about his agency's approach to homosexuality. Known as "the Great Needler from Brooklyn," Rooney was developing a reputation for badgering bureaucrats, particularly when they dared seek increased appropriations. Because of his veto power over appropriations that moved through his subcommittee, James Reston called him "one of the most powerful men in America." As one agency official explained about his power, "Anything we do here we do on the basis of 'Could I explain this to Rooney.'" So when Gladieux informed him that no Commerce Department employee had been dismissed in the past three years because of homosexuality, Rooney was flabbergasted. "Not one?" Rooney asked incredulously. "In the whole department?" he pressed. "That is incredible," the chairman exclaimed. Chastising his witness for a lack of aggressiveness in pursuing homosexuals, Rooney compared the situation negatively to that in the State Department. "It would seem with the Department of State weeding out as many homosexuals as it has, your statement that with 46,000 employees you have not been able to weed any out, just does not jibe," Rooney complained.[4]

Gladieux took cover behind the Federal Loyalty Program, suggesting that cases of homosexuality would generally "become known" through standard FBI screenings administered to all employees doing classified work. Rooney advocated a more aggressive approach. Noting that "the fact of homosexuality is a side issue in the loyalty check," he suggested that the department launch its own antigay program. He advised sending a directive "calling for the names of any people suspected of being homosexuals" to the heads of the various bureaus within the Department of Commerce "all the way down the line"—particularly those engaged in classified work, such as the Bureau of Standards. Gladieux objected that this might attract unwanted publicity to the situation and questioned whether he had enough staff to conduct investigations once names had been produced. Such excuses exasperated the chairman. "Are you not in control of your organization to the extent where you can get the word around that you wanted turned up any people who were so inclined?" Rooney asked. "Is it your idea that nothing should be done about it?" Calling upon his own experience as an assistant district attorney, Rooney highlighted the urgency of the situation. "The danger is that these people will meet other people who might satisfy their desires and, in return, divulge information with regard to the security of the Nation," the chairman explained. Somewhat cowed by the interrogation, Gladieux conceded the seriousness of the issue but was unsure of a course of action. Rooney had the answer. "They have the right approach on this in the Department of State," he offered, explaining how cooperative John Peurifoy had been with his committee on this issue. Although the Department of State was being excoriated in the press for its alleged harboring of homosexuals, its aggressive program of uncovering and removing them was becoming the model that Congress pressured other departments to follow. The State Department's approach, a security system with two principal targets—Communists and homosexuals—was becoming the standard for the entire federal government.[5]

Having been "hauled over the coals" by the appropriations committee—as one political columnist commented at the time—Department of Commerce officials implemented an antigay campaign of their own. Within months, Commerce Secretary Charles Sawyer had set up a new Office of Security Control to handle security matters and arranged for his top officials to receive a lecture on "perversion" from a St. Elizabeth Hospital psychiatrist. By November the department reported that it had uncovered forty-nine sex perverts, of whom twenty-five had resigned, sixteen had been dismissed, four had been cleared of allegations, and four were still under investigation. In the previous three years, by comparison, the department had reported only seventy-one loyalty separations. Although extensive publicity over a number of suspected Communists in the Department of Commerce—principally William Remington—contributed to the department's strengthened security program, both the substance of the congressional hearings and the dismissal statistics suggest that eliminating homosexuals was a primary concern. Pleased by the results, Rooney felt the program should be extended. "We probably could do the same thing in all of the departments of the Government," he observed at a later hearing. "This has been extensively advertised as a problem which is solely the State Department's, but the facts do not bear that out."[6]

That summer Congress handed the Commerce Department and other agencies a new tool in their efforts to eliminate homosexuals from their ranks. Since 1946, Congress had attached what was known as the "McCarran rider" to the appropriations bills of State and Defense Departments, giving the heads of these agencies "absolute discretion" to dismiss any government employee if such action was "deemed necessary in the interest of national security." Senator Homer Ferguson (R–Michigan), one of the original drafters of the McCarran rider, explained to a *Washington Star* reporter that it was specifically designed to assist the State Department in discharging homosexuals. He and many other legislators assumed that the infamous ninety-one had been ousted under this legislation. Congressman Rooney, after grilling Gladieux, asked if he would like a similar rider attached to the Commerce appropriations bill, pointing out that such legislation "would certainly help you with regard to the homosexual problem." Gladieux concurred. In congressional debates over the extension of the rider, Senator Bridges argued that it was necessary precisely because some of the "sex perverts" dismissed from the State Department had been hired by other agencies. In a lengthy diatribe to a medical association in his home state of Nebraska on the evils of homosexuals in government, Congressman Arthur Miller cited the extension of the McCarran rider as the best way to remove them from government. "The Congress is writing into several appropriation bills a clause which will permit the secretary of a department to dismiss individuals who might be security risks. It always includes homosexuals," he assured his audience. That summer Congress extended these summary dismissal powers to eleven federal agencies and authorized the president to extend it to the entire federal government if deemed necessary. Although often characterized by historians as a broadening of the loyalty program to include persons whose loyalty was in doubt—fellow travelers and Leftists—this piece of legislation was understood by members of Congress as a means to fire security risks. And as Representative Cliff Clevenger (R–Ohio) reminded his colleagues, "The most flagrant example is the homosexual." As with much of the nation's burgeoning Cold War internal security apparatus, Congress created the McCarran rider first for the State and Defense Departments, and then extended it to much of the federal government. And like much of that apparatus, it was motivated by both the Red and Lavender Scares.[7]

Senator Wherry Investigates

In the spring of 1950, many members of Congress highlighted the threat posed by homosexuals in government and pushed for new policies and procedures to ferret them out. Among those pushing to expand the Lavender Scare, none was more crucial than Senator Kenneth Wherry. Labeled by the *New York Times* as "Washington's leading symbol and rallying point of die-hard conservatism," Wherry was one of the most powerful Republicans in Congress. First elected to the Senate in 1942, he quickly developed a reputation as "the most practical rough-and-tumble politician" among Senate Republicans. Elected party whip in his first term, by 1950 he was Senate Republican Floor Leader. Known for "moving about the Senate floor with the ability and bounce of a prize fighter," he spoke with a deep baritone voice and emphasized points by pounding his chest with both fists. "When he is against anything, he is against it totally, four-square, 100 percent—and at the top of his lungs," commented one frequent observer from the Senate press gallery. Though the dour and aristocratic Republican leader, Robert Taft, was known as "Mr. Republican," some thought Wherry—with a more energetic, combative style—was more deserving of the title. There was even talk of a run for the Republican presidential nomination in 1952.[8]

As a member of the powerful Senate Appropriations Committee, Kenneth Wherry had played a key role in launching the State Department's quiet purge of homosexuals in 1947 and would now become one of the driving forces behind the extension of the Lavender Scare to the entire federal government. He was among the senators—along with Styles Bridges—who first alerted Secretary of State George Marshall that the employment of homosexuals in "highly classified positions" in the department posed a threat to national security. In the ensuing years, Wherry continued to exert quiet pressure on the department. Now that the menace of homosexuals in government was a public issue, Wherry wanted credit for his past efforts and a leading role in the continuing purge. During the Tydings committee hearings, he had labeled himself "the expert on homosexuality in the State Department." When McCarthy failed to prove his charge that State Department advisor Owen Lattimore was a top Russian spy—after promising his campaign would "stand or fall" on this one case—Wherry tried unsuccessfully to find evidence that Lattimore was homosexual. Unlike McCarthy, Wherry was no Johnny-come-lately to the cause. As he was quick to point out, he was not *reacting* to the ouster of ninety-one homosexuals; he was largely *responsible* for it. Now he would attempt to widen the search.[9]

In March 1950, Wherry had made national headlines by criticizing President Truman for refusing to release loyalty files to the Tydings committee. Alarmed by the Truman administration's lack of cooperation, Wherry thought he might get access to government files by taking advantage of his position on the appropriations subcommittee for the District of Columbia. Realizing that many "sexual perverts" and subversives working for the government might have come in contact with local police, Wherry subpoenaed the heads of the local "vice" and "spy" squads. He hoped that District of Columbia officials, reliant on Congress for their funding, might be more compliant than President Truman when it came to providing information on federal personnel. Though less than a quarter of the entire federal work force was located in and around Washington, D.C., most Americans associated the federal bureaucracy with Washington. Newspapers labeled calls for the investigation of homosexuals in government as a "Probe of D.C. Morals." Even more important than the symbolic connection was Congress's political control over Washington, D.C. Since creating the District of Columbia "ten miles square" in 1790, as provided for in Article One of the U.S. Constitution, Congress enjoyed "exclusive jurisdiction" over the federal city. Congress determined its form of local government, exercised veto power over its laws, and provided it with financial support. Exercising his authority over the District's appropriations might allow Wherry to overcome what he viewed as the intransigence of the executive branch.[10]

Wherry subpoenaed Lieutenant Roy Blick, head of the Metropolitan

Police vice squad, and Sergeant James Hunter, chief of the Special Investigations, or "Spy Squad." Hunter testified to connections between the subversives he tracked and the homosexuals Blick hunted. Having attended many meetings of Communist-front organizations in Washington, Hunter observed that "a pervert is very susceptible. You find quite a few perverts attending these meetings." Leaks about his testimony led newspapers to assert not only that "sex offenders" were being blackmailed by "Red agents," but that "some of the perverts, the committee has been informed, are Communists." Although it underscored the national security implications of the homosexual problem by associating it with subversive activity, Hunter's testimony was overshadowed by that of Blick. His claim that 5,000 homosexuals lived in the nation's capital and that 3,750 worked for the federal government made national headlines. Hunter estimated that the nation's capital had only 1,000 Communists, a figure later corroborated by the *Washington Star* using estimates released by J. Edgar Hoover. Blick's estimate suggested that the real menace facing the capital was perversion.[11]

Blick's numbers were, at best, speculation. When interviewed by columnist Max Lerner of the liberal *New York Post*, Blick gave conflicting stories about the method he used to arrive at the oft-quoted statistics. He first suggested that he derived the 5,000 figure by extrapolating from the number of people arrested on homosexual charges in Washington. "We have these police records," Blick explained. "You take the list. Well, every one of these fellows has friends. You multiply the list by a certain percentage—say 3 or 4 percent." But he later told Lerner that when a man was arrested and interrogated about his friends, those names were also added to the list. Suspicious of this double manipulation, Lerner asked, "[W]hich do you do? Multiply by five, or add all the friends you find out about?" Blick responded that he did both. "Well, it's 60–40," he elaborated. "Sixty percent of it I put the friends down on the list, and 40 percent of it I multiply by five." His estimate that 300 homosexuals worked for the State Department was based on another creative accounting scheme. He took the number of "perverts" discharged (91) and multiplied that by 10, he explained, because the U.S. Public Health Bureau estimated that one-tenth of people with a venereal disease report their illness. Then, to be conservative, he cut the total in half, thus arriving at a total of 455—a figure still 50 percent larger than his original estimate of 300. In attempting to couch his public estimates with a patina of statistical sophistication, Blick inadvertently revealed their groundlessness. As Blick later told Lerner, "The figures I gave them were guesses, my own guesses, not official figures."[12]

Blick's claims to have organized files on Washington's homosexuals—some newspapers reported they were cross-indexed by name, age, and occupation—were similarly dubious. When the Senate subcommittee demanded to see Blick's records, Police Chief Robert Barrett refused to release them. "I've got the key and I'm going to keep it. Nobody is going to get to them," Barrett proclaimed.[13] This saved his department from revealing that they did not have such records, at least not in any systematized form. When State Department security officers talked to Blick about his claims to have lists of known homosexuals on their payroll, Blick admitted not only that his estimates were "not based on factual knowledge" but also that "there are no private files." The only files he had were regular police arrest records, which were a matter of public record. Nor did he have any specific information on any current State Department employees indicating homosexuality. Wherry and Blick were using a favorite McCarthyite tactic—claiming they had records that did not exist or that could not legally be made public to create the impression that officials were protecting subversives.[14]

Blick's exaggerated claims were the statements of an ambitious local police officer looking for a bigger budget and national recognition. One federal personnel manager dismissed his claims as a "cheap demagogic attempt to enlarge the size of the vice squad." Although Blick had been on the vice squad for eighteen years, this was his moment in the spotlight, a chance for empire building. Ben Bradlee, then a lowly *Washington Post* reporter on the police beat, thought Blick "a nasty little man," who, until the homosexual scandal broke, "hadn't gotten any ink at all in the vice squad because nobody was particularly interested in rubbing out prostitution or little after-hours clubs." And the Washington police had historically been in competition for federal funds with other law enforcement units operating in the District of Columbia, such as the U.S. Park Police and the U.S. Secret Service. Testifying before the people who determined his budget, Blick thus had every incentive to highlight the danger posed to the city and his ability to manage it. He boasted to the committee how one night he led a raid on Lafayette Park that resulted in the arrest of sixty-five homosexuals, all of whom "admitted guilt."[15] Blick already had four men who devoted full time to arresting homosexuals—mostly men—but now wanted a "lesbian squad." He also had national ambitions. "There is a need in this country for a central bureau for records of homosexuals and perverts of all types," Blick argued. He let it be known, not so subtly, that if chosen to direct such a bureau, he would make the files available to "all government agencies." In its report, the subcommittee praised his work and recommended increased appropriations for his squad. It proposed the establishment of a special Washington police squad to "work exclusively on connections between Communists and sex perverts" and "sufficient police personnel for the adequate policing of crimes involving homosexualism."[16]

Revising the Kinsey Report

While many people expressed shock at Blick's estimate of Washington's homosexual population, others saw it as an underestimate. Medical professionals and scientists, drawing on the data of their colleague Alfred Kinsey, were among the most critical of Blick's estimates. Dr. Benjamin Karpman, chief of psychotherapy at Washington's St. Elizabeth Hospital, characterized the investigations as a "witch hunt" and ridiculed the 5,000 figure, saying there "probably are 50,000 of them in Washington." Pointing to Kinsey's finding that 4 percent of the white adult males in the United States were "exclusively homosexual," editors at the widely syndicated Science News Service argued that probably 56,787 male civil servants were gay. They argued that if security officials were correct in considering one homosexual contact enough "for Communist blackmailer's purposes," than the more relevant statistic was Kinsey's finding that 37 percent of adult men had at least one homosexual experience. If these findings were accurate, the editors warned, more than 500,000 civil servants and 192 members of Congress would be considered security risks. Francis Biddle, former U.S. Attorney General and head of Americans for Democratic Action (ADA), echoed this sentiment, suggesting that a quick reading of the Kinsey report would demonstrate that "there are no more abnormal people in Government than anywhere else—no more than in Congress itself, for that matter." Kinsey, known for being highly sensitive about interpretations of his data, weighed in with his approval of these extrapolations. "The reality of the total situation needs to be drawn to the attention of the country," Kinsey cautioned. "Hysteria thrives best when only a small segment of the picture is understood."[17]

Debate over the truth and usefulness of Kinsey's findings on male homosexuality remained a central feature of the Lavender Scare. Those who opposed or at least questioned the necessity of the purges would inevitably cite Kinsey to suggest not only the futility but also the danger in trying to effectively quarantine such a large percentage of the population from any work touching on national security. Kinsey's findings even made it into the report of Senator Lister Hill (D–Alabama), the chairman of the District of Columbia appropriations subcommittee. In a separate report from that of Wherry, Hill conceded that homosexuals posed a security risk in sensitive positions but argued that there were no more homosexuals in the government or in Washington, D.C., than anywhere else. He cited the director of the National Institute of Mental Health, Dr. Robert H. Felix, who quoted unnamed "statistical samplings" suggesting that "perhaps as many as 4 percent of the white males in the country as a whole are confirmed homosexuals." Though obviously referring to the Kinsey study, Felix kept his source anonymous, aware of the controversial nature of the Indiana University professor's findings. But extrapolating from Kinsey, he showed how Blick's figures were ridiculously small. With a total 1950 population of 800,000, of whom approximately 300,000 were adult men, the District of Columbia, according to Felix's figures, should have as many as 12,000 homosexuals. Including women or suburbanites would easily have doubled the figure.[18]

Blick's estimate that there were 5,000 homosexuals in Washington was an implicit repudiation of the Kinsey study. It represented a rejection of the expert opinion of a scientist and university professor in favor of common police sense. One contemporary commentator suggested that all the congressional inquiries into homosexuality amounted to "writing a supplement to the Kinsey report." In fact, they offered a critique. Those who believed homosexuals posed a threat to national security portrayed them as a small, secretive, underground menace concentrated in Washington, D.C. Although wanting to suggest that the homosexual problem was large enough to pose a danger to national security, they had to guard against suggestions that it was so large as to seem a naturally occurring anomaly. Focusing on Blick's estimate rather than Kinsey's allowed them to suggest the enormity and the uniqueness of the homosexual menace in Washington. They had no use for national averages. When questioned about Kinsey's figures by Max Lerner, Senator Wherry pounded his desk saying, "Take this straight. I don't agree with the figures. I've read them all, but I don't agree with them." Besides, he considered federal civil servants a select group to whom averages did not apply. "By the same reasoning one could argue, but not very intelligently," Wherry stated, "that because there are an estimated 55,000 Communists in the United States, the Federal Government . . . should have [its] pro rata share." In rejecting Kinsey's estimates, Wherry rejected the notion that homosexuals were a significant minority population throughout the country, implying instead that they represented an unusual, but containable, clique in Washington.[19]

Despite their ridiculousness, Blick's figures became widely accepted in American popular culture. Blick's estimates would be repeated, misquoted, and exaggerated for years, solidifying a perceived connection between sexual perversion, Washington, D.C., and government bureaucracy. In their best-selling 1951 exposé *Washington Confidential*, Jack Lait and Lee Mortimer reported that "there are at least 6,000 homosexuals on the government payroll, most of them known, and these comprise only a fraction of the total of their kind in the city." Suggesting that the city was "a garden of pansies," they told readers, "if you're wondering where your wandering semi-boy is tonight, he's probably in Washington." In the following year's expanded exposé, *U.S.A. Confidential*, Lait and Mortimer increased the figure to 10,000. Arthur Guy Mathews, in his 1957 book *Is Homosexuality a Menace?* similarly exaggerated the estimate to 7,000 and dubbed the city a "Platonic and Socratic homosexual playground." Mathews claimed that having been "booted out" of Washington, a large number of homosexuals had come to New York City to work at the headquarters of the newly established United Nations. While homosexuality had formerly been confined to Greenwich Village and the theater district, he argued that "with the coming of the U.N., homosexuality in New York has increased tremendously." He suggested government security officers visit U.N. headquarters, "where they will find the largest congregation of homosexuals they have ever seen in their lives." He implicated all levels of government in this explosion. "New York has about 7,000 homosexuals, the majority of them males, working in federal, county, city, and state jobs," Mathews claimed.[20]

Lait and Mortimer borrowed the rhetoric about Washington's homosexual menace from Wherry, Bridges, and other politicians. They added names of actual gay bars and newspaper accounts of government officials arrested on morals charges, and served it up as an indictment of the New Deal. They painted an image of a Washington teeming with prostitutes, gamblers, Communists, drug dealers, "fairies and Fair Dealers." A city overtaken by a "gigantic governmental apparatus," it had become a crime-infested cesspool. They blamed Roosevelt's Supreme Court appointment of Felix Frankfurter, "the brains of the New Deal," for allowing the city to be invaded by a "whole nest of appeasers, left-wingers, welfare-staters, do-gooders and queer intellectuals." Questioning both the loyalty and the manliness of the New Deal braintrusters, they derided them as "crackpots from the campuses, communists, ballet-dancers, and economic planners." They claimed that Georgetown, previously a mostly black, working-class neighborhood, had been discovered by Eleanor Roosevelt and had since become a haven for her privileged New Dealer friends who engaged in deviant sexuality. "Not all who reside in Georgetown are rich, red, or queer," Lait and Mortimer conceded, "But if you know anyone who fulfills at least two of these foregoing three qualifications," he probably "prances" behind one of the restored colonial townhouses there. Driving home the association, they likened Georgetown to New York's Greenwich Village, home to a thriving subculture of gay men, lesbians, bohemians, and political radicals since the 1910s. The "hands on hip" set, they summarized, had "won the battle of Washington."[21]

Lait and Mortimer took particular aim at the civil service as a haven for lesbians, gay men, and other "eunuchs." Their investigation led them to conclude that though "the exceptional ones do drift to Broadway and to Hollywood," traditional haunts of artists and actors, "now we know where the dull, dumb deviates go." The security of the civil service attracted these less talented queers, they reasoned. "There, in the mediocrity and virtual anonymity of commonplace tasks, the sexes—all four of them—are equal in the robot requirements and qualifications." Not only had the civil service erased gender distinctions, but "there is no color line, no social selectivity; not even citizenship is always a prerequisite." To Lait and Mortimer, and their millions of readers, the civil service represented a breakdown in all the hierarchies of civilized societies. But it was the gender and sexual breakdown that most concerned them. Speculating that Washington harbored ten thousand more women than men, they labeled the city a "femmocracy" where "lesbianism is scandalously rampant." The self-sufficient G-girl, her marriage prospects bleak, was "a push-over for a predatory Lesbian," they argued. Not merely the absence of men but the way in which women had invaded the male workspace led to this inversion of the natural order. Even if they did not succumb to lesbianism, female civil servants were forced to hunt aggressively for men, pick up the check on dates, and even pay for sex, Lait and Mortimer argued. "They are a hard, efficient lot, doing men's work, thinking like men, and sometimes driven to take the place of men—in the proscribed zones of desperate flings of love and sex." Having usurped the role of men in the workplace, they were doing it in the bedroom as well.[22]

Such tabloid journalism that asserted a link between New Deal bureaucracy and sexual deviance was wildly popular in the 1950s. *Washington Confidential* sold more than 150,000 hardcover copies in its first three weeks of publication. Within a month it was number one on the *New York Times* bestseller list. By the next year, when Dell came out with a thirty-five-cent paperback edition, sales were in the millions. It spawned a veritable cottage industry of similar exposés and led one year later to the founding of the tabloid magazine *Confidential*, which carried on the tradition for the rest of the decade. "Everyone knew the book," commented *Washington Star* columnist Emelda Dixon. Writing in the *New Republic*, John Mallon warned that, despite their obvious exaggerations and inaccuracies, the Lait and Mortimer books would be used by Republicans in the upcoming election to smear Democrats. "They are reaching a large and growing audience which," he argued "cannot digest the pompous dullness of William F. Buckley's attack on academic freedom or John Flynn's ponderous assault on the Welfare State."[23]

Lait and Mortimer's book so tarnished the reputation of Washington and its bureaucrats that the Civil Service Commission felt compelled to respond. Chairman Robert Ramspeck feared that the publicity about the "sordid conditions" in Washington was hindering recruitment of federal workers. Ramspeck launched a program known as the "Truth Campaign" to set the record straight. As a public relations effort, it sought to disseminate information extolling the recreational, cultural, religious, and educational opportunities available in the nation's capital. "Many government departments are doing an outstanding job in encouraging wholesome outside activities for their employees," Ramspeck noted, and he wanted to see that these efforts received as much publicity as the writings of "sensationalists" like Lait and Mortimer.[24]

Deviant Bureaucrats

As McCarthy had solidified the association between homosexuals and Communists, Wherry's investigation solidified an association between homosexuals and government bureaucrats. This association enjoyed such widespread acceptance and caused such concern because, like McCarthy's claims about Communists in government, it crystallized long-held suspicions about the federal bureaucracy—suspicions that pre-dated the Cold War. The federal workforce had long been considered a site of gender nonconformity. In the nineteenth century, middle-class ideology insisted that men be self-employed entrepreneurs or professionals. To work for a salary was considered demeaning and emasculating. Though small by modern standards, the federal government in the late nineteenth century was among the first large-scale bureaucracies. To travel to Washington to seek work from a politician—to thus give up one's independence—was considered a sign of unmanliness. Labeling them "weak-limbed" and "wizened," popular literature from the period derided government workers as emasculated, lazy, and sycophantic. One Thomas Nast cartoon effectively illustrated the supposedly feminizing nature of government work by depicting male office-seekers in Washington wearing women's clothes. As historian Cindy Aron has argued, "[G]overnment workers were trapped between an ethic that encouraged them to make it as independent, autonomous professionals and entrepreneurs and an economic reality that required them to take their place within an increasingly white-collar world." Exacerbating the situation, the federal government was among the first large-scale employers to hire women in white-collar occupations. The large numbers of women in government offices made working there even more demeaning for middle-class men and, she argues, "heightened the connection between federal jobs and weakness."[25]

The tremendous expansion of the federal government under the New

Deal brought in thousands of new civil servants—many of them women—and saw the rise of a new type of government worker, the intellectual. The myriad of New Deal government agencies brought economists, social scientists, statisticians, and other experts to Washington to fight the Depression and help regulate the nation's economy. One observer described the typical New Dealer as "an entirely new type of public servant . . . young, enthusiastic, idealistic, able, and hard-working. He knew the difference between fudge and a fugue, had read books, could talk intelligently, and had ideas." Though such talented civil servants were valued by champions of the New Deal, its critics dismissed them as meddling "eggheads." Louis Bromfield's 1952 definition of an "egghead" made clear that such persons lacked masculinity: "a person of spurious intellectual pretensions, often a professor or the protégé of a professor; fundamentally superficial; overemotional and feminine in reactions to any problems." Many Americans resented the new breed of geeky social scientists with slide rules and pocket protectors running the new federal relief and regulatory agencies. One congressman dismissed such New Dealers as "short-haired women and long-haired men messing into everybody's personal affairs and lives, inquiring whether they love their wives or do not love them." During a debate over funding for the National Science Foundation, he argued that "the average American does not want some expert running around prying into his life and his personal affairs and deciding for him how he should live." During the Roosevelt administration, resentment was already growing not only against new federal government programs, but against the kinds of people who administered them.[26]

As the size and scope of the executive branch grew rapidly during the New Deal and World War II, legislators saw the balance of power shifting away from Congress. As the expert administrator became more crucial to the running of government and waging war, the legislator resented his perceived loss of power. As Richard Hofstadter put it, "In the management of public affairs and private business, where small politicians and small businessmen used to feel that most matters were within their control, these men have been forced, since the days of FDR, to confront better educated and more sophisticated experts, to their continuing frustration." Legislators were elected generalists, often from small-town America, whereas civil servants were unelected specialists, usually from a more urban, cosmopolitan culture. That civil servants were often better educated and of a higher social origin than the lawmakers only exacerbated what sociologist Edward A. Shils called "the legislative war on the civil service." When economists and other specialists from the executive branch took the witness stand in congressional hearings, "the congressmen were simply overwhelmed," noted David Brinkley. Fearful of such bureaucratic knowledge, legislators came to suspect that bureaucrats were both keeping secrets from them and turning secrets over to enemy agents. Key to both these fears was the notion that bureaucrats had important secrets, or types of knowledge and expertise, that they controlled. Legislators were jealous of the new power and expertise of bureaucrats and imagined them using and abusing that power either by withholding information from them or giving it to others.[27]

Concern about the rising power of bureaucrats was fueled by the notion that they constituted an antidemocratic force, a new branch of government with no constitutional basis, taking power away from the people's elected officials. As Shils wrote, "[T]he administrator is regarded as the usurping rival of the legislator, and sometimes as an actual obstruction to the realization of the people's will." Some commentators put the threat bureaucrats posed to sacred notions of republicanism even more starkly, calling them "princes of privilege" and comparing them with the absolutist monarchy of pre-Revolutionary France. "The sight of an army of Federal workers descending on every village and city in the country, building fortresses in the local squares, with the intent of intimidating the citizenry, would horrify Americans," wrote Edna Lonigan. "They would be shocked to learn of an even stronger Bastille erected in Washington. But politically, that is what has occurred." Several studies published during the late 1940s and early 1950s argued that bureaucrats were a heterogeneous group, more representative of the average American than elected officials, and therefore did not constitute a cohesive bureaucratic class. That social scientists felt compelled to make such arguments suggests how widespread was the perception that bureaucracy posed a threat to American democracy. Government workers had become so numerous and so powerful, their enemies imagined, as to constitute an influential voting block. *The Saturday Evening Post* editorialized that Truman won his surprise victory in 1948 over Dewey not because of his whistle-stop tour or the overconfidence of the Republican candidate but because of the votes of federal workers, "who have grown so numerous that they, with their wives and in-laws, now hold the balance of power in any close election." The magazine cited the example of Ohio, which Truman won by only 7,000 votes, and which was home to 80,000 federal employees. Since the federal payroll was increasing each year, the writers wondered whether the party in power could ever be defeated at the polls. A "despotism of bureaucracy" seemed to be forming.[28]

Many Americans were also concerned about the effect of this increasingly powerful bureaucracy on society. They saw the large-scale government programs of the New Deal and Fair Deal as threats to traditional American notions of individualism and self-reliance. By making citizens dependent on government largess, they argued, such programs imitated the effects of communism by limiting personal initiative and weakening moral fiber. As Senator Taft declared in a speech to the U.S. Chamber of Commerce, "We have become infected with the totalitarian idea that no longer is an individual responsible for his own life, but that all problems must be solved by Washington." Such lack of individual responsibility, warned a Chicago Presbyterian minister, led to a decline in morals. "When the state becomes a god, morals seem to go," he told his congregation. Under the new trend toward state idolatry, he explained, the people "exchange their free manhood for the manna from Washington." As Senator Thomas Pryor Gore (D–Oklahoma) wrote of the New Deal, "It has spoiled the character and the morals, spoiled the souls of millions of people." Such critics believed that as government bureaucracy increased, individual responsibility and determination declined. Socialism made citizens lazy and stunted their independence. Men became weak, and women flouted standards of proper decorum. With their moral fiber sapped, both would succumb to immoral temptations such as homosexuality and would ultimately be seduced by communism.[29]

To many of its critics, bureaucracy was guilty of smothering the individual will of American citizens, particularly male citizens. It was accomplishing on a societal level what parents, especially mothers, were feared to be doing on a familial level. Mid-century social critics and psychologists labeled the problem "momism." They imagined that overprotective mothers were smothering their children—particularly their sons—to such an extent that they were to blame for an apparent rise in homosexuality. Since the American Revolution, women had been assigned the task of raising and educating virtuous male citizens who would ensure the survival of the republic. While in some ways empowering to women, this special role also set them up for blame if the character of the nation's citizens was perceived to be declining—as it was in Cold War America. Philip Wylie first coined the term "momism" in his best-selling 1942 book *Generation of Vipers* to describe the problem of domineering mothers who produced weak and neurotic sons and husbands—men who lacked independent will. "Her boy," Wylie wrote, "'protected' by her love, and carefully, even shudderingly shielded from his logical development . . . is cushioned against any major step in his progress toward maturity." Affection that should have focused on a young girl gets channeled into sentimentality toward the mother. Rather than strike out on his own, such a boy would remain tied to his mother's apron strings and, according to Wylie, "take a stockroom job in the hairpin factory and try to work up to the vice-presidency." He would become a neutered bureaucrat.[30]

By the 1940s, many Americans believed that bureaucracy was a powerful, emasculating, immoral force subverting America's democratic traditions. A Gallup poll before the 1944 presidential election reported that the principal issue to Republicans voters was "bureaucracy."[31] Two years later, in his first campaign for the U.S. Senate, McCarthy ran against the Washington bureaucrat, about whom he was already speaking in gendered terms. Projecting the image of a virile farmer and war veteran, McCarthy promised to confront Washington's "bureaucratic nightmare" and turn back the New Deal. "Tired of Being Pushed Around?" asked a McCarthy campaign advertisement. "Do you like to have some government bureaucrat tell you how to manage your life?" If not, the answer was to elect "a Tail-gunner" like Joseph McCarthy. "Now, when Washington is in confusion, when BUREAUCRATS are seeking to perpetuate themselves FOREVER upon the American way of Life, AMERICA NEEDS FIGHTING MEN," urged another flyer. McCarthy dismissed his opponent Howard McMurray, a political science professor from the University of Wisconsin–Madison, as a bureaucratic expert who was part of the problem. When McMurray boasted of his Ph.D., McCarthy responded, "I'm no professor—just a farm boy." As one of McCarthy's ads said of Washington, "There are too many professors there now." News coverage of the campaign emphasized McCarthy's manliness—particularly his reputation as a college boxing champ and his "barrel-chested appearance." One paper reported that he sharpened his razor not with a hone but on the palm of his hand. As a self-made man, McCarthy was reported to be winning voters away from "the false Gods of bureaucracy, socialism, communism and back to the American way of life." Though McCarthy's attack on the virility of federal bureaucrats at this early stage was mostly made by contrasting them with his own masculine demeanor, the attacks would later become much more explicit.[32]

Like McCarthy, Wherry too came to his antigay campaign after years fighting the New Deal bureaucracy. Wherry got his start in politics as mayor of Pawnee City, Nebraska, and president of the local county fair association. Born in 1892, he had inherited a family furniture business and expanded it into an automobile dealership, farm implement store, and funeral parlor. Drew Pearson derided him as the "Merry Mortician." As a small-town businessman, Wherry harbored a life-long resentment of government intervention into private enterprise and became a die-hard opponent of Roosevelt's New Deal and Truman's Fair Deal social programs. Rejecting the label "conservative" as an inadequate reflection of his views, Wherry called himself a "fundamentalist" in his opposition to the "socialistic welfare state." He advocated a return to a "simpler past" before large-scale government bureaucracy. Like many midwestern legislators, Wherry was also an ardent isolationist. He railed against the World Bank, the United Nations, and other international efforts as "schemes" that would lead to the "end of self-government in the United States." He characterized postwar Washington as a "confusion planned by those in high places, who mean that it shall produce a state of mental futility on the part of our people," allowing them to seize power and establish communism in the United States. His opposition to both federal and international agencies knew few bounds. To suggest that they were full of homosexuals was part of his ongoing campaign to discredit them.[33]

Long before the spring of 1950, concern about the rising power and effect of government bureaucrats was being articulated in moral and gendered terms. To many Americans in the postwar era, Washington, D.C., was perceived as a white-collar town full of long-haired men and short-haired women trying to tell everybody what to do. Its smothering bureaucracy was seen as threatening the moral character and individualism of American society. So when McCarthy, Bridges, Wherry, and other politicians began to produce "evidence" that the State Department had ninety-one homosexuals and the federal government thousands more, such revelations seemed completely plausible. To label such people homosexuals and Communists was only to make explicit suspicions that pre-dated the Cold War. Those who perceived bureaucracy as a force which was emasculating and morally weakening American society were quick to suggest—and to believe—that it was full of homosexuals who were themselves emasculated moral weaklings. Though sharpened in the context of the Cold War, both the Red and Lavender Scares were outgrowths of a broader campaign led by members of Congress to halt the expansion of the bureaucracy they had neither the expertise nor the power to control. They were reactions against a major transformation in the role of government and in the city of Washington over the course of the New Deal and World War II. They expressed a fear of what was imagined as a faceless, gender-less, family-less welfare state. What leaders of both the Red and Lavender scares feared most was not communism as identified in the Soviet Union as much as the communism of the New Deal and all it implied—that Americans were becoming a nation of immoral, materialistic, bureaucrats.

"Information is accumulating," wrote Westbrook Pegler in June 1950, "which shows that perversion has been so kindly regarded in the New Deal cult as to amount to a characteristic of that administration." Throughout the 1950s Americans continued to associate a perceived increase in sexual immorality with the New Deal, even if it occurred thousands of miles from

Washington. In 1955, a "homosexual panic" erupted in Boise, Idaho, after a front-page story in the *Idaho Daily Statesman* announced that three men had been arrested for having sex with teenage boys. Believing they had uncovered the tip of a large "homosexual ring," police began interviewing hundreds of Boise citizens. Over the next year, sixteen men were arrested on various morals charges, including a bank vice president and other prominent community leaders. The trials, covered extensively in the local press, resulted in lengthy prison terms—the first man convicted was sentenced to life in prison. *Time* magazine reported that "Boiseans were shocked to learn that their city had sheltered a widespread homosexual underworld." In their search not only for an explanation but also for a cure, many of them turned to Washington. The local prosecutor, looking for an expert on uncovering homosexuals, hired a former government security officer whose "claim to fame" had been his investigation of homosexuals in the State Department. And a Boise banker, trying to explain what he saw as the new-found presence of homosexuals in his community, pointed to the New Deal. "The homosexual scandal took me by surprise," he noted. "Such things did not exist when I was a boy. I can tell you exactly when the moral degeneration of America began: It began with the election of Franklin Roosevelt."[34]

A Full Investigation

By crystallizing the association between the federal bureaucracy and immorality, the Wherry investigation ensured an expansion of the Lavender Scare. It inspired many government agencies to step up efforts to uncover and remove homosexuals from their ranks. Many established new security offices, promulgated new policies, and established alliances with local police and the FBI. By May 1950, Lieutenant Blick noted, "[N]early every one of the agencies of the Government has had their men down here to see me since your investigation began." As a result of these new procedures, the antigay purges were spreading. "From what I can learn and by my own personal observation," Blick concluded, "between ninety and one hundred moral perverts have recently resigned while under investigation. That covers all branches of government." The FBI offered assistance by turning over lists of all persons with arrest records for "sex aberration." As one Washington paper reported, "[N]umerous individual agencies quietly have been conducting their own drives" against "perverts." Not wanting to be called before an oversight committee to explain why they had done nothing to eradicate the homosexual menace, agencies began purges on their own.[35]

Most important, Wherry's investigation convinced his Senate colleagues to launch a full-scale congressional inquiry into homosexuals in the government. Senator Ferguson rose in support of the resolution, urging that "the evidence was so shocking that action should be taken immediately." Vice President Alben Barkley, as president of the Senate, assigned the recommended investigation to the Committee on Expenditures in Executive Departments; the Rules committee authorized funding; and the full Senate unanimously authorized an investigation into sexual perversion in the federal workforce. With outrage building from the Peurifoy and then the Blick revelations, no Democrat dared speak against it. Senator McCarthy called the investigation "an excellent idea" and predicted that "if the thousands of perverts are removed from the government payroll, a very serious blow will be dealt to Communist espionage activities in our government." Elmer Davis, a liberal radio commentator, derided what he called the Senate's new role as "guardian of public morals," but admitted, "it looks as if the enemies of the State Department, and of the administration generally, have got hold of a more profitable issue than communism." The full-scale congressional probe Republicans had been angling for since March was underway.[36]

Secretary of State Dean Acheson (right) and Assistant Secretary John Peurifoy
*answer questions from a Senate appropriations committee on February 28, 1950, about
Senator Joseph McCarthy's charges that the State Department harbored "security
risks." Peurifoy set off a Lavender Scare when he revealed that among those ousted from
the department as security risks were ninety-one homosexuals. (Courtesy AP/Wide
World Photos.)*

Senator Joseph McCarthy's popularity
*stemmed as much from his campaign against
Communists as his campaign against homosexuals. The phrase "treason and dishonor" on this
1954 campaign matchbook cover signals the dual
nature of McCarthy's attack.*

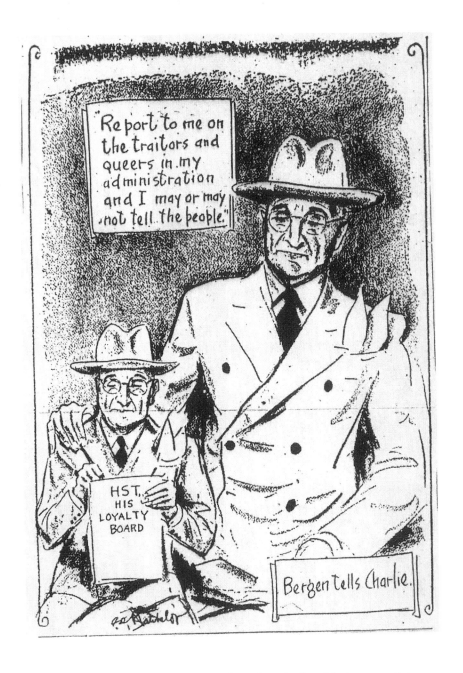

By March 1950, *Republicans were calling for an investigation of the homosexuals-in-government problem. When President Truman's loyalty board refused, political cartoons like this one from the* Washington Times-Herald, *the city's most widely read newspaper, accused Truman of protecting "traitors and queers." (C. D. Batchelor,* Washington Times-Herald, *March 31, 1950. © New York Daily News, L.P., reprinted with permission.)*

"It's true, sir, that the State Department let me go, but that was solely because of incompetence."

The State Department *became so associated in the public imagination with both disloyalty and homosexuality that employees grew defensive. In this* New Yorker *cartoon from June 1950, a fired employee feels the need to distance himself from these charges, no matter what the cost. (Alan Dunn,* New Yorker, *June 17, 1950. © The New Yorker Collection 1950 Alan Dunn from cartoonbank.com. All rights reserved.)*

WE ACCUSE

...SUMNER

By TRUXTON DECATUR

EDITOR'S NOTE: Authorities tell us homosexuals are security risks in time of war, and the State Department is a prime target for espionage. No government at war could commit greater folly than to retain a confirmed homosexual in its No. 2 Foreign Policy post.

This magazine feels the American people have a pressing right to know that their wartime Under Secretary — SUMNER WELLES — was such a man. Continued suppression of the Welles story can no longer be justified in view of the need of public awareness of this danger and public support of our Federal Security Program. It must not happen again, and an informed citizenry will not let it happen again.

THE AMERICAN PUBLIC was jarred a seismograph in an earthquake in when the Senate disclosed a Washing police estimate of 3,500 homosexuals in fed jobs—many of them in the State Departme

The Senate's announcement that its Comm tee on Executive Department Expenditures wo investigate this shocking estimate was the real inkling citizens of the United States of the grandiose scale on which the governm had been infiltrated by sex deviates during Roosevelt and Truman administrations.

Homosexuals are said by FBI director J. E

12

FDR's Undersecretary of State Sumner Welles *was forced to resign in 1943 when senators threatened to reveal a homosexual scandal from his past. Though hushed up at the time, the truth behind Welles's resignation helped associate diplomatic "cookie pushers in striped pants" with deviant sexuality. The popular tabloid* Confidential *"outed" Welles in this May 1956 cover story.*

Those persistent whispers are all true!

He had that lavender stripe even when he was second in command of the State Department

WELLES

er and other authorities to be security risks
...e of war or international tension for two
...s: 1) They are promiscuous to the point of
...ting with strangers who might be spies; 2)
...are open to blackmail by espionage agents
... the necessity of hiding their perversion.

...all wonder then that the knowledge that
...sexuals had virtually saturated the State De-
...ent — the treasury of America's foreign
... secrets—caused a wave of public indig-
...n.

...sequent firings and resignations of several
...ed State Department employes who either
...ted or were proved by investigation to be
...sexuals has served to turn the heat down on
...zzling post-war political issue; but the whole

TURN THE PAGE

Republican senators such as Kenneth Wherry (R–Nebraska) *vigorously pursued the campaign McCarthy helped unleash against homosexuals in the federal government. He held special hearings on the subject and asked his Senate colleagues, "Can [you] think of a person who could be more dangerous to the United States of America than a pervert?" (Courtesy of the Senate Historical Office.)*

Lieutenant Roy Blick, *head of the Washington, D.C., vice squad, oversaw the arrest of hundreds of gay men and lesbians. In March 1950 he told a congressional committee that Washington was home to five thousand homosexuals and estimated that three-quarters of them worked for the federal government. (Courtesy AP / Wide World Photos.)*

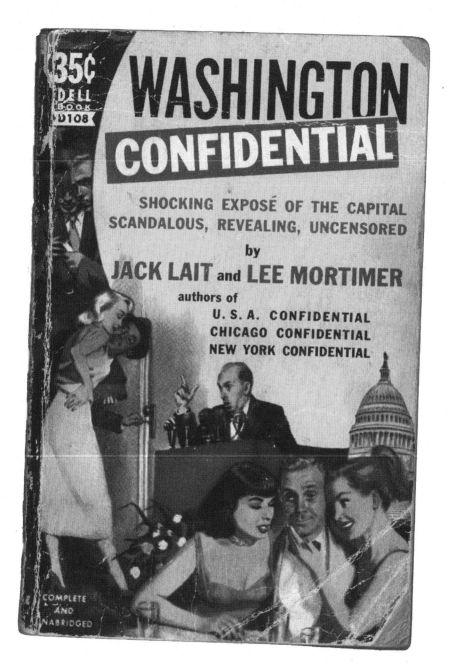

Jack Lait and Lee Mortimer's 1951 best-selling exposé *Washington Confidential* helped popularize the notion that the nation's capital was a haven for homosexuals. They charged that the city was a "garden of pansies" — a city not only teeming with prostitutes, gamblers, and Communists, but "fairies and Fair Dealers." (Reproduced with permission of Random House, Inc.)

In June 1950 the Senate authorized a full investigation *into the "employment of homosexuals and other sex perverts in government." Senator Clyde Hoey (D–North Carolina, second from right), a man first elected to public office in 1898, headed the investigation. Senator Margaret Chase Smith (R–Maine, far right) condemned McCarthy but participated fully in the homosexuals-in-government investigation. (Courtesy of the Senate Historical Office.)*

Liberal cartoonist Herb Block of the Washington Post— *known for coining the term "McCarthyism"— also lampooned the Hoey Committee's investigation of homosexuals in government. The cartoon suggested that the interest senators took in "perversion" was itself an example of "abnormal psychology."* (Copyright 1950 by Herblock in The Washington Post, *reproduced with permission.)*

Homosexuals were considered *security risks because they could allegedly be blackmailed into revealing state secrets. The only evidence the Hoey Committee found to substantiate this claim was the case of Colonel Alfred Redl, head of Austrian intelligence before World War I. Though Redl was homosexual and did give secrets to the Russians, government officials exaggerated the uncertain role blackmail may have played in his espionage.*

The F.B.I. knew those two code experts were fruity fellow
off to Moscow. How many more pansies do we have, in str
caught on cameras by cunning Commie agents, to be use

Behind The Scandal Of Those Two Traitors: HOW

BLACKMA
INTO SPYIN

The Reds are using a
in recruiting spies and t
it's working. The new
gain access to American
using — homosexuals!

It is a pattern that is
familiar to Western counte
agents. The Reds trap th
men in indiscretions and
mail them. They tell the
that if he won't give the
they want, they'll see th
posed in his sex peculiari

It was thru two highly
characters of this ilk th
sians were able to get acc
ments in the hush-hush I
curity Agency.

The treason of two N
perts, Bernon F. Mitchell
H. Martin, finally brough
all the agencies of gove
SHOULD have been on
ago. And the investigatio
agencies — and especia
gress—have turned up m
so explosive they'll neve
suppress it, try as they n

Maybe the governmen
who're supposed to look a
matters just aren't hip e
any Washington corres
any alert (and normal)
capital, for that matter, a
you that this is an old,
in Miss Liberty's home
Potomac.

William H. Martin (left) and Bernon F. Mitchell, the two lavender lads who were code experts for the U.S. before becoming turncoats and flitting off to Russia

BY JAMES SHAWCROSS

THE recent case of the two American defectors — or, to put it more
bluntly, traitors — who went over
to the Reds after slipping away from
their work at a super-secret U. S.
security agency, has come as a great
shock to many people.

No one could understand how two
young men like these — clean-cut
fellows who looked like typical all-
14

American boys — could betray their
own homeland to the Russians. After
all, these men came from solid,
church-going families, lived in the
kind of small towns for which this
country is famous, and seemed as safe
from subversion as two young men
could be.

You've read about this case in the
newspapers and heard about it on
the air. But the BIG TRUTH behind
it has not yet been told!

For the truth is this:

In 1960, Bernon Mitchell and William Martin, *both analysts with the National Security Agency, defected to the Soviet Union for political reasons. The press erroneously dubbed them a homosexual "love team" who fell victim to Soviet blackmail. (*Top Secret, *February 1961.)*

g was done about it until the boys had already minced
ans, whose perverted pursuits in hotel rooms have been
nail bait to make the homos turn against their homeland?

HE REDS
OMOSEXUALS
OR THEM!

World War II, for example, top men in the State De- was widely known as a , and yet he was untouch- one lavender lad get into d before you know it the arming with limp-wristed couldn't wiggle their hips ey were Marilyn Monroe y wish they were). And happened at State. The crawling with fairies, but nothing good about this ry. Most of the agencies gton have been afflicted curse at one time or an- ne dismay of the govern-

ut Washington, Prince ounty in adjacent Mary- arts of Virginia just across c, there are scores of places lmost exclusively to homo- e fairies call them "gay" e are night clubs specializ- male impersonators, some bars and grills, and some tly innocuous restaurants. ts are heavily patronized that you sometimes can't way into them — and s fall into two groups a ducky idea, from their warped point of view): omosexuals, living it up. ussian agents, setting their

In dimly lit cocktail lounges and in the glare of fluorescence in less subtle homo hangouts, the agents strike up conversations with men they've been watching, men who seem to work for the government but don't say what agency. This is the tell- tale sign of the man who works for a secret agency and has security clear- ance. For a standing rule at all the

hush-hush security agencies — NSA, Central Intelligence Agency, and the like — is: Never tell anyone you work here.

The agents proposition the eager homo, and off he goes with them to a private room where anything can (and does) happen. But what the homo doesn't know, until too late, is that hidden cameras have photo-

Aerial view of the grounds of the National Security Agency, at Fort Meade, Mary- land, which was a very hush-hush agency — until these two spies queered things.

Bruce Scott (right) and Gordon Fahey *met at the Chicken Hut, Washington's most popular gay bar in the 1950s. They are pictured here in front of the townhouse they shared in Georgetown, then a neigh-borhood heavily populated by gay men and lesbians.*

Lafayette Park, across Pennsylvania Avenue from the White House, *was the center of gay male life in Washington for much of the early twentieth century. After World War II, the U.S. Park Police launched a "Pervert Elimination Campaign" to clean up the park. The building housing the public men's room is visible at the far left. (Courtesy of the Library of Congress.)*

Bruce Scott began working for the Department of Labor in 1938. *He is pictured here with his secretary (left) and boss (right) in 1954. Two years later he lost his job on suspicion of homosexuality, after the government learned that he lived with a homosexual and had been arrested for loitering in Lafayette Park.*

Despite the devastating affect of the antigay purges, *gay men in 1950s Washington continued to socialize together. Here an unidentified group of gay men enjoy an outing at Arlington Cemetery.*

A gay party in 1953 *at the suburban Alexandria, Virginia, home of Bruce Scott and Paul Glaman (far right). Glaman lost his job with the CIA for being gay.*

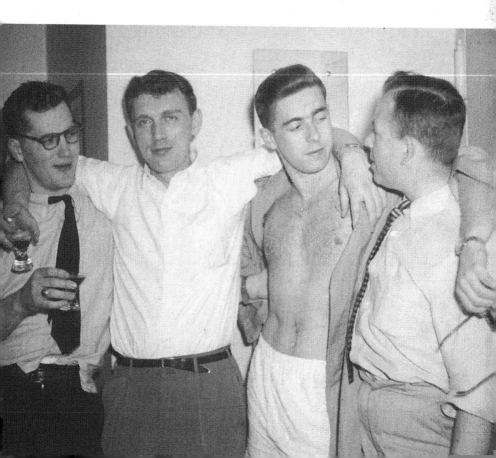

In 1957, *at the beginning of the space race with the Soviet Union, Frank Kameny, with a Ph.D. from Harvard, was one of a handful of astronomers in the United States. Despite the need for his expertise, the government fired him for suspicion of homosexuality. Kameny fought his dismissal all the way up to the Supreme Court. When his legal efforts failed, he organized the Mattachine Society of Washington, which adapted the tactics of the civil rights movement to the cause of gays and lesbians. (Courtesy of Kay Tobin Lahusen.)*

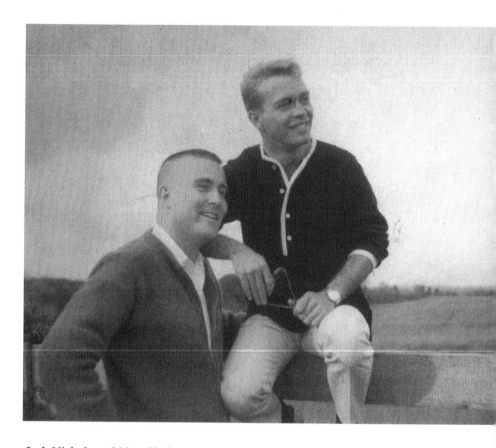

Jack Nichols and Lige Clarke *organized the Mattachine Society of Washington's first public pickets in front of the White House in April 1965. "The [Mattachine] Society gave us a rallying point, a cause, around which we centered our lives," Nichols remembered. (Courtesy of Jack Nichols.)*

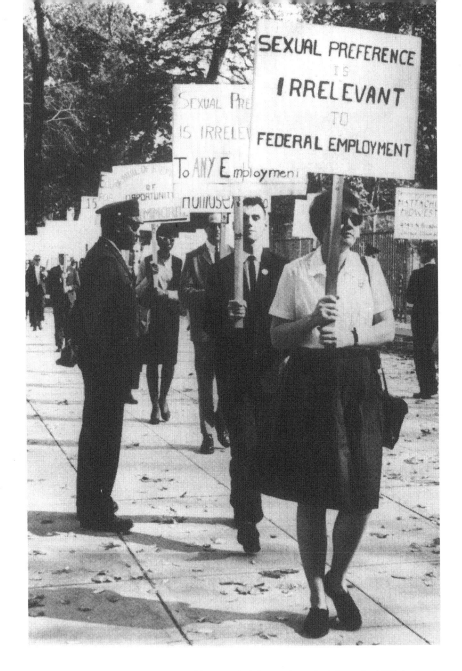

The Mattachine Society of Washington held a series of pickets in 1965 *in front of federal government buildings to call attention to the exclusion of gays and lesbians from both civilian and military jobs. The October 1965 picket in front of the White House drew forty-five participants, from as far away as New York, Philadelphia, Chicago, and Florida. Barbara Gittings of Philadelphia is pictured here at the front of the picket line. (Courtesy of Kay Tobin Lahusen.)*

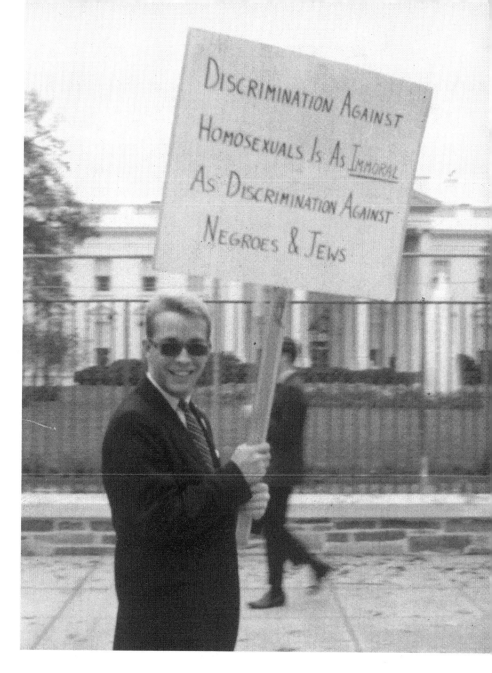

Lige Clarke, *a civilian who worked in the Office of the Army chief of staff, risked his job to participate in the October 1965 picket in front of the White House. Like many of his fellow picketers, he wore sunglasses to partially mask his identity. (Courtesy of Jack Nichols.)*

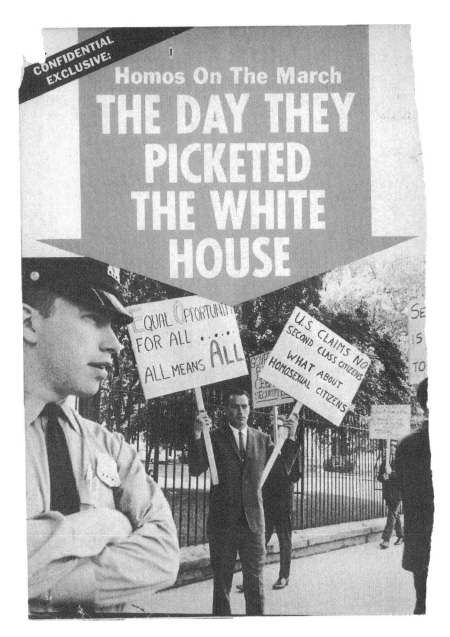

Homos On The March

THE DAY THEY PICKETED THE WHITE HOUSE

Mainstream television and print media *covered the unprecedented White House pickets for gay rights, but tabloid magazines like* Confidential *gave them the most prominent coverage. Though sensationalistic, this October 1965 story effectively publicized the groups' claims: "Emboldened by the gains made by other minority groups, homosexuals are banding together to put pressure on the politicians and change the laws which discriminate against homos and Lesbians." (*Confidential, *October 1965.)*

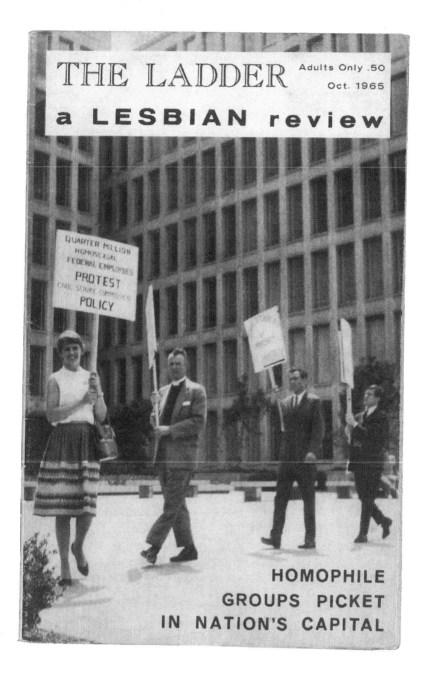

THE LADDER

Adults Only .50
Oct. 1965

a LESBIAN review

QUARTER MILLION
HOMOSEXUAL
FEDERAL EMPLOYEES
PROTEST
CIVIL SERVICE COMMISSION
POLICY

HOMOPHILE
GROUPS PICKET
IN NATION'S CAPITAL

Lilli Vincenz *leads twenty-three picketers in front of the Civil Service Commission in June 1965. One of the first and most active lesbian members of the Mattachine Society of Washington, Vincenz edited the group's news magazine. This photo appeared on the cover of* The Ladder, *a 1960s lesbian magazine with a small national circulation.*

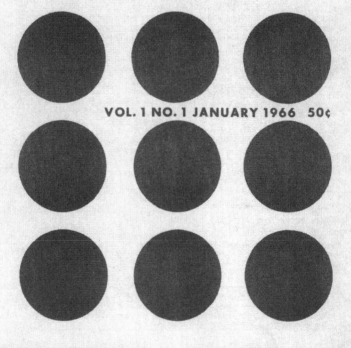

THE HOMOSEXUAL CITIZEN

- **NEWS OF CIVIL LIBERTIES**
- **AND SOCIAL RIGHTS**
- **FOR HOMOSEXUALS**

VOL. 1 NO. 1 JANUARY 1966 50¢

The Mattachine Society of Washington *began publishing a small monthly news magazine,* The Homosexual Citizen, *in 1966. The title suggested that homosexuals, though members of a minority group, remained patriotic and responsible participants in American democracy. (Reproduced with permission of the Mattachine Society of Washington.)*

Employ homosexuals??! Please leave
me alone -- I want to retire in peace!

After years of letter writing, *court cases, and public demonstrations, on September 8, 1965, members of the Mattachine Society of Washington finally succeeded in meeting with representatives of the Civil Service Commission to discuss its policy of excluding gay men and lesbians. This cartoon from the* Homosexual Citizen *depicts CSC Chairman John Macy attempting to dismiss the MSW and its concerns. The U.S. Court of Appeals eventually forced the CSC to stop excluding gay men and lesbians from the civil service. (Robert Hayden,* Homosexual Citizen, *May 1966. Reproduced with permission of the Mattachine Society of Washington.)*

In November 1986, *former members of the Mattachine Society of Washington reunited to celebrate the twenty-fifth anniversary of the organization's founding. Because members had been required to use pseudonyms in the 1960s, it was the first time many learned of their colleagues' true names. Pictured (standing left to right) Martha Becker, Eugene Baker, Nancy Tucker, Lilli Vincenz, Otto Ulrich, John Swanson, Perren Schafer, Eva Freund, Robert Bellanger, Ron Balen, and Frank Kameny, (kneeling left to right) Bruce Scott, Tony Jacubosky, and Paul Kuntzler.* (Washington Blade, *November 21, 1986. Photo by Doug Hinckle. Reproduced with permission of the* Washington Blade.)

5

The Hoey Investigation
Searching for a Homosexual Spy

In the spring of 1950, when Senator Clyde Hoey heard that he had been given the task of investigating homosexuals in the government, he "almost jumped out the window," according to his chief counsel. "God damn. I don't want to investigate that stuff," he told Francis Flanagan. "It's baloney, I don't want to get involved in it." Hoey was one of the last of the nineteenth-century Southern statesmen, what his biographer called, "the Hollywood version of a senator." He could be easily spotted on Capitol Hill wearing a traditional English walking coat, striped trousers, and spats, with a carnation adorning his lapel, a cane at his side, and a gray fedora covering his flowing white hair. First elected to public office in 1898 on a white supremacist platform, Hoey was the only North Carolinian to serve as a member of both houses of the state legislature, governor, and member of both houses of Congress. He had gained national attention during his investigation in 1949 into "Five-Percenters"—men who allegedly obtained government contracts for a 5 percent fee. But at the age of seventy-three and near the end of a long and distinguished career, Hoey was not interested in overseeing a probe into what he viewed as the seamier side of the nation's capital. He feared it might become a "witch hunt" that would discredit him, his committee, and the Senate.[1]

Although his was "a dirty job which he did not want," Hoey was determined to carry it out in a quiet and dignified manner. He called his chief counsel in and said, "I don't want any public hearings at all on this matter, I want it as low key as possible. Do it thoroughly—investigate it from hell to breakfast—but we're not going to have any hearings that McCarthy can make big headlines out of." Though sympathetic to McCarthy's cause, Hoey disapproved of his tactics. As early as 1940 he had charged that Communists were "mixed up" in every level of government and called for their dismissal. As a southern Democrat, Hoey opposed government programs he saw as "socialistic," particularly those that threatened "state's rights" or racial segregation. He saw the South as a bulwark against the rising tide of federal power and governmental bureaucracy. But Hoey dismissed McCarthy as a publicity hound and recommended ignoring his "wild" charges. As chair of the Committee on Expenditures in Executive Departments, Hoey developed a reputation for keeping McCarthy, the committee's most notorious member and future chair, "in check." He was particularly adamant about the need to keep the homosexual investigation from becoming a "circus." Clearing the way for Hoey, McCarthy recused himself entirely from the hearings. Some reporters claimed he did this "to avoid being in a position of judging his own accusation," a position which normally caused him little concern. Whatever the reason, it suggests that by the summer of 1950 the drive to purge the federal government of homosexuals had moved well beyond McCarthy.[2]

Hoey's views on homosexuality were not atypical for a man born in the nineteenth century. To him it represented a sinful, immoral behavior that he was not terribly familiar with nor comfortable debating. He tried to prevent the only female member of the committee, Margaret Chase Smith, from attending the hearings, fearing that the presence of a "lady" would inhibit the discussion. Nonetheless, Senator Smith insisted on attending and took an active part in questioning witnesses. Francis Flanagan recounted that one day after an eminent doctor had testified before the committee, Hoey called him over to the Senate cloak room, led him into a private corner, and said, "Frip, that was an excellent witness, I wanted to ask him a few questions but that god-damn Margaret Chase Smith was there." He then asked Flanagan the question he had refrained from posing to the doctor. "He mentioned about these women homosexuals, but he didn't explain it to us," Hoey complained. "Can you please tell me, what can two women possibly do?" As Flanagan recalled years later, Senator Hoey "had never heard of that. . . . He couldn't imagine." The man charged with conducting the first full-scale congressional inquiry into homosexuality was completely unfamiliar with the topic.[3]

As with many congressional investigations, the driving force behind the Hoey Committee's investigation of homosexuals was its chief counsel, Francis Flanagan. Hoey's discomfort and ignorance regarding the subject only increased Flanagan's responsibility. That the investigation was handled behind closed doors further enhanced his power, eliminating any concerns about overshadowing his boss in public. "I handled that investigation," Flanagan boasted when later questioned about the homosexuals-in-government inquiry. Flanagan managed the research effort, chose the witnesses who would testify before the committee, and wrote the final report. He also consulted with the White House and served as liaison with all federal departments and local law enforcement agencies. As Flanagan would later remark, if the hearings had been public, "I'd have made a world-wide reputation as a great investigator of homosexuals." Instead, his role has been largely obscured. Although commonly known as the Hoey Committee investigation, its outcome was determined at least as much by Francis Flanagan as it was by Clyde Hoey.

Flanagan had begun working on Capitol Hill as an investigator for the committee under Senator Harry Truman, who came to national prominence directing the committee's aggressive investigation of fraud and waste in the national defense industry during World War II. A Georgetown Law School graduate and former special agent for the FBI, Flanagan became chief counsel of the committee when it was reorganized as the Committee on Expenditures in Executive Departments after the war. He also became friends with Joseph McCarthy, a minority member of the committee and a fellow Irish Catholic. Both men were fond of hunting and would travel together on weekend trips to the hunting ranch of wealthy Texas oilman Clinton Murchison, one of McCarthy's principal financial supporters. In 1953, when the Republicans won the majority in the Senate and McCarthy became committee chair, Flanagan was poised to become McCarthy's right-hand man. But Flanagan was considered a "Democratic holdover" too close to members of the Truman administration. Under pressure from his right-wing backers, McCarthy hired Roy Cohn, a young New York district attorney. For a few months Flanagan and Cohn both worked under McCarthy as equals with two separate staffs, until McCarthy's backers found Flanagan a position in private industry. Once again he would narrowly escape national prominence.[4]

The White House Liaison

The White House was also heavily involved in managing the investigation. Already alarmed by the political implications of the continuing charges that the administration was harboring homosexuals, Truman aides worried that the Hoey investigation might lead to an escalation. "The pressure to make political hay out of the investigation while it is going on will be very great," cautioned Truman aide David Lloyd. Though pleased that McCarthy had recused himself from the hearings, they were concerned that committee member Senator Karl Mundt, cosponsor of the Nixon-Mundt bill requiring the registration of Communists, "might very well step into McCarthy's shoes." On June 22, President Truman and Undersecretary of State James Webb met to discuss how the Hoey Committee and the White House might "work together on the homosexual investigation." Truman told the undersecretary "he was sure we could find a proper basis for cooperation" and agreed that Webb and two White House aides should meet with Hoey to establish a *modus operandi*. Though Truman did not meet directly with Hoey—perhaps to insulate the president from charges of undue influence—he was closely involved in the administration's approach to the committee.[5]

The task of White House liaison to the Hoey Committee fell to Stephen Spingarn, one of the president's administrative assistants. In late June and early July, Spingarn, accompanied by Charles Murphy, special counsel to the president and one of his closest advisors, met repeatedly with Hoey and Flanagan to communicate the White House's position. One of their key concerns was how the committee should conduct its deliberations—whether its hearings should be closed or open to the public. While not wanting to draw attention to the investigation, the White House also did not want to be accused of a cover-up. Spingarn sought the advice of the entire White House staff as well as the Surgeon General and representatives of the departments of Justice and State. A small minority favored public hearings, at least for the medical professionals who might provide more scientific, less sensational, testimony. Presidential advisor and anthropologist Philleo Nash thought that closed hearings would only perpetuate the current "tendency to distort the facts." But the vast majority agreed with Spingarn that the entire investigation should be held in executive session. As White House aide George Elsey argued emphatically, "Executive, by all means. The McCarthys would have a Roman Circus otherwise." Hoey, who wanted to minimize publicity, convinced the Republicans on the committee to acquiesce to this position and the hearings were held entirely in secret. Even the transcripts remained closed to the public for almost fifty years.[6]

The issue of committee access to executive department files proved more contentious. The day after the Senate authorized the investigation, Flanagan began sending requests to department heads for the files of known or suspected homosexuals. Though not yet authorized by the committee, Flanagan's plan was to establish "a central card index" of homosexuals, a tool that government agencies could consult in screening potential or current employees. To maximize its effectiveness, the list was to include names of anyone a government agency had reason to suspect of homosexuality, whether a government employee or private citizen. Flanagan's ambitions were inspired by the practices of the notorious House Committee on Un-American Activities, which for years had maintained its own extensive files of suspected Communists and fascists. At the very least, Flanagan hoped to consolidate a number of existing lists of sex deviants already compiled by various government agencies. He learned that the Navy had a file of nearly 8,000 names, while the Army had compiled one of nearly 5,000. Those kept by the State Department and the Washington, D.C., police each had approximately 3,000 names. The smallest was that of the U.S. Park Police, which had only a few hundred. Acquiring just these five lists would give Flanagan the names of 16,500 suspected homosexuals.[7]

The White House quickly squashed Flanagan's hope for a central homosexual clearinghouse. Alerted to Flanagan's plans, Spingarn met with Hoey and reached an agreement that the requests would be ignored. Spingarn explained that a 1948 presidential order concerning loyalty files prohibited executive agencies from giving investigative information on individual employees to congressional committees. Agencies would be forced to refer such requests to the White House, putting them "squarely in the President's lap," Spingarn noted, with potentially damaging political repercussions. One newspaper had already reported that the White House was refusing to release sex pervert files to the committee and predicted "President Truman seems almost certainly headed for a hot clash with Congress." Hoey agreed that rather than request actual names, the committee would only gather statistics on the number of homosexuals fired or investigated in each agency. But when called to the White House to meet with Spingarn, Flanagan continued to press for access to the files. He asserted that the Republican members of the subcommittee, particularly Senator Mundt, might insist on seeing actual files. Flanagan personally thought that the committee could not determine if agencies were handling the matter properly without them. This caused one White House staffer to predict "a very sordid smear campaign to the effect that the President is protecting the homos." But the White House and the executive departments held firm, denying Flanagan his central card index of homosexuals and permitting him only to compile statistics and policy statements from the agencies.[8]

In addition to favoring closed hearings and closed files, the White House implemented a strategy to emphasize the "medical" aspects of the problem and downplay security concerns. They provided the committee with a list of "qualified medical witnesses" to consider, recommending that the medical authorities testify before the security experts and that their testimony be made public prior to release of the committee's final report. There was also talk of creating a "medical advisory board" to assist the committee and to appear publicly to handle questions from the press. All this would serve, according to Spingarn, to put the problem in "proper perspective."[9] To advance the notion that homosexuality was the domain of psychiatrists and not security experts, the White House launched a series of seminars run by Robert Felix, head of psychiatry at the National Institute of Mental Health. Titled "Perversion among Government Workers," the informal seminars for government personnel managers were reportedly so popular they were conducted in "three jam-packed sections" and quickly acquired the nickname "School for Scandal." Felix cautioned that homosexuals should be excluded from sensitive positions, but that they posed no more of a problem then "promiscuous persons, gossips, thieves, alcoholics, and horseplayers." If they served in positions that did not involve classified material and were discreet in their behavior, Felix argued they should be allowed to serve the government. Felix had advocated a similarly tolerant position while serving as a Naval officer, where he recommended retaining gay men who were discreet and did excellent work. "Because the boy is 'queer' is no more reason to condemn him than to condemn you or me because we enjoy the company of pretty girls," Felix had told his fellow naval officers. But Felix's tolerant approach was poorly received by the government personnel officers. One seminar participant dismissed it as "fol-de-rol about what makes one man like this and another like that." As another complained, "All I learned is that it is supposed to be okay to keep queers on in non-sensitive jobs." These personnel managers knew it was members of Congress, not government psychiatrists, that they needed to please. According to Hoey Committee staffer Jerome Adler, who attended one of the sessions, personnel managers looked to the Hill for direction. "They appear to be very anxious to have someone address them from our subcommittee to advise them in what procedures to follow."[10]

In its struggle to highlight the medical rather than the security implications of the investigation, the White House found allies among several liberal journalists. Max Lerner ran a lengthy series of columns in the *New York Post* criticizing the purges as the "Panic on the Potomac." Like the White

House, Lerner argued that homosexuality was an illness that needed to be treated on an individual basis by competent psychiatrists, not an issue of national security. Joseph and Stewart Alsop labeled the idea that the government was "honeycombed with perversion" a "lunatic notion" and dismissed as "vulgar folly" efforts to raise homosexuality to the level of a "serious political issue." In his June 16, 1950, broadcast, Eric Sevareid stressed how the ninety-one State Department terminations involved "office morale and efficient administration" and had been handled in "a routine manner" by personnel officials rather than security officials. Arguing that a "frank and open homosexual" was less vulnerable to blackmail than a philandering heterosexual, Sevareid concluded that homosexuality was "marginal" to the nation's security concerns. Some critics went even further, attacking the character of the purgers themselves. *Washington Post* political cartoonist Herbert Block—famous for coining the term "McCarthyism"—suggested that the members of Congress investigating perversion were taking a prurient interest in their subject. He portrayed a Walrus-like member of the Senate expenditures committee in a darkened room, shades drawn, eagerly reading a book on sexual perversion with a handkerchief dangling from his pocket, indicative of overactive salivary glands. He placed the entire scene, Congressman and all, under the rubric "abnormal psychology." Lerner made a similar point in characterizing the investigation as "a case of the sick being pursued by the sicker."[11]

The attempt to frame the debate in medical terms left Francis Flanagan unimpressed. At a meeting at the White House on July 8, Flanagan told Spingarn that he did not think scientists like Kinsey had "a very practical approach to the matter." Like Wherry, Blick, and others before him, he was uncomfortable with claims that a significant percentage of the population engaged in such practices. He falsely accused authorities like Kinsey of dealing with the fuzzy issue of "tendencies" rather than overt behaviors, which was the focus of his committee investigation. Echoing the sentiments of Senator Wherry, Flanagan said, "Kinsey doesn't know anything. He's a god-damn statistician." Flanagan wanted witnesses who could talk about the causes of and cures for homosexuality, not how widespread it was in the population. He eventually found government physicians and private medical experts more to his liking, especially George Henry, a New York physician who for years had been studying the cause, rather than the incidence, of homosexuality. But even with these witnesses, Flanagan was not entirely comfortable. "The medical experts," he claimed, "knew less than anyone else."[12]

Flanagan preferred the argument of government security officials that homosexuals threatened national security. Like many of these officials,

Flanagan was a former FBI agent. While serving on director J. Edgar Hoover's staff, Flanagan had become familiar with the investigation of Undersecretary of State Sumner Welles's sexual advances to railroad porters and the notion that a highly placed homosexual could be blackmailed into revealing government secrets. As a trained attorney, Flanagan sought evidence to back up the claim, but concluded from conversations with his former colleagues that "they were not able to produce much dope in documented instances in which homosexualism had endangered security." Even without any evidence, Flanagan remained committed to the security risk argument. As Steven Spingarn wrote after one of his meetings with Flanagan, "Despite the lack of documentation, he seemed convinced that homosexualism represents a serious security threat." Spingarn, a former counterespionage and security officer, believed that other types of security threats were more dangerous, especially heterosexual men with an "exceptional weakness for women." Unable to persuade Flanagan on this point, he lamented that Flanagan "seems to regard the fact that there is scant documentation of this an unfortunate accident." A State Department staffer who also met with Flanagan came to the same conclusion. "I got the impression," he wrote, "that Flanagan has already concluded that homosexuals should not be employed in government under any circumstances." Assessing that Flanagan had "pre-judged" the central issue of the investigation, Spingarn predicted that the White House "might have some difficulties from his direction."[13]

The Blackmail of Colonel Redl

In July, when the committee began to hear testimony in a small room on the third floor of the Senate Office Building, Flanagan's focus on security set the tone for the hearings. Despite White House pleas to emphasize the medical approach, the lead witness was Admiral Roscoe Hillenkoetter, director of the Central Intelligence Agency. A creation of the 1947 National Security Act, the CIA was so new that Hillenkoetter had to explain to the committee that his agency gathered intelligence on foreign countries. He provided the one piece of evidence that Flanagan would cite in his final report to prove that homosexuals posed a threat to national security. Hillenkoetter told the story of Colonel Alfred Redl, head of Austrian intelligence before World War I, one of the most infamous double agents in the history of international espionage. Hillenkoetter testified that the Russians learned of his sexual preferences, supplied him with an attractive "newsboy," and burst in on them in a hotel room engaged "in an act of perversion." Because the Austrian army had a strict policy against homosexuality, Hillenkoetter asserted, the Russians were then able to blackmail Redl into working for them. For more than a decade, Redl provided hundreds of important documents to the Russians, including the Austrian war mobilization plans, in exchange for large sums of cash. As a result of his deceit, Austrian intelligence was "completely neutralized" at the start of World War I. Calling it an old but "classic case" of sexual perversion leading to espionage, he warned that it was a concrete example of "what can be done to a country's security by a homosexual strategically placed."[14]

As recounted by Hillenkoetter, the Redl example had dubious relevance to the situation of the average American civil servant in the Cold War. Redl's espionage had occurred two world wars and an ocean away, and in the military rather than the civil service. Moreover, unbeknownst to the committee, Hillenkoetter had manipulated and exaggerated elements of the Redl story. By all accounts Redl was a homosexual double agent, but because he committed suicide within hours of the discovery of his duplicity, how he began his espionage has remained obscured. Most accounts point to Redl's greed as the prime motivation, his need to support a "sybaritic homosexual life." Although from humble origins, Redl lived lavishly as an army officer, supporting a handsome, young lieutenant and driving flashy automobiles. Most renditions of the Redl affair emphasize his callousness and the demands *he* placed on his Russian "employers," including information about Russian agents that he used to enhance his standing in the Austrian intelligence hierarchy. One historian of the Austro-Hungarian empire notes that the army was "fairly broadminded about its officers' private failings, as long as they were somehow connected with sex" and thereby cast doubt on the blackmail theory. "There may have been some hint of blackmail, but it is not likely that before the first act of treason it was a compelling factor," he concluded. A recent study by a Viennese journalist, Georg Markus, who had access to Soviet archives, suggests that Redl's Russian handler threatened to reveal that Redl was having an affair with a "Lieutenant X." But he also suggests that greed quickly became the predominant motivating factor. If blackmail played a role in the Redl spy story, Hillenkoetter's version exaggerated the connection. His claim that Russians planted a newsboy in his hotel room and caught him in the act was pure fabrication.[15]

Hillenkoetter was the only official to testify before the Hoey Committee who offered any concrete evidence to support the blackmail argument. Subsequent testimony from Army, Navy, and Air Force security officers cast doubt on his claims. Though they all expressed the opinion that homosexuals posed a security risk if involved in classified work, none could offer any evidence. Colonel Hamilton Howze from the Army's G-2 intelligence unit testified that "we have no information to the effect that foreign governments have [considered] or are considering the homosexual class as a special target for espionage purposes." He had heard rumors of a Nazi list of homosexuals, but admitted it had never been located. The Air Force representative from the Office of Special Investigations, after delineating a number of ways in which a homosexual posed a security risk, admitted that in the history of his office, "no specific cases have come to light which would demonstrate these points." A representative from the Office of Naval Intelligence concurred, noting that "the Navy had no actual records to indicate that either the Germans or the Russians used homosexuals in any manner." As another representative of the Office of Naval Intelligence told a Hoey staffer, "there was too much stress on blackmail in connection with homosexuals." As the committee knew, the military had a very aggressive policy of excluding homosexuals, but it was not based on concerns about blackmail or national security. Instituted at the beginning of World War II, it was part of a general psychiatric screening of applicants designed to eliminate those unfit for service who might become postwar psychiatric causalities.[16]

The committee also heard from the Washington, D.C., police about blackmail, though these accounts involved only demands for cash, not state secrets. One police lieutenant told of a State Department employee who met a man in Farragut Square—a downtown Washington park known as a place where gay men congregated. After accompanying the stranger home, he was robbed at gunpoint and forced to pose for compromising photographs. When the blackmailer tried to extort more money, the State Department employee approached the Metropolitan police, who set up a sting operation with marked bills and caught the blackmailer. But rather than see this failed attempt at blackmail as an example of how a homosexual could resist coercion, the committee interpreted it as further proof that homosexuals were particularly vulnerable. The police argued that their story demonstrated that blackmailers "only work on homosexuals for the reason that the homosexual will not make a report to the police."[17] Because the man had come forward to seek police assistance, they assumed he was innocent. Whether it was a failed attempt at blackmailing a homosexual or a false attempt at blackmailing a nonhomosexual, the example undermined the claim that homosexuals were uniquely vulnerable.

Stories of "normal men" being falsely accused of homosexuality and blackmailed permeated Cold War culture. Government officials, tabloid journals, and gay intellectuals alike agreed this was a constant threat. Hillenkoetter recounted the story of a Nazi who was drummed out of the party on false charges of homosexuality. The *Washington Times-Herald* reported that "a known pervert—or an innocent person who realizes a trumped-up charge might irreparably damage his reputation—would do 'anything' to keep from being exposed." In his novel *Washington, D.C.*, Gore Vidal described an attempt by D.C. police officers to blackmail a gay journalist—loosely based on Joseph Alsop—whom they arrested in a theater for lewd behavior. When a U.S. congressman intervened on the journalist's behalf, the police threatened to falsely arrest him as well. "There is nothing to stop us saying you was picked up, too, Mr. Big Shot," they asserted. The Hoey Committee's own files contain numerous letters from men claiming they were falsely arrested, and evidence that a Washington police officer admitted to lying about one such arrest. Stories of false arrests on sex charges were a staple of 1950s magazines. *Confidential* warned its readers of the widespread racket it called "the Homo Frame-Up," a scheme involving a team of men who worked men's restrooms, created compromising situations, and then threatened to arrest the victim. Initially limited to "known homosexuals," it had since spread to "men who, for the very reason that they were NOT perverts, would be doubly anxious to avoid any hint of homosexual practices." *Esquire* ran a similar story to warn its assumed heterosexual readers that "you can be framed on a perversion rap." In a rabidly homophobic atmosphere such as 1950s America, everyone was a potential victim of antigay extortion.[18]

As even CIA director Hillenkoetter acknowledged, part of the reason that charges of homosexuality posed such a potent weapon in the hands of blackmailers was a function of governmental policies and societal stigma. "Coercion and blackmail of homosexuals is particularly effective when homosexuality is universally condemned and actively attacked by the society in which the subject lives," he noted. Colonel Redl, for example, was vulnerable to blackmail only because of the Austrian emperor's alleged strict ban on homosexuals in his military. Flanagan, too, seemed to acknowledge that government policies played a role in creating the blackmail threat. If, as Hillenkoetter claimed, "enforcing the laws with vigor makes these people more susceptible to blackmail," Flanagan wondered what would happen if Congress enacted stronger penalties against homosexual conduct. Hillenkoetter predicted it would make homosexuals even more of a security risk and therefore called for an even more aggressive program of removal. "You have got to find those people in Government and get them out," he warned. The committee was caught in a conundrum—blackmail served as both a cause and effect of government antigay policies.[19]

But it was not just government policies that made homosexuals vulnerable to blackmail. Hillenkoetter, and many other witnesses, told the committee that homosexuals were particularly likely victims because they were intrinsically weak, cowardly, unstable, neurotic, and lacking in moral fiber. "The consistent symptoms of weakness and instability which accompany homosexuality always represent danger points of susceptibility from the standpoint of security," Hillenkoetter argued. They tended to be indiscreet in both mannerisms and speech, free to talk about themselves and their partners. Their combination of promiscuity and indiscretion made them, according to the director of the CIA, "the center of gossip, rumor, derision, and so forth." Because they congregated in known hangouts, they were easily identified and approached by foreign agents. They were overly emotional, and their relationships "involve emotions as strong and usually stronger than a normal love relationship between men and women." To Hillenkoetter, the intense bonds of loyalty within the homosexual community not only made them vulnerable to blackmail but also made them a dangerous presence in any government. "They belong to the lodge, the fraternity. One pervert brings other perverts into an agency, they move from position to position, and advance them usually in the interest of furthering the romance of the moment." This created, he warned, the concept of "a government within a government."[20]

No gay men or lesbians testified before the committee to refute these stereotypes. But they did hear second-hand, from a government psychiatrist, what one gay man thought of the security risk argument. In his mid-thirties, the man had left the military with a clean record and high recommendations to work for the State Department. During his preliminary screening he had volunteered to take a lie detector test, confessed to homosexual behavior, and was rejected. Barred from government service and lacking experience in private industry, he sought advice from his friend George Raines, who coincidentally had been called to testify before the Hoey Committee. Raines asked his friend what he would do if he were blackmailed. "He had an entire procedure. He knew how to approach the intelligence agency of our government," Raines told the committee. "He said . . . he would volunteer for counterespionage." And, according to the testimony of many security officials, his offer would have been accepted. Hillenkoetter admitted that the CIA sometimes gave protection to homosexuals who came forward in exchange for their cooperation. "While this agency will never employ a homosexual on its rolls," he insisted, "it might conceivably be necessary, and in the past has actually been valuable, to use known homosexuals as agents in the field." The FBI had a similar policy of using and protecting homosexual informers. So while claiming homosexuals threatened national security, government officials also used them to protect it.[21]

Medical Testimony

By the time the committee got around to hearing testimony from the medical community, only two senators other than the chairman bothered to attend. As the Truman administration predicted, they provided the most tolerant approach to the problem. Many of the physicians complicated the committee's task by suggesting that gender and sexuality were fluid. Leonard A. Scheele, the surgeon general of the United States, suggested, "Physiologically, in terms of chemical processes and living process within the body, we are not just a hundred percent male or a hundred percent female, no matter who we are." He stressed the similarity between homosexuals and heterosexuals, even on the all-important question of weakness and vulnerability to outside pressures. "I think we have something approaching the range of susceptibility to blackmail and that sort of thing even in homosexuals that we might have in other elements of the population or in the population at large." Senator Margaret Chase Smith was caught off guard by this statement. "You mean by that they are not any weaker in mind than any other group?" she inquired. Equating weakness of mind with intelligence, Scheele responded that homosexuality "runs through the whole range of IQ levels." Senator Smith was again surprised. "It is not necessarily the mentally deficient then?" she pressed. Scheele intimated that the real problem was the stigma against homosexuality. "They are not nearly as unusual people as sometimes, in this taboo which is built up in people's minds, they appear to be."[22]

George Raines, a captain in the U.S. Navy and former chief of psychiatry at the Bethesda Naval Hospital, cautioned the committee that even the testimony of his fellow physicians was based on a skewed sampling of homosexuals seeking medical treatment. "The homosexual in the drawing room," Raines noted, "is quite a different individual than the homosexual the psychiatrist sees in his office. Only sick people go to a doctor." He testified about his own social contacts with "thousands" of homosexuals rather than the "hundreds" he encountered in his psychiatric practice. As a teenager playing in a small jazz band in rural Mississippi, Raines had learned that homosexuals included "prominent businessmen, bankers, ministers, doctors, all sorts." He told the committee that "you can no more classify an individual by homosexual behavior than you can by religion or politics." To illustrate his point, he told a story related to him by one of his naval patients, a married man who would hitchhike home to his family on weekends and proposition the male drivers who offered him rides. The patient estimated that three out of five drivers accepted his sexual advances. Allowing for some measure of self-selection, Raines felt that "this is the sort of thing that leaves you a little bit uneasy about where any general attack on the homosexual in Government may lead." These experiences seemed to corroborate Kinsey's findings, which Raines recommended the committee read. Raines even suggested that the government's policy of excluding gay people, by creating an embittered and economically marginalized group, might pose more of a danger than allowing homosexuals to serve in the government.[23]

The complicated portrait drawn by the medical experts exasperated the senators, who were mainly interested in hearing practical advice on how to identify and possibly cure homosexuality. "There is no quick test like an X-ray that discloses these things?" Senator Smith asked one witness hopefully. The possibility presented by the physicians that there was no way to identify them and that they were legion angered and frightened Senator Mundt. "This committee is confronted with quite a problem," he summarized. Security experts, he claimed, had given "unanimous testimony" that homosexuals were "the worst conceivable security risk." Now, he said, you doctors tell us "there is no means of detecting them and [if] the percentage is as high as you indicate, we just are not going to have any security in this country." The committee's task was not about medical ethics or philosophy, he warned, but about "securing the freedoms of a country."[24]

Final Report

Since the homosexuals-in-government scandal broke at the beginning of 1950, newspapers, politicians, and commentators had repeated the claim like a mantra—homosexuals were vulnerable to blackmail and therefore threatened national security. After months of investigation, the committee had discovered little evidence to back up the claim. It had never found a single example of a homosexual American citizen who had been blackmailed into revealing state secrets. And it had uncovered considerable difference of opinion, even within the U.S. government, over whether foreign governments attempted to blackmail homosexuals. Still, the Hoey Committee's final report, issued in December 1950, ignored this ambiguity and stated emphatically that all of the intelligence agencies of the government that testified "are in complete agreement that sex perverts in Government constitute security risks." It asserted that Russian intelligence agents had been given orders to find weaknesses in the private lives of American government workers. And while acknowledging that other weaknesses might pose as much of a threat, it asserted that such comparisons were beyond the committee's mandate. Through the Hoey Committee's final report, the notion that homosexuals threatened national security received the imprimatur of the U.S. Congress and became accepted as official fact. The report was sent to American embassies and foreign intelligence agencies around the world, became part of federal security manuals, and would be quoted for years by the government of the United States and its allies as justification for excluding homosexuals.[25]

Subsequent government investigations would be highly critical of the Hoey Committee's conclusions. As early as 1957 a report of the U.S. Navy, an in-depth investigation of policies and practices dealing with homosexuals, credited the Hoey Committee with originating the notion that gays posed a security risk but faulted it for its lack of evidence. "No intelligence agency, as far as can be learned, adduced any factual data before that committee with which to support these opinions," the Crittenden Report concluded. It dismissed the testimony of the intelligence officers as only offering "isolated cases" that needed to be measured against security breaches by non-homosexuals. Countering the case of Redl, for example, the navy report offered the example of Mata Hari, the heterosexual female spy in World War II Japan that Senator Tydings had mentioned during his 1950 hearings. It found that the number of cases of homosexual blackmail was "negligible" and concluded, "the concept that homosexuals necessarily pose a security risk is unsupported by adequate factual data." But the Pentagon kept the Crittenden Report secret and repeatedly denied its existence until it was discovered by attorneys in 1976. The Navy's findings were bolstered decades later by the Defense Personnel Security Research and Education Center (PERSEREC), which noted in a 1991 study that of the 117 cases of American spies uncovered since World War II, only 6 were homosexual and that homosexuality was not a significant factor in any of those cases. Another study noted that a 1962 KGB training manual did not single out homosexuals as "persons to be cultivated for exploitation." In 1985, the very same senate committee—renamed the Senate Committee on Government Operations—reviewed American cases of espionage and found that none involved homosexual blackmail.[26]

The Hoey Committee report gave widespread currency to the myth that homosexuals threatened national security. It emboldened security officers to assume blackmail was involved whenever they discovered a homosexual engaged in nefarious contacts with foreigners. It provided a distorting lens through which government officials would interpret subsequent discoveries of homosexuals involved in criminal activity. In 1951, for example, John Wayne Clarke Williams, vice counsel in the Hong Kong embassy, was convicted in federal court for accepting bribes from Chinese nationals in exchange for travel visas. Like Redl, Williams was motivated by greed. He had told a close friend that he wanted to "make a killing in the next few months and leave the foreign service." But the case made international headlines because according to the chief investigator, "there were homosexual aspects to the case." In addition to accepting bribes—which netted him between $20,000 and $50,000—Williams was sexually involved with a Chinese man with whom he shared an apartment, and under interrogation he revealed the names of several other men "he had had relations with." Having uncovered between three to six other homosexuals in the Hong Kong office, a State Department official described the situation as a "flourishing pansy patch." Testifying before Congress, Carlisle Humelsine, Peurifoy's successor as head of State Department Security, gratuitously attributed the bribery scandal to Williams's homosexuality. "The fact that he was a homosexual they used against him, and they bribed him," Humelsine told the committee, his very syntax revealing a lack of causality. Humelsine took a proven case of a homosexual accepting bribes and imagined a blackmail connection. To the eyes of most government security officials at the time, if a homosexual was involved in illegal activity—particularly something related to espionage or foreign affairs—they assumed a causal relationship between the two. In Humelsine's telling, Williams's greed became part of a Communist conspiracy.[27]

In some ways, the validity of the claim that homosexuals posed a security risk was irrelevant. The Hoey Committee offered a second, broader justification for removing them from the federal bureaucracy that would apply to all government employees, whether or not they worked with sensitive materials. The moral weakness and cliquishness that made homosexuals vulnerable to blackmail, according to the final report, also made them "unsuitable" employees. As violators of sodomy laws and "normal accepted standards of social behavior," homosexuals engaged in acts of moral perversion that weakened their "moral fiber" and "emotional stability" to such an extent that they could not be trusted in positions of responsibility. Echoing the concerns of the earlier sex crime panic over child molestation, the report asserted that they exerted a "corrosive influence" on their co-workers and posed a particular danger to young men and women entering government service whom they might entice into acts of perversion. Echoing concerns about the "nest" of homosexuals discovered in the State Department, the report asserted that they tended to "gather other perverts" into the government, creating dangerous cliques. In what was perhaps the Hoey Committee report's most memorable assertion, it warned that "one homosexual can pollute a Government office."[28]

The committee saw no need for any new legislation. It simply recommended that government agencies end what it called their "head-in-the-sand" mentality when it came to homosexuality and begin aggressively enforcing the long-standing civil service ban on "immoral conduct." By demanding statistics and policy statements from each federal agency on its efforts to identify and eliminate homosexuals, the committee had already made it clear that Congress would be monitoring their efforts closely. Between April and November 1950, the pressure exerted by the Wherry and Hoey investigations had already led to the ouster of 382 homosexuals. Many were men who had been arrested on sex charges in the postwar years, but whose arrests went unnoticed until the public scandal over the Peurifoy revelation inaugurated a regular reporting system between local police, the FBI, and the Civil Service Commission. To strengthen that enforcement mechanism, the committee also called for stricter enforcement of sex crime legislation in the District of Columbia. Despite the passage of the Miller Sexual Psychopath law in 1947, most men arrested for homosexual activity in the District were only charged with disorderly conduct and allowed to post twenty-five dollars collateral. In effect, they were simply fined at the police precinct and released. To put an end to this "slipshod" policy, Flanagan met with George Barse, the chief judge of the D.C. municipal court, and persuaded him to issue an order that all persons charged with sex offenses in the District of Columbia appear in court and post a minimum of three hundred dollars collateral.[29]

With the Hoey Committee investigation, the Lavender Scare began to move beyond partisan rhetoric to enjoy bipartisan support and become part of standard, government-wide policy. The avid participation of the Democratic members of the committee suggests that the notion that homosexuals in government posed a threat to national security was becoming part of a national consensus. Margaret Chase Smith had been one of a handful of Republican senators to issue a "declaration of conscience" condemning McCarthy and his "four horsemen of calumny—Fear, Ignorance, Bigotry, and Smear." But she participated fully in the Hoey Committee hearings and approved its final conclusions.[30] The Hoey Committee's final report received general praise, even from those who had been critical of its original mandate. The *Washington Post* thought it showed "good sense, a decent restraint, and enlightened tolerance." Because of its secret hearings, it had subjected no witnesses to "shame or ridicule" as the newspaper had feared at the outset. And it had seemed to squelch the accusations of the Wherry investigation that the government was full of sex perverts, since only a few hundred had been uncovered in the interim. Its seemingly rational deliberative process had cooled the sensationalistic charges from earlier in the year. But the newspaper warned that the Hoey Committee's conclusion that homosexuals should be barred from all government jobs, no matter the position or the discretion they exercised, posed a danger: "It opens the way to idle, ignorant, and malicious charges which are difficult to disprove."[31]

6

"Let's Clean House"
The Eisenhower Security Program

On the morning of March 13, 1953, "Miss Blevins," a fifty-five-year-old, single secretary-clerk at the State Department, read in her morning paper that eight homosexuals had been dismissed from the department in the last week. The *Washington Post* called it "the first major 'clean-up'" under the newly inaugurated Eisenhower administration, which had campaigned under the slogan "Let's Clean House." Blevins had long harbored suspicions about her boss, Miss McCoy, the recording secretary for an interdepartmental trade agreements group. Blevins found McCoy to be difficult to work for and felt "nauseous" and "uncomfortable" in her presence. Blevins was particularly suspicious of McCoy's relationship with an older female co-worker with a "mannish voice." The two telephoned each other several times a day—upon arriving for work in the morning and again before going to lunch. Although Blevins found McCoy's general appearance to be feminine, she noted certain anomalies—"peculiar lips, not large but odd-shaped." Prompted by the newspaper story, Blevins typed an anonymous memorandum to the new head of State Department security. "I have thought about this for at least two years," she wrote. "I have not been able to get the prodding idea out of my head that (God forgive me if I am wrong) Miss . . . McCoy tends towards lesbian characteristics." Having read that the new administration was dismissing a moral deviate every three days, Blevins wanted to "contribute something to help get them out of the government." She added a postscript to underscore the seriousness of the charge, noting that McCoy worked on "very secret matters."

A civil servant since 1933, Blevins had only been working for Miss Mc-Coy for the last three years. Unsatisfied with her performance, McCoy had recently placed her on probation. A State Department investigation quickly revealed that Blevins's anonymous note was the result of this "personality situation." Despite their determination that Blevins was a disgruntled employee of "questionable reliability," security officials pressed her for more information about McCoy and her other co-workers. Pleased to be taken seriously, Blevins unburdened herself of all the suspicions she had accumulated. She told officials that she had "a funny feeling" about one man she described as having "a feminine complexion, a peculiar girlish walk." She cast suspicion on a female co-worker for having "a deep voice, an unusual face for a woman, not at all feminine. She has peculiar shaped lips and very little in the way of hips." Even more ominously, Blevins noted, "she is single, has spent a lot of time in China." Security officials collected four pages of such comments from Blevins, which were placed into these individuals' personnel files and prompted further investigations. Blevins named eighteen people as potential security risks. In some cases she noted common cultural codes for homosexuality, such as gender nonconformity or a tendency to associate only with members of the same sex. In other instances she pointed to unusual physical traits, particularly "odd-shaped lips" for suspected lesbians. But often her suspicions were entirely unfocused. "Something about Miss X pushes me away," was Blevins's case against one woman. Another woman gave her "an uncomfortable feeling." Though Blevins mentioned that some of her suspects had spent time in Communist countries, her concerns were not about the loyalty of her fellow government workers, but the possibility that they were homosexual security risks.[1]

Blevins's cooperation with security officials reflected how the Eisenhower administration institutionalized within the executive branch the security concerns that Republican politicians had been railing about since February 1950. Security officers rather than legislators would take the lead in overseeing the new security program, as the focus on security shifted from congressional hearing rooms to agency interrogation rooms. The Eisenhower administration expanded the government's security apparatus from a few federal agencies to cover the entire federal workforce while simultaneously broadening its focus from specific concerns about loyalty to vaguer notions of "national security." Blevins's anonymous note illustrated how the notion that homosexuals posed a threat to national security, once the rationale of a few politicians and security officials, was becoming the common assumption of average Americans who saw it as their duty to assist the government in weeding them out.

1952 Presidential Politics: "That Stevenson Rumor"

The presidential election of 1952 was the first national election since the rise of Joseph McCarthy and the beginnings of the Lavender Scare. The Republican Party campaign slogan "Let's Clean House" promised to rid the federal bureaucracy of a host of problems, including communism, corruption and sexual perversion. Although Republican presidential candidate Dwight Eisenhower and vice presidential candidate Richard Nixon most frequently attacked the Truman administration for graft, influence-peddling, and other financial improprieties, their general attack on the "mess in Washington" hinted at more salacious behavior. Eisenhower's references to "wickedness in government" and the Republican platform's charges of "immorality" among top policy makers implicitly raised the specter of homosexuality within the Truman administration. Republican rhetoric emphasized how Eisenhower and Nixon were "regular guys" and "God-fearing men" who were "for morality." Throughout the campaign, Mamie and Dwight Eisenhower made joint appearances to call attention to the divorced status of the opponent. Indeed, Democratic candidate Adlai Stevenson, portrayed as an intellectual "egghead" with a "fruity" voice, represented the kind of man many wanted to remove from Washington, not send there—wealthy, urbane, and a former State Department official rumored to be a homosexual.[2]

Charges of immorality tainted both the incumbent administration and the Democratic presidential candidate. Intent on helping Eisenhower and Nixon win election, FBI director J. Edgar Hoover circulated information that Stevenson had been arrested in New York on a homosexual offense. Though there was no documentation, Hoover had added Stevenson to his burgeoning "sex deviate" card file. Ellen Borden Stevenson, the candidate's ex-wife, was also known to tell dinner guests that her former husband was a homosexual. But as a divorced woman diagnosed with "persecutory paranoia" who also spread rumors that Stevenson was having affairs with numerous women, she had little credibility. Newspapers were reluctant to publicize such rumors, but Senator Joseph McCarthy was less reticent. When he threatened to attack the Stevenson campaign on national television as full of "pinks, punks, and pansies," the Democrats threatened to reveal a letter from General George C. Marshall discussing Eisenhower's postwar plans to divorce Mamie and marry his WAC driver and secretary Kay Summersby, whose relationship with Eisenhower had been the subject of rumors and gossip during World War II.[3]

Although never appearing explicitly in print, the rumors about Stevenson's alleged homosexuality were widespread. They had such nationwide currency that one tabloid magazine ran a story on "How That Stevenson Rumor Started," without ever having to reveal its contents. The rumor, according to *Confidential*, was "the nastiest, most widely circulated hearsay in the annals of rumor-mongering" and was so pervasive that "it burned the ears of a nation." It was also false, according to the tabloid, "a dastardly and deliberate lie" perpetrated by an angry ex-wife. The former Mrs. Stevenson had reportedly told a journalist "off the record" about "the deeper, sinister, never-revealed reason for her divorce," something which "reflected on the manhood of the father of her three sons." The tabloid further hinted at the contents of the rumor by linking it with "the recent State Department scandals." Attacks on Stevenson's manhood became even more explicit in the 1956 election—a rematch between Stevenson and Eisenhower. On election night, noted gossip columnist Walter Winchell, a friend and ally of J. Edgar Hoover, announced on his radio program, "A vote for Adlai Stevenson is a vote for Christine Jorgensen," a reference to the nation's first male-to-female transsexual.[4]

Issues of gender and sexuality permeated the Eisenhower-Stevenson contest. The notion that Stevenson was homosexual was so widespread that many gay men at the time considered him "the first gay candidate for president." Although acknowledging that the claim was "an irresistible fantasy," they had a sense that, with all the locker room attacks on Stevenson's masculinity, "it seemed to be what the election was really about." One group of gay men in New York even hosted a champagne dinner party on election night to celebrate what they quixotically hoped would be their hero's victory. "We had the good sense not to turn on the radio to listen to the election returns until after dinner," one of the hosts explained. Identifying with the purportedly contrasting sexualities of one of the two candidates was not limited to homosexuals. As the strong, silent war hero, "Ike" was supposed to appeal to the heterosexual female vote. Women who supported Stevenson were forced to defend not only the manly appeal of their candidate but their own femininity. As one supporter wrote in a letter to Stevenson, "the papers keep saying that all the women in the country voted for Ike. I just want you to know that I and all my girlfriends voted for *you*. We are singers and dancers in a Broadway show and we are gorgeous and

100% women."[5] More than a partisan endeavor, voting for Eisenhower or Stevenson was also, for many, a means of gender and sexual self-identification.

After the election, with Republicans in the White House for the first time in twenty years, they began in earnest to implement their mandate to "clean up the mess in Washington." Within three months of taking office, Eisenhower issued an executive order replacing Truman's loyalty system with an entirely new security system, with new criteria and procedures for ensuring that the employment of every federal employee was "clearly consistent with the interests of national security." Executive Order 10450 signaled a change in emphasis from issues of political loyalty to broader notions of general character and suitability. Even before specifying the need of government employees to exhibit "complete and unswerving loyalty," the order stated that employees must be "reliable," "trustworthy," and "of good conduct and character." An individual would be disqualified for employment for "any behavior which suggests the individual is not reliable or trustworthy." The order went on to delineate specific proscribed behaviors: "Any criminal, infamous, dishonest, immoral, or notoriously disgraceful conduct, habitual use of intoxicants to excess, drug addiction, or sexual perversion." Although the generic language of "criminal" and "immoral" conduct was drawn from preexisting civil service policies—and had already been used to bar homosexuals—the inclusion of the more specific reference to "sexual perversion" was unprecedented. By combining issues of loyalty and security, and granting final authority to agency heads, it effectively expanded the security authority originally given to the State Department and a few military agencies at the start of the Cold War to the entire federal government. Under the Eisenhower administration, national security would require not only political loyalty but also proper morality.[6]

During his first television appearance, Eisenhower had his Attorney General, Herbert Brownell Jr., explain the new program to the American people. Broadcasting from the Conference Room at the White House, Brownell explained how loyalty and security were very different types of risks. "Employees could be a security risk and still not be disloyal or have any traitorous thoughts, but it may be that their personal habits are such that they might be subject to blackmail by people who seek to destroy the safety of our country." In a subsequent presidential news conference, Eisenhower singled out the same example. "We are talking security risks: if a man has done certain things that, you know, make him, well, a security risk in delicate positions—and I don't care what they are—where he is subject to a bit of blackmail or weakness." Eisenhower's halting and embarrassed language suggested that what made one vulnerable to blackmail was unspeakable, but anyone who had followed the previous three years of publicity about homosexuals in the State Department understood. In the privacy of his presidential memoirs, Eisenhower was more explicit: "Many loyal Americans, by reason of instability, alcoholism, homosexuality, or previous tendencies to associate with Communist-front groups, are unintentionally security risks." He then seemed to single out homosexuality for special consideration, writing how, "in some instances, because of moral lapses, they become subjected to the threat of blackmail by enemy agents."[7]

The press was somewhat more explicit in its explanations. As Joseph Young, the *Washington Star* reporter on the civil service, explained, "Security risks have little or nothing to do with communism or Communist membership or sympathies." They included several types, such as "a person who drinks too much," "an incorrigible gossip," "homosexuals," "neurotics," as well as persons with large debts or those who "run around with a disreputable crowd." All might reveal secrets to the enemy, either inadvertently or under duress. "Security," one commentator noted, "covers a multitude of sins." The *Washington Post* even suggested that the new executive order, by looking at "trustworthiness, personal habits, and susceptibility to coercion," essentially instituted a "suitability test." It suggested that "unsuitability" would be a more appropriate label for dismissals under the new order. Some members of the administration, trying to distance the new program from the loyalty program, began referring to it as the "integrity-security" program. It was designed to ensure, they argued, that all federal employees were "persons of integrity" and of "high moral character."[8]

McLeod's "Miscellaneous M Unit"

The new administration's campaign to "clean up the mess in Washington" was most sharply focused on the State Department. "It was the mess in the State Department and the outraged indignation of the rank and file citizens all over the country that played a major part in the defeat of the Truman administration," observed Fulton Lewis Jr. on his Mutual Radio broadcast. Like other commentators, Lewis thought the department "smelled to high heavens" and viewed the election as a mandate for it to be "cleaned out from top to bottom and fumigated." As the new head of the State Department's Bureau of Security and Consular Affairs, R. W. Scott McLeod personified the Eisenhower administration's aggressive approach to security. The department's outspoken new enforcer of security regulations, McLeod quickly became a "bogeyman" to employees, "a shadow that lurk[ed] over every desk and over every conference table at Foggy Bottom," as one columnist described him. His tactics were said to have struck fear in the hearts of foreign service officers and brought eavesdropping and informing to new levels. Tales of steam opening of mail were rampant, and allegations of a Gestapo mentality pervaded discussions of McLeod's operation. With speaking tours and frequent press interviews, he raised the profile of the security situation in the department to new levels. Because of all the publicity, one reporter dubbed McLeod "one of the most powerful and controversial officials in the United States government." As did McCarthy's, his behavior even led to the coining of a new word: "McLeodism," which Stewart Alsop defined as "the State Department's dutiful imitation of McCarthyism."[9]

Like Francis Flanagan and many of the security officers he oversaw, McLeod began working for the government as an FBI special agent. Assigned to the FBI office in Concord, New Hampshire, he soon became the protégé of Senator Styles Bridges, who hired him in 1949 as his administrative assistant in Washington. He also became a confidant of Joseph McCarthy. "He used to call me up and ask my advice," McLeod bragged to one reporter. He prominently displayed a photograph of McCarthy on his desk with the inscription, "To a great American." Although journalists and historians have made much of his purported connections to McCarthy—Joseph and Stewart Alsop called him McCarthy's "personal Ambassador to the State Department"—his more direct contact with Senator Bridges may have been even more formative. It was Bridges, after all, who helped instigate the State Department purges in 1947 and coerced John Peurifoy into revealing that the department had fired ninety-one homosexuals. A principal backer of the antigay purges, he advocated a more quiet, behind-the-scenes approach than his more famous senatorial colleague. As head of State Department security, McLeod would borrow tactics from both of these mentors.[10]

To "clean up" the State Department, McLeod intensified the campaign against homosexuals. During his first appearance before a congressional committee, McLeod articulated the new priorities of the Bureau of Security and Consular Affairs. Second only to a general call for tighter investigative procedures and terminology, McLeod promised a crackdown on homosexuals. "The campaign toward eliminating all types of sex perverts from the rolls of the department," McLeod assured congressional leaders, "will be pressed with increased vigor. All forms of immorality will be rooted out and banished from the service." Within ten days of his appointment, sixteen employees had been terminated as "moral deviates" and five as "security risks." The swiftness of the firings suggested that the Truman administration had protected homosexuals and highlighted a new "get tough" policy aimed more at immorality than disloyalty. As his friend John Haines remembered, McLeod "was deeply suspicious of the things in the State Department that he didn't understand, like the intellectuals. He knew shortly from his own records and investigations . . . what he had suspected viscerally—there was a part of the foreign service that had been infiltrated by fairies." According to Haines, McLeod's approach to the issue was influenced by his experience in law enforcement. "Scotty had the essentially simple approach to a fairy that you will find in a cop who has never had the benefit of, let us say, courses in abnormal psychology at Yale. . . . Scotty had a very black and white kind of approach—and this wasn't white."[11]

In both public presentations and internal meetings, McLeod treated homosexuals as a special class of security risks. Meeting for the first time with department security officials, he outlined a fairly liberal policy concerning the evaluation of much employee behavior. He cautioned evaluators to weigh the behavior of employees in the distant past against their more recent conduct, implying that a brief association with a Communist-front organization during the Depression would not necessarily disqualify someone who otherwise had a clean record. But his tolerance did not extend to moral issues. With regard to homosexuality, the standard was to be absolute—one offense meant expulsion. Since one homosexual act made one susceptible to blackmail, McLeod reasoned, no amount of intervening good behavior could compensate. In a much-publicized speech to the American Legion convention in Topeka, Kansas, McLeod discussed the security risks to which he was giving top priority—Communist agents, fellow travelers, and homosexuals. He made no mention of alcoholics, blabbermouths, or any other risks. Nor did he couch his clean-up campaign in euphemisms. "I have attempted very frankly and honestly," McLeod told this sympathetic audience, "to face the issue of sexual perversion—the practice of sodomy—in the State Department." Calling it both a "security risk" and a "condition which calls for psychiatric treatment," he assured the audience that he was doing all in his power to remove such practices from the department. Since 1947 allegations concerning such behavior had led to the removal of more than five hundred department employees. To replace these security risks, McLeod was looking to recruit men "well-grounded in the moral principles which have made our Democratic republic a model form of government." The ideal candidates, according to McLeod, would be "red-blooded men of initiative." He made no mention of women.[12]

McLeod's right-wing connections and obsession with homosexuality became a thorn in President Eisenhower's side when he nominated career foreign service officer Charles Bohlen to be ambassador to Moscow. A right-wing Republican alliance composed of McCarthy, Bridges, McLeod, and others tried to prevent his nomination, claiming he was a security risk. They were suspicious of Bohlen's political leanings, since he had accompanied Roosevelt to the Yalta conference, where critics claimed Roosevelt sold out to Stalin by conceding to him a sphere of influence in Eastern Europe. But what almost scuttled his nomination was his close association with three State Department employees suspected of homosexuality, particularly Charles Thayer, a Soviet expert and former head of the Voice of America. Thayer was implicated in several homosexual acts and had admitted to one, though he had also fathered a child out of wedlock. Conceding that homosexuality was "a very hard thing to prove," J. Edgar Hoover asserted that Bohlen's association with homosexuals cast sufficient doubt, since "normally a person did not associate with individuals of that type." At the very least, according to Hoover, Bohlen had "used bad judgment in associating with homosexuals." That Thayer was Bohlen's brother-in-law and colleague when both were stationed in Moscow—situations that would have necessitated at least a modicum of association—did not seem to matter. Undersecretary Donald Lourie told Dulles privately that "those who study this type of thing feel [Bohlen] is one of them, and work on the criteria that once one, always one, and consequently a security risk." Publicly, McLeod said that he could not approve of Bohlen from a security perspective. Senator Robert Taft, after being allowed to read Bohlen's security file, rejected the "guilt by association" argument and reported to the Senate Foreign Relations Committee that although he had associated with known homosexuals, Bohlen was not, in his opinion, a homosexual. Bohlen was confirmed, but in exchange Thayer was ousted from the department. After Bohlen was named ambassador to Moscow, Secretary of State Dulles told him to travel to Moscow with his wife to dispel rumors about his association with homosexuals, adding, "Why do you think Mrs. Eisenhower traveled with the President during the election campaign?" Although considered the Eisenhower administration's first victory over McCarthy, it also underscored how the administration's own emphasis on rooting out immorality could be used against it.[13]

Within the McLeod security office, a special investigative branch known as the "Miscellaneous M Unit" handled homosexual cases. Although responsible for investigating any type of moral deviation, the unit had a caseload that was overwhelmingly focused on homosexuality. During one three-month period in 1954, all but one of the Miscellaneous M Unit's twenty-seven separations were for homosexuality. Indeed the office was so focused that it divided its work into only two categories—"homosexual cases" and "other morals cases." With two full-time agents, several part-time agents, and clerical help, the unit was considered to be understaffed by the head of the security office. In a request for additional personnel, he indicated the office had a backlog of 266 pending cases. In spite of the handicaps it had to endure, the unit was proud to report that it was responsible for ninety-nine separations during calendar year 1953—one every two to three days. It projected even higher levels for 1954, since it had already removed twenty-seven individuals in the first three months.[14]

The Miscellaneous M Unit used many techniques to detect homosexuals, but the most successful were personal interviews and polygraph tests. According to the State Department *Investigative Manual*, all male applicants were to be personally interviewed to help detect sex deviates. Investigators were to note "any unusual traits of speech, appearance and mannerisms." Such personal observations, the manual predicted, could provide a "tip-off" indicating "sex deviation," which might lead to other information. If information suggested an applicant or an employee was homosexual, the Miscellaneous M Unit would confront the individual and attempt to procure a confession, offering the "opportunity" of a polygraph examination to the recalcitrant. Since its first use of the polygraph in 1950, the State Department had used it almost exclusively in morals cases. Although the State Department denied that it confined use of the polygraph to such cases, internal records suggests that by 1955, of the seventy-four persons subjected to such an examination, all but two were suspected of immorality, which almost always meant homosexuality. The Miscellaneous M Unit staff was quite confident about the effectiveness of this method. As one member put it, "only a few, by the way, have ever 'beat' the polygraph machine, and there are questions about these."[15]

One of those who failed to "beat" the polygraph was C. L., an administrative liaison between the State Department and the CIA. During his standard security investigation, questions arose concerning both "moral issues" and "past associations with alleged Communists." Although security officers somehow resolved their concerns about the Communist allegations without any follow-up, they took the morality questions more seriously. In June 1954 they interrogated C. L. about his homosexual activity. He not only denied such activity but also refused to take a polygraph. But two months later, under pressure from the CIA, which wanted the situation resolved, C. L. "elected" to submit to a lie detector. When he was asked about recent homosexual acts with State Department employees, the polygraph recorded "pronounced positive reactions." When security officers pressed C. L. to name names, he agreed to resign. Whether C. L. was caught by the polygraph, or simply fell victim to the coercive nature of such a performance, is unclear. But in the hands of State Department security officers, the polygraph was an effective tool in forcing homosexuals to resign.[16]

To the Miscellaneous M Unit staff, there were only two possible results from a homosexual investigation—they cleared the person of charges or forced him to resign. Fred Traband, special agent in charge of sexual deviation investigations, told a conference of regional security supervisors in 1953 that 80 percent of homosexual interrogations ended in confessions. Failure to answer charges was considered virtually the same as an admission. In addition to a confession of guilt, interrogators sought detailed descriptions of homosexual acts and the names of participants. Using a classic "good cop/bad cop" technique, they threatened to reveal the employee's homosexuality if he didn't name names. After such interrogations, there were rarely any hearings. As security agent Szluk commented, "Hearings . . . what the hell for? That was a waste of time! No, I was the hatchet man. Szluk says the son of a bitch is a queer, out he goes!" Through 1956, the unit reported only one case of a person accused of homosexuality who refused to resign. That employee was terminated and appealed the case to the Civil Service Commission under the Veterans' Preference Act, but was denied reinstatement. Despite their near total independence, security officials in the unit acknowledged an increasing ambiguity in these cases. They complained that the work was presenting "more and more difficulties." The unit's small staff often had to rely on old background investigations that did not pay sufficient attention to moral issues. More important, they had to deal with "many cases that are far closer to the borderline than previously existed." This reflects an increasingly aggressive stance toward homosexuality—a no-tolerance policy—where every rumor and innuendo, no matter how unreliable, was sent to them for investigation. The frustration with being "closer to the borderline" suggests that, although their experience led them to see a continuum of human sexuality—cases could be closer or further away from some dividing line—they had only been given two categories to place everyone into, homosexual or heterosexual.[17]

By 1956 the difficulties and ambiguities in homosexual security cases became so great that the department attempted to set out a policy regarding the handling of "homosexually inclined persons." According to McLeod, a "considerable difference of opinion, if not confusion" had arisen regarding such cases, particularly concerning persons who had engaged in homosexual activities in the "remote past" but who had since exhibited a "clear pattern of normal activity." McLeod, predictably, took a hard-line approach, arguing that any homosexual activity, no matter when it occurred and despite evidence of "rehabilitation," still represented a "considerable risk." "It is frequently the case," McLeod argued, "that such early demonstrations are not completely arrested but come to a renaissance in later life." CIA director Hillenkoetter had expressed a similar understanding during the Hoey Committee hearings. Despite McLeod's position, the department's draft policy statement established a very precise cut-off point for homosexual activity it would consider relevant: an employee's eighteenth birthday. Activity before that date could be overlooked, but after one turned eighteen years old, any sort of same-sex eroticism—including kissing, embracing, and fondling—constituted grounds for exclusion. Neither genital contact nor orgasm was necessary. McLeod submitted this strict policy statement to Thomas Donegan, chairman of the president's Personnel Security Advisory Committee, an interdepartmental group that coordinated security issues throughout the federal government. McLeod hoped it would become "a standard for Government-wide application." Whether it was formally adopted or not, its consideration in such a forum ensured it would have an influence on security practices throughout the civil service.[18]

Under McLeod, the State Department security office became a *de facto* sex squad. In both the statistics they compiled and the language they used to record them, officials demonstrated an overwhelming focus on homosexuality. In a memorandum to McLeod conveying terminations during the first nine months of 1953, security officer Dennis Flinn reported that 192 persons had been removed for "Security (Exclusive of Homosexuality)" while 114 had been removed for "Security (Homosexuals)." Homosexuality had become such a dominant category that the generic term "security" had to be defined in relation to it. In January 1955 Flinn reported that, of the cases under investigation by the security office, almost all were for homosexuality or other moral indiscretions. His office was investigating 111 "derogatory cases," ninety of them "morals cases." Although the FBI was investigating another hundred of the department's cases, this suggests that uncovering immorality and homosexuality was not a peripheral but a central mission of the State Department security office. While McLeod and his men considered each security dismissal to be another "scalp" on their belts, as one political columnist noted, they considered the hunt for homosexuals a particularly rewarding sport. A month after taking office, in an internal memorandum concerning the elimination of homosexuals, one security officer boasted, "Our batting average [is] now one a day."[19]

Despite their coercive tactics, State Department investigators believed they were helping the men and women whose careers they were ending. In a lecture to administrative officers about the security program, John F. Ford, head of the department's office of security, boasted about the "assistance" his office had given to the homosexuals it encountered in its investigative work, even as it engineered their dismissals. He characterized his office's treatment of suspected homosexuals as "similar to interrogations made by psychiatrists." Ford even cited "letters of praise and gratitude" the security office had received from "confessed homosexuals" who had lost their jobs. He insisted that his investigative staff was justified in being "proud of the assistance they [had] afforded in straightening out the lives of these unfortunate people."[20]

The publicity surrounding the State Department's aggressive security stance toward homosexuality led many in the department to inform on their fellow employees, effectively widening the gaze of the security officers. Anonymous letters poured into the security office implicating individuals or giving general advice on where to search for homosexuals. One such letter suggested that "in your search for homosexuals in your department you look very carefully into the backgrounds of the following people," listing the names of half a dozen men and women at diplomatic posts in Europe and Asia. "How is it you have allowed yourself to be duped by certain of the older F[oreign] S[ervice] O[fficer]'s who have gotten married since 1950 when McCarthy began his reign of terror?" the informant wondered. "I think you will find a good number of deviates who are hiding behind marriage if you look closely into their backgrounds." After searching its own files, the office of security discovered that one of the men had also been named as a former sex partner in a Miscellaneous M Unit interrogation of an "admitted homosexual." He was ordered to return to Washington for an interrogation. In another case, the wife of a foreign service officer complained about her husband's male secretary. The desire to dismiss homosexuals was not limited to security officials but permeated the department. And as McLeod promised, "every allegation is now being investigated."[21]

Purging the United Nations

Not content with removing from its own ranks anyone who had ever engaged in a homosexual act, officials in the State Department pressured international organizations to carry out similar purges. The United Nations had long been a favorite target of conservatives and anti-Communist crusaders, who associated it with Roosevelt, Yalta, and threats to American sovereignty. Senator McCarran's Internal Security Subcommittee and a federal grand jury had already conducted investigations into the employment of Communists among the U.N.'s American delegation. Shortly before leaving office, President Truman had signed an executive order requiring

loyalty checks on American citizens working for international organizations, and the U.N. had agreed to remove employees who were found to be
"disloyal" to member nations. However, the new International Organizations Employees Loyalty Board (IOELB) that was set up to administer this
system had no authority to look into broader issues of character and "suitability." But the Eisenhower State Department, which relayed the results of
these investigations to the U.N. and forty-six other international organizations, took on the extralegal function of forwarding information regarding the "suitability" of employees, exerting considerable pressure to have
its recommendations followed. During the first year of the Eisenhower administration, the State Department furnished the U.N. with derogatory
"suitability" information on 238 employees, but the U.N. terminated only
41 of them. U.N. authorities did not consider such information "definitive"
and often found it to be "irrelevant." This failure to follow the State Department's security advice raised the hackles of officials, prompting them
to increase the pressure.[22]

State Department officials were particularly concerned that homosexuals fired from the State Department were finding refuge with international
organizations. They feared a homosexual scandal at the United Nations
would be blamed on them. As one official speculated, "in time Congress or
an aroused public will charge officials of this department with sweeping
homosexuals out of the back door of the State Department into the front
door of the U.N." Indeed, some members of Congress had raised this concern hypothetically soon after the Peurifoy revelation in February 1950.
While even McLeod had to acknowledge that "in large and important parts
of the world homosexuality apparently does not excite the same degree of
opprobrium as in the United States," he wanted the U.N. to understand the
"pitfalls" of employing homosexuals fired from the U.S. government. Desperate to avoid such a public relations scandal, officials argued that fired
homosexuals—unlike others fired as unsuitable—showed no remorse, resented their dismissals, and therefore should be considered untrustworthy.
"They are so far from being friendly and sympathetic to [this country's]
ideals and principles," he argued, "as to raise a reasonable doubt as to their
continued loyalty." Such persons could not be trusted to work coopera-
tively with the State Department.[23]

The State Department undertook an extensive lobbying campaign to ensure the ouster of homosexuals from all international organizations of
which the United States was a member. In their routine briefings to twenty-
six specialized international agencies, such as UNESCO, department officials included appeals for the need to purge homosexuals. They called
upon their security colleagues at the Treasury Department to deliver the

same message to the World Bank and the International Monetary Fund. McLeod made it clear to U.N. officials that a homosexual scandal in their organization could threaten U.S. financial support. "Notoriety accompanying some revelation of homosexual conduct among U.N. personnel," warned Scott McLeod, "scandalous to the American public, might very easily have echoes in Congress unfavorable to the U.N." Henry Cabot Lodge, U.S. Ambassador to the United Nations, conveyed this message directly to U.N. Secretary General Trygve Lie, noting that U.S. support would be "seriously undermined" if the U.N. retained homosexual American employees. The Secretary General agreed to the request, but insisted that the department provide definitive information, such as a criminal conviction record, documenting homosexual activities. The Secretary General had already dismissed nineteen of twenty-seven employees about whom the State Department had forwarded derogatory homosexual information. Unrelenting in its pursuit, the State Department wanted the remaining eight employees—all in clerical positions—removed as well, even though the charges against them were mostly "allegations and rumor." It promised to reopen investigations to find more definitive proof. Although the U.S. government had no authority to provide such suitability information to international organizations, it continued to do so until 1972.[24]

The Eisenhower administration also put pressure on its allies to exclude homosexuals from government positions. As early as 1951, officials in the British Foreign Office had informal contacts with State Department officials about their policies and procedures regarding "the homosexual problem." A few years later an interdepartmental committee looking into the control of military information found deficiencies in the British personnel security system, specifically its lack of attention to "personal associations and to defects in character and personal traits." Britain's unique relationship with the United States and a series of homosexual scandals among British government officials led the United States to put extreme pressure on the British to follow its lead in matters of security and pay closer attention to the issue of homosexuality in its personnel security program.[25] In 1953, a top-ranking member of Scotland Yard spent three weeks in Washington consulting with FBI officials on a plan to weed out homosexuals from the government. The British, Canadian and Australian security agencies all studied and copied, to varying degrees, the antigay policies and investigative procedures developed by the United States government. Whether or not they subscribed to the same beliefs about homosexuals, each feared that the disclosure that one of their secret agencies employed a homosexual would jeopardize their close relationship with American intelligence officials. When Canadian officials discovered a homosexual working in a highly secret agency monitoring radio signals from the Soviet Union in 1952, they immediately sought his resignation. As a Canadian intelligence expert explained, "The authorities feared more than anything that the Americans would find out." If countries like Canada did not conform to American standards of security, they risked being cut off from America's intelligence-gathering apparatus. Once the model for the rest of the federal government, the State Department's antigay policies and procedures had become the model for much of the NATO alliance.[26]

The Numbers Game

In his 1954 State of the Union Address, President Eisenhower announced the preliminary results of his administration's efforts to "clean house": 2,200 security risks had been removed from the federal workforce. Like the numbers bandied about by McCarthy and the State Department in 1950, the statistics quickly became embroiled in controversy. In what became known as the "numbers game," less precise officials claimed the administration had ousted that many "Reds" or "subversives" despite the fact that "security risk" included many sins. Thomas Dewey cited the figures as evidence that the government was "infested with spies and traitors." Vice President Richard Nixon claimed famously that "we are kicking the Communists and the fellow-travelers out not by the hundreds but by the thousands." Senator McCarthy asserted on a national radio and television broadcast that 90 percent of the security-risk dismissals were for "Communist connection and activities or perversion." Many used the figures as vindication of McCarthy's first charges against the government. Given the freewheeling manner in which Republicans used the figures, the press sought clarification. Reporters wanted to know what agencies the employees worked for, when they had been hired, whether they were male or female, and the specific grounds for their removal. One reporter queried White House Press Secretary James Hagerty, "Could you tell us a little more about the reasons for them—morals, loyalty, or what?" Another asked, "How many of 2,200 firings were on loyalty grounds? How many for sex deviationism [sic] or other immorality? How many for drunkenness, habitual loose talk, etc.?"[27]

Though he admitted that many security dismissals involved issues of blackmail and weakness rather than disloyalty, Eisenhower resisted pressure from the press to give more specific information. As politicians had long known, using the generic term "security risk" was a very useful way to invoke treason, espionage, and disloyalty while referring to less serious indiscretions. Giving a precise breakdown would reveal the wide range of behaviors covered under "security." Administration officials and congressional allies argued that there was no need for such a disclosure. "I, as a tax-payer, am not interested in whether a person was discharged for being dis-loyal or for being drunk, and I don't think the average person is," asserted Philip Young, chair of the Civil Service Commission. On a speaking tour through Wyoming, McLeod insisted that people "aren't interested whether loyalty risks are drunks, dope fiends, sex perverts or Communists." They just wanted them out of the government, he argued. "What difference does it make if a man is no good because he cannot keep his mouth shut on atomic secrets, or spills confidential information under the influence of in-toxicants, or does the same thing because he is a drug addict, pervert, or just a plain sap?" inquired Congressman George Bender (R–Ohio). "A risk is a risk is a risk," he summarized, ironically paraphrasing lesbian writer Gertrude Stein. Like many defenders of the administration's security pro-gram, Bender blurred the lines even further between loyalty and security. His examples presumed that alcoholics, blabbermouths, and other secu-rity risks were fired because they had *already* committed treasonous acts—not because of their *potential* to do so.[28]

The press continued to criticize the administration for lumping together serious cases of espionage with minor incidences of drunkenness. Murrey Marder, best known for his thorough and often critical coverage of Joseph McCarthy, pointed out that many of the dismissals would have occurred under routine civil service procedures in the previous administration with-out earning the label "security risk." Joseph and Stewart Alsop charged that the State Department scoured the files of employees who happened to be resigning for bits of derogatory information so that their resignations could be added to the total number of security ousters. "In short," the Al-sops reported, "there was not a single case of actual subversion in all the State Department's security firings—and it is doubtful if there was one such case throughout the Government." Journalists like Joseph and Stew-art Alsop criticized McLeod and the rest of the Eisenhower administration for what they called "palpably dishonest" tactics in the numbers game. Pointing out that in the vast majority of cases there was no question of dis-loyalty or pro-communism, Alsop charged that nineteen out of twenty cases were for "drinking, temperamental unsuitability, or the like."[29]

This increased scrutiny of the security program also revealed some of its excesses, further angering the public. It became apparent that even some heterosexuals were being charged with immorality under the system. In a Pulitzer Prize–winning, seven-part series on the security system for the *Washington Daily News*, Anthony Lewis disclosed that a female language specialist at the State Department had been discharged for "immorality" because she had conceived a child out of wedlock, even though she had subsequently married the child's father. Acknowledging that the practice of considering immorality a security violation had originated with the Truman administration, where it applied principally to homosexuals, he noted that application of this principle had broadened. As Lewis concluded, "The Eisenhower security program's strictures on immorality apply not only to sexual perversion, as has been well publicized, but to intimate heterosexual (normal) relations out of wedlock." In an article devoted to the homosexual as security risk, Lewis pointed out that the government's emphasis on morality actually contributed to a climate that allowed blackmail to flourish. "Critics of the morality-security concept," Lewis wrote, "say it may lead to a form of blackmail by the Government itself." Other newspapers came out with similar stories critical of the program. "The State Department is currently giving official 'sin' a broad, new interpretation," proclaimed the liberal *New York Post*. "It now goes beyond communism and homosexuality to suspected drunkenness, adolescent indiscretions, 'loose' talking and a free-wheeling category known as 'moral turpitude.'" It highlighted the case of a man who married a woman shortly before his divorce from his first wife was finalized and another married man who had been involved in a "minor homosexual affair" at the age of sixteen. The government was dismissing them both on morals grounds. Other press reports noted that one unmarried "government girl" in her twenties was given a lie-detector test and asked these questions: Have you had sexual relations with a man? Have you had sexual relations with a woman? When did you last have intercourse?[30]

Perhaps the most celebrated case of a federal employee being charged with heterosexual sexual immorality was that of Marcelle Henry. A French-born, naturalized American, Henry worked for the Voice of America. She had been investigated under the loyalty program for Communist sympathies and exonerated. But under the security program, State Department security officials called her in again. "Have you ever had sexual intercourse without being married?" they asked her during an hour-and-a-half interrogation. "When did you last buy contraceptives?" the security agents continued. "When did you last have sexual intercourse? With whom?" She was told that sexual relations outside of marriage were both illicit and illegal, and that the moral standards in this country were not those of France. In May 1953, Henry was "separated" from the service because she had "manifested a disregard for the generally accepted standards of conventional behavior and that this has resulted in . . . criticism of the Department." Having admitted to "having sexual relations with a number of men," Henry posed a threat not to security but rather to the reputation of the department. What was extraordinary about the Henry case was not the sexual nature of the questioning but the heterosexual nature of the relationships. "I am not accused of being a Lesbian," Henry noted, "I am accused of loving the other sex too much." By contrasting herself with the standard, well-accepted type of security risk—the homosexual—she sought to highlight the ridiculousness of the charges against her. Not only was she not a homosexual, she was claiming to be the opposite, someone whose attraction to the other sex was manifest. How, Henry wondered, could both homosexuality and heterosexuality be dangerous to the nation?[31]

The Eisenhower security program came under increasing criticism not only because it was affecting heterosexuals, but also because it was affecting millions of Americans, even those who did not work for the government. An independent study in 1958 estimated that one of every five employed adults in America had been given some form of loyalty or security screening. This included the five million present and former federal civilian employees, five million military personnel, and three million private-sector workers connected with defense contracts. It also included a half million who worked on Atomic Energy Commission projects and another half million seaport workers. Even citizens volunteering their expertise at one-day, government-sponsored conferences had to confront security officers. For example, public health experts and pharmaceutical executives who consulted with the Department of Health, Education, and Welfare on the Salk antipolio vaccine were fingerprinted, asked to sign a loyalty oath, and warned against "drunkenness, sexual perversion and associating with spies."[32]

Under mounting pressure, the administration agreed to release a limited breakdown of the security figures. Individual agencies, called before congressional committees, were already being forced to provide more precise statistics. In February, for example, Commerce Department officials revealed under questioning that of the 132 employees they had recently removed, only 23 were accused of disloyalty. Of the remaining 109 security cases, more than a third were removed for homosexuality.[33] The administration's breakdown, however, would be limited to four broad categories. It lumped all evidence of subversive or Communist entanglements into one category, rather than following the six separate loyalty breaches outlined in Executive Order 10450—from actual sabotage and treason, to membership in a Communist organization, to mere association with Communists. This had the effect of hiding the lack of any actual espionage uncovered through the security program and met with widespread criticism. The *Washington Post* called it "security by concealment." In the case of persons fired for security or suitability reasons, the Civil Service Commission (CSC) created three new categories—those convicted of felonies or misdemeanors, those guilty of sex perversion, and "all others." In this new schema, sexual perversion was the only security issue to receive its own unique category.[34]

By creating three new categories, the administration was also concealing the emphasis it had placed on homosexuality. It reported only 190 firings for sex perversion in the first year. But in individual reports for the same period, State, Commerce, and the CIA alone reported 180 dismissals for sex perversion. In these agencies, sex perversion cases accounted for between a quarter and a half of all security dismissals.[35] Although these departments were known to be particularly aggressive in their homosexual investigations, their statistics are of an entirely different order than those the administration claimed for the entire federal government, where homosexuals accounted for only 10 percent of the total. Though eventually the total number of dismissals in the "sex perversion" category would top 800, it always remained approximately 10 percent of the total. One explanation for this discrepancy can be found in the most conspicuous of the administration's new categories—"felonies and misdemeanors." Though never before part of the discussion about loyalty or security, it now accounted for 504 dismissals, the second largest category. Since many gay men had police records for disorderly conduct earned while cruising in known gay venues, the administration may have used this new category to conceal the number of homosexual firings. It undoubtedly wanted to avoid the error committed by John Peurifoy in 1950 of bragging too loudly about the number of homosexuals removed, for fear of creating another uproar over the character of the federal work force.[36]

Another explanation for the comparatively low figures for homosexual dismissals is that government security officials often used technical violations to obscure the substantive issue behind a firing. Applications for federal employment contained questions about past arrests and membership in subversive organizations that were designed less to solicit information than to provide a clear basis for firing those who lied about their pasts. If, for example, a gay male employee was found to have been arrested on a sex charge in a known gay cruising area but had failed to properly disclose it on his federal application form, he could be terminated for the criminal offense of falsifying a federal form. As Civil Service Commission general counsel H. Patrick Swygert acknowledged, "These questions are primarily used to impeach persons who falsely answered the questions in the negative or to dissuade persons from applying who believe their backgrounds might raise suspicions."[37]

Even the president was critical of the administration's one-size-fits-all security program. In cabinet meetings, Eisenhower exhibited considerable sympathy for those affected by the program, frequently suggesting the desirability of transferring "lesser security risks, as distinguished from disloyal individuals," to nonsensitive positions within the government. He envisioned the plight of "the man who has performed a great number of years of honorable service in the Government, who has no outside income," but who loses his job on security grounds not involving subversion. When CSC chairman Philip Young suggested that such transfers of terminated employees did occur, but only when they reapplied for government employment, Eisenhower suggested a more direct approach—that such persons be offered reassignment to less sensitive positions. He thought the General Services Administration ought to be able to find room for such individuals. "We ought to try to do something about it," Eisenhower insisted. But Secretary of Defense Charles Wilson disagreed and argued that all the individuals removed under the security program were "no good." Whether his sympathies with "lesser security risks" extended to homosexuals is impossible to determine, although he must have been aware that homosexuals were a prominent component of this category.[38]

Earlier in his career, Eisenhower had exhibited a similarly tolerant attitude toward homosexuality. One story from his service in the U.S. Army suggests he was less than zealous in enforcing its then relatively new exclusion of gay men and lesbians. The general once reportedly asked a WAC sergeant on his staff to provide a list of lesbians in the WAC battalion. When she suggested that firing lesbian members of the battalion would mean losing some of the most competent members of his staff, including herself, Eisenhower reportedly told her to forget the order. This tolerant attitude was also reflected in a project Eisenhower initiated while president of Columbia University. He wanted to study the military's experience with screening, rejecting, and training millions of applicants during World War II and use the findings to improve civilian personnel management decisions. To coordinate this five-year study of the "Conservation of Human Resources," Eisenhower appointed his friend and personal physician, Marine Corp Major General Howard Snyder. Snyder was extremely critical of the wholesale removal of all homosexuals from the military and suggested, "each case should be judged upon its merits." He found most homosexuals "used discretion" and caused few administrative problems. Because of the huge costs to manpower involved, he argued that the military should not be forced to reflect public prejudice. "As is true in the Negro problem," Snyder noted, "we may have to point the way." Eisenhower remained close to both Snyder and the project at Columbia, whose reports reflected this tolerant attitude.[39]

But rather than reform the program, Eisenhower's cabinet decided that the real problem was public relations. A consensus developed in the cabinet for a "campaign for public understanding" to explain the security program to the American people and repair its damaged reputation. As part of this campaign, Vice President Nixon suggested the placement of a favorable article in a widely read magazine such as the *Reader's Digest*. The result, written by Richard and Gladys Harkness, was a two-part article under the typically breezy title "How About Those Security Risks?" Reprinted in *U.S. News & World Report*, it sought to counter the criticism that the program was an unnecessary invasion into the private lives of government workers. It was a masterpiece of manipulation and innuendo, confusing rather than differentiating between loyalty and security. The Harknesses highlighted not a security risk case—someone who might reveal secrets because of some vulnerability—but someone who already had given secrets to a foreign government. Joseph S. Petersen Jr., a physicist with the National Security Agency, had been found guilty in federal district court for passing classified cryptographic information to a friend in the Netherlands. His motivation was unclear, although it seems to have been the continuation of a practice of collaboration with a scientific colleague begun during World War II. The Harknesses cast this case in sinister tones, suggesting that Petersen's espionage was tied to his "instability" and "aberrant habits," both code words for homosexual. The Harknesses implied that the "tall, gaunt, bespectacled code clerk" was queer, noting that he "lived quietly in a modest apartment in Arlington, Va.," while neglecting to mention his wife. The Harknesses claimed that the Eisenhower security program's focus on personal behavior had uncovered this important incident of espionage. In fact, it was the counterespionage technique of checking Petersen's international correspondence that led to his arrest. Most important, the Harknesses framed the story within a larger discussion of homosexuality and its connection with blackmail, thereby seeming to account for Petersen's treason. "The sordid combination of immorality or homosexuality and blackmail has been a tool of espionage through the ages," the Harknesses asserted by way of explanation. Although the article also discussed how heterosexuals could be security risks, it concluded without substantiation that "the Communists prey mainly on homosexuals." By insinuating that Petersen was a blackmailed homosexual spy caught by the Eisenhower security program, the Harknesses made the security program look not only reasonable but also necessary.[40]

Senatorial Suicide

In October 1953, Roy Blick's vice squad arrested yet another government employee in Lafayette Park on a morals charge. All such arrests in 1950s

Washington were potential fodder for partisan political intrigue, but in this case the stakes were even higher. Lester C. Hunt Jr. was the son of Senator Lester Hunt (D–Wyoming), who was up for reelection in 1954. The Republicans held control of the Senate by the narrowest of margins—only through the votes of Wayne Morse of Oregon, an independent, and the tie-breaking vote of Vice President Richard Nixon. Desperate for another Republican senator, Hunt's political opponents, led by Styles Bridges, then head of the Republican Campaign Committee, threatened to raise the issue in the 1954 campaign if he did not withdraw from the race. When Hunt refused, Bridges exerted pressure on Blick to prosecute his son, even though the initial charges had been dropped. The subsequent trial and publicity left Senator Hunt emotionally distraught and he began to seclude himself in his office. "He just didn't want to face the innuendo and rumors regarding his boy during the election campaign," columnist Drew Pearson wrote in his diary. On June 8 Senator Hunt announced that due to failing health he was withdrawing from the race. Ten days later, on a Saturday afternoon, he went to his senate office and shot himself with a .22 caliber shotgun. Styles Bridges, the man responsible for the Peurifoy revelation in February 1950, the political mentor of Scott McLeod, and a principal backer of the Lavender Scare, was also the man behind its most brazenly cynical act.[41]

Although press coverage of the resignation and suicide focused on Hunt's failing health, Washington insiders like Allen Drury, who covered the Senate for the *New York Times*, knew the story. It became the inspiration for Drury's 1959 best-selling novel *Advise and Consent*, about the suicide of a prominent U.S. senator when his political opponents threatened to reveal a past homosexual affair in the midst of a battle over a presidential nominee for secretary of state. Many considered it the best novel ever written about the workings of the U.S. government. Both John Kennedy and Richard Nixon were photographed reading it before the 1960 election. After remaining on the best-seller list for almost two years, *Advise and Consent* became the basis for the first Hollywood film to openly treat the subject of homosexuality. Both the novel and the episode it was based on highlighted the excesses of the hunt for homosexuals and how it was less about national security than about partisan politics.[42]

In Drury's telling, the blackmailed senator is Brigham Anderson, a handsome, clean-cut, entirely sympathetic character in a conventional, if not passionate, marriage. As the junior senator from Utah, he was a rising star with a photogenic family, an adoring electorate, and the respect of his colleagues. His one homosexual affair occurred during World War II. It was an event he had almost forgotten, having little to do with his current character, behavior, trustworthiness, or politics. "People go off the track sometimes, under pressures like the war. That's what happened to me," Anderson explained to his wife when the story came out. Anderson was one of the 37 percent of American men who, according to Kinsey, had had a homosexual experience. But Anderson was also the lone opponent to the president's nomination of Robert Leffingwell to be secretary of state, a man who had lied about his pro-Communist past. Leffingwell was a Machiavellian figure portrayed as ready to sell the country out to the Russians. "A liar and a cheat and a double-dealing son of a bitch," Anderson called him. Drury's explicit contrast of the two men's pasts offered a critique of a security system that weighed political disloyalty and deviant sexual behavior equally. What Anderson was concealing was "purely personal and harmed no one else," Drury wrote, while Leffingwell's Communist leanings "went to his public philosophies and could conceivably be of great harm to his country." As he has Anderson exclaim, "It isn't comparable. . . . How could foreign policy possibly be affected by what I—what I. . . ." The president conceded his claim but noted that the public would not agree. "But try to tell Main Street," he quipped. While acknowledging that Anderson's homosexual dalliance had no connection to national security, he knew that the connection was so ingrained in mainstream thought that there would be no defense against it. In Drury's novel the gay-baiters are the unprincipled menace to the country, using every available tool for partisan advantage. By portraying their victim as a courageous man whose homosexual experience was limited to one wartime encounter, Drury effectively spotlighted the excesses of Washington's obsession with homosexuality for millions of readers.[43]

By mid-decade there was mounting pressure from the public, the media, intellectuals, the courts and even administration officials for a review of the Eisenhower security program. The Fund for the Republic and the Rockefeller Foundation both launched independent studies of the program. *The Bulletin of Atomic Scientists* and *The Annals of the American Academy of Political and Social Science* devoted entire issues to critiques of the program. In *Cole v. Young*, the Supreme Court limited its scope, finding that the program could not be applied to every government position, only to those actually involving national security. Stating that "the public has lost a great deal of confidence in the security program," even Eisenhower administration officials felt that a public advisory commission should study the problem. The head of one executive agency wrote that Executive Order 10450 was "leading toward national insecurity rather than security." He argued that the public sympathized with those who had lost jobs, often failed to cooperate with investigators, and were increasingly unwilling to serve the government. The disrepute into which government work had fallen was, he warned, "undermining the source of American scientific leadership." In-creasingly, critiques focused on the system's mixing of loyalty and suitabil-ity as one of its major problems. As one administrative official admitted, "the criterion should be loyalty and not a person's conduct or morals."[44]

A number of prominent psychiatrists publicly criticized the way the Eisenhower security program targeted homosexuals. In 1955, a commit-tee of the Group for the Advancement of Psychiatry (GAP) warned of the dangers of trying to eliminate all persons who have engaged in homo-sexual behavior from federal employment. In a published report, the committee concluded that although the homosexual was an "emotionally immature individual" who could benefit from psychotherapy, the gov-ernment's exclusion of anyone who ever engaged in a homosexual act went too far. "Inflexible application of the rules now in effect in most Government agencies, including the Armed Services," the committee cautioned, "in many instances results in injustice." Persons who merely as-sociated with homosexuals might be caught up in "witch hunts," the psychiatrists warned. Citing how many homosexuals had "functioned with distinction, and without disruption of morale or efficiency" in both government and private settings, the psychiatrists argued against an across-the-board policy of exclusion and recommended that such cases should be evaluated on an individual basis.[45] At the 1955 meeting of the American Psychiatric Association, Dr. Karl M. Bowman, its former presi-dent, deplored the "wave of hysteria" in Washington regarding homosex-uality, where "the person even suspected of homosexuality is banned from government work." Warning that if the present program continued, gay men and lesbians might find it "impossible to earn a living," he called for a national commission to study sex offenses and consider the revision of sodomy laws.[46]

After the Democrats won control of Congress in the 1954 election, a number of congressional committees began to review the security pro-gram. Chief among them was the Senate Government Operations subcom-mittee chaired by Hubert H. Humphrey (D–Minnesota). Humphrey found that the standards of E.O. 10450, thrown together in the first months of the Eisenhower administration, were so vague as to leave almost total discre-tion to the individual agencies. This lack of uniformity in its administration led Humphrey to refer to the security program derisively as a "government of men and not of laws." He reserved special venom for the burgeoning profession of security officers, of which the Civil Service Commission alone employed some nine hundred. "As a group, they represent one of the most powerful and influential forces within the Government itself and within American life generally," Humphrey warned. "They hold in their hands the future economic well-being and personal happiness of millions of Americans." He argued that such delicate positions required the combined skills of a lawyer, a social worker, and a psychologist, but that most security officers were "alumni of investigative and intelligence organizations . . . trained to look for evil." Humphrey and his colleagues were astonished to hear from a security officer for Douglas Aircraft that when one of its employees was denied a security clearance by the federal government, he was immediately fired. "We feel that if a man is a security risk when he has access to classified materials," the Douglas official explained, "he is a security risk wherever he is in our plant." Humphrey protested that a homosexual might be considered a security risk by the government, but might still be a highly skilled employee. "Michelangelo might not be able to get a job under such terms," quipped Senator Humphrey.[47]

Martin and Mitchell: The M&M Boys

By the end of the 1950s, pressure seemed to be building to moderate the Lavender Scare. The Supreme Court had reined in the Eisenhower security program, congressional committees were highlighting its excesses, and a sense seemed to be building that it had gone too far. McCarthy had been censured by the Senate and subsequently drank himself to death. But in September 1960, the image of an alleged homosexual traitor on the nation's television screens breathed new life into the Lavender Scare. He was Bernon F. Mitchell, a National Security Agency (NSA) analyst who, with his friend William H. Martin, defected to the Soviet Union and became one of the most renowned defectors in American history. As they explained to the cameras from Moscow's House of Journalists, Martin and Mitchell left out of disgust with what they saw as dangerous and unethical intelligence-gathering practices of the United States. They were particularly worried that the American U-2 spy plane missions over the Soviet Union might needlessly lead to war. But the press attention and congressional investigations quickly focused on Mitchell's homosexual past. Under polygraph interviews for his security clearance, Mitchell had refused to answer questions about sexual perversion and blackmail, which authorities interpreted as evidence of "homosexual tendencies." During a second round of interviews he admitted to sexual experimentation with dogs and chickens as an adolescent. FBI director J. Edgar Hoover claimed that a dismissed federal employee "had been involved in homosexual activities with Mitchell." Although his friend Martin seems to have had a perfectly heterosexual record, this crumb of sexual perversion on the part of Mitchell was all the authorities needed to attribute the entire defection to homosexuality. That they were two single men only added fuel to the fire. As in many previous cases, starting with that of Colonel Redl, officials and the public would use the flimsiest of evidence to draw causal connections between homosexuality and espionage.[48]

Newspaper coverage of the Martin and Mitchell defection regurgitated much of the rhetoric surrounding the Peurifoy and Blick revelations of 1950. The *Los Angeles Times* reported that one Congressman was investigating reports of a "government ring of homosexuals which work [*sic*] for promotions of 'the clique' and recruit other sex deviates for federal jobs." The conservative newsletter *Human Events* repeated a story from 1952 on the international homosexual conspiracy. The Hearst newspaper chain, particularly blatant in its sensationalism, referred to "the two defecting blackmailed homosexual specialists in NSA" as a "love team." Denying nearly a decade of an aggressively enforced government policy of excluding homosexuals, they claimed there was an "amazing increase in the numbers of homosexuals in government." Journalists and politicians began calling for a new campaign to rid the government of homosexuals. One conservative columnist asked, "Is it not time to face the question of homosexuals frankly and courageously?"—as if the past ten years of congressional hearings, press coverage, security policies, and thousands of dismissals had never happened. If not expressing ignorance of the federal government's policy of exclusion, commentators saw the Martin and Mitchell incident as evidence of its failure. "Obviously there is no all-out and effective campaign against homosexuals in the federal service," one journalist concluded.[49]

In a National Security Council (NSC) meeting that October, top administration officials discussed how to step up the security program to respond to the Martin and Mitchell defection. They focused solely on how homosexuals threatened national security, ignoring the concerns raised by the NSA analysts about American spy missions. "The Soviets are exploiting sex situations" and "seem to have a list of homosexuals," argued Attorney General William Rogers. He saw a need to "sound the alert throughout the Government to be stricter in these matters." He feared that Martin and Mitchell might not have acted alone and that "there [was] an organized group of these people." Along with Secretary of State John Foster Dulles and FBI director J. Edgar Hoover, Rogers thought the polygraph was particularly effective in uncovering such sex deviates. Eisenhower felt that the available lists of homosexuals compiled by the various government agencies should be coordinated by a central authority—a role Roy Blick, Francis Flanagan, and others had tried to assume in 1950. Any doubt in such cases, Eisenhower asserted, "should be resolved in favor of the government."[50]

Because of the way the defection of the two NSA analysts was interpreted, homosexuality would continue to be linked in the public mind with threats to national security and remain a priority of government security officials, perhaps an even higher one. After the defection, NSA reviewed the records of all employees and fired twenty-six for suspected homosexuality. As one government employee from the 1960s remembered about her periodic security briefings, "Whenever security people talked about homosexuals as this major risk to security, they always said, 'remember the M & M boys,' and everybody knew who they meant."[51]

★

To those who viewed McCarthy's accusations against innocent men and women as wild and dangerous, the Eisenhower security program appeared more methodical, discreet, and just. Eisenhower himself contrasted the tactics of his own security program with those of McCarthy. "Where, without proof of guilt, or because of some accidental or early-in-life association with suspected persons, a man or woman had lost a job or the confidence and trust of superiors and associates," Eisenhower noted, "the cost was often tragic, both emotionally and occupationally."[52] Yet exactly the same critique could be launched at the Eisenhower security program, which explicitly set out not to prove guilt or disloyalty but to prevent potential disloyalty. Security risks were by definition innocent of any wrongdoing, yet were subject to the humiliating and often economically wrenching fate of losing their employment, sometimes their very employability. During the 1952 presidential election, Adlai Stevenson chastised the Republicans for "slandering innocent people" in their zeal to weed out Communists from the government and called instead for "quiet professional work" by the FBI.[53] The distinction, however, was a false one. It was the job of FBI agents and departmental security officers to identify, interrogate, and seek the removal of innocent civil servants and government contractors who might potentially commit a crime. While what happened in thousands of civil service interrogation rooms did not receive the publicity of McCarthy's pronouncements from a senate committee room, the harm to loyal American citizens was just as great. The work of government security officers and the charges of informers like Blevins may not have provoked the kind of publicity that Senator McCarthy did, but it was their quiet work as part of the Eisenhower security program that represented the apogee of the Lavender Scare as it became institutionalized within the national security state.

7

Interrogations and Disappearances
Gay and Lesbian Subculture in 1950s Washington

Madeleine Tress remembers that she was wearing a pale blue suit and high heels when she came to work at the Department of Commerce building in Washington that day at the end of April 1958. It was already hot in Washington, and there was no air conditioning in the room where two civil service investigators had brought the twenty-four-year-old woman for an interrogation. As the meeting began, the two male investigators noted Tress's "feminine apparel" but also recorded what they regarded as a telltale defect—two buttons were missing from the front of her dress. "Miss Tress," one investigator began, "your voluntary appearance here today has been requested in order to afford you an opportunity to answer questions concerning information which has been received by the U.S. Civil Service Commission." Tress had been working for the Commerce Department as a business economist for only a few months, and her employment, like that of all civil servants under the Eisenhower administration, was conditional on passing a security investigation. The investigator asked Tress if she objected to taking an oath before they began to take her statement. Realizing the seriousness of the situation, Tress asked if she could consult an attorney and was told that she could, but that the attorney could not be present in the room during the "interview." Tress took the oath and began to answer mundane questions concerning her name, address, and date of birth. "Miss Tress," the investigator intoned, finally getting to the heart of the matter, "the Commission has information that you are an admitted homosexual. What comment do you wish to make regarding this matter?"[1]

Tress froze. Which would be worse, she wondered, admitting being gay or lying? Tress said she had no comment, and adamantly refused to discuss the matter. The investigators had more subtle questions for her. "Were you ever at the Redskins Lounge?" one of them demanded to know. Figuring there was nothing illegal involved, she admitted she had been to the lesbian bar. Asserting that she "enjoyed the orchestra there," Tress denied that she went there "for the purpose of making homosexual contacts," as the officials suggested. "Do you know Kate so-and-so?" the investigator continued, dropping the name of a lesbian acquaintance of hers. He named a host of her gay friends, demanding to know if she associated with any of them. Again, thinking that this was not illegal, Tress admitted knowing what the investigators termed "known homosexuals" but insisted she was attracted only by their "intellectual appeal." "How do you like having sex with women?" one of them sneered. "You've never had it good until you've had it from a man," he taunted. Under intense questioning, Tress eventually admitted to some homosexual activity in her youth, but claimed she had "broken away" from that since coming to Washington. At the end of the interrogation she refused to sign a statement prepared by the investigators but knew that she had only one option—resignation. The interrogation was the most demeaning experience of her life. With World War II a fresh memory, Tress thought this was what it must have been like in Nazi Germany. The next day she submitted her resignation.

Tress's feelings of defeat and powerlessness were tempered with anger. As she walked back to her office, she saw Bob, the "mealy mouthed" man who worked across from her and answered her phone when she was away. Suspecting that Bob had informed on her, Tress went over and pounded on his desk. "Did you speak to the FBI about me," she demanded, towering over him. When he admitted that he had, she became furious and began crying. "Did you give them names, you fucking son-of-a-bitch?" Tress had to be taken away from Bob's desk by her co-workers. Bob was only one of dozens of acquaintances, co-workers, and neighbors who, during a routine investigation by the FBI, raised questions about Tress's mode of dress, associations, and character. He had told the FBI she was "unstable" in dress and thinking, "bohemian" in lifestyle, and received calls from many single women. Although Tress suspected Bob was informing to differentiate himself from his brother, a union organizer accused of being a Communist, his comments differed little from a host of others suggesting she was "mannish," "a tom boy," or had "personality problems." In perhaps the most damaging comments, a Georgetown professor charged that "she is homosexual admittedly and known." But it was Bob upon whom she and her friends vented their wrath by organizing an around-the-clock vendetta. "We would call him at two in the morning, and say, 'You son of a bitch,' and hang up." Because of that day, Tress recalled, "My whole fucking life had changed."

Madeleine Tress's experience was typical of what happened to thousands of men and women who lived and worked in Washington, D.C., in the 1950s. Even for those who never experienced such an inquisition, the threat of it hung over their lives like a sword of Damocles. It altered their work routines, their socializing, and the way they made love. To some people the Lavender Scare was a tactic in a political struggle to turn back the New Deal. To others it was a necessary measure to protect national security and counter what they saw as a nation in moral decline. But to gay and lesbian civil servants, it represented a real threat to their economic, social, and psychological well-being. Though it affected millions of individuals across the country, both gay and straight, federal employees and private-sector employees alike, the effects of the Lavender Scare were most acute in the gay and lesbian community of Washington, D.C. For nearly twenty-five years it was part of their daily experience. Theirs was a community under siege.

"I Can't Describe That Kind of Fear"

With the Metropolitan Police, the U.S. Park Police, the FBI, and the CSC all engaged in a hunt for homosexuals, Washington's gay community was permeated with fear. Government workers felt particularly vulnerable. They wondered every time the phone rang if this was the call that would lead to accusations of homosexual behavior and a grueling interrogation about their sex life. Friends began to mysteriously change jobs or disappear entirely. As one gay man who worked as a civilian for the army remembered, "You would go to work and you would ask, 'Where is lieutenant so-and-so?' They wouldn't answer. They had discovered that he was gay, and he was separated. His desk was cleaned out. You never saw the man again." Having seen it happen to others, they knew it could happen to them. Every morning as she reported for work, Joan Cassidy remembered, "I wondered whether there was going to be somebody standing there with a piece of paper saying 'Joan Cassidy, come with us please.'" Since mere suspicion about one's sexuality might lead to an investigation, gay and lesbian federal workers acted with discretion. Many self-censored their communications. "All they had to do was have somebody say that they doubted your orientation," explained David Bowling, who worked in Washington. Fearing that gay bars and even private parties were being watched, people would park blocks away to avoid the chance of having their license plate numbers recorded. Men who lived together as a couple would sleep in separate beds.[2]

Madeleine Tress remembered the fear that permeated her white, middle-class, gay social network in 1950s Washington. She had arrived in the fall of 1950 to attend college. Working as a mail clerk at the National Science Foundation to support herself, she met an eclectic mix of people in her night classes—young people like herself, veterans, and seasoned government employees. Among her largely male classmates were many gay men with whom she began socializing and going to parties. "They were raiding bars then," Tress noted, so the middle-class homosexuals with whom she socialized held private parties, which, "for protection," were largely integrated with both gay men and lesbians. "The guys were very handsome, wore smart clothes," Tress observed. "It was not a jeans set." She wore "sexy" feminine clothes, which, she thought, offered some protection from any immediate association with lesbianism. "Underneath it all there was a subdued hysteria. You lived not knowing what would happen next," Tress observed. "You would be socializing with somebody, and then they disappeared, they had gotten kicked out and left town." Even among your gay friends, you never knew who might be pressured to inform on you. "I can't describe that kind of fear," Tress confessed. In her case the fear was not misplaced. In the summer of 1958, after losing her position with the Department of Commerce, she, like many of the men and women she socialized with, disappeared from the Washington scene and relocated to San Francisco.[3]

The close networks established by gay men and lesbians would now become their undoing, since merely socializing with known homosexuals was often sufficient cause for dismissal. Guilt by association, a favorite tactic used to malign suspected Communists and fellow travelers, was also a standard tool in the antigay purges. Tress, for example, was asked repeatedly during her interrogation if she knew various lesbians, as if the mere acquaintance with a known lesbian established her guilt. J. R. lived in Paris after the war and applied for a low-level job with the Marshall Plan with the aid of a Texas congressman. Summoned to appear before government security agents, he was informed that because he had "associated with known homosexuals" in the London theater during the war, he could not be cleared for government work. "He never accused me of being one," J. R. said of the security officer. A past association with known homosexuals was sufficient to preclude him from the job. When State Department security officers in Paris interrogated B. F., their main charge against him was that he was "living with a notorious homosexual." He had met an Italian jeweler during the war and began sharing his flat after being assigned to the Paris embassy. The officials had also learned from his maid that the two roommates held all-male parties—the maid thought she was doing them a favor by insisting that no women were involved. B. F. confessed to homosexual activity and resigned his position as vice counsel in 1953. The way in which acquaintance and friendship networks were being used against them fostered a rumor in the gay community that the government had constructed a master list of homosexuals. Many lived in fear that their names were on it. After moving to a new apartment in Washington, John Edward Collins discovered that his roommate had been discharged from the military for homosexuality. When FBI agents came to the apartment to ask questions about another friend who worked for the government, they recorded Collins's name and that of his current roommate, as well as his previous address, where his former boyfriend still resided. Both he and his former boyfriend were then linked to a known homosexual. "I knew for a certainty that from that day on, Jay's name and mine would definitely be on that famed list. The chain reaction had caught up with me," Collins feared. He kept asking himself, "When will my turn come?"[4]

With government officials pressuring people to "name names," the problem of informing only intensified the fear. "Everybody was suspicious because everybody was squealing on everybody else. You were afraid to make friends with anybody," remembered Raymond Mailloux, who moved to Washington in 1949. As Paul Clark, a long-time State Department security officer commented, "The sources of our information on these people generally came from a co-participant. . . . We were fortunate in that when we interviewed some of these people—which we were required to do before they left the department—they furnished us with a long list of names of others who were similarly involved." Although security officials attributed this behavior to a penchant among homosexuals toward garrulousness, threats to reveal an employee's homosexuality to his family and friends if no names were offered was no doubt a prime motivation. When Edward Kellar was interrogated by State Department security officials, he realized that a friend had apparently implicated him in a similar interrogation. "He was trying to defend himself by implicating others, which makes him sound like a real shit," Kellar noted. But the brutality of his own interrogation caused him to feel more sympathy than anger. "It was the good cop/bad cop thing, the kind of thing none of us is prepared to go through. . . . These guys can squeeze you until you end up saying things you wish you hadn't. So I don't hold it against him." As Madeleine Tress summarized the problem, "You didn't know who your friends were."[5]

For those with government jobs to protect, concealing their homosexuality became a prime occupation, a matter of survival. During much of his almost thirty years in government service, Phil Hannema remembers avoiding other gay people, especially if they were "obvious." "I played the game," he noted of his attempt to conceal his homosexuality to protect his job. As one gay man noted, "It has been my observation and experience that the responsible homosexual executive is apt to lean over backward, perhaps to his own discredit, to avoid hiring anyone whom he knows to be or suspects of being homosexual." Someone with a government job did not want to have to worry about being associated with "others over whose conduct and discretion he [had] no control," he noted. Nat Fowler recalls dating a man who worked for the State Department who would not accompany him to Fire Island. "He wouldn't dare be caught here. Joe McCarthy somehow would find out." Such protective strategies stood in marked contrast to the prevailing notion of politicians and government security officials, who assumed that the homosexual sought to surround himself with "his own kind" both in his social and business life.[6]

Government employees who wanted to protect their jobs distanced themselves from gays and lesbians who worked in less sensitive jobs and had less reason to hide. Joan Cassidy held a managerial post as a civilian with Naval Intelligence. She had such high-level security clearances that she was restricted from going "behind the Iron Curtain" for ten years after her retirement. She did not frequent lesbian bars. "It was very dangerous," she recounted. "We were told that you never knew if there was a plant there. The gossip in the community was—you go there, you could get picked up by someone whose job it is to report you. . . . Not only that, there were rumors that there were actually people assigned to take photographs of everybody going in and out." So she and her friends would have private parties. As she explained, "The rule always was with the women I lived with, we never invited anyone who didn't have as much to lose as we did. So there was no way someone who wasn't in a protected job would get into this house—a job they would have lost immediately. So school teachers, military officers, etc. [came]." When asked about the possibility of socializing with hairdressers, Cassidy was unequivocal. "No. Sorry. You can be as gay as you want to be and you're not going to get fired. I couldn't afford to associate with somebody like that." As Donald Webster Cory wrote in the first book-length, insider account of the gay subculture, "If a homosexual must wear the mask, he cannot associate with those who have discarded it." The purges facilitated the formation not of a singular community but several insular ones divided by class interests and the need to protect one's job.[7]

But within such insular groups, the purges created a sense of solidarity, particularly between lesbians and gay men, who came to rely on one another in social settings requiring a display of heterosexuality. As L. D. said, "Of course there was one feeling in the 50s and 60s when all this was going on, being under surveillance by the city vice squad, constantly, and all the government agencies . . . there was a wonderful feeling of comradeship." Within her very respectable, middle-class, professional group, Joan too found a high degree of solidarity and community. "We formed this chain," Cassidy remarked about the way gay men and lesbians would serve as discreet character references for one another on security clearance checks. They would also socialize together as a way of passing as straight. "We found gay guys and we paired up because when you're in your twenties and thirties you have to be dating," Cassidy explained. "You have to show up at social gatherings from your office with a guy if you are carrying security clearances." Even when socializing privately, Cassidy's circle included a careful mixture of gay male and lesbian couples. Cassidy remembers such a dinner party at the home of a lesbian couple. All the same-sex couples were sitting together around the table when the mother of one of the hostesses rang the doorbell. "By the time her mother walked in the door," Cassidy recalled, "we were boy/girl, boy/girl, with the guys' arms draped over the back of the women's chairs and the women leaning toward them." They had made "the switch" instinctively. "We hadn't said a word, we just did this automatically."[8]

"They Didn't Have Anything on Me"

With all the publicity surrounding increased enforcement in Lafayette Park, most gay men in Washington abandoned it as a cruising site. "Anybody with a brain in their head never went anywhere near any of those parks," commented L. D., a gay Washingtonian. "Everyone who did was arrested, and the word spread." Although he worked for a time in a building facing Lafayette Park, he would go out of his way to avoid traversing the park. "I wouldn't go near it at night," he insisted emphatically. U.S. Park Police statistics show a significant decline in arrests by 1950, suggestive of a decline in actual activity. While the Pervert Elimination Campaign picked up 109 men in October 1947, a year later it processed only 25. By the fall of 1950—after the Hoey Committee convinced judges to require alleged sex offenders to appear in court—the figures dipped into the single digits. "Pervert activity around the public comfort stations has dwindled away to a minimum," reported the U.S. Park Police sergeant in November. "Local perverts seemed to have disappeared from their known gathering places, such as Lafayette and the Monument Grounds," he concluded after questioning those few still using the parks. "Arrests show only newcomers and an occasional service man." Word had quickly spread within the gay community to stay away from Lafayette Park. Washington newspapers reported that those arrested since the crackdown included a touring actor, a federal job seeker, and an English professor from Louisiana. As a further deterrent, gangs of male teenagers came to Lafayette Park for the express purpose of "knocking off a queer." Some wanted to help police enforce the law, while others sought to profit financially by "rolling" gay men. When Jack Frey first came to Washington in 1952, he learned from reading *Washington Confidential* that Lafayette Park was the place to find gay men. But on his first foray there, Frey was picked up by a man who robbed him of all his money at knifepoint. He soon found other, more hospitable cruising venues, such as Connecticut Avenue and DuPont Circle.[9]

While men who frequented gay bars and cruising areas were most vulnerable, those who led more discreet lives were still at risk. Given the fear and watchfulness that pervaded 1950s Washington, inviting someone of the same sex back to one's own apartment could result in an arrest. In February 1952, residents of 21st Street NW in the Foggy Bottom neighborhood adjacent to the State Department noticed that soldiers frequently entered the apartment of forty-three-year-old Thomas Heinze, a salesman for a manufacturing firm. Around the same time residents of Wisconsin Avenue in upper Georgetown noticed similar behavior at the apartment of forty-year-old James Dykes, a civilian employee of the Army quartermaster general's landscape architect office. What caught the attention of the neighbors was not only the frequency of the visits, and the military uniforms of visitors, but their relative youth compared with that of the men they were visiting. Residents complained to the local police, and Roy Blick's vice squad launched an eighteen-month investigation. In July 1953 both Heinze and Dykes were arrested for sodomy, along with a nineteen-year-old private and a seventeen-year-old soldier of unidentified rank. Fraternizing with members of the same sex, even in one's own home, if there was no clear, nonsexual explanation for it, suggested deviance serious enough to raise the eyebrows of neighbors and warrant investigation by law enforcement.[10]

Even gay men and lesbians in stable relationships who exercised extreme discretion were not immune from the preying eye of the security apparatus. Charles Gruenberger and Jack Kersey had been together for six years in 1953 when security officials visited their home. They wanted to know who decorated the apartment and what Kersey's feelings were for his "roommate," who worked as a dentist at the Pentagon. Knowing he might lose his position, Gruenberger decided to leave government service a year later. A State Department official in a relationship with the same man for eight years was not so lucky. As he told a gay publication in 1967, "I knew that the government had this policy against homosexuals, but, really, I didn't see myself being affected by it." His parents had accepted his lover into the family, he never discussed the issue with friends, and didn't travel in gay circles. "I do not drink, nor have I had a large number of sexual partners," he explained, "I certainly do not frequent public places such as men's rooms for sexual contacts." Despite his conservative behavior, the State Department drummed him out in 1965. Marriage to a member of the opposite sex was often not protection either. Edward Kellar had been married for many years and hadn't even had a homosexual experience when he was interrogated about his sexuality. Security officials questioned him intensely about problems in his marriage and his friendship with several other men who had become part of a gay subculture. No amount of middle-class respectability could protect them.[11]

Lesbians have traditionally had less access to public space then men and therefore were less vulnerable to arrest and prosecution for their homosexuality. As one psychiatrist wrote about the disparity in the policing of gay men and lesbians, "I learned from authoritative sources [in Washington, D.C.] that there have been no cases of female homosexuality which came to the attention of the police that were prosecuted. The usual practice has been to dismiss the complaint, and to regard the incident as 'misbehavior.'" Close relationships between women were more socially acceptable than those between men and also provided some protective cover. "No one thinks anything of two women who put their arms around each other and kiss each other, live together, sleep in double beds," a government psychiatrist told the Hoey committee. "There are thousands of Government girls who do that thing." But given the thoroughness of government security investigations, women who acted on their homosexuality only in private were also at risk of losing their well-paid government jobs. And because the federal government was one of few places where women had opportunities for responsible jobs above the level of a secretary, the stakes were particularly high. Their very ambition to rise to positions of responsibility in male-dominated environments cast doubt on their femininity. When President Truman nominated Kathryn McHale, longtime executive director of the American Association of University Women, to the Subversive Activities Control Board, her nomination had to be withdrawn after Senator Pat

McCarran threatened to reveal that she was a lesbian. Less public but still powerful women suffered similar fates. In the early 1960s Betty Deran worked as an economist in the Treasury Department, writing reports that went to the White House. But in 1962 she failed to pass a security clearance review despite what she considered an extremely discreet private life. "They really didn't have anything against me . . . as long as I didn't live my private life, they didn't have anything on me," she protested. She had to leave Washington and take a job as an economist in New York. "I took a sort of lesser job because of the circumstances," Deran noted. Joan Cassidy knew that because she had risen to manage a division within the Office of Naval Intelligence, both men and women uneasy with her authority watched her particularly closely.[12]

This fear and division was not unique to the gay community but permeated Cold War Washington. One of Barbara Kraft's most vivid memories of Washington in the 1950s is how quiet people were while riding the bus. "People were afraid to talk to one another," she remembered. A government security officer and his wife moved into a Washington housing development and refused to speak to or socialize with their new neighbors. When one of the snubbed neighbors remarked on their aloofness, the wife responded, "You see, my husband has told me that under no circumstances should I associate with any of the neighbors who haven't been given a full security clearance."[13]

"I Held Out Longer Than Many"

For gay and lesbian civil servants and contractors, the loyalty/security system posed a constant threat. Never knowing when an investigation might be opened heightened the uncertainty. For some, like Tress, the interrogation came soon after accepting a position. Others passed initial screenings and worked for years without incident until a new level of security, a promotion, or a complaint precipitated a more thorough investigation. Bruce Scott was arrested in October 1947 for loitering in Lafayette Park yet kept his job with the Department of Labor until 1956, when security in his office was upgraded, and all employees were required to obtain clearances. His 1947 arrest was subsequently discovered—as well as his living situation with a fired gay federal employee—and his boss suggested he resign. The official notice in his personnel file hid the truth, recording that he had left "to enter private industry." "I held out longer than many," Scott said, referring to his seventeen years of service in the Department of Labor. All along Scott lived with the notion that "my time might come."[14] Fear of being subjected to a new investigation prevented many gay men and lesbians from seeking pro-

motions or transferring to other agencies. Ted Richards began working for
the Veteran's Administration as a clerk-typist during summers while attending Duke University. But when his supervisors recognized his talents
and urged him to pursue "an executive kind of situation," his fear of discovery held him back. "I know that my fear, my terror at the time, was that
if I became anything other than a clerk-typist, then I might get found out,
and then I would lose my job. . . . I had the ambition, but I was frightened."[15]

Those forced to resign often lost more than just a job. Many suffered
from long-term unemployment or underemployment, resulting in severe
financial or health problems. Many were forced to relocate. As a gay publication reported, "Among homosexuals, learning that someone of the group
has lost a job is commonplace. Many can list acquaintances who have gone
long periods without steady gainful employment." One scientist fired from
the government was without work for almost two years, during which time
he lived on a diet of twenty cents worth of potatoes and frankfurters a day.
He lost so much weight it became uncomfortable for him to sleep on his
side. Such fired gay and lesbian civil servants often ended up in low-paying
jobs for which they were overqualified or ill-suited. One man who lost a
government job after being arrested by a vice squad officer was out of work
for "three or four years." Despite having a master's degree, he dug ditches,
because such a job did not require a government security check. "You get a
good education and you end up doing menial work," commented one gay
man about he and his Georgetown University friends barred from government service. Others described being discharged from the military and
working as hair stylists or in similar positions where being gay was not considered problematic. Losing one's career and being forced into another occupation was a common fate of gay men and lesbians.[16]

For many gay men and lesbians, once the ax fell, losing a promising government career was only the beginning of their torment, as the apparatus
of the national security state continued to limit their job prospects. The federal government's influence on other industries and institutions was so
great that many found their paths blocked at every turn. After being forced
out of the Department of Commerce, Madeleine Tress won a Fulbright Fellowship to study abroad, but the State Department vetoed her award because her government file had been "flagged" with the note "questionable
loyalty and morals (lesbian)." This was the final blow that made her abandon a career in international economics and go into private industry. "That
whole area was, I felt, shut off," Tress remembered. After Bruce Scott was
forced to resign from the Department of Labor in 1956, he worked tem-
porarily in a local bank and warehouse until forced to leave those jobs
when his past record caught up with him. After seventeen years of service

in the government, few private-sector jobs were open to him. "It was a rough time," he remembered of those eight years of underemployment and unemployment. Scott applied for a job in the personnel office of Fairfax County, Virginia. His truthful answer to a question on the application about prior arrests prevented him from landing the job. When he later reapplied to the same office, he omitted any information about his arrest. "In such penurious circumstances, I saw no reason to quibble about whether . . . a 'loitering' arrest was technically different from a 'parking' arrest," which the instructions indicated could be omitted. He got the job, but lost it sixteen months later when the agency discovered his previous application. As he wrote in 1962 as a fifty-year-old man, "It has now become virtually impossible for me to find employment for which I am qualified by training, experience, and prior job performance." Eventually living in Northern Virginia on fifty cents a day and heating his bedroom with a kerosene heater, he fell behind on his mortgage payments. When the bank foreclosed on his house, Scott was forced to return to his native Chicago.[17]

An unknown number of gay men and lesbians, stripped of their livelihoods, facing embarrassment and unemployment, took their own lives. "The only thing I regret in my campaign to rid the State Department of that type of individual [sodomites]," confessed Peter Szluk, a self-described "hatchet man for the State Department," was "when within minutes, and sometimes maybe a week, they would commit suicide." Such suicides were rarely linked publicly to the actions of the government security program. As Szluk explained, "One guy, he barely left my office and he must've had this thing in his coat pocket—and boom!—right on the corner of Twenty-first and Virginia. . . . Of course, nobody knew that he had been in to see me. It remained a mystery except to me and the security people." An official of the General Services Administration told a congressional investigator that one government employee confronted with "charges of perversion" had committed suicide by leaping from a bridge. John Montgomery, a forty-two-year-old bachelor and manager of the Finnish Desk at the State Department, committed suicide by hanging himself from the second floor balcony overlooking the foyer of the Georgetown townhouse he shared with A. Marvin Braverman, a Washington attorney. Suspicious of the secrecy surrounding the suicide, a congressional committee investigated and issued a report criticizing the department for hiring a man who exhibited "mental and emotional instability" and had even been rejected from the military for "psychoneurosis." Pointedly noting that the problem of homosexuals in government had only been "brought into national focus" since Montgomery's hiring in 1946 and that security had since been improved, it anticipated that such a mistake would not be repeated.[18]

Government security officers knew that suicide was sometimes the end result of their investigations and went to great lengths to cover up their role. During two days of interrogations by State Department security officers in August 1954, Andrew Ference, an administrative assistant at the American Embassy in Paris, admitted homosexual activities, including with his roommate, Robert Kennerly, who served as an embassy courier. Four days later, Kennerly returned to their apartment to find Ference lying on the floor dead, having asphyxiated himself with gas from the kitchen stove. The State Department notified Ference's parents in Uniontown, Pennsylvania, of their son's suicide, informing them that he was despondent because of bad health, making no mention of the repeated interrogations or homosexual admissions. Security officials instead pointed to an embassy physician's report that a recent X-ray examination disclosed that Ference had an "inactive lung lesion." Despite the department's cover-up, the news spread quickly among gay Americans in Paris that "Drew" had committed suicide over his resignation. A gay man who had been forced out of a job at the Paris embassy but remained in the city remembers hearing the rumor. Soon Ference's parents heard conflicting stories from Robert Kennerly and began to suspect "foul play." They even had his body exhumed to determine the cause of death. Two years later, through the intervention of a member of Congress, Ference's parents learned the truth behind their son's suicide.[19]

The government was well aware of the harm its security procedures were causing. At a 1953 conference, State Department security supervisors discussed how to prevent "the threat of suicide" in homosexual cases by providing psychiatric counseling prior to an interrogation. There is no evidence that any such counseling was ever provided. The deputy undersecretary of state for security affairs confessed before Congress that "we have had several of them that have done away with their lives after we discharged them."[20] Though clear documentation of only a handful of suicides exists, the quiet handling of many of the gay interrogations and resignations suggests the possibility of many more. Washington newspapers from the period contain numerous stories of single male government workers, often State Department employees, who committed suicide for no known reason.[21]

Suicide was the most dramatic manifestation of the psychological anguish that resulted from an encounter with government security officers. Though most of the evidence available comes from those who identified as gay or lesbian, the Lavender Scare had a significant impact on many people who did not. Because of the "one encounter" policy, men who had only occasionally dabbled in homosexual behavior were also at risk. Because they could not draw on the knowledge of the gay community, they were in some ways more vulnerable. One such man, a thirty-seven-year-old State Department official, was arrested for having sex with another man in his car while parked by the Ellipse in the summer of 1950. He admitted to the offense, and resigned his position, but denied that he was a homosexual. "This is not something I do all the time. It happened this once. I was drunk. I'm not a drinking man," he told a reporter. Moreover, he saw the arrest as a chance to change his behavior. "I realize the impulse is there. Now I've got to straighten myself out," he pledged. "I'm not going to give in." For many men in mid-century America, homosexual behavior was seen as a temptation to be resisted, not an inborn characteristic or orientation. When Bill Youngblood lost his job as a technician with the Defense Department in 1956, he too tried to change. Youngblood had frequented the Chicken Hut and other gay establishments, but the loss of his job over an encounter at Lafayette Park filled him with guilt and made him withdraw from gay circles. He had "lost everything," he told historian Brett Beemyn. Traumatized over his situation, with both his health and his savings deteriorating, he began seeing a psychiatrist, hoping to "get straight." John Forbes Nash Jr., the Nobel Prize–winning mathematician, had a similar experience. According to his biographer, Nash was arrested in a Santa Monica, California, rest room on a morals charge and subsequently lost his post at the RAND Corporation along with his security clearance. After this traumatic series of career-threatening events, he decided to marry.[22]

For some who tried to put their homosexual past behind them, part of that process involved cooperating with authorities. As Victor Navasky wrote about the situation of former Communists, informing on others was seen as "test of character," a way to prove that one's "break with the past was genuine." One foreign service officer returned to the State Department security office several months after his interrogation, confession, and resignation, and offered his cooperation in identifying several homosexuals in the department. The officials attributed his helpfulness to their own "sympathetic and understanding treatment of homosexuals." During the summer of 1950, one man who had given up his life of homosexuality offered to assist the Hoey Committee in its efforts to identify homosexuals in government. As Senator Mundt told his colleagues, "He had been a solicitor for a long time. . . . He said he could tell who they were." Although Mundt apparently did not take him up on the offer, government security officers were less reticent. After Thomas H. Tattersall left his government job in 1953, he frequently offered his services to security agents in identifying homosexuals. Tattersall was a married man with a history of mental disorder who had spent time at St. Elizabeth's Hospital. Agents would show him photographs of suspected homosexuals, and Tattersall would identify those he knew to be gay, based on either a personal sexual encounter or observation of them in known gay cruising areas. In 1955 he signed a twelve-page, handwritten affidavit for the Civil Service Commission identifying dozens of men and women as homosexual. Tattersall once telephoned a friend at the Department of the Interior and allowed the conversation to be monitored by an investigator, who reported that "various homosexual terms were used" and that the "tone of the conversation and the tone of voice" of the Interior official were "definitely homosexual." Such men saw it as their duty to help the government identify people at risk for blackmail by enemy agents.[23]

Making such a clean break with one's homosexual past was precisely the effect security agents and law enforcement officers behind the antigay crackdown hoped to achieve. But the effect of losing one's career and hope for the future led some in another direction, pushing them into the gay subculture. L. D., for example, came to Washington from South Dakota to attend Georgetown's School of Foreign Service. There he met many openly gay students and did some experimenting himself, but felt conflicted about his sexuality. When his roommate invited him to attended gay parties, L. D. resisted, preferring to stay home and avoid temptation. His withdrawal from his friends earned him the nickname "Matilda-sit-by-the-fire." He joined the Roman Catholic Church to strengthen his resolve not to succumb to sins of the flesh. Upon graduation in 1951, L. D. was reluctant to take the stringent foreign service examination. Not only did he feel academically unprepared, but he recently heard that a friend had been "snagged off the boat" on the way to a foreign service post in Europe because the department found out he was gay. Instead, L. D. cautiously applied for a position as a State Department clerk. Upon being accepted, he went to the department to register and was told, "There are some people that want to see you." Reporting to one of the temporary, World War II–era buildings along the Mall, he was interrogated by two men whom he dubbed "Dr. Jekyll and Mr. Hyde." "They wanted me to admit that I was gay," he remembered, "and that everyone I'd ever known or lived with as a student was gay." If he did not cooperate, the security officers threatened to "tell everybody [he]'d ever known" that he was gay, including his parents. Though they coerced a confession from L. D., he refused to give information about his friends, pleading that he had no knowledge of their sexual behavior. "It was very frightening, really frightening. I don't know how people who are interrogated with a threat of torture can stand it. I wasn't threatened with torture, but how do people stand that? . . . I was on the verge of passing out with fright."[24]

L. D.'s treatment by the State Department security officers resolved the remaining conflict he felt about his homosexuality. "It did help really make me decide," L. D. recalled about the interrogation. "If [homosexuality] is that bad in their eyes, there must be something pretty good about it," he reasoned. Moreover, the future he had envisioned for himself had now been foreclosed. "It helped at that point that I had been shoved out of anything I had hoped to do, so I could go ahead and start over and face facts. As long as I was labeled as unacceptable, then I'd do the things that were previously unacceptable. And I did them with vengeance. I was rather popular and young and handsome." L. D. took a much less prestigious job in the private sector and took on a homosexual identity, becoming a fixture at gay bars and Georgetown parties.[25]

Other gay men and lesbians had similar encounters with government security officials that pushed them further into the gay subculture. E. M. was working for a private refugee relief agency in Germany in 1950. Her life had been "full of [the] turmoil and confusion known by all maladjusted homosexuals who have not recognized their plight." She experienced a series of attachments to straight women, suffered a nervous collapse, and was treated at a psychiatric clinic. In Europe, however, she found satisfaction in her work, was beginning to feel an interest in men, and thought she had put her "troubled past" behind her. But the State Department, which oversaw all relief efforts in occupied territory, discovered her psychiatric record and demanded her immediate expulsion from Germany. Humiliated and defeated, E. M. moved to New York and discovered the gay world, which she had scarcely been aware of before her dismissal. "Now that I was persecuted for having such inclinations, I felt a close identification with others like myself. I remembered that in my own city there had been places where homosexuals congregated. I combed the streets of New York and finally one night found such a place. That night I met and talked with a kind of people I had never known, who spoke to me in a language I had never heard. Since this experience a whole new world has opened for me."[26]

By stigmatizing homosexual behavior and labeling anyone with even one such encounter in their past as homosexual, the purges enforced a rigid homosexual/heterosexual divide. They thus facilitated the demise of an older sexual system based on gender identity and encouraged the classification of individuals based on their "sexual orientation." As historians of sexuality have demonstrated, earlier in the century individuals had a gender identity rather than a sexual identity. The mark of the true sexual deviant was the conscious inversion of gender norms—such as men wearing flamboyant clothing, using make-up, and displaying exaggerated mannerisms—not sexual contact with individuals of the same sex. Men could have sex with effeminate "fairies" and still consider themselves "normal" and masculine, so long as they performed the insertive role. Under such a sexual system, not all homosexual contact was stigmatized. But by the 1950s, the sex of one's sexual partner was increasingly more determinative of one's status than was one's self-presentation or role. By defining anyone with one adult homosexual experience—whether insertive or receptive—as a homosexual, the security system greatly strengthened the focus on sexual object choice. One man interviewed by government security officers, for example, admitted to several acts of fellatio with a "known homosexual" but claimed his actions were not homosexual since he was merely the "passive" partner. Despite his protests, he lost his position with the U.S. Information Agency. By stigmatizing all homosexual behavior, the purges forced people to make choices and thereby reified a homosexual/heterosexual divide. While trying to contain perversion, the Lavender Scare also helped to redefine it, forcing people to think of their behavior in new ways. Confronted with the possibility of being labeled "a homosexual," some abandoned same-sex behavior, while others adopted the new identity and became part of the gay subculture.[27]

Singing at the Chicken Hut

For those who embraced a gay identity in 1950s Washington and wanted to meet others like themselves, the Chicken Hut was the place to go. Located at 1720 H Street, less than a block from Lafayette Park, Washington's most popular gay bar had the relaxed atmosphere of a college hangout. Known affectionately as "the Hut," it was "the center of gay social life in the city in the late 40s and 50s," recalled Peter Morris, then a student at Catholic University. "Everybody knew everybody," he said. It was at the Chicken Hut in 1954 that Morris met Jack Frey, who remained his lover for the next four decades. While a restaurant occupied the first floor, the bar and tables on the second floor were often so crowded that patrons had to tip the waitresses downstairs to secure a seat. The most popular table was one closest to the piano, where Howard, who had begun entertaining gay crowds at Margaret's in the 1930s, held court. Known as "Miss Hattie" to the bar's regulars, Howard was a short, bald man with glasses who created a festive mood with his renditions of show tunes and ballads with campy lyrics. People would sing along, especially as the beer flowed more freely. As regular patrons made their way up one of two staircases—often after having dinner on the first floor—Howard would play tunes to welcome them and spoof their character. When romantic Jack Nichols mounted the stairs, Howard would play "Falling in Love Again." The entrance of Jack's friend

Ben would elicit a less charitable "Ten Cents a Dance." Jack Frey, who came from Cincinnati, was greeted with the first line to Leonard Bernstein's "Ohio"—"Why Oh Why Oh Why Oh Why Did I Ever Leave Ohio?" Commenting on the continued popularity of such bars even during the purges, one man noted, "It was obvious that the government-agency exposé hadn't affected trade."[28]

Within several blocks of the Chicken Hut, several other bars catered to a lively gay and lesbian clientele. The men's bars in the Mayflower and Statler hotels had long been a meeting spot for homosexual men. Soon after the war a bar opened up on L Street midway between the two hotels and was known as the "MayStat." While it initially attracted gay men who frequented the other nearby bars, it soon developed a lesbian following and changed its name to the Redskin Lounge. By the 1950s it featured a small band and a butch lesbian entertainer who sang and told jokes. The Derby Room, at the corner of Eighteenth and H Streets, NW, was a popular downtown lunch spot by day, but at night it was filled with gay men. Considered more "classy" and respectable, the Derby Room featured a maître d' who would greet patrons at the door, ask how many were in the group, and fit them into remaining space in one of the bar's many booths. "On any given night, gay men were present in droves" on the street between the Chicken Hut and the Derby Room, Nichols remembered. After the bars closed, the California Kitchen on Connecticut Avenue "served burgers to the bleary-eyed." It also offered a chance for those who hadn't met anyone that night to continue socializing. Later renamed the Copper Skillet, it also earned the nickname the "Last Chance Café." "Everybody knew that was where the gay crowd would end up," commented a frequent patron.[29]

When Raymond Mailloux first moved to Washington in 1949, he lived in suburban Takoma Park but made occasional forays into the city to meet other men. He first went to Lafayette Park, but after getting beat up by two undercover police officers, he moved on to the bars, which seemed safer. "I would go to Washington and have a little bit of an affair for one night," he recalled, but the guilt would keep him from returning. "I wouldn't leave the house where I was living for six or eight months before I had enough courage to go back downtown," he explained. He would dress up in a suit and necktie to go out and would often be placed in a booth with strangers. Despite the crowded conditions, "nobody would talk to each other," Mailloux commented. But one night in 1953 after the Derby Room closed, Raymond was milling about with the crowd on the sidewalk and noticed a handsome young man who winked at him. Later at the California Kitchen the two men finally talked. Mailloux summoned the courage to ask him back to his house, and within a month the two moved in together. It was the beginning of a twenty-year relationship. Since two men living together were suspect, they would tell inquiring neighbors and acquaintances that they had met during the war in Okinawa. "We had to fabricate," Mailloux explained. Though they both worked as civilians for the Defense Department, they managed to elude security officials and keep their jobs.[30]

Though a haven for many people, Washington's gay bars were not immune from the tensions gays and lesbians faced every day. Local vice squad officers kept them under observation, but apparently never closed them down. Henry Yaffe remembers going out to the bars every weekend. "If I didn't go out every Friday and Saturday night in those days, I thought my world would collapse," he commented. Because most of the bars served food, he would often have dinner there as well. "You got to know everybody," he remembered. But because of the purges, he noted, "You never knew what people did . . . they never told you where they worked." Yaffe had been forced out of the military for his homosexuality and worked cutting hair, so he had little to hide. Many middle-class gay people concerned with respectability and protecting their jobs shied away from the bars. Not only were they concerned about bars being raided or watched, but they often found the campy atmosphere distasteful. Ramon G., who worked as a Portuguese language specialist at the Library of Congress, was repelled by the bar scene. "In those days at the bars you would find people screaming 'darling,' and being campy, campy. . . . I dreaded that," he explained. Ted Richards, a government clerk who became a high school teacher and classical pianist, was intimidated by the flamboyance of the bar crowd. He found the banter in bars "contrived" and "exaggerated," the clientele mostly "ribbon clerks." They neither wanted to be nor could risk being that openly gay.[31]

Washington's liquor laws and the codes of conduct established by bar owners also limited the conviviality. Patrons could neither walk around the bar with a drink in hand nor dance. Any open display of affection between same-sex couples would elicit a lecture from a worried bar owner. African American patrons were unwelcome, even after the Supreme Court ordered restaurants in Washington to end segregation in 1953. Management would put "Reserved" signs on tables to justify refusing people they wanted to turn away. The married Italian couple who owned the Chicken Hut hired only female servers, fearing gay male servers might lead to disreputable behavior. The song that would close out the night at the Chicken Hut captured both the celebration and the guilt of the bar experience. Patrons would sing along to Howard's rendition of the Yale "Whiffenpoof Song," a hit 1946 recording featured in the Bob Hope film, *Road to Bali*. The lyrics invoked the solace of convivial drinking among a group of friends at their favorite watering hole: "To the dear old Temple bar we love so well, / Sing the Whiffenpoofs assembled, with their glasses raised on high." While celebrating the bar, the song also evoked the outcast nature of the patrons in some of the closing lyrics: "We're poor little lambs who have lost our way. . . . We're little black sheep who have gone astray."[32]

"About One Every Day"

The total number of men and women affected by the anti-homosexual purge is incalculable.[33] Many agencies did not keep records of such dismissals. Many were never recorded as dismissals, since the individual, confronted with accusations of homosexuality, "resigned voluntarily." Nevertheless, some published figures give a sense of the scale of the antigay purges. According to the carefully compiled statistics of a congressional committee, during the approximately four years between January 1947 and November 1950, more than four hundred federal employees resigned or were dismissed for sexual perversion—about one hundred per year. This figure represents only the first few years of the purges, before much publicity and calls to "clean house." In the two years between May 1953 and June 1955, as the purges accelerated, over eight hundred federal employees either resigned or were terminated with files containing information indicating sex perversion—about four hundred per year. During the height of the witch-hunts in 1953, Undersecretary of State Donald B. Lourie testified before a congressional committee that homosexual firings were averaging "about one every day" from his department alone. By the 1960s the State Department, the most aggressive federal agency in ferreting out homosexuals, had fired approximately one thousand suspected homosexuals. Since statistics indicate that State Department firings represented about 20 percent of the total, as many as five thousand suspected gay or lesbian employees may have lost their jobs with the federal government during the early days of the Cold War. At the very least, these partial statistics suggest that the total number of federal employees fired for homosexuality is well into the thousands.[34]

These partial figures represent only those at the center of a storm whose effects rippled throughout both public and private employment. Many dismissals occurred on a more informal basis—ostensibly to protect the reputation of the employee—and were not recorded as dismissals for homosexuality. Other gay and lesbian civil servants resigned before their sexual orientation was discovered. Ray Mann, for example, decided to leave the State Department in the summer of 1954 because "being unmarried, I just didn't think my future lay working for the U.S. government in the Mc-

Carthy era." Though never accused, he moved to the airline industry because, as a gay government employee, he felt "watched."[35] When George Poe, a civilian with the Navy, became aware that he was under investigation, he "saw the handwriting on the wall" and decided to resign before he was asked to leave. Soon thereafter his partner, Nils Skavang, also under investigation, was fired from the State Department. A Chicagoan who moved to Washington, amazed at the level of fear and repression in the capital, related a similar story. "I remember having a neighbor, very nice fellow, who worked for the Navy department. I know he was followed to gay bars—we lived in the same building. He finally quit. They didn't force him to quit. He knew it was coming because they started to question him." In addition to such preemptive resignations, thousands of federal job applicants were rejected because of their sexual orientation. Between 1947 and 1950, 1,700 applicants were rejected because of "a record of homosexuality or other sex perversion," more than four times the number of incumbent employees dismissed on similar charges during that period. These figures also exclude the thousands of men and women discharged for their sexual orientation from the military, where the witch hunt was even more severe.[36]

The impact of the purges was not limited to federal employees. Millions of private-sector employees who worked for government contractors were required to have security clearances. Although those denied a security clearance could theoretically do nonclassified work for such companies, in practice they were often fired. Because the government did not reveal to private companies the reason for a security clearance denial, it cast a shroud of mystery over the employee. As Bernard F. Fitzsimmons, a security officer for Douglas Aircraft, told a congressional committee in 1955, "We feel that if a man is a security risk when he has access to classified materials, he is a security risk wherever he is in our plant." Other private industries, with no direct federal contracts, adopted the policies of the federal government—the nation's largest single employer. When Bob Adams left his job with U.S. Army radio in Europe in 1952 and returned to the states, he thought he had left the threat of losing his job for being gay behind. In Europe he encountered "hellish grilling," suicides, people jumping out of windows. "Each time somebody would disappear, I thought, 'Oh God, what's going on?' We were all scared," he remembered. But when he got a job in commercial radio, the situation was only marginally better. He found out that CBS had "swept out a whole raft of its people." The Mattachine Society received numerous letters from gay men, many of whom had been arrested on a morals charge, who were finding it nearly impossible to find employment. One man wrote in from the South, "I have been selected out of large groups of applicants for good jobs, but as soon as an investigation is made of my past, I am dropped abruptly." The Chicago chapter of Mattachine reported in 1955 that the practice of targeting homosexuals as undesirable employees "has been widely adopted by private business."[37]

Witch hunts in the business world were so common they spawned a new industry, as investigative agencies formed to act as "miniature FBIs." Fidelifacts, Inc., offered "fact-finding and personnel reporting services for business organizations" in thirty cities. Staffed largely by former FBI officers, these consulting businesses used high-pressure promotional techniques that stressed the importance of following the government's lead in probing the lives of veteran and potential employees alike. One such agency in Chicago listed "homosexuals" in bold print on its letterhead among the types of "undesirables" it specialized in uncovering. After one West Coast airline hired such an agency, agents interrogated a large segment of the staff suspected of being homosexual. When employees refused to answer the question, "Is it true that you're a homosexual?" investigators coerced confessions by claiming the employees had forfeited the right not to answer when they signed loyalty oaths on their job applications. According to a 1950s gay publication, over half of the company's technicians were subsequently fired. "Almost no corporation or other private business will hire a man with such a stigma on his record," warned a prominent Washington psychiatrist. "If the present wave of public sentiment continues, certain male and female homosexuals will become persons without a country, since they may find it practically impossible to earn a living."[38]

As the obsession with Communist infiltration spread to the nation's universities in the 1950s, so did the obsession with homosexuality. In the spring of 1955, Robert Bellah, a graduate student at Harvard, was nominated for a one-year instructorship. Bellah had suffered some harassment at Harvard as a former member of the Communist Party, but the winning of this fellowship suggested the school no longer had doubts about his loyalty. But the instructorship came with a request from McGeorge Bundy, dean of the Faculty of Arts and Sciences, that Bellah submit to an interview with an official of the Harvard Health Service. "He began after a few pleasantries with a story about someone who worked for the State Department who decorated his apartment with pictures of naked women to hide the fact that he was homosexual," Bellah wrote years later. "He became less indirect and began asking whether I had ever engaged in sexual acts for which I could be blackmailed." Amazed at the line of questioning, Bellah remembered that as a Harvard undergraduate he had consulted a doctor about "feelings and anxieties not uncommon to college undergraduates." Bellah was not homosexual and apparently convinced the Harvard Health Service of his heterosexuality. He went on to become a famous and prolific sociologist of religion. Though a single anecdote, his encounter illustrates how the reasoning and tactics of government security officers served as models for private institutions. It also underscores how even a rumor of homosexuality was often considered a graver transgression in 1950s America than an admission of former membership in the Communist Party.[39]

"Something Ought to Be Done": Early Political Organizing

Although throughout the 1950s no gay man or lesbian came out publicly to decry the homosexual witch-hunts, more subtle forms of resistance were exercised every day. Not cooperating with security officials was one simple, common way of standing up to the security process—whether by refusing to name names or by actively lying to the authorities. Other gay people in positions of authority offered each other more powerful forms of protection. As an attorney in the personnel office of the U.S. Department of Health, Education, and Welfare, "Patrick" was once asked to initiate a dismissal against a male employee who had allegedly propositioned another male at an office Christmas party. "I had an in-box that deep of things that were important," he recalled, "and I put this at the bottom. I thought, 'Some day they will come after me and say, "How are you coming on that case?" and I'll say, 'I'll get to work on it.'''" Nothing ever came of the dismissal. Joan Cassidy also had a gay friend in high places. When her commanding officer at the Office of Naval Intelligence got a report that she was a lesbian, he asked her supervisor what should be done. As a gay man, he knew many people on his staff were gay or lesbian and anticipated the devastation such an investigation might cause. "If you start this kind of investigation, it's going to be massive, disruptive, and you are going to lose some of the best people you have. Do you want that to happen?" he asked the commanding officer. Again, no investigation was launched.[40]

In addition to fostering these common forms of resistance, the purges played a pivotal role in the formation of an organized gay movement, both at the national and local levels. At the same time the purges were making headlines in Washington, a small group of gay men in California were founding the Mattachine Society, the first sustained gay political organization in the United States. The organization was named for Matachinos, masked court jesters of the Italian Renaissance who were free to speak the truth. Harry Hay, the group's principal founder, remembers that the firing of perverts from government offices was in the papers and on the evening television news in 1950, just as the organization was getting off the ground. He had been alerted of the purges in the State Department two years earlier, when he first drew up a prospectus for the group. Bill Lewis, a gay secretary in the industrial office in which Hay worked, had a college friend named Chuck who worked as a secretary in the State Department in Washington. Lewis was interested in Hay's ideas about organizing homosexuals. When Chuck came home to Los Angeles for a vacation in May 1948, the two friends "came down to our factory during lunch-time so I could hear what was going on [in Washington]," Hay remembered. Chuck told Hay about the rash of firings going on in the department and how "everybody was terrified." Chuck, thirty-five years old and in a pool of "top secretaries," had been trying to figure why all the gay men in the department were being fired. They had come to the conclusion that "the boys who slept with 'Andrew,' a gorgeous 'dream-boat' who'd been reassigned to D.C. from elsewhere, were the ones who were being given the third degree and being fired."[41]

Although Chuck's intention was to warn Hay of the possible consequences of forming a gay organization, stories of government purges were a prime motivation in Hay's decision to form the Mattachine Society. "The purge of homosexuals from the State Department took place," Hay noted when asked about the context for the founding of the Mattachine Society. "It was obvious McCarthy was setting up the pattern for a new scapegoat, and it was going to be us—Gays." Blacks were already organized, he reasoned, and Jews could not be attacked because of the "painful example of Germany." He began drafting a proposal for an organization that, by the summer of 1950, he was calling "Society's Androgynous Minority." In his preliminary notes from July 1950, Hay warned that "the government indictment against Androgynous Civil Servants" was part of an "encroaching American Fascism." Through references to "concentration camps" and extermination, Hay raised the specter of Nazi Germany. Hay noted how tactics of "guilt by association" and reliance on "anonymous and malicious informers" characterized both the persecution of Communists and homosexuals. More ominously, in light of the Korean conflict, Hay feared that this governmental policy would eventually spread to the private sector. With "the Government's announced plans for eventual 100% war production mobilization," Hay reasoned that all commerce would be conducted by government contract, "making it impossible for Androgynes to secure employment." Working in Southern California, an area already heavily dependent on government contracts for much of its manufacturing base, Hay knew very well the influence the federal government could have on private enterprise. Fully half of the area's economic growth in the decade following World War II could be attributed to defense contracts. California as a whole, with 250,000 federal workers, was becoming known as "a second United States Capital." Like many of his friends, Hay had worked for aircraft manufacturers with large government contracts and therefore knew from personal experience the effect government policies could have on private enterprise. Hay had declined to go into the new discipline of systems engineering, despite the urgings of his supervisors, because of "security clearance problems" stemming from his involvement in the Communist Party. Given this experience and his fears about the future, Hay felt that homosexuals in California had to organize a response to the encroaching federal purges.[42]

In order to find others who shared his beliefs, Hay canvassed the gay beaches of Los Angeles in the summer of 1950. He and a friend would first ask people if they would sign a petition against the Korean War. Figuring most would find this too radical, they would then raise the comparatively moderate proposal of a gay organization. "Then we'd get into the gay purges in U.S. government agencies of the year before and what a fraud that was." Hay remembered asking the beach goers, "Isn't it high time we all got together to do something about it?" Despite Hay's expectations, most people signed the antiwar petition, but no one was interested in forming a gay organization to combat the witch-hunts. But by that fall, Hay had found a small group of like-minded men who helped him form the Mattachine Society. After a brief period of activism, the group engaged in what historian John D'Emilio has termed "a retreat to respectability," disavowing any political involvement while relying on educational and research efforts to further their cause.[43]

Throughout the 1950s, the nascent movement articulated a sustained critique of the federal government's security program and its effect on gays and lesbians. Both of the movement's California-based publications, the *Mattachine Review* and *One*, ran frequent news items and critical essays concerning the government security system, suggesting it was a major concern of their readership, which by the end of the decade exceeded five thousand. Such articles refuted the alleged connection between homosexuality and communism, pointing out that the Communist Party also excluded homosexuals and that the life of the average gay person was too stressful for political activities of any kind. "Too many of our people are involved in their social oppression, their personal love adventures in an atmosphere of legal persecution, and their day-to-day problems of making a living and paying their bills to have any energy, let alone inclination, to participate in revolutionary movements." The very first volume of the *Mattachine Review* in 1955 featured a lengthy response from an anonymous, gay Republican Party official to Senator Everett Dirksen (R–Illinois), who had complained that kicking all the "security risks and homosexuals" out of the government was "no picnic." The gay official argued that all branches of the government were well staffed with homosexual men and women whose "hearts are not less full of pride and honor at the sight of massed American flags because [they] are homosexual." Such published statements offered a strong critique of the Lavender Scare and kept gay men and lesbians informed of government policy and media coverage of the issue. Sometimes they even suggested corrective action. As the anonymous letter writer reminded Senator Dirksen, "Homosexuals vote too, in greater numbers than you can possibly know." By the early 1960s, these publications would also provide a communications network among people beginning to challenge those policies. As historian John D'Emilio points out, these early gay publications were "creating a common vocabulary" and "inventing a form of pubic discourse" that would prove key tools as the gay and lesbian community began to fight federal government policy.[44]

Throughout the 1950s gay men and lesbians in New York, Chicago, and other cities formed Mattachine Society chapters—sometimes called "area councils." Generally they followed the California group's example in focusing on research, education, and social services. But in 1956, Buell Dwight Huggins, a federal clerk-typist, formed a Washington chapter that set itself apart. Calling itself "the Council for Repeal of Unjust Laws," the Washington chapter had attracted thirteen members by August 1956, had elected officers, rented a post office box, and begun publishing a monthly newsletter. With an ambitious goal of legal reform, the group discussed the civil rights bill then before Congress—the first since the Civil War era— and lamented that "civil rights never seem to apply to homosexuals." They noted with irony that many of the Congressmen who favored this legislation had been "those who had spoken the loudest against homosexuals," singling out Congressmen Miller and Rooney. Calling Republicans the party of the "homo-haters," they revealed that an employee of the Republican National Committee had been seen frequenting Washington's gay bars. The group demonstrated a keen sense of the political origins of the purges in 1950 and how they continued to affect the daily lives of Washington's gay residents. Referring to the 1950 Wherry Committee testimony that the Washington police had a list of thousands of D.C. homosexuals, one newsletter urged people to join the new chapter. "The risks you will assume with us are far less than the risks many take in their daily and nocturnal rounds of the parks, theatres, and bars," the newsletter noted.[45]

Huggins, the group's founder, newsletter publisher, and guiding light, had moved to Washington to work for the government in 1942, after being forced to leave the University of Illinois for making a pass at a male student. Huggins had followed the rise of the Lavender Scare very carefully, clipping newspaper stories and swapping accounts with friends. Given his public record of homosexuality at the university, he assumed his government job was at risk. Though never fired, Huggins watched as friends and acquaintances lost their jobs. One friend with a master's degree had been unemployed for three years since losing his government job and forced to do manual labor. Another had been out of work for a year. "So great is the fear which grips him because of his misfortune that he cannot bring himself to make the final step in approaching a prospective employer," Huggins complained. One had been arrested by a plainclothes police officer, while the other had been turned in by a former boyfriend who was blackmailing him for money. Huggins, who was involved in ongoing struggle with the University of Illinois over his dismissal, thought it time to do something about the federal situation.[46]

But when Huggins wrote the national Mattachine Society about the Washington chapter's desire to "change unjust laws," the leaders insisted that Huggins and his group would have to forgo such militancy. The Mattachine Society charter, they pointed out, limited its activities to "research and education." Direct lobbying or other political involvements would endanger their charter, they warned.[47] As a result of this reprimand from the national group, the Washington chapter retreated from its initial activist agenda. It removed "the council for repeal of unjust laws" from the masthead of its monthly *Washington Newsletter*, but it remained active, holding monthly meetings, sponsoring speakers, and maintaining a lending library. Conforming to the Mattachine strategy of assisting the work of heterosexual professionals, the chapter invited the ACLU to send a speaker to its meetings—an offer the ACLU declined. Among those who did agree to speak to the group were St. Elizabeth psychiatrist Benjamin Karpman, a critic of the government purges, and attorney Edward Kehoe, who had defended several gay men who fell victim to Washington's vice squad. By 1957 the Washington chapter had nearly as many active, dues-paying members, as recognized by the national organization, as New York and Los Angeles, cities more than twice its size. By May 1958, with approximately forty members, the group had outgrown its meeting space in private homes and had begun holding meetings in the parish hall of St. James Episcopal Church on Capitol Hill. Although it toed the Mattachine line and stayed out of politics, the group kept a watchful eye on the entrapment activities of the D.C. morals squad, spreading word through its newsletter of men who had successfully fought their arrests in court.[48]

Despite the activist intentions of its leader, the Washington chapter remained out of the headlines and became dormant by the end of the decade. In December 1957 the group lost Huggins, who moved back to southern Illinois to attend to family business. "Mattachine's growth in this area is largely due to his efforts," members lamented at the founder's decision to leave town. Equally devastating may have been the organization's decision to hold public meetings, which caught the attention of both the local police and the FBI. By the end of 1958 the group was again meeting in private homes, and its newsletter was increasingly devoted to book reviews and other cultural notes rather than political commentary. Most gay men and women who were active in the gay subculture of 1950s Washington were unaware of the chapter's existence. By the 1960s it was remembered, if at all, only as a "social group." Nevertheless, the existence of a gay organization in the nation's capital in the 1950s, and its initial desire to move beyond the limited mission of the parent organization in California, suggested that the purges were creating a uniquely potent level of frustration and sense of injustice in the nation's capital. Just a few years later, after the collapse of the national Mattachine structure, a new organization under new leadership would take hold in Washington, fulfilling the agenda of this earlier group and taking the entire gay movement in a new direction.[49]

Challenging the Morals Squad

As this early Washington chapter of Mattachine recognized, the biggest immediate threat to gay men and lesbians in Washington was the local morals squad. "The rottenest I have ever experienced," complained one well-traveled man about the local police's notoriously aggressive pursuit of homosexuals. Simply making eye contact with another man in a known gay cruising area could lead to an arrest, even physical violence. Two men from suburban Virginia reported that moral squad officers beat them during an interrogation, resulting in a broken rib and toe. Challenging the employment policies of the federal government seemed a daunting task, but contesting one of its key enforcement mechanisms proved more feasible. The Washington chapter publicized important legal struggles mounted by a few courageous individuals—court challenges that set legal precedents for future cases, curbed police behavior, and emboldened others to bring more suits: Individual challenges to the excesses of the Washington police would be the first attempts at legal reform launched by the victims of the Lavender Scare.[50]

At 1:30 A.M. on a Saturday morning in September 1948, Edward F. Kelly, an analyst with the Public Health Service, was sitting on a bench in Franklin Park. Kelly, forty-one, had been in Washington three years, having been transferred to headquarters from a field office. He struck up a conversation with a man on an adjacent bench about the beautiful fall weather. The man claimed to be a "plastics salesman from Atlanta." The two discussed the difficulty of getting a drink after hours in Washington, and Kelly said he had some liquor they could share in his apartment at the corner of Twenty-first and Pennsylvania Avenue. According to later court testimony, Kelly also suggested they could "have a lot of fun" and described in detail particular sexual acts they might also share. When the two men got to Kelly's car, the man flashed a badge and arrested Kelly for "unlawfully inviting another to accompany him for lewd and immoral purposes."[51]

The arresting officer was Frank Manthos, one of the most notorious representatives of the D.C. morals squad. A twenty-two-year-old former boot black, Manthos had joined the vice squad in early 1948 and quickly developed a reputation as a "vice crusader." Dubbed by the press a "fine-featured, one-man vice squad," Manthos claimed more than one hundred and fifty vice convictions in eight months on the force.[52] That night he had already made six similar arrests. Kelly contested his conviction in D.C. municipal court, claiming that on the night of the arrest he was returning from a date with a woman when he decided to grab something to eat at the "White Tower" all-night restaurant several blocks from Franklin Park. He claimed that Manthos had initiated the conversation and that he was just acting "congenial" toward an out-of-towner looking for a drink. Despite his legal strategy of denying any sexual aspect to the encounter, the circumstances suggested otherwise. Kelly was an unmarried, forty-one-year-old man in a known gay cruising area late on a Friday night who invited an attractive, twenty-two-year-old strange man to his apartment for a drink. The case came down to who had more credibility—civil servant Edward Kelly or vice officer Frank Manthos. Kelly produced numerous witnesses who testified to his good character. He also produced evidence that Manthos had made false statements to the probation office and the court. After an initial defeat, Kelly appealed to the U.S. Court of Appeals, which found Manthos's uncorroborated statements insufficient for a conviction. The court noted that while the offense was technically a misdemeanor "less serious than reckless driving," in the real world it amounted to a serious accusation and was the "easiest of blackmail methods." Kelly had lost his government job because of the arrest. If the evidence of a single witness—even a plainclothes police officer—were all that were required for conviction, the court warned, "any citizen who answers a stranger's inquiry as to direction, or time, or a request for a dime or a match is liable to be threatened with an accusation of this sort." The testimony of a single witness claiming solicitation for a homosexual act, the court counseled, "should be received and considered with great caution."[53]

Kelly's 1952 victory at the U.S. Court of Appeals was a significant victory for men who cruised Washington's parks and theaters, establishing what became known as the "Kelly counsels"—rules of evidence that courts had to consider in deciding similar cases. If there was only one witness to a verbal invitation to sodomy—as was usually the case—the court had to consider that testimony with "great caution." Evidence of the good character of the defendant had to be considered. Finally, in order to sustain a conviction, the circumstances surrounding the alleged crime had to be corroborated. The Kelly counsels played a significant role in impeding convictions in many subsequent gay sex cases and encouraged more men to challenge their arrests, particularly when the evidence was limited to the word of the police officer. Their impact was immediate. A federal building guard convicted of soliciting a vice squad officer for lewd and immoral purposes the day the Kelly decision came down received a new hearing a month later and was acquitted. By 1954 conviction rates for morals offenses fell below 40 percent—lower than for any other type of crime in the District.[54]

The effect of the Kelly counsels angered the U.S. attorneys who prosecuted such cases in the District of Columbia. Calling Washington "a hotbed of perversion," prosecutor Paul Leonard complained that the ruling impeded his ability to prosecute crime and claimed that judges had interpreted it too broadly. U.S. Attorney Leo Rover took the extraordinary step of meeting with police court judges to discuss how to increase conviction rates in homosexual cases and provided them with a twenty-five-page interpretation to guide their rulings. He even threatened to go over their heads by insisting on jury trials if he thought a bench trial might lead to an acquittal. Some judges, and one member of Congress, denounced this attempt at manipulating the court, while other judges welcomed Rover's advice and delayed scheduled morals cases until the report arrived. Newspapers reported that conviction rates were up to 62 percent a month later.[55] In their "drive for convictions," prosecutors also met with vice officers to advise them how to overcome the limitations of the Kelly counsels. If vice officers lured their prey into making actual physical contact—rather than just the kind of verbal invitation Kelly had made—prosecutors could charge them with assault. With this encouragement from the U.S. Attorney's office, the morals squad became even more aggressive.

On January 3, 1955, Ernesto Guarro, a twenty-two-year-old secretary, went to the Follies theater, a well-known cruising area across the street from Lafayette Park. In the men's room he encountered Louis Fochett, a morals squad officer in plainclothes. Fochett exchanged glances with Guarro and then followed him to the theater balcony, where he positioned himself against the back wall. Interpreting these as signs of sexual interest,

Guarro approached Fochett, asked him why he was not watching the movie, and touched Fochett below the waist—Guarro claims he brushed his open coat, while Fochett maintains he touched his genitals. Fochett asked Guarro if he "wanted to take it," and when he got what he interpreted as an affirmative response he arrested Guarro and charged him with assault. Though Guarro confessed to previous homosexual conduct, the trial focused on Lieutenant Fochett's conduct and whether or not he gave consent to the touching. Fochett testified that he was not shocked, embarrassed, or humiliated at Guarro's touching, since he did this sort of thing for a living. Though Guarro lost at the lower court level, in 1956 the U.S. Court of Appeals ruled that vice officers who conversed with other men and accompanied them to new venues effectively "gave consent" and therefore could not claim assault. The court even accused him of engaging in a "flirtation" with Guarro. The first duty of a police officer is to prevent crime, the court noted, not create it. The Guarro case represented a setback for the prosecutors' new strategy and resulted in the dismissal of many similar cases in which plainclothesmen enticed men and then claimed assault.[56]

Both the local chapter of Mattachine and the national organization in California viewed the Guarro case as a major victory. "Mattachine salutes what citizens everywhere will agree upholds a vital intention in our laws," the *Mattachine Review* editorialized. The Washington chapter called it a "brilliant opinion" and noted that the testimony made "interesting reading on a long winter's evening." Gay men in Washington could find some solace in the Guarro decision. They knew that local sex-crime arrests and the federal government's antigay policies formed a reinforcing circle. Such arrests were used as evidence to fire gay civil servants, and the alleged security risk posed by gay civil servants served as justification for stepped-up enforcement and prosecution. Whether the legal charge was disorderly conduct, solicitation, or assault, police were essentially arresting these men for being homosexual. To ensure conviction, prosecutors would often use evidence of a defendant's homosexuality, including use of words and phrases which "had special significance among sexual deviants." One prosecutor pressed for a conviction by arguing that "all the security agencies of the United States immediately fire these people as weak security risks." But as the judge pointed out, the man was not charged with being homosexual but with a particular incident of assault. "Perhaps defendant is a homosexual; perhaps he had engaged in homosexual acts; perhaps on the night in question he solicited the officer to engage in a homosexual act," the judge argued. "He was not charged with any of these things. He was charged with assault and convicted on proof of homosexuality." Edward

Kelly, Ernesto Guarro, and many other courageous men succeeded in placing limits on notorious D.C. morals officers, an important enforcement mechanism for the government purges. Their willingness to contest their convictions and the sympathetic hearing they received from the U.S. Court of Appeals suggested that the best chance for legal reform might be in the courts.[57]

8

"Homosexual Citizens"
The Mattachine Society of Washington

In October 1957, Frank Kameny was on assignment for the Army Map Service on the slopes of Mauna Loa, Hawaii. A recent Ph.D. in astronomy from Harvard University, Kameny had joined the army as a civilian employee in a project to map accurate distances around the globe. Using astronomical observations, government scientists like Kameny would permit the military to accurately target the intercontinental missiles it was developing. While in Hawaii measuring occultations of the moon, Kameny received a letter instructing him to return to Washington within forty-eight hours to attend to "certain administrative requirements." Kameny thought finishing his observations seemed more important than this vague bureaucratic summons and stayed on to complete the project. Once back in Washington, he was interrogated by two civil service investigators. "Information has come to the attention of the U.S. Civil Service Commission that you are a homosexual," they informed him. "What comment, if any, do you care to make?" Kameny responded by asking what sort of "information" they had, but the investigators refused to be specific. Despite their own reticence, they pressured him for information about the time of his most recent sexual encounter and what types of homosexual activities he had engaged in. By Christmas the Army Map Service had dismissed him with the trumped-up charge of falsifying a federal application form—Kameny had mis-identified an arrest for "lewd and indecent acts" as "disorderly conduct," though he made no attempt to hide it. As with many gay men in the 1950s, the record of an arrest in a known gay cruising area—Key Terminal in San Francisco—forwarded to the FBI precipitated this interrogation and dismissal.[1]

That same month the Soviet Union had launched Sputnik, the earth's first artificial satellite. Americans were shocked to find themselves behind in the space race, and politicians called on American educators to focus on the study of science and engineering to prevent the country from falling further behind. As one of only a few hundred astronomers in the country, Kameny envisioned a prosperous future working in the U.S. space program and imagined that his dismissal would only be temporary. A newcomer to the gay world and to Washington, he was unaware of the origins of the Lavender Scare and the toll it continued to take on the community. Kameny naively began appeals through the proper administrative channels within the Army Map Service and the Civil Service Commission. When these failed, he spent much of the next year engaged in a letter-writing campaign targeting President Eisenhower, the chairmen of the House and Senate Civil Service Committees, and the chairman of the Civil Service Commission, all to no avail. As an astronomer at the advent of the space race, he was "flown in luxury for interviews all over the country," but the wooing always ended when the issue of a security clearance arose. When he had exhausted his unemployment insurance and savings, he sought charity from the Salvation Army. Unable to find work in his chosen profession, he decided to find a lawyer and fight his dismissal in court.

Kameny had trained his entire life to be an astronomer. As a six-year-old boy growing up in Queens, New York, he became fascinated with the stars. "He was always interested in astronomy," his mother remembered. "I bought him a telescope [when he was] a little boy." After skipping several grades and graduating from Richmond Hill High School at the age of sixteen, where he had formed an astronomy club, he majored in physics at New York's Queens College only because it offered no astronomy courses. In 1942 Kameny welcomed America's entrance into World War II because it meant nightly blackouts, which enhanced his stargazing possibilities. The war eventually interrupted his studies and took him to Europe, where he served as a U.S. Army mortar crewman. After the war he finished his undergraduate education and was determined to pursue a career in astronomy, despite his parents' disapproval. "What kind of a career is that for a

Jewish boy? How will you ever get anywhere in astronomy?" his mother argued. But winning a full scholarship to Harvard helped overcome his parents' objections. It was a job as a research associate in the astronomy department at Georgetown University that brought him to Washington, but he soon decided that teaching at a conservative Catholic school was not to his liking. The federal government, then sponsoring much of the research in his field, seemed more promising. His dismissal represented the loss not simply of a job or even a career, but a life-long passion.[2]

It was no accident that the first federal employee fired for homosexuality to launch a sustained fight with the government was a scientist. Given the technological basis of the Cold War contest between the United States and the Soviet Union, the requirements of the national security state fell hardest upon scientists. The federal government was quickly becoming the nation's leading employer of scientists and engineers. But the scientific community was becoming displeased with the government's security program, particularly its secrecy requirements, which clashed with the free flow of ideas necessary to the scientific method. As Edward Shils noted in 1955, scientists "have come to bear the brunt of the loyalty-security measures," and as such they "stood practically alone in their criticism of the loyalty-security program." Kameny's field was particularly narrow and extremely dependent on government funds. "Being an astronomer," Kameny explained, "is like living in a very, very small town; all astronomers know all other astronomers." Since much of the work was government-sponsored, Kameny's back was to the wall. The fear expressed by Harry Hay and others that increasing governmental control of the economy would render gay men and lesbians unemployable was already a cruel reality for Kameny's world of astronomy.[3]

Kameny's initial court pleadings sought to distance himself from the charge of homosexuality, asking that he be examined as an individual and not be judged like other homosexuals. But by 1960, when he brought his case to the U.S. Supreme Court, Kameny realized that his case was not about him as an individual at all. When his attorney abandoned his case as futile, Kameny wrote his own petition to the Supreme Court for *certiorari*. Kameny's brief represented a monumental shift in thinking about the issue of gays in government. He charged that he and fifteen million other Americans were being treated as second-class citizens. He argued that he was not being persecuted for illegal conduct but for his sexual identity, a practice he labeled "no less illegal than discrimination based on religious or racial grounds." He not only compared homosexuals to racial and religious minorities, but also claimed the discrimination they faced was even more severe. "Instead of being mitigated and ameliorated by the government's attitudes and practices," Kameny argued, antigay sentiment "has instead been intensified by them." While governmental rhetoric and policy, however ineffective, sought to protect the rights of religious and racial minorities, homosexuals were the only group "barred, *in toto*, from Federal employment." He did not challenge the facts of his case, nor the procedures involved, but asked the court to decide on the constitutionality of the government's blanket policy of excluding homosexuals from government employment.[4]

Kameny's assertion that gays and lesbians constituted an oppressed minority group was not entirely unprecedented. As early as 1951, sociologist Edward Sagarin, using the pseudonym "Donald Webster Cory" had published *The Homosexual in America*, a first-person account of the gay subculture. There he called gays and lesbians "the unrecognized minority" and predicted that they would take their place beside blacks, Jews, and other groups demanding equal treatment. On the West Coast Harry Hay had articulated a similar philosophy in founding the Mattachine Society. And Buell Dwight Huggins of Mattachine's Washington chapter had likened the federal treatment of gays and lesbians to racial discrimination. But Kameny, because of his dismissal, brought this fomenting idea into the judicial and political process. The Supreme Court, predictably, refused to hear his case. But the political position Kameny outlined in his brief was one he carried out in the years ahead as he became the nation's foremost gay activist and the leader of the struggle to overturn the government's ban on gay and lesbian employees. He would reframe the homosexuals-in-government issue as a matter not of morality, criminality, or national security but of civil rights.[5]

Organizing the Mattachine Society of Washington

When the Supreme Court denied his petition in 1961, Kameny began looking to form an organization in Washington to enlarge his fight against federal antigay discrimination. While fighting his case in the courts, Kameny had turned to the handful of gay organizations in the country for help, particularly the chapters of the Mattachine Society in New York and San Francisco. All they could offer was moral support and small financial contributions for his legal bills. But when Kameny proposed founding a gay organization in Washington, officers of the New York Mattachine Society agreed to contact the Washington-area residents on its mailing list and set up an organizational meeting. Since the national Mattachine structure had recently collapsed, each group was now independent, and the New York group hoped to expand its sphere of influence by establishing a field office or affiliate in the nation's capital. Kameny also recruited friends and contacts in Washington's gay bar and party scene. That August, this combination of personal and organizational contacts drew sixteen people to the Hay-Adams Hotel. The group chose to set up an independent organization, but voted to use the name "Mattachine" because it had come to be associated with gay organizations over the previous decade. By November 15, 1961, they had written a constitution for the Mattachine Society of Washington (MSW) and elected Kameny as president.[6]

The first organizational meeting at the Hay-Adams Hotel suggested how the MSW would bring a new approach to familiar problems facing homosexual Washingtonians. Looking around the room at the other fifteen white men assembled, one participant thought he recognized Lieutenant Louis Fochett of the Metropolitan Police Department's Morals Division, notorious for entrapping gay men in Washington's parks and theaters. He pulled Kameny aside and told him of his suspicions. Kameny noticed that there indeed seemed to be a gun holster protruding from the suspected man's sport coat. Kameny proceeded with his presentation, but during the question and answer period, knowing that police officers were required to identify themselves, decided to call his bluff. "I understand that there is a member of the Metropolitan Police Department here," Kameny announced to the group. "Could he please identify himself and tell us why he's here?" Visibly flustered, Fochett explained that he had received an invitation and quickly left the room. The police department had somehow infiltrated the New York Mattachine mailing list. The Federal Bureau of Investigation had also been alerted to this first meeting and immediately began a program of surveillance and information gathering. FBI investigators interviewed Hay-Adams Hotel staff about the homosexual meeting and attempted to obtain informers from within the organization and acquire a membership roster. When Kameny discovered the FBI had interrogated people about the organization, he sent a letter of protest to Attorney General Robert Kennedy calling it "improper harassment and intimidation."[7]

Because of the continuing climate of fear and surveillance, the Mattachine Society of Washington adopted a series of restrictive and cumbersome security measures for joining the organization and maintaining membership rolls. An applicant for membership had to be sponsored by two members and be approved by a majority of the executive board in order to become a *probationary* member. During this probationary period of three months, the executive board could terminate membership by majority vote at any time. The secretary could only keep two sets of membership records and they were only open to MSW officers. Anyone who "breached the security" of the organization could be expelled by a two-thirds vote of the membership. Pseudonyms were the norm, not only in meeting minutes and publications, but also in conversations at meetings. When conducting the affairs of the organization, MSW officers were required to use pseudonyms unless given dispensation by the executive board. As one former officer explained, one "had to very carefully rehearse the fact that you would never slip with a real name," whether referring to people one knew in public or at meetings. Some members never learned the true names of their colleagues until the group reunited in 1986 for a twenty-fifth anniversary celebration. The concern with security would become a stumbling block in the effort to attract a larger and more diverse membership, but in 1961 the need to protect the organization and its members was paramount.[8]

Though secretive about its membership, the MSW was demonstrative about its goals. In contrast to the secretive genesis of almost all previous gay organizations, the MSW distributed press releases announcing its formation to every member of Congress, the president, and the cabinet. Two members of Congress, William Fitts Ryan of New York City and Robert Nix of Philadelphia, responded favorably and agreed to meet with MSW representatives. Invoking the founding documents of American democracy, the group promised to "act by any lawful means . . . to secure for homosexuals the right to life, liberty, and the pursuit of happiness, as proclaimed for all men by the Declaration of Independence and . . . the basic rights and liberties established by the word and spirit of the Constitution of the United States." While the few other gay organizations were dedicated to sponsoring research, educating the public, or, helping homosexuals adjust to society, the MSW quickly struck out in a new direction. It boldly claimed that homosexuals deserved full American citizenship and that it would speak on their behalf to end the injustices they experienced, particularly at the hands of the federal government. Under Kameny's leadership, the MSW would not remain underground and seek heterosexual authorities to speak on its behalf. Kameny, as the MSW's first president and principal spokesperson, would speak for it. On issues of homosexuality, Kameny argued, "we are the experts and the authorities." As historian John D'Emilio argued, "Kameny spearheaded the new militancy in the gay movement." While its use of pseudonyms looked back to the 1950s, its tactics and goals spoke of a new activist approach.[9]

One of the earliest and most influential members of the MSW was Jack Nichols. At one Saturday night, after-the-bars party in Washington, as Kameny was discussing the virtues of Donald Webster Cory's book for gay people, his booming voice caught the attention of Jack Nichols. A twenty-two-year-old man who had grown up in suburban Maryland, Nichols had read Cory's book soon after realizing he was gay at age fourteen. A precocious teenager, Nichols's openness about his budding homosexuality had led to great torment from his family, especially his father, a special agent for the FBI. They tried military school, psychiatry, even a female prostitute to cure him. Nichols found solace in the early 1950s only in a sympathetic, fifty-year-old lesbian school principal, who introduced him to the writings of Walt Whitman, Edward Carpenter, and Donald Webster Cory. "I read and re-read it, marking sentences that lit up new avenues to self-acceptance," Nichols recalled of Cory years later. When he got to high school he gave Cory's book to his friends to read. "Several indicated that they too were gay and the rest, fence sitters and tag-alongs, found the company of admitted homosexuals too interesting to disparage," Nichols remembered. Soon he had a "coterie" of gay friends, who, by the time Nichols turned seventeen, were exploring Washington's gay bars and parks. So when Nichols heard Kameny discussing the book that had been so instrumental in his life, he had to meet him. He, his friends, and his lover Lige Clarke, who worked in the Office of the Army Chief of Staff, became immersed in the work of the organization. "The Society gave us a rallying point, a cause, around which we centered our lives," he remembered.[10]

Congressman Dowdy's Charitable Contribution

As the fledgling organization became more active—sending out press releases, writing letters, and holding meetings with the few federal officials who responded—it increasingly needed money. Over a drink one night at the Hideaway, a small, basement-level gay bar along the seedy strip of theaters and newsstands on Ninth Street, Frank Kameny was discussing the group's financial needs with a friend. "Whenever money is involved, there are laws. You'd better check," the friend advised. Kameny discovered that to raise money in the District of Columbia, one needed a license. In 1957 Congress had passed the Charitable Solicitations Act to ensure that donations from District citizens went to legitimate charities. The registration procedure was fairly simple, requiring only the payment of a small fee and the recording of an organization's name, purpose, and the names of its officers. When the superintendent of licenses and permits, C. T. Nottingham, was confronted with the application for Washington Mattachine, however, he tried to deny the license. He hounded Kameny for a complete membership roster and procured an unfavorable report from the D.C. police. Despite his efforts, Nottingham lacked the authority under the law to deny a license to an applicant who provided the necessary information. Begrudgingly granting the license, Nottingham promised to be scrupulous in reviewing the MSW's financial records. If the group solicited "as much as one dollar," he asserted, it would be required to open its books, and any improprieties would result in the revocation of the license. Although far from an endorsement, the license was a modest form of public recognition that the group did not hesitate to publicize.[11]

Reading the Sunday edition of the *Washington Star* on September 16, 1962, Washingtonians saw an unusual headline: "Group Aiding Deviates Issued Charity License." The group was raising funds, the newspaper reported, to "help give the homosexual equal status with his fellow men." The story, which hinted at civic misconduct, infuriated John Dowdy (D–Texas), the ranking Democratic member of the House Committee on the District of Columbia. Dowdy felt responsibility for the welfare and morals of the nation's capital. His subcommittee was then overseeing the "urban renewal" projects that were transforming the District's poorer neighborhoods south of the National Mall. He was determined that the D.C. government, which reported to his committee, should not be in the business of sanctioning an organization of homosexuals. The fifty-year-old Congressman from rural East Texas, a graduate of East Texas Baptist University and former district attorney, quickly introduced a remedial bill in Congress, explaining that it was necessary to prohibit governmental recognition of a group "whose illegal activities are revolting to normal society." The acts of these people, Dowdy told his colleagues, "are banned under the laws of God, the laws of nature, and are in violation of the laws of man." They did not deserve a license from the government of the nation's capital "to promote their sexual deviations." His remedy was twofold. First, it required the District government to determine that any group granted a solicitation license contributed to "the health, welfare, and the morals" of the District of Columbia. Secondly, removing any doubt about Dowdy's real aim, the bill specifically revoked the license granted to the Mattachine Society of Washington.[12]

Threatened with revocation of its only piece of public recognition, the MSW sprang into action to defend its license. MSW representatives contacted the D.C. commissioners and the local chapter of the American Civil Liberties Union (ACLU), both of which came out in opposition to the bill. Discussions with local newspapers resulted in a *Washington Post* editorial opposing the bill, calling it "a very serious crimp in the right of expression and petition," and a violation of the First Amendment's intent to protect "unpopular causes" such as Mattachine's. Most important, the group wrote each member of the House District Committee requesting hearings on the bill and the right for an MSW representative to testify. They were astonished when the request was granted. Frank Kameny had been invited to give what would be the first congressional testimony by an openly gay person in the history of the United States government. As he prepared for his appearance, he had three important allies—the ACLU, the D.C. government, and the *Washington Post*.[13]

In this unprecedented appearance, Kameny testified for more than four hours over two days to explain his group's agenda. The MSW, Kameny told the committee, comprised citizens who had come together to express their views and agitate for social change. They were a "civil liberties group" devoted to "social action." Emphasizing that the group was "orderly and fully lawful," he invited the lawmakers to attend one of its monthly meetings. Dowdy, however, saw the group not in political but moral terms. "Aren't your meetings, in fact, introductions which lead to certain groups?" Dowdy inquired. While Kameny tried to talk about prejudice and injustice, Dowdy and the other members fixated on homosexual acts. They quoted from the D.C. sodomy statute and the Biblical books of Leviticus and Paul. Dowdy talked of "homosexual orgies," bestiality, and rumors of men gaining weight on "a diet of semen."[14] Trying to pull the hearings out of the realm of local regulatory law and into the context of national security, Dowdy recalled an alleged diplomatic incident in which persons attached to a Communist embassy in Washington had "sexual orgies" and took photographs of the participants to use for blackmail. "Permitting a bunch of homosexuals to call themselves a charitable organization," Dowdy charged, constituted "a security problem." To prove his point, he noted that the government had discharged Kameny as a security risk.[15]

To further highlight the national security angle, Dowdy suggested that homosexuality was a problem unique to Washington, D.C. "In my part of the country," Dowdy declared, "I don't think we run into any of these perverts." Wondering "whether all the homosexuals in the country have come to Washington," Dowdy raised the specter of a powerful coterie of homosexual Washington insiders opposed to his legislation. He asserted that the MSW was part of a "national and international organization" that had "up in the millions" of members. At first Kameny seemed to corroborate Dowdy's assertions, when he estimated that there were a quarter of a million homosexuals in Washington, and a similar number who worked nationally for the federal government. Kameny based his estimates on figures extrapolated from Kinsey that 10 percent of the population was homosexual. But when he revealed that his group had only thirty to forty members, and only a hundred names on its mailing list, the legislators were incredulous, making him repeat the figure three times. They were equally stunned to learn that the group had only one bank account of less than $500, no stocks, and no other assets. The incongruity between the estimated size of the homosexual population and the size of the Mattachine Society of Washington confused the committee. "You stated earlier that there are a quarter of a million homosexuals in this area," noted Congressman Frank Horton, "You are telling me that this communication that you send out once a month to the public goes to only possibly a hundred people?" These members of Congress held the assumption that homosexuals were inherently drawn into the same clique and would somehow all be on the same mailing list. For them, the problem was not that homosexuals were unorganized—as Kameny saw it—but that they were already too organized and too powerful.[16]

To further promote the notion that the MSW was a subversive organization, the committee frequently compared its proposed legislation to the Smith Act, which sought to outlaw the Communist Party. Intent on uncovering a conspiracy, members of Congress grilled Kameny about his conversations with lawyers, the length of time he spent with the D.C. corporate counsel's office, and the origin of his charge that the proposed legislation constituted an illegal bill of attainder. Dowdy tried to get Kameny to reveal the occupations of the other officers of the group, particularly whether or not they worked for the federal government. He got nowhere, until he happened to ask whether or not their names, as listed on their D.C. license application, were "true names." Kameny responded, "Those are the names with which they are registered in the society. I know of no others, as president of the society." Kameny's final qualifier gave away the secret. "So that isn't their names," Dowdy exclaimed, having finally caught the group in what he imagined to be fraud. "You have got dummies registered with the District as officers of your society." Kameny tried to justify the members' use of pseudonyms, arguing that if their identities were made public, they would likely lose their jobs. "An unemployed and starving member of the Mattachine Society or of any other group is a rather ineffective member," Kameny asserted. But the use of pseudonyms on a public document not only seemed fraudulent but also gave the impression of an underground, subversive group not unlike the Communist Party. It gave credence to Dowdy's charge that the MSW was "a secret organization dedicated to changing laws that were designed for the public good."[17]

The revelation that the MSW had used pseudonyms to obtain its fundraising license led to new attempts at revocation. Armed with this information, the D.C. Department of Licenses and Inspections ordered the MSW to show cause why its license should not be suspended. An attorney advised the group that since its fund-raising efforts amounted to less than $200 per year, they did not need a license. The D.C. Charitable Solicitation Act exempted solicitations under $1,500. Citing this exemption, the MSW turned in its license and avoided any further hearings. Unsatisfied with the voluntary relinquishing of the license, Dowdy reintroduced his legislation in 1964 and got it introduced for debate on the floor of the House. There Dowdy and his allies highlighted the danger and power of homosexuals in the nation's capital that had to be thwarted. "This Kameny fellow claims 10 percent of the employees in all the departments of Government are qualified for membership in his society," he warned. Citing the "power of the homosexuals in Washington," Dowdy claimed that the *Washington Post* had been attacking him for two years because of his sponsorship of this legislation. Despite a minority report from nine members of the House District Committee, which labeled the proposed legislation "ill-considered, unnecessary, unwise, and unconstitutional," Dowdy's bill overwhelmingly passed the House, 301–81.[18]

In a sense, Dowdy had won the battle because he had succeeded in revoking the MSW's license. But he did not stop it from raising funds. More important, he gave the organization the kind of publicity that years of solicitations never could have financed—more than fifty newspaper articles and editorials, according to one source. "Capital Is Called Homosexual Hub," proclaimed one Midwestern paper, noting that "homosexuals have their own 'club' in Washington." *Drum*, the most widely read gay publication of the 1960s, published the roll call on H.R. 5990 so every gay subscriber could know how his or her representative voted. Kameny, whose number was listed in the Washington telephone directory, received many favorable calls from people offering money, time, and moral support. He also got anxious calls from beleaguered gay civil servants wanting advice about their interrogations. Being attacked by Dowdy was the best thing that had ever happened to the MSW. The East Coast Homophile Organizations (ECHO), a small confederation of gay groups, voted Dowdy the man who contributed the most to the homophile cause that year. "By virtue of the energetic efforts of Representative Dowdy," Kameny told his group "we are now known throughout the informed Washington community—heterosexual as well as homosexual—and known in the best possible light. We are accepted by the Government of the District of Columbia as a reputable, respectable organization. We are known to church groups, to political groups, to civil liberties groups, as spokesmen for the homosexual minority."[19]

The new prominence of the MSW seemed to confirm fears first voiced in the 1950s that large nests of homosexuals had invaded the federal government and posed a threat to the nation. Indeed the Dowdy hearings evoked the series of congressional hearings of the spring of 1950 that started the homosexuals-in-government scandal. Both had mixed local and national politics by raising the specter of a large clique of homosexuals in the nation's capital and turned a local regulatory issue into one allegedly involving national security. But there were a number of important differences. Most notable was the presence of an open homosexual, who used a new vocabulary of civil liberties to talk about the situation of homosexuals in the federal government. While Dowdy used the language of criminal acts, blackmail, espionage, and national security, Kameny spoke of social action, rights of expression and privacy, political protest, and, above all, citizenship. Dowdy was engaged in a 1950s discourse on homosexuality, whereas Kameny was creating a new one. And there were other differences. Now it was the homosexuals themselves, rather than their enemies, who were claiming they constituted a significant portion of the federal workforce. And they had powerful allies in the form of another civil liberties group, the local government, and the Washington media—all united by the lack of home rule in the District and all eager to point out any injustices carried out by their congressional overseers.

Winning the support of the local ACLU chapter was crucial to the MSW's struggle with the federal government. In the 1950s, the national ACLU had declared that "the most important civil liberties problem is the way our government employees are treated today," but this concern did not apply to homosexuals. It ruled in 1957 that "homosexuality is a valid consideration in evaluating the security risk factor in sensitive positions." Since homosexuality was a crime in every state, the ACLU was only concerned with the denial of due process to those accused of sodomy and related crimes. At the time one of the national ACLU board members, Merle Miller, was secretly gay, and he described himself as "the most silent of all." But when Frank Kameny and other MSW members helped found a Washington chapter in 1961, this new National Capital Area affiliate (ACLU/NCA) began to take an interest in the issue of homosexuality and government employment. Not only did it send a representative to testify in defense of the MSW at the Dowdy hearings, but it inaugurated a broad study of the issue of homosexuals and government employment. In August 1964 the ACLU/NCA issued a report calling upon the federal government to "end its policy of rejection of all homosexuals on that ground alone." It labeled this policy "discriminatory" because it was based on attributes that "bear no necessary relation to job qualifications." It rejected the arguments that homosexuals affected the efficiency and morale of the government or posed an undue security risk and was troubled by the "demoralizing, degrading, and oppressive" methods the government used to uncover the private, consensual sexual activities of its employees. At the 1964 ACLU national conference, delegates referred the D.C. chapter's white paper to the national board for study. After more than two years of consideration

and mounting pressure from a number of gay groups and local ACLU af-
filiates, the national ACLU board of directors also came out against the
CSC policy as "discriminatory, unfair, and illogical." Although it conceded
that homosexuality might be a relevant factor in certain jobs, it placed a
high burden of proof on the government and rejected any blanket policy
excluding all homosexuals from all jobs. Perhaps even more important
than these policy statements was the legal counsel the ACLU/NCA provided to a number of test discrimination cases the MSW helped instigate.[20]

One of the phone calls Kameny received after the publicity of the Dowdy
hearings came from Clifford Norton. A budget analyst with the National
Aeronautics and Space Administration (NASA), Norton told Kameny how
on a recent Saturday night he met a man at Lafayette Park and invited him
home for a drink. When the two men arrived in the parking lot of Norton's
apartment in separate cars, they discovered that they had been followed by
two District of Columbia police officers assigned to the Morals Division.
The officers questioned the men about their interaction at the park and, because they had followed them at speeds exceeding forty-five miles per
hour, brought them in to issue them "a traffic violation." At police headquarters, Roy Blick interrogated them for two hours concerning their activities that night and their sexual histories in general. Since Norton had
revealed his place of employment, Blick telephoned NASA's security
director, who continued the interrogation until 6:30 A.M. Though he had
committed no crime worse than speeding and had a fifteen-year record of
exemplary government service, several days later NASA discharged Norton for "immoral, indecent and disgraceful conduct."[21]

As Kameny would later do for a host of distraught gay and lesbian civil
servants, he began to gather the facts of the case and referred Norton to a
sympathetic ACLU attorney. Concerned that Norton had told the police
where he worked and admitted homosexual behavior in his past, Kameny
was beginning to develop a strategy for such interrogations that he would
publicize at every opportunity. The advice soon crystallized into a pamphlet called "If You Are Arrested," which stressed the right of the person
arrested to remain silent. "Experience has shown that the worst tragedies
frequently occur not on account of arrests themselves but through unnecessary disclosure of information, including, most importantly, place of
employment." A second MSW pamphlet, "How to Handle a Federal Interrogation," asserted that it was "the patriotic duty of every American citizen" to thwart the government's policies toward homosexuals, since they
were "gravely injurious to the national interest." If questioned about one's
homosexuality, the pamphlet insisted, one should respond: "These are
matters which are of no proper concern to the federal government of the

United States under any circumstances whatever." It also advised against being "stampeded" into resigning and called on those fired to contest their dismissals. The MSW stood ready to provide advice and legal representation to those interested in contesting their treatment by the government.[22]

Among the other men who took up the MSW's offer of legal assistance was Bruce Scott. Having lost jobs with both the federal and state governments over a 1947 arrest in Lafayette Park, Scott was virtually destitute when he learned about Frank Kameny and his struggle through the Mattachine Society of California. He became a charter member and officer of the Mattachine Society of Washington and almost simultaneously reapplied to the federal government. This time he would not go away without a fight. After predictably being denied employment because of "immoral conduct," and exhausting administrative appeals, Scott filed suit in April 1963 and received national media attention. Scott told a reporter that he wanted to make himself a symbol that would prompt the federal government to reexamine the relationship between homosexuality and job performance. His suit claimed that the disqualification of persons from federal employment for homosexual conduct was "arbitrary and discriminatory" and beyond the authority of the commission. His ACLU counsel, David Carliner, underscored the importance of the case by saying he expected to take it to the U.S. Supreme Court. Some in the gay press called it "one of the most important [legal cases] ever fought in the area of civil rights for sexual minorities." In 1963 Judge George L. Hart of the U.S. District Court ruled against Scott, finding that "homosexuality is immoral under the present mores of society and is abhorrent to the great majority of Americans." The *Washington Post* called his decision "dangerous" because many homosexuals "lead thoroughly useful, successful and apparently normal lives." As his attorney promised, Scott appealed the decision.[23]

Evolution of the Mattachine Society of Washington

While Kameny's focus on lobbying government officials and encouraging judicial cases garnered positive publicity outside the organization, internally it created tension. Few members were as zealous in their commitment as Kameny. Only a small minority of members had been discharged from the government—mostly the military—and only a minority were current government employees or contractors. The largest contingent of active members were young men and women, many drawn to Washington for college, who harbored a sense of injustice and wanted to do something. They were not professionals with titles and incomes to lose, but persons with administrative or service industry jobs. Many had taken less demanding jobs than their educational or class position might have allowed, either because of the lack of opportunity or because this permitted them to express a gay identity. As Lilli Vincenz, who had dropped out of a graduate program at Columbia to explore her sexuality reported, the MSW "tended to attract idealists as well as lonely people who wanted to meet somebody and didn't want to go to bars, but they didn't stay long after they met somebody." Jack Nichols, who worked in a series of hotel administrative jobs, commented that many Mattachine members were more interested in "personal affairs and romantic hopes" than in ideological debate. Soon a split developed between those who wanted interesting meetings that served the needs of the members and those, like Kameny, who wanted to focus single-mindedly on changing the status of the homosexual in the larger society. Although the group had sponsored public talks, including one by Donald Webster Cory, the group's constitution did not allow it to function as "a social group or as an agency for personal introductions." The policy was so strictly enforced that the group declined to have an official party for visiting activists during a regional homophile conference. Kameny viewed any attempt to serve the interests of the gay community as a retreat to 1950s self-help tactics. Although not personally antagonistic to the bars—having recruited many Mattachine members there himself—he objected to official group events that focused solely on the gay community. While Kameny, the group president from 1961 to 1964, boasted that the group had been recognized by the local government, other civil liberties groups, and government officials, it had a tenuous relationship to its own gay constituency.[24]

The Mattachine Society of Washington may have spoken for the homosexual minority, but it never became a grassroots gay organization. Membership never exceeded one hundred people. Only half of the full membership was ever active, and a group of ten to fifteen people formed the core of the organization. For the first several years, meetings were held in private homes. Not until the mid-1960s did the MSW grow large enough to move its meetings to St. Mark's Church on Capitol Hill. Nor was the group representative of Washington's gay population. Although the first organizational meeting was attended entirely by white men, the MSW soon attracted a number of white women, many of whom were recruited by Lilli Vincenz. Integrating the group racially proved more problematic. Despite recruitment drives at the Nob Hill, an African American gay bar, and membership committee meetings devoted to issues like "How Can We Bring the Negro into the Homophile Movement?" the MSW never attracted more than a few African Americans. Personally, Kameny had considered himself an opponent of racism and segregation. Whenever he was asked for his "race" on an official form, he wrote "human," considering such designations "residual relics of racism and segregation." He and several other members of the MSW attended the 1963 March on Washington led by Dr. Martin Luther King Jr. But Kameny and the other members of the group did not understand the pervasiveness of racism in American society, how African American gay men and lesbians were faced with much more overt forms of oppression for their race than for their more covert sexual orientation. The *de facto* segregation that permeated life in Washington extended to the Mattachine membership. The MSW's strict policies of secrecy and sponsorship requirements for new members kept the group insular and cut off from potential new members.[25]

Though MSW members recognized that Kameny was a "life-giving, hard-driving force" with many talents, some found him "too dictatorial for the presidency." The society's direction had been determined by Kameny's interests, rather than those of the membership, they complained. Bruce Scott, who ran against Kameny for the presidency, distinguished himself from his opponent by promising to respect parliamentary authority, delegate responsibility, and share the workload.[26] Kameny was unapologetic about his role, claiming credit for most of the organization's successes. For his presumed hubris, he was voted out of office in 1965 and replaced as president of the MSW by Robert King, who had coordinated one of the group's few service projects aimed at the gay community, the publication of a venereal disease pamphlet in conjunction with the D.C. public health service. The group distributed thousands of these pamphlets in area bars, theaters, and rest rooms. Some saw the change in leadership as a change from a "one-man organization" to a "membership organization." The MSW no longer functioned solely as a legal reform society but adopted larger purposes. It instituted a number of new committees to establish programs and do outreach to the gay community. It began monthly efforts to recruit the bar crowd, including visits to white lesbian bars and African American gay male bars. Not a retreat to the self-help techniques of previous homophile groups, as Kameny feared, this change was a self-conscious attempt to combine political activism with service to and affirmation of the gay subculture.[27]

Kameny continued to direct a number of projects for the MSW, including its relationship with the federal government. He was acquiring a national reputation in the small homophile movement, and, through speeches, participation in regional federations, and a lively correspondence with officers in other gay organizations, he developed a constituency outside of Washington. When he spoke to Philadelphia's Janus Society he drew a crowd of 150 people and garnered the city's first mainstream newspaper coverage of a homophile event. In July 1964 Kameny made a speech to the New York chapter of the Mattachine Society intended to radicalize that organization, challenging it to follow Washington's lead and move from research and education efforts to "social action." Six months later, president Julian Hodges called it "an address that caused, and is still causing, more active participation in our projects, and more positive, actionist attitude in those who direct our projects." The speech was so popular that a transcript of it appeared in the Mattachine New York newsletter available in select newsstands in New York.[28] The New York group even elected Kameny to serve on its board. Meanwhile Kameny continued to be plagued by job loss. Twice he found work with government contractors where he could use his background in physics and astronomy, only to lose them when his application for a government security clearance was denied. During one twelve-month period of unemployment he depended upon loans from friends. "Bills are piling up, rent is unpaid, and I cannot—very often—underwrite the fare to and from New York," he wrote a friend in 1965. Dick Leitsch, president of New York Mattachine, called Kameny "the most valuable single item the homophile movement possesses" and sharply criticized the Washington group for rebuffing him. "To remove him from office would be a victory for the Dowdys . . . and the Bull Conners of the World." What divided Kameny from most others in the movement, said Leitsch, was his willingness to fight publicly using his own name, to be a "martyr."[29]

Civil Rights and the Civil Service

Under increasing pressure from the black civil rights movement, the federal government began taking steps to advance the cause of racial equality. In addition to passing the Voting Rights Act and the Civil Rights Act, the federal government also tried to become a model for the nation in employment practices. The Civil Service Commission increasingly encouraged hiring women and racial minorities. Kennedy signed a presidential order requiring civil service to hire "without regard to sex." Johnson set up an Equal Employment Opportunity program designed to act as a model for private industry. In public statements, CSC Chairman John Macy insisted that the government "assure equal opportunity to all groups for entry and advancement by rejecting discriminatory standards such as race, creed, color, sex, or other non-quality measures." The results in increased minority hiring were modest but steady. African American employment in the civil service rose 3.2 percent in 1964, the fourth consecutive year of employment gains for all minority groups, according to the commission.

Macy was publicly committed to making the civil service "a showcase of equal opportunity." He even initiated a program to employ the mentally handicapped. But the commission's understanding of civil rights did not extend to homosexuals. Macy even refused repeated requests to meet with representatives of the MSW.[30]

The commission was also loosening its concern with private heterosexual sex. With pressure from Congress and the media, the commission stopped requiring applicants to take personality tests or answer questions about their sexual attitudes. The 1964 edition of the *Federal Personnel Manual*, acknowledged that the ban on "immoral conduct" raised tremendous difficulties of interpretation for investigators and personnel managers. Not only were such matters generally considered a "private affair," but the authors of the manual acknowledged a "wide variation in views" concerning immoral conduct, depending upon one's class, social group, age, and geographic location. "The Commission does not consider itself to be the guardian of the public's morals," the manual stated emphatically. If an individual generally had a good reputation, the commission would not exhume "skeleton[s] in the closet" or otherwise "probe into the intimacies of his private life." As an example, persons of the opposite sex living together would not automatically be disqualified, as long as the relationship was "stable" and "socially accepted in the community." Only if investigators discovered a "gross or flagrant abuse of generally accepted standards of moral conduct" or something that would be "seriously offensive to the sensibilities of the average person," would they have to disqualify the offender from federal employment. In the case of homosexual conduct, however, the standard was much more strict. "Persons about whom there is evidence that they have engaged in or solicited others to engage in homosexual or sexually perverted acts with them, without evidence of rehabilitation," according to the *Federal Personnel Manual*, "are not suitable for Federal employment." Although in evaluating potentially "immoral conduct" the commission was generally willing to consider a host of mitigating factors, including the notoriety of the activity and the person's general reputation, in the case of homosexuality, one solicitation, no matter how discreet, was disqualifying.[31]

Following these guidelines, the government continued to oust homosexuals from its ranks and prevent others from gaining access. All federal applicants continued to be asked, "Have you ever had, or have you now, homosexual tendencies?" on the medical history portion of Standard Form 89. New government programs created during the Kennedy and Johnson administrations made special efforts to screen out homosexuals. Cuban refugees seeking training in U.S.-sponsored military training camps to assist the overthrow of the Communist government in their home country had to undergo an extensive security procedure that included a lie-detector test and questions about "homosexual relations." The federal Job Corps program, part of Johnson's antipoverty program, designed to train boys between sixteen and twenty-one in useful trades, specifically barred those with "homosexual tendencies." The Peace Corps also screened its applicants for homosexual activity.[32] The State Department—the agency most meticulous in keeping and publicizing dismissal statistics—continued to fire thirty to forty homosexuals a year in the early 1960s. Though the absolute number of homosexual dismissals had declined since the 1950s, they accounted for an increasing percentage of the total number of security dismissals. Of the thirty persons fired from the State Department on security grounds in 1965, for example, twenty-eight were fired for homosexuality. Moreover, now that all incumbent employees had been investigated—many of them on several occasions—the real focus fell on applicants. In 1960, ninety-two State Department applicants were rejected because of suspected homosexuality, nearly a third of the total. Testifying before a House appropriations subcommittee in 1966, William Crockett, deputy undersecretary of state, testified that all male applicants to the department were asked directly, "Have you ever engaged in a homosexual act?"[33]

Of the many government employees who lost their jobs in the 1960s because of a homosexual encounter, none was better known than Walter Jenkins. On the night of October 7, 1964, Jenkins, one of President Lyndon Johnson's closest advisors, attended a cocktail party with his wife to celebrate the new offices of *Newsweek* magazine. He left the party ostensibly to return to the White House to finish some work but instead visited a basement restroom at the YMCA a few blocks away, where he was arrested on a morals charge with another man. Johnson aides lobbied Washington newspaper publishers to ignore the arrest, but when the head of the Republican National Committee announced that the White House was suppressing a story "affecting the national security," it became public. White House officials tried to frame the incident in the language of mental health. They admitted Jenkins to George Washington University hospital to "recover," claiming he suffered from high blood pressure, exhaustion, and depression due to overwork. Johnson also immediately ordered the FBI to investigate whether Jenkins, who had a high security clearance and was known as "the last one to leave the White House at night," had breached national security. When it was discovered that Jenkins had a prior arrest record from a similar incident in the same restroom in 1959, attention immediately focused on the state of the security screening process in the

White House. Because of a recording error, Jenkins's earlier arrest had only been reported to the FBI as an investigation of a "suspicious person," with no mention of the sexual nature of the suspicion. Coming in the midst of Johnson's presidential campaign, the Jenkins affair provided fodder for the Republican presidential candidate Barry Goldwater, who was already hammering the Johnson administration for its lack of morality. President Johnson privately told an aide he feared "it could mean the whole ballgame."[34]

Although press coverage exuded sympathy for Jenkins, a married man with six children, it uniformly agreed that such a man could not hold a position of trust in the government. Though Goldwater pledged not to exploit the Jenkins affair, his campaign speeches regularly referred to the president's attempt to "cover up one of the sorriest rumors we have ever had in the nation's capital"—a reference to the Bobby Baker influence-peddling case that was ambiguous enough to refer to Jenkins as well. Goldwater's vice presidential running mate was much more explicit. William Miller told crowds that the Jenkins affair raised "very, very serious questions" because "if this type of man had information vital to our survival, it could be compromised very quickly and very dangerously." A few days later, Miller excited a partisan crowd of more than a thousand in California by reminding them that, "[Jenkins] was sitting in the highest councils of government when this was a matter of public record available to any Soviet agent." Echoing the rhetoric of the 1952 election, the chairman of the national Republican congressional committee charged that "the state of morality in Washington has sunk to perhaps its lowest point in history" and called for a GOP victory "to help clean up the mess in Washington and clean out the security risks from Government." Tabloids warned of "Washington's growing homosexual menace" and how just one blackmailed government employee could precipitate a "holocaust which would destroy the world." Even President Johnson was taken in by all the rhetoric about national security. In private conversations with his attorneys, he wondered if there was "any chance that anybody could have been getting any secrets from him." Abe Fortas had to explain to Johnson that the national security language was being invoked because homosexuals were considered security *risks*, not because Jenkins or any other homosexuals were actually involved in espionage. As in 1950, journalist Max Lerner stood almost alone in asserting that there was no factual basis for the notion that homosexuals posed a security risk.[35]

Though the Jenkins arrest brought the homosexuals-in-government issue into national headlines, the MSW did not exploit them. Jenkins was not the face they wanted to put on their struggle. Though homosexually active, Jenkins was not part of Washington's gay community. Though the YMCA had been a gathering site for gay men since the 1930s, local gay men who frequented it in the 1960s met in the pool and sauna but avoided the basement restrooms where Jenkins was arrested. "People from out of town . . . would go down there and oftentimes get picked up by the vice squad. All of us locals knew that was not the place to go. You went upstairs to the roof, which was wonderful for sunning," remembered one gay man. The Jenkins publicity tended to stress how one very high-powered homosexual had managed to elude authorities for years rather than the plight of the lowly government worker hounded out of his job by government security officials. Right-wing conspiracy theorists even used the incident to substantiate New Orleans District Attorney Jim Garrison's theory that a group of homosexual conspirators assassinated President Kennedy, claiming they were part of a plot to bring Jenkins and his ilk more power. By reprising much of the rhetoric from the 1950s, the Jenkins affair represented a setback to the Mattachine Society. Although Johnson won the election in a landslide, embarrassment over the Jenkins affair made it politically impossible for the administration to respond favorably to the MSW's demands to liberalize policies toward homosexual civil servants.[36]

Picketing the White House

The combination of affirmative action toward racial minorities, liberalization of policies concerning heterosexual conduct, and a continuing hardline toward homosexuals created a great deal of frustration. With their eyes on the rising tide of public protest over both civil rights and the war in Vietnam, Mattachine groups in D.C. and New York had discussed the possibility of public demonstrations, but no particular event sparked emotions high enough to precipitate action. Then on Friday, April 16, 1965, a lengthy article appeared in the *New York Times* and other papers on the establishment of homosexual labor camps in Cuba.[37] Kameny got two calls suggesting this was the moment to launch a gay demonstration—one from members of Mattachine in New York, and one from Jack Nichols in Washington. Nichols was considerably younger than Kameny and more of a bohemian—he would go on to participate in the burgeoning hippie counterculture. Kameny was at first reluctant to picket, since Cuba had no embassy in Washington. Nichols suggested the White House as a target. "The U.S. government persecutes us and so does the Cuban government," he told Kameny, suggesting that they combine their grievances against the two governments. That night they called other Mattachine members and got ten people to agree to picket. They made signs with slogans like "Russia, Cuba, and the United States Unite to Persecute Homosexuals." Within twenty-four hours of Nichols's suggestion, on Saturday afternoon, seven men and three women picketed the White House for gay rights. Because of the precipitous nature of the planning, the demonstration was reported by only one newspaper—the *Washington Afro-American*. The African American press, sympathetic to protests charging the government with inequitable treatment, had a long history of giving more prominent coverage than the mainstream press to gay events.[38]

The fears many had about public picketing—and the initial cause of homosexual internment in Cuba—were soon forgotten. The MSW quickly formed a Committee on Picketing and Other Lawful Demonstrations and launched a series of carefully orchestrated pickets at the Pentagon, the State Department, the Civil Service Commission, and again at the White House. Unlike their first tentative efforts, on these occasions they were careful to alert the media—even hand-delivering press releases to offices throughout Washington's Press Building—and were rewarded with coverage by all the major wire services and several television networks. The June picket in front of the Civil Service Commission headquarters drew twenty-five marchers. By October 1965 another White House picket drew forty-five participants, some from as far away as New York, Philadelphia, Chicago, and Florida. After distributing more than one thousand leaflets to passersby, the group celebrated with a buffet reception at the Chicken Hut. Those who participated in the pickets described the experience as life-changing. One man, initially reluctant to march, decided in the middle of a demonstration to give a taped interview with CBS-TV. Because of this public avowal of his sexuality, he felt as if he had "gained a little piece of his soul." Kameny characterized the event for many of the picketers as "one of the more meaningful and rewarding of our lives."[39]

In both its planning and rhetoric, the MSW strove to place itself squarely within the tradition of lawful American protest. Before each picket members sent letters to the appropriate governmental official requesting a meeting and warning that failure to grant the request would result in a public demonstration. Picket organizers emphasized that they were only picketing as "an avenue of last resort," when all attempts at seeking redress had failed. "What is there left to do, for a group of American citizens who feel that they have a genuine grievance, in order to get the constructive attention of their government?" they asked.[40] The only demonstration organized outside of the nation's capital was at Independence Hall in Philadelphia, a setting calculated to invoke the Declaration of Independence and its assertion that "all men are created equal." Because they had long been seen as subversive and a threat to national security—perhaps even connected with the Communist Party—MSW members were exceedingly careful to highlight not only that they were homosexuals but that they enjoyed rights as American citizens. Because the federal government, local police, and others had treated them merely as "homosexuals," the MSW adopted the strategy of referring to themselves as "homosexual citizens." In all its public pronouncements, picket signs, correspondence, and publications, the MSW used the term "homosexual citizens," suggesting that sexual identity and political rights were not incompatible. It asserted that gays and lesbians should enjoy equal rights without having to efface their sexuality. While coming out publicly as homosexuals, they were simultaneously wrapping themselves, metaphorically at least, in the American flag.[41]

Wanting to be seen not only as American citizens but also as potential employees of the civil service, picketers dressed conservatively—women in dresses, men in suits and ties. The MSW drew up strict regulations stating that "picketing is not an occasion for an assertion of personality, individuality, ego, rebellion, generalized non-conformity or anti-conformity." Dress and appearance were to be "conservative and conventional." Signs had to be approved, neatly lettered, and carried in a prearranged order. Talking among picketers, smoking on line, and acknowledging passersby (who might be gay) were discouraged. As one picketer asserted, "We are not wild-eyed, dungareed radicals throwing ourselves beneath the wheels of police vans."[42] Kameny did not rule out the possibility of unlawful sit-ins in the future, but felt that, given the novel character of the protest, an ordered, dignified approach would ensure the best response. Kameny threatened that continued government intransigence on these issues could lead to "popular demonstrations by the homosexual community at large, which will be far less responsible, controlled, and orderly." But for now, Kameny and the MSW practiced a strategy of what historian Marc Stein has labeled "militant respectability."[43]

Despite their tame appearance, many within the gay community thought these MSW picketers were crazy. Leroy Aarons, a reporter for the *Washington Post*, was listening to the police radio when he heard that ten homosexual picketers were in front of the White House. "I thought they must be totally reckless or weird," he told journalist Ed Alwood years later. Though Aarons was gay, he remembered feeling uncomfortable that the picketers threatened to bring the highly compartmentalized parts of his life together. "What does this have to do with me," he thought, "I had my job, I had my gay life, and I had my straight life." Aarons described the same sort of compartmentalization that people like Kameny, Scott, and many others had also attempted to maintain until the Civil Service Commission intervened. Still, there was much resistance in the gay community to picketing. "We were alarmed by them. Wouldn't touch them with a ten-foot pole," commented L. D., who had been denied a job in the State Department in the early 1950s. Raymond G. heard that picketers were often beaten and abused. Even many other homophile groups thought picketing would be counterproductive. When ECHO, a small, east coast federation of gay organizations came out in support of picketing in the summer of 1965, the Daughters of Bilitis withdrew its membership.[44]

Meeting with the Civil Service Commission

Before their June 1965 picket in front of the Civil Service Commission, Mattachine members sent repeated notices to Chairman Macy promising to cancel the demonstration if he would agree to a meeting. Placing their cause within the tradition of the fight for racial equality, their signs proclaimed that Chairman Macy was "Washington's Governor Wallace," barring the doorway to jobs for homosexuals as Wallace barred the school door to blacks in Alabama. In that same month came news that would convince Macy to open the door slightly. In one of the first major gay rights legal victories, the U.S. Court of Appeals ruled in favor of Bruce Scott. In his majority opinion, Chief Judge Bazelon faulted the CSC for charging Scott with unspecified "homosexual conduct" without ever presenting any evidence. Citing the CSC's sloppy language, the court ruled that "such vague labels as 'homosexual' or 'homosexual conduct'" were not grounds for determining that Scott was guilty of "immoral conduct." The court demanded that the commission define its terms and "at least specify the conduct it finds 'immoral.'" For fifteen years the government had been discharging people like Scott, Kameny, and Tress without providing any evidence of the charges against them. With the *Scott v. Macy* decision, the commission was now required to document its charges. "No federal court has gone as far as this opinion in strongly suggesting that homosexual conduct may not be an absolute disqualification for Government jobs," commented the *Washington Post*. Although only a partial victory, and one that would lead to further litigation, one contemporary gay observer noted that with the Scott decision "a candle has indeed been lighted" in the struggle for gay rights. Congratulatory messages for Scott came in from around the country. "You have done us all a great service," wrote a gay activist from California. The Scott decision, another wrote, had "shaken the walls of the Federal Jericho."[45]

The 1965 *Scott* decision by the U.S. Court of Appeals affected the legal situation of federal workers across the board. It established the principle that an applicant, as opposed to a probationary or permanent employee, had grounds to sue the government. This applied to all job applicants who wanted to sue for any inequities they perceived in their treatment. It also forced the commission to specify the charges against an employee or applicant it deemed "unsuitable." After the Scott case, those who inquired about the charges against them received detailed lists of names, dates, addresses, and physical acts, if the commission had such information. This requirement made the commission move beyond relying on rumor, association, and suspicious arrests in known gay cruising areas, significantly raising the burden of proof on the commission. It discouraged the commission from pursuing cases where the evidence was weak, and at the very least provided the employee with a basis to refute the charges. Finally, combined with the MSW's picket lines, it convinced the commission to agree to meet with members of the homosexual community, opening a dialogue that would force the government to explain its antigay policy.[46]

At 7:30 P.M. on September 8, 1965, three men and two women from the MSW were escorted into the Civil Service Commission headquarters on Virginia Avenue to meet with Lawrence Meloy, CSC General Counsel, and Kimbell Johnson, director of the Bureau of Personnel Investigations. It had taken three years of letter writing, court suits, and demonstrations to get this unprecedented meeting. Cognizant of the historic nature of the event, Kameny and the other members met as a group all Sunday afternoon to prepare. Meloy and Johnson were "exceedingly cordial and anxious to please," reported Kameny, but "squeamish" on the topic of homosexuality. "I'm not accusing any of you of being gay," Johnson said to the assembled MSW representatives, thereby missing the unprecedented nature of the meeting—the first dialogue between openly gay individuals and the CSC. According to Kameny, Johnson was "clearly very uneasy about even talking about the issue." A fifty-two-year-old Alabaman, Johnson had been a teacher before joining the CSC as an investigator and had been chief of the Bureau of Personnel Investigations since it was established in 1961. Kameny and the others tried to point out problems and inconsistencies in the CSC policies. They noted the vagueness of the commission's term "unfit," the selective enforcement of its claim to disqualify all criminals, when no one had ever been fired for miscegenation, a crime in many states. Lilli Vincenz, who attended the meeting, somewhat idealistically felt that she was "bringing the truth" to people "who had been misled." Kameny, more hardened, conceded that "we didn't really convince them of anything." At the conclusion of the hour-and-a-half meeting, the commission representatives requested that the MSW submit a formal statement of its position to John Macy and promised a response.[47]

As a result of this exchange, the CSC made the first attempt to explain its position on homosexuality, the first formal statement on the topic by any branch of the government since the 1950 Hoey Committee report. In a letter to the MSW, Macy asserted that the commission did not discriminate against a class of people but simply excluded individuals based on illegal or immoral conduct. It denied the very existence of homosexual individuals, stating that the adjective "homosexual" could only be applied to actions. "We see no third sex, no oppressed minority or secret society" wrote Macy, rejecting the MSW's claim to represent millions of homosexual American citizens. Claiming it did not pry into the private sex lives of federal employees, the commission asserted it was only concerned with homosexual activity that became public knowledge through an arrest record or "public disclosure and notoriety." If an individual "publicly proclaim[s] that he engages in homosexual conduct, that he prefers such relationships," for example, then the commission was bound to disqualify him. The commission had to consider how the public would react to transacting government business with "a known or admitted sexual deviate," a category it had earlier claimed did not exist. As Kimbell Johnson later clarified in a public interview, "to retain public confidence" the commission disqualified employees the general public considered "repugnant." Since the public considered lesbians "less repugnant" than gay men, they were less likely to be investigated. The CSC had to conform to what it considered acceptable community standards.[48]

When once their secretiveness had made homosexuals potential blackmail victims, now their very openness created a danger. Macy's new rationale reflected the new reality of homosexuals identifying themselves publicly and forming picket lines in front of government buildings. If the Hoey Committee in 1950 constructed the image of a cowering, emotionally unstable, blackmailed sex pervert, CSC Chairman Macy in 1966 located the real danger in the open, militant, homosexual proclaiming that "he is not sick, or emotionally disturbed," and that "he simply has different sexual preferences." By placing the emphasis on overt conduct and suggesting that private homosexual behavior was not investigated, the letter was an admonishment for gay and lesbian employees to cease any public avowals of their "sexual preferences" and remain hidden. In subsequent dismissals that made it to trial, the CSC would charge civil servants with "flaunting" their sexuality, gender-deviation, or membership in gay political organizations as examples of "notoriously disgraceful conduct."[49] But the courts found the policy letter to be full of "anomalies and contradictions." Citing the letter's vagueness, one court wondered whether the commission was concerned only with current or also with past homosexual acts. Its simultaneous claim that homosexual acts were illegal, but that it only acted when such acts became public, prompted the court to remark that "qualification for federal employment thus appears to turn not upon whether one is a law violator but whether one gets caught." Charging the commission with hypocrisy, the *Washington Post* pointed out that more than half of the commission's annual budget went to "probing into the lives of present and prospective jobholders."[50]

Though the civil service in general was concerned about pubic opinion, agencies working with classified information continued to invoke the blackmail rationale. In the fall of 1965 the MSW picketed the State Department, calling it "the last resolute bastion of McCarthyism in our government." During a televised press conference the day before the picket, a reporter asked Secretary of State Dean Rusk for a reaction to this "self-described 'minority group'" and the "personnel policies at issue"—carefully avoiding the word "homosexual." Rusk had clearly been forewarned. "I understand that we are being picketed by a group of homosexuals," Rusk clarified, prompting the journalists in the room to break out in derisive laughter. "The policy of the department," Rusk carefully explained, "is that we do not employ homosexuals knowingly, and that if we discover homosexuals in our department, we discharge them." This policy was not, he said, based on "medical or humane considerations" but rather on the department's involvement with "the security of the United States" and its need therefore to impose standards of conduct that were "far higher" than in society at large. "This has to do with problems of blackmail and problems of personal instability, and all sorts of things," Rusk asserted, "so that I don't think that we can give any comfort to those who might be tempted to picket us." Although by 1965 the issue of security was rarely the internal reason for homosexual dismissals, even in sensitive agencies, it remained the public rationale of the department.[51]

Two years later, a man accused of being a "security risk" held his own press conference. In November 1967, just outside the New York bureau of the Defense Department's Industrial Security Clearance Review Office (ISCRO), Benning Wentworth admitted that he was being blackmailed—by the U.S. government. An electronics technician at Bell Laboratories, Wentworth had held a security clearance for seven years without incident. One reporter called him "soft spoken and shy . . . anything but a crusader" and noted that "nothing in his manner evokes the stereotyped homosexual." But the Defense Department wanted to revoke his clearance on the basis of the coerced testimony of an enlisted man discharged from the Air Force for being gay. The Air Force had seized the enlisted man's address book, found Wentworth's name, and elicited testimony about alleged sexual activity between the two men. The Defense Department asserted that

Wentworth "may be subject to coercion, influence, or pressure which may be likely to cause action contrary to the national interest." Called in for an interrogation, Wentworth, with Kameny acting as counsel, decided to plead his case to the press. Wentworth denied having sexual relations with the enlisted man, but freely admitted to being homosexual. By appearing publicly as an openly gay man—with stories about him in newspapers throughout the country—Wentworth argued that he could not possibly be blackmailed. "The only one exerting coercion, influence, or pressure," Kameny insisted, "is the Defense Department." Wentworth became "something of a minor national hero" in the gay community and the press conference became a standard part of Kameny's approach to subsequent security clearance cases.[52]

As more and more fired gay federal employees and contractors contested their dismissals, others became more aggressive in their own defense when confronted by government investigators. Knowing that organizational resources were available to defend them emboldened gay and lesbian civil servants. In 1968 when a young man employed by the federal government for less than a year was called in for an interrogation, he asked representatives of the MSW to accompany him. At the interrogation, the CSC confronted him with evidence that he had "engaged in numerous perverted acts of a lascivious nature with various males over the years." Several years before, State Department investigators had coerced him into confessing to several acts of mutual masturbation. MSW representatives asserted that not only was the behavior not immoral and not notorious, but that it had been "wormed" out of the young man in direct violation of the commission's claim that it would not invade anyone's private sex life. To emphasize their point, they read aloud to investigators relevant portions of Macy's 1966 letter to the MSW. A few weeks later the CSC informed the young man that it had closed his case and would take no further action. Such informal victories never made it into the headlines but helped chip away at what had been a blanket policy of expelling anyone who admitted homosexual conduct.[53]

By the late 1960s the CSC was beginning to acknowledge that, due not only to court pressure but changes in societal mores, it could no longer automatically fire all gay men and lesbians. "Attitudes toward what consenting adults do in private are changing," the CSC acknowledged. Other government entities were liberalizing their personnel policies. New York City, for example, began quietly hiring unwed mothers and homosexuals in 1966. In its 1968 annual report titled "Challenge and Change," the CSC admitted that "as long as he behaved himself on the job and did satisfactory work, Michelangelo would probably be permitted to paint a post office ceiling." But if a federal employee "has the right to be different," the report warned, he did not have the right to "debauch his fellow-workers, to debase his agency, or to bring disgrace on his Government." The CSC still reserved the right to fire gays and lesbians if it found them not to be discreet.[54]

Victory in the Courts

Over the next few years, as the MSW brought several other test cases, the courts consistently criticized the commission's rationale. The most decisive of these cases was that of Clifford Norton, whose Lafayette Park "traffic violation" had caused him to lose his position with NASA in 1963. Since that time the MSW and the local ACLU chapter had helped shepherd the case through the judicial system. In *Norton*, the CSC not only had evidence of a particular homosexual overture at Lafayette Park, confirmed by a third party, but a confession of previous homosexual activity. This allowed the court to look beyond issues of evidence and consider the connection between homosexual conduct and the "efficiency of the service." Writing for the U.S. Court of Appeals, Judge Bazelon, also the author of the *Scott* decision, attacked the Civil Service Commission for automatically concluding that a finding of "immorality" constituted "adequate rational cause" for removal. A judgment of morality, Bazelon wrote, "connotes a violation of divine, Olympian, or otherwise universal standards of rectitude" which the commission had "neither the expertise nor the requisite anointment to make." The commission, the court chided, was simply imposing "the prevailing mores of our society." While admitting that homosexual conduct might bear on the efficiency of the service—particularly if the behavior was "notorious"—Bazelon noted that Norton "neither openly flaunts nor carelessly displays" his homosexuality in public. He did not work with the public, and his co-workers were unaware of his "immorality." "We do not doubt that NASA blushes whenever one of its own is caught *in flagrante delicto*," Bazelon wrote, but "an agency cannot support a dismissal as promoting the efficiency of the service merely by turning its head and crying 'shame.'" Since the dismissal effectively imposed a "badge of infamy" upon the dismissed employee, the court demanded a rational connection between an employee's off-duty conduct and his dismissal. Neither NASA nor the CSC had provided one.[55]

The CSC never appealed the *Norton* decision. In lieu of reinstating Norton, they paid him a hundred thousand dollars and provided him with a government pension. Over the next six years they would delay, call for new legislation, and hunt for more favorable judicial decisions, but with the July 1, 1969, *Norton* decision, the CSC had clearly lost the battle. The court had ruled that federal civil servants could no longer be fired solely on the grounds that they were homosexual. Combined with the *Scott* decision, it marked what the *Advocate* called a "homosexual Bill of Rights."[56]

Epilogue

The demise of the federal government's campaign against homosexual civil servants, like its genesis, was a slow process. As decisive as the 1969 U.S. Court of Appeals decision in favor of Clifford Norton and against the civil service seemed, it did not result in an immediate reversal of policy. Fearful that it would lose at the Supreme Court, the Civil Service Commission never appealed the *Norton* decision. But it was not ready to capitulate. It complained that Judge Bazelon's opinion had placed an "unwarranted burden on the executive branch" by requiring proof of a connection between the individual's off-duty misconduct and his government duties. It took advantage of some ambiguity in the decision, which acknowledged that the exclusion of homosexuals might be justified under special circumstances. And, hoping for more favorable decisions, it continued to fight similar cases that were making their way through the judicial process. The commission was rewarded in *Schlegel v. U.S.*, the case of a civilian employee of the army dismissed when his homosexual activity came to light during a re-investigation for an upgraded security clearance. The court sustained Schlegel's dismissal, finding that "the presence of known homosexuals in an executive agency will bring the agency into hatred, ridicule, and con-tempt." With discrepancies between the *Norton* and *Schlegel* decisions, the CSC called on Congress to "clear the air" by passing new legislation con-cerning suitability and security in the civil service.[1]

But Judge Bazelon's demand in the *Norton* decision that the government demonstrate a "rational nexus" between an employee's off-duty conduct and his reliability as a government employee was becoming an important legal precedent, reaffirmed in numerous cases involving an array of pro-scribed behaviors. Relying on *Norton*, a federal court reinstated a Public Health Service official who had been denied a commission for expressing opposition to the Vietnam war. In California a federal court reinstated a San Francisco postal clerk who had been removed for living with a woman who was not his wife.[2] And by 1973 the same court finally forced the Civil Ser-vice Commission to end its exclusion of homosexuals. In deciding a class action suit filed by Donald Hickerson and the San Francisco–based Society for Individual Rights, the court not only reinstated Hickerson to his job a as a clerk-typist with the Department of Agriculture but forbade the com-mission to dismiss other employees for "immoral conduct." In his majority opinion, Judge Alfonso Zirpoli argued that "the notion that it could be an appropriate function of the federal bureaucracy to enforce the majority's conventional moral code of conduct in the private lives of its employees is at war with elementary concepts of liberty, privacy, and diversity." It was time, the court noted, for the CSC to stop disobeying the U.S. Court of Ap-peals order in *Norton*.[3]

A month later, in December 1973, the commission finally began to com-ply by issuing a bulletin proposing revisions to its "suitability" regulation. Acknowledging it could no longer enforce a blanket exclusion, the CSC continued to insist that "particular circumstances" might justify dismiss-ing an employee for homosexual conduct. Although still trying to reserve the right to exclude certain homosexuals, it was clearly fighting a losing battle. "They've been pushed back to the wall in case after case," Kameny observed. It would take another eighteen months for the changes to be-come effective. On July 3, 1975, Frank Kameny received a telephone call from the general counsel of the Civil Service Commission. The commission was issuing new regulations that day, he told Kameny. It had removed just two words from the list of disqualifications for federal government em-ployment: "immoral conduct." As its official press release explained, the CSC would now apply "the same standards in evaluating sexual conduct, whether heterosexual or homosexual." Praising the decision, the *New York Times* editorialized that the Civil Service Commission had struck "an important blow against the glacier of bias that imprisons the vast majority of homosexuals in America."[4]

★

For twenty-five years, the federal government's systematic and aggressive exclusion of gays and lesbians had been fomenting not only frustration but action. In 1950, in California, State Department firings of gay men helped convince Harry Hay to found the first Mattachine Society. In the 1960s Frank Kameny and the Mattachine Society of Washington radicalized the movement as it began a program of social action aimed at changing federal policy. When Clark Polak, a Philadelphia-based gay activist and publisher, explained to readers of a national magazine "what organized homosexuals want," he focused on overturning their exclusion from federal civil and military service. When the Mattachine Society of New York sent questionnaires to 125 state and national candidates during the 1968 election, the first four questions concerned federal employment policies. Speaking before the Democratic National Convention in 1972, New York gay activist Jim Foster denounced the Civil Service Commission for wasting $12 million a year investigating gay civil servants. Because it affected both men and women, the federal government's exclusion served as a unifying force. For over two decades, the struggle with the federal government was a main rallying cry of the movement.[5]

Because the struggle over federal employment policies had no decisive or dramatic conclusion, its importance to the early gay rights movement has been obscured. The *Norton* decision has been overshadowed by an event that took place the same week—the June 1969 riots at the Stonewall Inn in New York's Greenwich Village. Though this event is commonly seen as the beginning of the gay rights movement, by the time those gay, lesbian, and transsexual bar patrons fought a routine police raid, the movement had already won its first major legal victory and had established much of the rhetoric and tactics it would deploy over the next thirty years. Because the Civil Service Commission's reversal of policy did not officially occur until 1975, it has been labeled an achievement of the post-Stonewall generation. Although the commission was influenced by the rising tide of antidiscrimination laws and other gay-supportive measures around the country and in the District of Columbia, the pivotal decision that drove the Civil Service Commission to change its policy was the *Norton* decision of 1969, from a case initially brought in 1964. As historian Marc Stein has argued, the story of the pre- and post-Stonewall gay and lesbian rights movement is "more continuous than we have wanted to believe."[6] Although now overshadowed by the Stonewall riots in New York's Greenwich Village, the White House pickets against federal government discrimination were once seen as the watershed moment in the gay rights struggle. Mainstream news stories on the "newly visible" homosexual community written soon after Stonewall used the pickets at the White House and Kameny's testimony before a congressional committee—along with the riots in New York—as evidence of a new militancy. For more than two decades, the struggle with the civil service was a driving force behind the gay rights movement. Perhaps it is also because the movement succeeded in winning this struggle that its historical importance has been overlooked.[7]

The struggle for workplace equity for lesbians and gay men remains a mainstay of the gay rights movement. What is often forgotten is that ending the federal government's antigay policies was the first part of that battle. No progress could be made in the private sector as long as the federal government continued to consider gay men and lesbians "unsuitable" employees. Prior to 1975, all discussions of antigay employment discrimination, whether by journalists, legal scholars, or activists, began with and focused on federal policy. "There seems to be little likelihood of changing the situation of discrimination in non-federal employment as long as the federal government continues to set its present example," observed Kameny. Not only was the federal government the nation's largest employer, but its policies were imitated and followed by private employers. As Kameny told an audience in New York in 1964, "Prejudiced official attitudes and policies reinforce private discrimination. The private employer, for example, may or may not hire homosexuals if the government *does* hire them; he will *not* hire them if the government does *not*."[8]

Although the reversal of the antigay policies in the federal civil service was ultimately brought about through judicial order, the men and women behind these court cases were the true agents of change—the gay men who acted as plaintiffs, the heterosexual lawyers who defended them, and the activists like Kameny who acted behind the scenes to bring the cases to court. Kameny's strategy of deploying a civil rights rhetoric, building coalitions with other civil liberties groups, and most of all seeking publicity for his cause provided the tools that would allow other disgruntled employees to win in the courts. Without the resources of the MSW, people like Clifford Norton would have joined the long line of dismissed gay civil servants. In the process of fighting the federal government, Kameny and the MSW formulated many of the tactics and strategies that were adopted throughout the movement. Barbara Gittings had been active in homophile circles for several years before Kameny, yet she dates her activism to her encounter with him. "Before I met Frank," she said, "I was going around speaking out of my own experience, but I wasn't really getting anywhere. Frank put everything together in a political sense. My contribution really started with Frank." Gittings would later become the editor of the *Ladder*, the premier lesbian publication of the 1960s.[9] As another movement leader said in 1966, "If the homophile movement, as an active, effective weapon for social change, can claim a father, it would certainly be [Frank Kameny]." More than a decade later, Steve Endean, the movement's first full-time Washington lobbyist, called Kameny "the grandfather" of the movement and praised him by saying, "Kameny . . . has probably done more for lesbian and gay Americans than any other person." The recent chroniclers of the post-Stonewall phase of the movement credited Kameny with "almost single-handedly" forming and popularizing "the ideological foundations of the gay rights movement in the 1960s."[10]

Washington's gay and lesbian activists went on to become one of the most potent political constituencies in the nation's capital. After Congress granted the District of Columbia limited home-rule, local gay and lesbian leaders began to focus on local politics. In 1971, Frank Kameny was one of six candidates to become the District of Columbia's first nonvoting delegate to the House of Representatives. Throughout the campaign, Kameny stressed themes that originated with the Mattachine Society of Washington. "As homosexuals we are fed up with a government that wages a relentless war against us," Kameny insisted. "We are homosexual American citizens. We intend to see to it that the second and third words of that phrase, 'American citizen,' are no longer ignored with regard to us." Although he came in fourth in the six-way race, he succeeded in using the election to increase publicity for his "personal freedoms" platform and to politicize the local gay community. After the election, Kameny's campaign committee reorganized into the Gay Activists Alliance (GAA), a nonpartisan group dedicated to securing "full rights and privileges" of citizenship for the gay and lesbian community of the District of Columbia through "peaceful participation in the political process." The GAA was instrumental in securing passage of the D.C. Human Rights Law in 1973, one of the nation's first laws to ban discrimination against gays and lesbians. To end police entrapment, GAA successfully lobbied to eliminate the city's funding for the Morals Division of the Metropolitan Police Department, thereby denying the Civil Service Commission what had functioned as one of its chief investigative arms.[11] By 1980, after the gay and lesbian community provided the decisive voting margin in Marion Barry's first election as mayor, headlines began asking if Washington had become the "Gay Capital" of America. "Washington is the most comfortable city in the world for gays. This is utopia," Kameny effused. "The police are no problem, we have a strong gay rights law, the local candidates come to us begging for endorsements; this year our gay pride day is a *week*, not a day, and it's a street fair, not a march, and we're celebrating that we *have* [rights] rather than agitating for denied rights."[12]

Crediting Kameny and the Mattachine Society of Washington with a key role in the modern gay rights movement necessarily implicates the federal government's McCarthy era antigay policies in that project as well. If the federal government had not "declared war" on him, as Kameny phrased it, he might have gone on to an illustrious career in the space program and never thought much about gay rights. Certainly in other places and in other ways, gay men and women experienced oppression because of their sexuality. But in 1950s and 1960s Washington, D.C., the policies of the federal government toward gay and lesbian employees so devastated a community that they helped launch a new civil rights struggle.

The irony is that in the 1950s, congressional conservatives claimed to fear that homosexuals constituted a large, powerful cabal that threatened the security of the nation. To counter this threat, they harnessed and expanded the burgeoning national security apparatus to expel homosexuals from the executive branch. This defensive effort became so successful and so routinized within the loyalty/security system that it created organized opposition. Through publicity, lobbying, demonstrations, and litigation, gay men and lesbians succeeded in dismantling the policies designed to exclude them from government service. Thus the policies meant to counter the power and influence of gay civil servants actually fostered the creation of an effective and influential political gay pressure group. The feared deviant bureaucrat who might pass secrets to the enemy or influence policy had now become something even more powerful—the homosexual citizen.

Notes

Note: *The following abbreviations are used to simplify citations in the footnotes.*

BSCA   Bureau of Security and Consular Affairs, U.S. State Department

CHS   Chicago Historical Society

DDE Library   Dwight D. Eisenhower Presidential Library

FEK Papers   Private Papers of Franklin E. Kameny

GLHSNC   Gay and Lesbian Historical Society of Northern California

HST Library   Harry S. Truman Presidential Library

Hoey Committee Report   U.S. Congress, Senate, Committee on Expenditures in the Executive Departments, *Employment of Homosexuals and Other Sex Perverts in Government*, Senate Doc. 241, 81st Cong., 2nd sess., 1950.

Hoey Committee Hearings   U.S. Congress, Senate, Committee on Expenditures in Executive Departments, Investigations Subcommittee, Hearings Pursuant to S. Res. 280, Executive

	Session Transcripts, 81st Cong., 2nd sess., July 14–September 8, 1950, RG 46, NARA.
IGIC	International Gay Information Center Archives, New York Public Library
LBJ Library	Lyndon Baynes Johnson Presidential Library
LC	Library of Congress
NARA	National Archives and Records Administration, Washington, D.C.
NSC	National Security Council
RG 46	Record Group 46, Records of the U.S. Senate
RG 48	Record Group 48, Records of the U.S. Department of Interior
RG 59	Record Group 59, Records of the U.S. Department of State
RG 146	Record Group 146, Records of the U.S. Civil Service Commission
RG 273	Record Group 273, Records of the National Security Council
WHCF	White House Central Files, Confidential Files

Introduction: "Panic on the Potomac"

1. I label the hysteria over homosexuals in government the Lavender Scare to demonstrate its parallels with the second Red Scare. In 1950s culture, lavender was the color commonly associated with homosexuality, as evidenced in references to the "lavender lads" in the State Department, whereas pink connoted fellow traveling and Communist sympathies. See Brooks Martin, "Lavender Skeletons in TV's Closet!" *Confidential*, July 1953, 2–3.

2. Westbrook Pegler, "Fair Enough," *Washington Times-Herald*, June 3, 1950; Elmer Davis, May 19 Radio Transcript, Box 20, Elmer Davis Collection, LC; Wherry quoted in *Congressional Record*, April 25, 1950, 5699; Charles S. Murphy, George M. Elsey, and Stephen J. Spingarn to the president, July 11, 1950, "Internal Security—McCarthy—Charges #4" folder, Box 70, George Elsey Papers, HST Library; Hoffman quoted in *Congressional Record*, March 24, 1950, 4065. Max Lerner called it "the homosexual panic" and the "homosexual scare," but credited unnamed senators for the term "purge of the perverts." Editors at the *New York Post* subtitled his story "Panic on the Potomac." See Max Lerner, "The Washington Sex Story," *New York Post*, July 10, 1950, 4.

3. See Athan Theoharis, *Seeds of Repression: Harry S. Truman and the Origins of McCarthyism* (New York: Quadrangle, 1971); Robert Griffith and Athan Theoharis,

eds., *The Specter: Original Essays in the Cold War and the Origins of McCarthyism* (New York: New Viewpoints, 1974); Robert Griffith, *The Politics of Fear: Joseph R. McCarthy and the Senate*, 2nd ed. (Amherst: University of Massachusetts Press, 1987); David Caute, *The Great Fear: The Anti-Communist Purge under Truman and Eisenhower* (New York: Simon & Schuster, 1978), 273; Donald F. Crosby, S.J., *God, Church, and Flag: Senator Joseph R. McCarthy and the Catholic Church, 1950–1957* (Chapel Hill: University of North Carolina Press, 1978), 3.

4. For a critique of McCarthyism, see Ellen Schrecker, *Many Are the Crimes: McCarthyism in America* (Boston: Little, Brown, 1998), 51, 148–49. For defenses of McCarthyism, see Arthur Herman, *Joseph McCarthy: Reexamining the Life and Legacy of America's Most Hated Senator* (New York: Free Press, 2000); Richard Gid Powers, *Not without Honor: The History of American Anticommunism* (New York: Free Press, 1998); Jacob Weisberg, "Cold War without End," *New York Times Magazine*, November 28, 1999. One of the few defenders of anticommunism to acknowledge the Lavender Scare is John Earl Haines, *Red Scare or Red Menace? American Communism and Anticommunism in the Cold War Era* (Chicago: Ivan R. Dee, 1996), 170.

5. John O'Donnell, "Capitol Stuff," *New York Daily News*, March 27, 1950, C4; *New York Times*, June 15, 1950, 6. Historians who de-emphasize McCarthy's role include Schrecker, *Many Are the Crimes*, and Richard M. Fried, *Nightmare in Red: The McCarthy Era in Perspective* (New York: Oxford University Press, 1990). On speculation about McCarthy's sexuality, see the *New York Post*, July 21, 1950; Nicholas Von Hoffman, *Citizen Cohn: The Life and Times of Roy Cohn* (New York: Bantam Books, 1988); Drew Pearson, *Diaries 1949–1959*, ed. Tyler Abell (New York: Holt, Rinehart, & Winston, 1974), 188–92; and Richard H. Rovere, *Senator Joe McCarthy* (New York: Meridian Books, 1959), 68.

6. Oliver Pilat and William V. Shannon, *New York Post*, September 17, 1951, 2 ff; see also Alfred Friendly, "The Noble Crusade of Senator McCarthy," *Harper's Magazine*, August 1950, 34–35.

7. Rovere, *Senator Joe McCarthy*, 137; Griffith, *Politics of Fear*, 54.

8. Interview with Frank Kameny, October 19, 1991, 21; see also Eric Marcus, *The Struggle for Gay and Lesbian Equal Rights, 1945–1990: An Oral History* (New York: Harper Collins, 1992), 97.

9. *Congressional Record*, April 4, 1950, 4669 and April 19, 1950, 5405; Robert C. Ruark, *New York World Telegram*, March 23, 1950; Max Lerner, "The Washington Sex Story," *New York Post*, July 10, 1950, 4; and "'Scandal' in the State Department," *New York Post*, July 11–22, 1950. Some of these columns were reprinted in Max Lerner, *The Unfinished Country* (New York: Simon & Schuster, 1959), 310–32. On the "deep appreciation of homosexuals" Lerner garnered for these columns, see Sanford Lakoff, *Max Lerner: Pilgrim in the Promised Land* (Chicago: University of Chicago Press, 1998), xx. Marc Stein makes a similar argument about the prolifer-

ation of stories on homosexuality in Philadelphia print media between 1945 and 1960 in *City of Sisterly and Brotherly Loves: Lesbian and Gay Philadelphia, 1945–1972* (Chicago: University of Chicago Press, 2000), 116.

10. Nat Finney, "State Department Is Dealing Quietly with Morals Problem," *Buffalo Evening News*, April 23, 1953, found in "Homosexuals in Civil Service" vertical file, Kinsey Institute.

11. *Washington Times-Herald*, April 24, 1950, 1; *New York Times*, April 25, 1950, 5; *Washington Daily News*, June 20, 1950, 7.

12. Governmental official, congressional leader, and security officer quoted in U.S. Congress, House, *Department of State Appropriations for 1952*, Hearings, Subcommittee of the Committee on Appropriations, 82nd Cong., 1st sess., March 2, 1951, 397–98. Though no alcoholics had been separated for security reasons, two had been separated by the Office of Personnel. For one historian who claims "alcoholism was the leading disqualifier," see John Earl Haynes, *Red Scare or Red Menace?: American Communism and Anticommunism in the Cold War Era* (Chicago: Ivan R. Dee, 1996), 170.

13. Peter Grose, *Gentleman Spy: The Life of Allen Dulles* (New York: Houghton Mifflin, 1994), 153–54.

14. "The Abnormal," *Time*, April 17, 1950, 86; Charles Jackson, *The Lost Weekend* (New York: Farrar & Rinehart, 1944), 144; see also John W. Crowley, *The White Logic: Alcoholism and Gender in American Modernist Fiction* (Amherst: University of Massachusetts Press, 1994); Mark Connelly, *Deadly Closets: The Fiction of Charles Jackson* (Lanham, MD: University Press of America, 2001); Kenneth Lewes, *The Psychoanalytic Theory of Male Homosexuality* (New York: Quartet, 1988), 141–47; Vito Russo, *The Celluloid Closet: Homosexuality in the Movies* (New York: Harper & Row, 1987), 96–97.

15. *New York Times*, December 20, 1951.

16. Marlowe, "Homos on the March: The Day They Picketed the White House," *Confidential*, October 1965, 60.

17. See Elaine Tyler May, *Homeward Bound: American Families in the Cold War Era* (New York: Basic Books, 1988), 92–113; Michael Paul Rogin, *Ronald Reagan, the Movie, and Other Episodes in Political Demonology* (Berkeley and Los Angeles: University of California Press, 1987); Robert J. Corber, *In the Name of National Security: Hitchcock, Homophobia, and the Political Construction of Gender in Postwar America* (Durham, NC: Duke University Press, 1993); Stephen J. Whitfield, *The Culture of the Cold War* (Baltimore: Johns Hopkins University Press, 1991), 43–45. Historians and social scientists from the late 1950s and early 1960s were also attentive to the ways in which McCarthy and his colleagues constructed their image of the subversive to include hints of homosexuality. See Daniel Bell, ed., *The Radical Right: The New American Right Expanded and Updated* (Garden City, NY: Doubleday, 1963), 119; Richard Hofstadter, *The Paranoid Style in American Politics and Other Essays*

(New York: Knopf, 1965), and *Anti-Intellectualism in American Life* (New York: Random House, 1962), 41; Michael Paul Rogin, *The Intellectuals and McCarthy: The Radical Specter* (Cambridge, MA: MIT Press, 1967).

18. John D'Emilio, *Sexual Politics, Sexual Communities: The Making of the Homosexual Minority, 1940–1970* (Chicago: University of Chicago Press, 1983), 40–53; see also John D'Emilio, *Making Trouble: Essays on Gay History, Politics, and the University* (New York: Routledge, 1992); George Chauncey, *Gay New York: Gender, Urban Culture, and the Making of a Gay Male World, 1890–1940* (New York: Basic Books, 1994); Allan Bérubé, *Coming Out under Fire: The History of Gay Men and Women in World War II* (New York: Free Press, 1990); Elizabeth Lapovsky Kennedy and Madeline Davis, *Boots of Leather, Slippers of Gold: The History of a Lesbian Community* (New York: Routledge, 1993).

19. Gayle Rubin, "Thinking Sex: Notes for a Radical Theory of the Politics of Sexuality," in *The Lesbian and Gay Studies Reader*, ed. Henry Abelove, Michele Aina Barale, and David M. Halperin (New York: Routledge, 1993), 3–44; Michael Paul Rogin, *Ronald Reagan, the Movie and Other Episodes in Political Demonology* (Berkeley and Los Angeles: University of California Press, 1987).

20. Robert Dean, *Imperial Brotherhood: Gender and the Making of Cold War Foreign Policy* (Amherst: University of Massachusetts Press, 2001); Geoffrey S. Smith, "National Security and Personal Isolation: Sex, Gender, and Disease in the Cold-War United States," *International History Review* 14 (May 1992): 307–37; Seth Jacobs, "Our System Demands the Supreme Being: The U.S. Religious Revival and the 'Diem Experiment,' 1945–55," *Diplomatic History* 25, no. 4 (fall 2001): 589–624.

21. Anthony Summers, *Official and Confidential: The Secret Life of J. Edgar Hoover* (New York: G. P. Putnam's Sons, 1993); Athan Theoharis, *J. Edgar Hoover, Sex, and Crime: An Historical Antidote* (Chicago: Ivan R. Dee, 1995). Former congressional investigator quoted in interview with Francis Flanagan, April 11, 1996; Ronald Kessler, *The Bureau: The Secret History of the FBI* (New York: St. Martin's Press, 2002), 107–11.

22. "Sex Hysteria," *Bulletin of the Association for Psychiatric Treatment of Offenders* 1, no. 3 (July–August 1951); see also the *Daily Compass*, July 25, 1951, 18.

23. Curt Gentry, *J. Edgar Hoover: The Man and the Secrets* (New York: W. W. Norton, 1991), 310.

24. Chauncey, *Gay New York*, 27; Leisa D. Meyer, *Creating G.I. Jane: Sexuality and Power in the Women's Army Corps during World War II* (New York: Columbia University Press, 1996), 156.

Chapter One: Puerifoy's Revelation

1. *Congressional Record*, February 20, 1950, pp. 1961, 1979; among the historians who quote McCarthy out of context, stripping his statement of its homophobic

reference, see Ellen Schrecker, *Many Are the Crimes: McCarthyism in America* (Boston: Little, Brown, 1998), 152.

2. Statement by Deputy Undersecretary Peurifoy, February 13, 1950, *Department of State Bulletin* 22: 327; U.S. Congress, Senate, Subcommittee of the Committee on Appropriations, *Departments of State, Justice, Commerce, and the Judiciary Appropriations for 1951*, 81st Cong., 2nd sess., February 28, 1950, 581–603.

3. John D'Emilio, the first historian to identify the significance of Peurifoy's revelation, labeled it a "chance revelation"; see his *Sexual Politics, Sexual Communities: The Making of the Homosexual Minority, 1940–1970* (Chicago: University of Chicago Press, 1983), 41.

4. *New York Times*, April 19, 1950; *New York World Telegram*, March 23, 1950; *Congressional Record*, April 4, 1950, 4669; *New York Post*, July 21, 1950; *Washington-Times Herald*, July 27, 1950, 2; transcript, "Meet the Press," April 14, 1950, "Internal Security—McCarthy Charges, Section 2" folder, Box 69, George Elsey Papers, HST Library. The Peurifoy revelation is cited in innumerable articles and speeches. Among the books which refer to the ninety-one, see John T. Flynn, *While You Slept: Our Tragedy in Asia and Who Made It* (Boston: Western Islands, 1951), 22; Jack Lait and Lee Mortimer, *Washington Confidential* (New York: Crown, 1951), 125; D. J. West, *Homosexuality* (London: Gerald Duckworth, 1955), 36.

5. *Washington Star*, April 2, 1950, C-5; *New York Daily News*, March 27 and 29, 1950; Constantine Brown, "This Changing World," *Washington Star*, n.d., quoted in *Appendix to the Congressional Record*, March 23, 1950, A2136. McCarthy's papers and correspondence at Marquette University remain closed to the public.

6. Noah Mason, *Appendix to the Congressional Record*, May 2, 1950, A3212; *Washington Sunday Star*, April 2, 1950, reprinted in the *Appendix to the Congressional Record*, April 3, 1950, A2492.

7. *Green Bay Press-Gazette* columnist and Thomas Coleman quoted in Michael O'Brien, *McCarthy and McCarthyism in Wisconsin* (Columbia: University of Missouri Press, 1980), 101–2. After citing an interview with Wayne Hood, chairman of Wisconsin Republican Voluntary Committee, suggesting that state party leaders were more concerned about sex perverts than Communists, O'Brien never mentions the issue again.

8. For the June 1947 letter to Secretary Marshall, see the *Congressional Record*, July 24, 1950, 10806; and Caute, *Great Fear*, 26. On the use of the McCarran rider against homosexuals, see *Washington Evening Star*, March 26, 1950, A-19, and chap. 4 below.

9. *Washington Star*, October 7, 1947, 1, and March 13, 1953, A-2; "Public Reaction to the Department's Security Principles," October 31, 1947, Box 20, E 568N Reports on Public Opinion on the State Department, 1944–1963, RG 59, NARA. On oversight hearings, see *Congressional Record*, April 19, 1950, 5405; U.S. Congress, House, Subcommittee of the Committee on Appropriations, *Department of State*

Appropriations for 1951, 81st Cong., 2nd sess., January 20, 1950, 673; and U.S. Congress, House, Subcommittee of the Committee on Appropriations, *Department of State Appropriations for 1952*, 82nd Cong., 1st sess., March 2, 1951.

10. Hugh Morrow, "He's De-Snobbing the State Department," *Saturday Evening Post*, August 27, 1949, 25 ff.

11. *Congressional Record*, June 27, 1950, 9294–95; and July 24, 1950, 10843; Richard H. Rovere, *The New Yorker*, April 22, 1950, 106; "New Stripes," *Time*, July 24, 1950, 18. Peurifoy went on to hold sensitive Cold War positions for the State Department. He was appointed ambassador to Greece in 1950 and Guatemala in 1953, where he played a prominent role in the overthrow of the Arbenz government, considered a "communist dictatorship" by the Eisenhower administration. He died in an automobile accident in Thailand in 1955. See Stephen C. Schlesinger et al., *Bitter Fruit: The Story of the American Coup in Guatemala* (Boston: Harvard University Press, 1999), 132–41.

12. Douglass Cater, "Senator Styles Bridges and His Far-Flung Constituents," *Reporter*, July 20, 1954, 8–21; James J. Kiepper, *Styles Bridges: Yankee Senator* (Sugar Hill, NH: Phoenix Publishing, 2001); Edwin R. Bayley, "McCarthy Charges 'Too Wild' at Start, Sen. Bridges Says," no newspaper title, April 16, 1950, Folder 4, Box 37, Rauh Collection, LC.

13. Robert Griffith, *The Politics of Fear: Joseph R. McCarthy and the Senate*, 2nd ed. (Amherst: University of Massachusetts Press, 1987), 40–41, 52–74; Richard Rovere, *Senator Joe McCarthy* (New York: Meridian Books, 1959), 131; Statement by John E. Peurifoy, May 2, 1950, *Department of State Bulletin*, 22: 752–53; Robert E. Lee, *In the Public Interest: The Life of Robert Emmet Lee from the FBI to the FCC* (Lanham, MD: University Press of America, 1996), 117–27.

14. *Congressional Record*, March 27, 1950, 4118–21; John O'Donell, "Capitol Stuff," *New York Daily News*, March 30, 1950.

15. *New York Times*, March 16, 1950. A critic of FDR, Krock was involved in the forced resignation of Undersecretary of State Sumner Welles in 1943 because of homosexual allegations. See Benjamin Welles, *Sumner Welles: FDR's Global Strategist* (New York: St. Martin's Press, 1997), 345–46; *Washington Times-Herald*, May 11, 1950, 4.

16. Transcript, "Meet the Press," April 14, 1950, "Internal Security—McCarthy Charges, Section 2" folder, Box 69, George Elsey Papers, HST Library.

17. Caroline H. Keith, *"For Hell and a Brown Mule": The Biography of Senator Millard E. Tydings* (Lanham, MD: Madison Books, 1991), 13; *Congressional Quarterly's Guide to Congress*, 4th ed. (Washington, DC: Congressional Quarterly, 1991), 239; Senate, Subcommittee of the Committee on Foreign Relations, *State Department Employee Loyalty Investigation*, 81st Cong., 2nd sess., March 8–June 28, 1950, 1–13. See also *Washington Daily News*, March 9, 1950, 5; *Washington Post*, March 9, 1950, 1; *Time*, March 20, 1950, 21; Griffith, *Politics of Fear*, 66. On Panuch, see William

Buckley and L. Brent Bozell, *McCarthy and His Enemies: The Record and Its Meaning* (Chicago: Henry Regnery, 1954), 9–17.

18. *Congressional Record*, April 24, 1950, 5574–77; *Washington Star*, April 25, 1950, A-9; *New York Times*, April 25, 1950, 5.

19. *Congressional Record*, April 25, 1950, 5697–5711; *New York Times*, April 26, 1950, 1.

20. *Washington Daily News*, March 14, 1950, 7; *New York Times*, March 15, 1950, 1; L. D. B. to Secretary of State, April 3, 1950, Box 487, Decimal Files 1950–1954, RG 59, NARA, reprinted in *Foreign Relations of the United States, 1952–1954*, vol. 1, pt. 2: 139. The original memo contains many typographical errors, all of which were corrected by hand; but "homogeneity" was not changed. This may reflect the State Department's discomfort with the issue and preference for euphemisms.

21. U.S. Congress, Senate, *State Department Employee Loyalty Investigation*, Report no. 2108, Committee on Foreign Relations, 81st Cong., 2nd sess., July 20, 1950; Jenner quoted in *Congressional Record*, July 21, 1950, 10792, and July 24, 1950, 10816; Richard M. Fried, *Men against McCarthy* (New York: Columbia University Press, 1976), 76–77; Holmes Alexander, *Los Angeles Times*, August 2, 1950. For a critique of the Tydings committee's narrow focus, see Griffith, *Politics of Fear*, 106–11.

22. David Lloyd to Stephen Spingarn, July 3, 1950, "Sex Perversion" folder, Box 32, WHCF, HST Library; *New York Daily News*, March 30, 1950; Charles S. Murphy, George M. Elsey, and Stephen J. Spingarn to the president, July 11, 1950, "Internal Security—McCarthy—Charges #4" folder, Box 70, George Elsey Papers, HST Library.

23. *Chicago Daily Tribune*, April 28, 1950, 10; *Washington Daily News*, April 25, 1950, quoted in the *Congressional Record*, May 2, 1950, 6128.

24. S. J. Spingarn, "Memorandum of Pros and Cons on the Proposal to Establish a Commission on Internal Security and Individual Rights," June 26, 1950, "Internal Security Files, Nimitz Commission" folder, Box 70, George Elsey Papers, HST Library; McCarthy quoted in Elmer Davis, April 4, 1950 Radio Transcript, Box 20, Elmer Davis Collection, LC. On the proposed commission, see Fried, *Men against McCarthy*, 161–68; Griffith, *Politics of Fear*, 109–14. See also Murphy, Elsey, Spingarn to the president, July 11, 1950; and S. J. Spingarn, "Proposal for Presidential Commission on Internal Security and Individual Rights," May 22, 1950, both in "Internal Security—McCarthy—Charges #4" folder, Box 70, George Elsey Papers, HST Library.

25. *Congressional Record*, March 31, 1950, 4527–28, 4535, and April 4, 1950, 4669; *Washington Times-Herald*, April 1, 1950, 2.

26. Dewey's attack reported in *New York Times*, May 5, 1950, 1; Wherry quoted in *Washington Times-Herald*, March 31, 1950; Sokolsky quoted in *Appendix to the Congressional Record*, April 4, 1950, A2545; cartoon in *New York Daily News*, March

30, 1950 and *Washington Times-Herald*, March 31, 1950; Jenner, *Congressional Record*, April 25, 1950, 5704.

27. *Muncie (Indiana) Star*, April 1, 1950, quoted in *Appendix to the Congressional Record*, April 4, 1950, A2519.

28. Margaret Chase Smith, Hoey Committee Testimony, 2242; *Washington Post*, March 17, 1950; *Washington Times-Herald*, March 27, 1950; Catholic newspaper cited is *Brooklyn Tablet*, June 10, 1950, 1, quoted in Crosby, *God, Church, and Flag*, 3; on the circulation and political affiliations of Washington papers, see Edwin R. Bayley, *Joe McCarthy and the Press* (New York: Pantheon, 1981), 151.

29. Allen Weinstein, *Perjury: The Hiss-Chambers Case* (New York: Knopf, 1978), 118–19, 166, 400, 582–84.

30. One psychiatrist quoted in Gilbert Van Tassel Hamilton, *On the Cause of Homosexuality: Two Essays, the Second in Reply to the First* (New York: Breaking Point, 1950), 30; the romantic obsession argument comes from Meyer A. Zeligs, *Friendship and Fratricide: An Analysis of Whittaker Chambers and Alger Hiss* (New York: Viking Press, 1967); interview with Murrey Marder, October 1996.

31. Whittaker Chambers FBI File #74-1333-2152, February 8, 1949; Robert C. Ruark, *Washington Daily News*, March 23, 1950, 45. See also Sam Tanenhaus, *Whittaker Chambers* (New York: Random House, 1997), 343–45.

32. For references to homosexual "cells," see the *Washington Daily News*, March 16, 1950, and March 17, 1950, 46; Jack Lait and Lee Mortimer, *U.S.A. Confidential* (New York: Crown, 1952), 52. Ralph S. Brown refers to "colonies of homosexuals" in *Loyalty and Security: Employment Tests in the United States* (New Haven, CT: Yale University Press, 1958), 258.

33. Hoey Committee Report; John McPartland, *Sex in Our Changing World* (New York: Rinehart, 1947), quoted in *New York Mattachine Newsletter*, November 1968. On Communists, see Burnham, *Web of Subversion*.

34. Michael Paul Rogin, *Ronald Reagan, the Movie and Other Episodes in Political Demonology* (Berkeley and Los Angeles: University of California Press, 1987), xiii.

35. Arthur Schlesinger Jr., *The Vital Center: The Politics of Freedom* (Boston: Houghton Mifflin, 1949), 127; *Congressional Record*, March 31, 1950, 4528; Gore Vidal, *The City and the Pillar*, rev. ed. (New York: E. P. Dutton, 1965), 156.

36. R. G. Waldeck, "Homosexual International," *Human Events*, April 16, 1952, 1. For other places where this article appeared, see *Congressional Record*, May 1, 1952, A2652; *Human Events*, September 29, 1960; and Bryton Barron, *The Untouchable State Department* (Springfield, VA: Crestwood Books, 1963), 54–58.

37. Hollister Barnes, "I Am Glad I Am Homosexual," *One*, August, 1958. This conflation of the emotional and sexual comradeship of gay men and the political comradeship of Communists dates back to at least the 1930s and discussions by literary critics of the writings of Walt Whitman. See Berry Werth, *The Scarlet Professor: Newton Arvin* (New York: Nan A. Talese, 2001), 65–75.

38. "Homintern" discussed in Patrick Higgins, *A Queer Reader: 2500 Years of Homosexuality* (New York: New Press, 1993), 287; "powerful coterie" from Alfred Town, "Homosexuality in American Culture: The New Taste in Literature," *American Mercury*, August 1951, 3–9; one commentator quoted in Arthur Guy Mathews, "Homosexuality Is Stalin's Atom Bomb to Destroy America," *Physical Culture*, April 1953, 13; see also "The Lavender Skeletons in TV's Closet," *Confidential*, July 53; "Why They Call Broadway the 'Gay' White Way," *TipOff*, April 1956, reprinted in Martin Bauml Duberman, *About Time: Exploring the Gay Past* (New York: Gay Presses of New York, 1986), 187–90.

39. James D. Steakley, "Iconography of a Scandal: Political Cartoons and the Eulenburg Affair in Wilhelmin Germany," in *Hidden from History: Reclaiming the Gay and Lesbian Past*, Martin Duberman, Martha Vicinus, and George Chauncey Jr., eds. (New York: New American Library, 1989), 233–57; Westbrook Pegler, *Washington Times-Herald*, April 16, 1950.

40. Kurt D. Singer, *The Men in the Trojan Horse* (Boston: Beacon Press, 1953); U.S. Civil Service Commission, "Report of Investigation," April 20–23, 1958, Madeleine Tress FBI File #133-153.

41. McCarthy speech reprinted in *Congressional Record*, February 20, 1950, 1954; "free love" from Lait and Mortimer, *U.S.A. Confidential*, 52; "bureaus of free love" from Samuel Saloman, *Red War on the Family* (New York, 1922); on FBI agents questioning marriage views, see Eleanor Bontecou, *The Federal Loyalty-Security Program* (Ithaca, NY: Cornell University Press, 1953), 141; Montgomery quoted in *Washington Times-Herald*, September 10, 1950, 5; *Congressional Record*, March 31, 1950, 4528. On the history of homosexuality in the Soviet Union, see Simon Karlinsky, "Russia's Gay Literature and Culture: The Impact of the October Revolution," in *Hidden from History*, ed. Duberman, Vicinus, and Chauncey, 347–64; and Daniel Healey, *Homosexual Desire in Revolutionary Russia: The Regulation of Sexual and Gender Dissent* (Chicago: University of Chicago Press, 2002).

42. Joe McCarthy to the editors of the *Saturday Evening Post*, August 8, 1950, reprinted in *Congressional Record*, August 8, 1950, 11979; see also *Washington Times-Herald*, August 9, 1950, 5; Edwin R. Bayley, *Joe McCarthy and the Press* (New York: Pantheon, 1981), 160–63.

43. John Koch to Carlisle Humelsine, March 31, 1951, "John Wayne Williams," 123-Personnel File, RG 59, NARA; Delmar Hill to Harry Truman, March 28, 1950, "Subcommittee on Loyalty of State Department Employees—Misc.," OF 419-K, WHCF, HST Library.

44. Lait and Mortimer, *U.S.A. Confidential*, 44; Mathews, "Homosexuality Is Stalin's Atom Bomb," 12–13.

45. Max Lerner, *New York Post*, July 17, 1950, quoted in Jonathan Ned Katz, *Gay American History: Lesbians and Gay Men in the U.S.A.* (New York: Thomas Y. Crowell, 1976), 95.

46. Max Lerner, "The Washington Sex Story," *New York Post*, July 10, 1950.

47. Interview with Ramon G. and "Patrick W." February 10, 1997. Similar views are expressed in Dr. Israel J. Gerber, *Man on a Pendulum: A Case History of an Invert* (New York: American Press, 1955), 202, 241.

Chapter Two: "This Used to Be a Very Gay City"

1. Ladd Forrester (pseudonym), "Washington in the 1930s: An Opportunity to Escape," *Washington Blade*, August 1, 1986, 1.

2. George Chauncey, *Gay New York: Gender, Urban Culture, and the Making of a Gay Male World, 1890–1940* (New York: Basic Books, 1994); John D'Emilio, *Making Trouble: Essays on Gay History, Politics, and the University* (New York: Routledge, 1992), 3–16 ("Capitalism and Gay Identity"); Elizabeth Lapovsky Kennedy and Madeline Davis, *Boots of Leather, Slippers of Gold: The History of a Lesbian Community* (New York: Routledge, 1993).

3. Population statistics and government economist quoted from D.C. History Curriculum Project, *City of Magnificent Intentions: A History of the District of Columbia* (Washington, DC: Intact, 1987), 355, 419, 439; 5,000-a-week figure from David Brinkley, *Washington Goes to War* (New York: Ballantine Books, 1988), 106; "another writer" quoted in Federal Writer's Project, *The WPA Guide to Washington, D.C.* (New York: Pantheon, 1942), 9; "Washington Ranks Ninth among American Cities," *Washington Daily News*, July 12, 1950; "Boom Town" quoted in Constance McLaughlin Green, *Washington, A History of the Capital, 1800–1950,* (Princeton, NJ: Princeton University Press, 1962), 393, 444. See also Carl Abbott, *Political Terrain: Washington, D.C., from Tidewater Town to Global Metropolis* (Chapel Hill: University of North Carolina Press, 1999).

4. Paul P. Van Riper, *History of the United States Civil Service* (Evanston, IL: Row, Peterson, 1958), 98–110, 241; Cindy Aron, *Ladies and Gentlemen of the Civil Service: Middle-Class Workers in Victorian America* (New York: Oxford University Press, 1987), 107–9; Desmond King, *Separate and Unequal: Black Americans and the U.S. Federal Government* (Oxford: Clarendon Press, 1995).

5. Aron, *Ladies and Gentlemen of the Civil Service,* 5–25; Margery Davies, *Woman's Place Is at the Typewriter: Office Work and Office Workers 1870–1930* (Philadelphia: Temple University Press, 1982); statistics quoted in Margaret C. Rung, "Paternalism and Pink Collars: Gender and Federal Employee Relations, 1941–50," *Business History Review* 71 (autumn 1997): 383; Anderson quoted in Margaret C. Rung, *Servants of the State: Managing Diversity and Democracy in the Federal Workforce, 1933–1953* (Athens: University of Georgia Press, 2002), 40; on the Classification Act, see Van Riper, *History of the United States Civil Service,* 260; tabloid journalist quoted in Jack Lait and Lee Mortimer, *Washington Confidential* (New York: Crown, 1951), 98–105.

6. David K. Johnson, "The Kids of Fairytown: Gay Male Culture on Chicago's

Near North Side in the 1930s," in *Creating a Place for Ourselves: Lesbian, Gay and Bisexual Community Histories*, ed. Brett Beemyn (New York: Routledge, 1997), 97–118; Margaret T. McFadden, "'America's Boy Friend Who Can't Get a Date': Gender, Race, and the Cultural Work of the Jack Benny Program, 1932–1946," *Journal of American History* 80 (June 1993): 128–29; Allan Bérubé, *Coming Out under Fire: The History of Gay Men and Women in World War II* (New York: Free Press, 1990), 57–66.

7. Ina Russell, ed., *Jeb and Dash: A Diary of a Gay Life, 1918–1945* (Boston: Faber & Faber, 1993), 59, 192. The story of "John Edward Collins" is told in Israel J. Gerber, *Man on a Pendulum: A Case History of an Invert* (New York: American Press, 1955), 189–92; Robert L. Thomas to One, Inc., February 17, 1955, "Washington, D.C." clippings file, One Institute. *Man on a Pendulum*, from the Library of Congress Rare Book room, is "presented by" Dr. Gerber, a rabbi and "religious counselor," as the narrative of a man cured of his homosexuality. The first-person account by the gay man, "John Edward Collins," ends not with a renunciation of homosexuality but a plea for societal and religious understanding.

8. Although no statistics are available to determine the gay population of Washington, D.C., even today, in the first U.S. census to ask about unmarried couples in 1990, Washington ranked as the second gayest city in the United States, after San Francisco. Nineteen percent of D.C. households with unmarried "partners" (excluding "roommates") were same-sex. The average percentage of same-sex households in the twenty largest U.S. cities was only 9 percent (*Washington Blade*, June 24, 1994, 1).

9. Russell, ed., *Jeb and Dash*, 63, 82, 141–50; Hoey Committee Report, 10.

10. Russell, ed., *Jeb and Dash*, 59, 227; Gerber, *Man on a Pendulum*, 189–92.

11. Irving C. Ross, "Sexual Hypochondria and Perversion of the Genesic Instinct," *Journal of Nervous and Mental Disease*, November 1892, 799–807, quoted in Jonathan Ned Katz, *Gay American History: Lesbians and Gay Men in the U.S.A.* (New York: Thomas Y. Crowell, 1976), 42; Alexander quoted in Russell, ed., *Jeb and Dash*, 42, 51, 62, and in Brett Beemyn, "A Queer Capital: Lesbian, Gay and Bisexual Life in Washington, D.C., 1890–1955" (Ph.D. diss., University of Iowa, 1997), 22. For one gay novel that refers to Lafayette Park, see Robert Scully, *Scarlet Pansy* (New York: William Faro, 1932), 165–70; the Washington exposé is Lait and Mortimer, *Washington Confidential*, 35, 118.

12. Baron Frederick von Steuben, a close aide to Prussia's King Frederick II, was accused of "taking familiarity with young boys." The resulting scandal was among the reasons he came to America to serve as drill master for the colonial troops in the Revolutionary War. It is unlikely that the men using the park in the twentieth century were aware of this historical coincidence. See Randy Shilts, *Conduct Unbecoming: Gays and Lesbians in the U.S. Military* (New York: St. Martin's Press, 1993), 7–10.

13. Russell, ed., *Jeb and Dash*, 62.

14. Chauncey, *Gay New York*, 179; "Lafayette Park Has Own Rich History," *Los Angeles Times*, December 8, 1977; "Be Seated, Lovers, on a 168-ft. Park Bench!" *Washington Times-Herald*, May 21, 1950, 28.

15. Ladd Forrester (pseudonym), "Rollerskating 'Round the 30s Grapevine in D.C.," *Washington Blade*, September 26, 1986, 1.

16. Russell, ed., *Jeb and Dash*, 30–32.

17. Russell, ed., *Jeb and Dash*, 139; interview with Charles B., September 1980, Gregory Sprague Collection, CHS. On rooming-house districts, see Joanne Meyerowitz, *Women Adrift: Independent Wage Earners in Chicago 1880–1930* (Chicago: University of Chicago Press, 1988); David Johnson, "The Kids of Fairytown." On the YMCA, see Chauncey, *Gay New York*, 151–58, and John Donald Gustav-Wrathall, *Take the Young Stranger by the Hand: Same-Sex Relations and the YMCA* (Chicago: University of Chicago Press, 1998); the G Street Y made national headlines as a gay hangout after the 1964 arrest of LBJ aide Walter Jenkins in the basement men's room.

18. New York gay bars in the 1930s experienced a major crackdown through enforcement of liquor laws forbidding licensed establishments from becoming "disorderly." No similar attempts at closing D.C. gay bars seem to have occurred, though an examination of the D.C. alcoholic beverage control board records is warranted. See Chauncey, *Gay New York*, 335–47; Brinkley, *Washington Goes to War*, 229; Brett Beemyn, "A Queer Capital: Race, Class, Gender and the Changing Social Landscape of Washington's Gay Communities, 1940–1955," in *Creating a Place for Ourselves: Lesbian, Gay and Bisexual Community Histories*, ed. Brett Beemyn. (New York: Routledge, 1997), 184–85.

19. The Horseshoe was at 1123 Seventeenth Street. After 1944 it was known as David's Grill (Ladd Forrester, *Washington Blade*, September 5, 1986, 1); interview with Henry Yaffe, March 1997. See also the Rainbow History Project at www.rainbowhistory.org.

20. Forrester, *Washington Blade*, September 5, 1986, 1; Haviland Ferris, *Washington Blade*, September 11, 1980, 5, and October 1, 1982; Beemyn, "Queer Capital" (Ph.D. diss.), 30–31. Haviland Ferris is a pseudonym for poet John Davis; see Haviland Ferris, *Runes for Faring Forth* (Champaign, IL: Finial Press, 1975).

21. Forrester, *Washington Blade*, September 5, 1986, 1; Ferris, *Washington Blade*, September 11, 1980, 5; and October 1, 1982.

22. Ferris, *Washington Blade*, October 1, 1982; Russell, ed., *Jeb and Dash*, 60–66, 99, 154.

23. Bérubé, *Coming Out under Fire*, 113; Russell, ed., *Jeb and Dash*, 261–83. On lesbians in the military during the war, see Leisa D. Meyer, *Creating G.I. Jane: Sexuality and Power in the Women's Army Corps during World War II* (New York: Columbia University Press, 1996), 148–78.

24. Green, *Washington: A History*, 472; David Brinkley, *David Brinkley: A Memoir*

(New York: Ballantine, 1995); *The More the Merrier* (dir. George Stevens, 1943); John Dos Passos, *State of the Nation* (New York: Houghton Mifflin, 1943), 166.

25. Gore Vidal, *Palimpsest: A Memoir* (New York: Random House, 1995), 101; Allan M. Brandt, *No Magic Bullet: A Social History of Venereal Disease in the United States Since 1880*, expanded ed. (New York: Oxford University Press, 1987), 170–74.

26. Interview with Madeleine Tress, November 11, 1998; interview with Peter Morris and Jack Frey, January 20, 1997; interview with Frank Kameny, October 19, 1991; U.S. Congress, House, Committee on D.C., *Crime and Law Enforcement in the District of Columbia*, 81st Cong., 2nd sess., February 27, 1950, 632.

27. On Kinsey sales and publicity, see David Halberstam, *The Fifties* (New York: Villard Books, 1993), 272–81; Alfred Kinsey, Wardell Pomeroy, and Clyde Martin, *Sexual Behavior in the Human Male* (Philadelphia: W. B. Saunders, 1948), 623, 659.

28. Edmund Bergler, "The Myth of a New National Disease," *Psychiatric Quarterly* 22 (1948): 86; Donald Porter Geddes and Enid Curie, eds., *About the Kinsey Report: Observations by Eleven Experts on* Sexual Behavior in the Human Male, (New York: New American Library, 1948), 109–10.

29. Samuel Steward, oral history interview, July 2, 1983, GLHSNC; Harry Hay, *Radically Gay: Gay Liberation in the Words of Its Founder*, ed. Will Roscoe (Boston: Beacon Press, 1996), 61.

30. Vidal, *Palimpsest*, 153; Burns and *New York Times* quoted in Roger Austen, *Playing the Game: The Homosexual Novel in America* (Indianapolis: Bobbs-Merrill, 1977), 110, 94; "one writer" quoted in Gilbert Van Tassel Hamilton, *On the Cause of Homosexuality: Two Essays, the Second in Reply to the First* (New York: Breaking Point, 1950), 23; critic quoted in *New York Times Book Review*, September 10, 1950, 33; see also Gore Vidal, *The City and the Pillar* (New York: E. P. Dutton, 1948).

31. John Cheever, *The Journals of John Cheever* (New York: Knopf, 1991), 157.

32. Fay quoted in *Washington Post*, November 7, 1948; Hoover quoted in R. K. McNickle, "Control of Sex Offenses," *Editorial Research Reports*, December 15, 1949; J. Edgar Hoover, "How Safe Is Your Daughter?" *American Magazine* 144 (July 1947): 32. For reporting of sex crimes, see *Washington Evening Star*, September 29, 1947, A-2, February 14, 1948, A-8, March 7, 1950, A-12, and February 24, 1955. See also George Chauncey, "The Postwar Sex Crime Panic," in *True Stories From the American Past*, ed. William Graebner (New York: McGraw-Hill, 1995), 160–78; Estelle B. Freedman, "'Uncontrolled Desires': The Response to the Sexual Psychopath, 1920–1960," in *Passion and Power: Sexuality in History*, ed. Kathy Peiss and Christina Simmons (Philadelphia: Temple University Press, 1989), 199–225; Neil Miller, *Sex Crime Panic: A Journey to the Paranoid Heart of the 1950s* (New York: Alyson Books, 2002).

33. Howard Whitman, "Terror in Washington," *Collier's*, June 24, 1950, 20 f;

Washington Star, July 13, 1946; April 11, August 23, 26, 27, 29, 1947; *Washington Post*, August 27, 1947.

34. *Washington Star*, August 23, 1947, February 10, 1948; U.S. Congress, House, Committee on D.C., *Law Enforcement in District of Columbia*, 81st Cong., 2nd sess., February 27, 1950, 620. On the concept of "trade," see Chauncey, *Gay New York*, 16–22.

35. U.S. Congress, House, Committee on the District of Columbia, *H.R. 2937 and H.R. 5264, Criminal Sexual Psychopaths*, February 20, 1948, 69–70, in Case File 40-17-A, Committee on Government Operations, Permanent Subcommittee on Investigations, RG 46, NARA.

36. Vito Russo, *The Celluloid Closet: Homosexuality in the Movies*, rev. ed. (New York: Harper & Row, 1987), 92–94; on Hitchcock's use of homosexual characters generally, see Robert J. Corber, *In the Name of National Security: Hitchcock, Homophobia, and the Political Construction of Gender in Postwar America* (Durham, NC: Duke University Press, 1993).

37. U.S. Congress, Senate, *Providing for the Treatment of Sexual Psychopaths in the District of Columbia*, Report no. 1377, 80th Cong., 2nd sess., May 21, 1948; Public Law 615, 80th Congress. The section of the law outlawing sodomy was only repealed in 1993, after years of lobbying by gay and lesbian activists (*Washington Blade*, September 17, 1993, 1).

38. *Washington Star*, September 7, 1948 and September 13, 1949; *Washington Times-Herald*, November 7, 1948, 5.

39. U.S. Congress, House, Committee on D.C., *Crime and Law Enforcement in the District of Columbia*, 81st Cong., 2nd sess., February 27, 1950, 617–33; Oscar Chapman to Harry Truman, April 12, 1950, "OF-6-P National Capital Park Service," Box 71, Official File, WHCF, HST Library; "Monthly Reports—Pervert Elimination Campaign," Box 24, Entry 768, Office Files of Secretary Oscar Chapman, 1933–1953, RG 48, NARA. I thank Brian Martin, vice president of History Associates, Inc., and an expert on federal government records, for bringing these records to my attention. For a discussion of the effects of police harassment, see Steven A. Rosen, "Police Harassment of Homosexual Women and Men in New York City, 1960–1980," *Columbia Human Rights Law Review* (fall/winter 1980–1981): 159–90.

40. United States Park Police, Pervert Records, Bulk Exhibit 40-0-B, Numbered Case Files, Permanent Subcommittee on Investigations, Committee on Government Operations, RG 46, NARA.

41. Interview with Bruce Scott, 1978, Gregory Sprague Collection, CHS; Bruce Scott's annotated photographs, author's collection; Kathryn Schneider Smith, "Georgetown," in *Washington at Home* (Northridge, CA: Windsor Publications, 1988); Green, *Washington: A History*, 399.

42. Bruce Scott to David Carliner, November 9, 1964, "Scott v. Macy" folder,

Box 29, Gregory Sprague Collection, CHS; "Joint Appendix," *Scott v. Macy et al.*, Civil Action no. 1050-63, U.S. District Court, D.C., Kinsey Institute.

43. U.S. Congress, House, Committee on the District of Columbia, Special Subcommittee to Investigate Crime and Law Enforcement, *Investigation of Crime and Law Enforcement in D.C.*, 81st Cong., 2nd sess., 617–33.

44. United States Park Police, Pervert Records, Bulk Exhibit 40-0-B, Numbered Case Files, Permanent Subcommittee on Investigations, Committee on Government Operations, Senate, RG 46, NARA.

45. Geddes and Curie, eds., *About the Kinsey Report*, 124–25.

46. J. Edgar Hoover to Sidney Souers, April 10, 1950, "FBI-S," Box 169, President's Secretary's Files, Subject Files, HST Library; "Draft Memorandum on Homosexual Hearings for Information of Senate Committee," Case File 40-1-17, Committee on Government Operations, Permanent Subcommittee on Investigations, RG 46, NARA; Miller quoted in *Washington Evening Star*, April 4, 1951, A-6.

47. *Washington Evening Star*, November 9, 1947; November 11, 1947; and September 20, 1950, B-1; *Hearings before the Board of the Foreign Service in the Matter of Eugene Desvernine*, November 28, 1950, 20–21, Box 587, Central Decimal File, 123-Personnel 1950–54, RG 59, NARA.

48. George Chauncey similarly argues that the openness of homosexuality in the public sphere in New York during Prohibition was quickly followed by a "a powerful cultural reaction." The situation in Washington suggests a similar pattern, but a different periodization, since Washington's gay and lesbian subculture began to flourish later than New York's. See Chauncey, *Gay New York*, 8–12.

Chapter Three: "Cookie Pushers in Striped Pants"

1. Hull quoted in Benjamin Welles, *Sumner Welles: FDR's Global Strategist* (New York: St. Martin's Press, 1997), 348; Irwin Gellman, *Secret Affairs: Franklin Roosevelt, Cordell Hull, and Sumner Welles* (Baltimore: Johns Hopkins University Press, 1995), 215–45, 302–17; Ted Morgan, *FDR: A Biography* (New York: Simon & Schuster, 1985), 677–85.

2. Robert C. Ruark, *Washington Daily News*, March 23 and 24, 1950; Westbrook Pegler, *Washington-Times Herald*, March 26, 1950; Joseph and Stewart Alsop, *Washington Evening Star*, May 18, 1938; Max Lerner, "The Washington Sex Story," *New York Post*, July 10, 1950; Peter Edson also pointed to "one former high official" as the cause of the problem; see *Washington Daily News*, March 17, 1950, 47; for the first explicit press report of the Welles scandal, see Truxton Decatur, "We Accuse Sumner Welles," *Confidential*, May 1956, 12–15.

3. "Best Laughs of 1950" quoted in "Earl Wilson Reports," January 1951, unidentified newspaper, "Homosexuals in Civil Service" vertical file, Kinsey Institute; Fitzpatrick joke from interview with Barbara S. Kraft, September 10, 1994;

taxi driver and concert ticket holders quoted in Joseph and Stewart Alsop, "Why Has Washington Gone Crazy," *Saturday Evening Post*, July 29, 1950, 60.

4. Interview with Joan Cassidy, February 13, 1997; U.S. Congress, Senate, "Loyalty-Security Problems in the Department of State," *Executive Sessions of the Senate Foreign Relations Committee, Historical Series*, vol. 5, 83rd Cong., 1st sess., February 5, 1953, 70.

5. Westbrook Pegler, *Washington Times-Herald*, March 31, 1950, 14; Oliver Pilat, *Pegler: Angry Man of the Press* (Boston: Beacon Press, 1963).

6. Edward Ronns [pseud. of Edward S. Aarons], *State Department Murders* (New York: Fawcett Press, 1950; reprint, New York: Gold Lion Books, 1973), 17, 38, 153; Chris Steinbrunner and Otto Penzler, *Encyclopedia of Mystery and Detection* (New York: McGraw-Hill, 1976). A novel by Constantine Fitz Gibbon, *When the Kissing Had to Stop* (New Rochelle, NY: Arlington House, 1973), first published in 1960, also featured a gay spy character.

7. Philip Wylie, *Generation of Vipers* (New York: Rinehart, 1942; reprint, New York: Pocket Books, 1960), 232–36. In the 1960 edition Wylie added a self-congratulatory footnote: "It was not McCarthy who made, ten years after this was noted down, the findings about homosexuality in the State Department."

8. Martin Weil, *A Pretty Good Club: The Founding Fathers of the U.S. Foreign Service* (New York: W. W. Norton, 1978), 20–25, 127; see also Heinrichs, *American Ambassadors: Joseph C. Grew and the Development of the U.S. Diplomatic Tradition* (Boston: Little, Brown, 1966) 15, 96; Bryton Barron, *Inside the State Department: A Candid Appraisal of the Bureaucracy* (New York: Comet, 1956), 12; Eric F. Goldman, *The Crucial Decade and After: America, 1945–1960* (New York: Random House, 1960), 123–25; Allen Weinstein, *Perjury: The Hiss-Chambers Case* (New York: Knopf, 1978).

9. "Powder puff" from *Chicago Daily Tribune*, May 17, 1950, 10; Granville Rice to Kenneth Wherry, April 26, 1951, quoted in Marvin E. Stromer, *The Making of a Political Leader: Kenneth S. Wherry and the United States Senate* (Lincoln: University of Nebraska Press, 1969), 77.

10. Lately Thomas, *When Even Angels Wept: The Senator Joseph McCarthy Affair—A Story without a Hero* (New York: William Morrow, 1973), 238; On the foreign policy implications of the Lavender Scare, see Geoffrey S. Smith, "National Security and Personal Isolation: Sex, Gender, and Disease in the Cold-War United States," *International History Review* 14, no. 2 (May 1992): 307–37; Robert Dean, *Imperial Brotherhood: Gender and the Making of Cold War Foreign Policy* (Amherst: University of Massachusetts Press, 2001).

11. *New York Daily News*, March 27, 1950; Arthur Herman, *Joseph McCarthy: Reexamining the Life and Legacy of America's Most Hated Senator* (New York: Free Press, 1999), 140.

12. L. A. Moyer to Francis Flanagan, September 5, 1950, Committee on Government Operations, Permanent Subcommittee on Investigations, Numbered Case Files, 40-19, RG 46, NARA; Harry Mitchell to Homer Ferguson, June 9, 1950, Reading files of Samuel Boykin, Box 5, "Information on Homosexuals," BSCA, RG 59, NARA.

13. Acheson quoted in *Appendix to the Congressional Record*, April 24, 1950, A2934; *Washington Times-Herald*, April 24, 1950, 1; congressman quoted in *Congressional Record*, April 25, 1950, 5748; Mundt quoted in *Congressional Record*, April 24, 1950, 5572; Acheson quoted again in *Washington Daily News*, June 20, 1950, 7.

14. *Washington Times-Herald*, June 11, 1950, 1; E. K. Meade to Marshall, October 27, 1952 (unlabeled folder), Box 478, Decimal Files 1950–54, RG 59, NARA; Jeff Broadwater, *Eisenhower and the Anti-Communist Crusade* (Chapel Hill: University of North Carolina Press, 1992), 135.

15. Boykin to Fletcher, "Proposed New Manual for Special Agents," February 29, 1952, "SY-General 1952" folder, Box 1, Security Division Subject Files, Lot 53-D-233, BSCA, RG 59, NARA; "mannerisms" from Thomas to Flanagan, July 11, 1950, Case File 40-20-14, Committee on Government Operations, Permanent Subcommittee on Investigations, RG 46, NARA; on the department's master list, see U.S. Congress, Senate, *Report of the Investigations of the Junior Senator of Nebraska, a Member of the Subcommittee Appointed by the Subcommittee on Appropriations for the District of Columbia, on the Infiltration of Subversives and Moral Perverts in the Executive Branch of the United States Government*, S. Doc. 4179, 81st Cong., 2nd sess., 1950, 6 [Wherry Report]; Carlisle H. Humelsine, *Executive Sessions of the Senate Foreign Relations Committee, Historical Series*, vol. 5, 83rd Cong., 1st sess., February 5, 1953, 85–86.

16. Humelsine to Webb, June 23, 1950, "Information on Homosexuals," Box 5, Reading Files of Samuel Boykin; Boykin to MacKenzie, August 23, 1951, "SY-General 1947–1951" folder, Box 1, Security Division Subject Files; McJenett to Humelsine, March 7, 1951, "Loyalty 1951," Box 6, Reading Files of Samuel Boykin, all in BSCA, RG 59, NARA; college student quoted in Elaine Tyler May, *Homeward Bound: American Families in the Cold War Era* (New York: Basic Books, 1988), 95.

17. Humelsine to Webb, June 23, 1950, "Information on Homosexuals," Box 5, Reading Files of Samuel Boykin, BSCA, RG 59, NARA; Nicholson to Ylitalo, August 27, 1951, "Review of 176 Closed Miscellaneous-M Files," Box 12, Lot 62-D-146, Decimal Files 1953–60, BSCA, RG 59, NARA.

18. Humelsine to Webb, June 23, 1950, and Jean to Peurifoy, June 20, 1950, "Information on Homosexuals," Box 5, Reading Files of Samuel Boykin, BSCA, RG 59, NARA.

19. *Hearings before the Board of the Foreign Service in the Matter of Eugene Desvernine*, Box 587, Central Decimal File, 123-Personnel 1950–54, RG 59, NARA; *Washington Daily News*, September 20, 1950, 13; *Appendix to the Congressional Record*, September 21, 1950, A6775.

20. Boykin to Martin, "Homosexual Problem," December 21, 1950, "SY-General 1947–51" folder, Box 1, Security Division Subject Files, Lot 53-D-233, BSCA, RG 59, NARA; see also U.S. Congress, House, Subcommittee of the Committee on Appropriations, *Department of State Appropriations for 1952*, 82nd Cong., 1st sess., March 2, 1951, 399–400.

21. Carlisle Humelsine, *Executive Sessions of the Senate Foreign Relations Committee, Historical Series*, vol. 5, 83rd Cong., 1st sess., February 5, 1953, 70–71; Scott to Boykin, November 28, 1950, "Loyalty 1947–1950" folder, Box 5, Reading Files of Samuel Boykin, BSCA, RG 59, NARA.

22. Szluk quoted in Griffin Fariello, *Red Scare: Memories of the American Inquisition, An Oral History* (New York: W. W. Norton, 1995), 123; U.S. Congress, House, *Department of State Appropriations for 1952*, Hearings, Subcommittee of the Committee on Appropriations, 82nd Cong., 1st sess., March 2, 1951, 390–95; U.S. Congress, Senate, *Executive Sessions of the Senate Foreign Relations Committee, Historical Series*, vol. 5, 83rd Cong., 1st sess., February 5, 1953, 72–76; Flinn to McLeod, January 26, 1955, "Statistics-Security" folder, Box 12, BSCA, 1953–60, RG 59, NARA; *San Francisco Chronicle*, April 7, 1955, 22, quoted in *Temple Law Quarterly* 29 (1956): 300.

23. House chairman quoted in *Washington Daily News*, June 29, 1953, 17; Reilly quoted in *The Ladder*, October 1963, 17; Ralph S. Brown, *Loyalty and Security: Employment Tests in the United States* (New Haven, CT: Yale University Press, 1958), 258; R. E. L. Masters, *The Homosexual Revolution* (New York: Julian Press, 1962), 143–44; Letters to the Editor, *Washington Post*, June 10, 1968, A-20.

Chapter Four: "Fairies and Fair Dealers"

1. *Washington Times-Herald*, April 1, 1950, 2; *Newsweek*, May 1, 1950, and May 29, 1950, 18. See also *Washington Times-Herald*, March 24, 1950, 1; *Washington Daily News*, March 24, 1950, 3; *Washington Post*, March 25, 1950; *Washington Star*, March 28, 1950, B-1.

2. "More sensational" from *Washington Daily News*, March 28, 1950, 5; "emergency condition" from *Washington Daily News*, May 20, 1950, 4; "Lesbianism" from *Washington Times-Herald*, March 19, 1950, 1; all other quotes from U.S. Congress, Senate, *Report of the Investigations of the Junior Senator of Nebraska, a Member of the Subcommittee Appointed by the Subcommittee on Appropriations for the District of Columbia, on the Infiltration of Subversives and Moral Perverts in the Executive Branch of the United States Government*, S. Doc. 4179, 81st Cong., 2nd sess., 1950, 10–15 [hereafter cited as Wherry Report].

3. *Washington Daily News*, March 16, 1950, 7; *Congressional Record*, July 24, 1950, 11006–7; Wherry Report, 10; Testimony of Frances Perkins, Hoey Committee Hearings, September 8, 1950, 2737–39, RG 46, NARA.

4. Reston and agency official quoted in Peter Wyden, "The Man Who Fright-

ens Bureaucrats," *Saturday Evening Post*, January 31, 1959, 27; U.S. Congress, House, Hearings before the Subcommittee of the Committee on Appropriations, *Department of Commerce Appropriations for 1951*, 81st Cong., 2nd sess., February 27, 1950, 2339–40.

5. House Subcommittee of the Committee on Appropriations, *Department of Commerce Appropriations for 1951*, 2340–42; see also *New York Times*, March 20, 1950, 5; John O'Donnell, *New York Daily News*, March 24, 1950, in *Appendix to the Congressional Record*, March 28, 1950, A2279. Although taken in executive session the day before the Peurifoy revelation, this testimony was not made public until March. This substantiates the argument that the revelation was no surprise to Congress.

6. *Washington Daily News*, March 20, 1950, 2, and June 3, 1950, 4; lecture noted in James Thomas to Francis Flanagan, June 16, 1950, Case File 40-9-2, Committee on Government Operations, Permanent Subcommittee on Investigations, RG 46, NARA; statistics cited in Hoey Committee Report, 25; Gary May, *Un-American Activities: The Trials of William Remington* (New York: Oxford University Press, 1994); Rooney quoted in U.S. Congress, House, Hearings before the Subcommittee of the Committee on Appropriations, *Department of State Appropriations for 1953*, 82nd Cong., 2nd sess., February 1952.

7. Ferguson cited in *Washington Star*, March 26, 1950, A-19; Rooney quoted in U.S. Congress, House, Subcommittee of the Committee on Appropriations, *Department of Commerce Appropriations for 1951*, 81st Cong., 2nd sess., February 27, 1950, 2344; Bridges quoted in *Washington Star*, July 20, 1950, A-1; Miller quoted in *Appendix to the Congressional Record*, May 15, 1950, A3660; Clevenger quoted in *Congressional Record*, April 19, 1950, 5402. On the extension of the McCarran rider, see Public Law 733, 81st Congress, August 26, 1950; *Congressional Record*, July 12, 1950, 10015–17; *Washington Star*, March 30, 1950, A-1, June 29, 1950, A-2, and July 14, 1950, A-8; *New York Times*, July 13, 1950, 1; Richard M. Fried, *Nightmare in Red: The McCarthy Era in Perspective* (New York: Oxford University Press, 1990), 62; David Caute, *The Great Fear* (New York: Simon & Schuster, 1978), 26.

8. William White, "Portrait of a 'Fundamentalist,'" *New York Times Magazine*, January 15, 1950, 14; William White, "Senator Wherry Dies at 59," *New York Times*, November 30, 1951. See also Paul Healy, "Big Noise from Nebraska," *Saturday Evening Post*, August 5, 1950, 22.

9. Wherry Report, 1; "expert" quoted in U.S. Congress, Senate, *State Department Loyalty Investigation*, Hearings before a subcommittee of the Committee on Foreign Relations pursuant to S. Res. 231, 81st Cong., 2nd sess., 1950, 1109; Max Lerner, *New York Post*, July 17, 1950, 2.

10. *Washington Times-Herald*, May 20, 1950, 1. By the 1960s, only 10 percent of the federal workforce was located in and around Washington. See Donald R. Harvey, *The Civil Service Commission* (New York: Praeger, 1970), 46; and Kenneth R.

Bowling, *The Creation of Washington, D.C.: The Idea and Location of the American Capital* (Fairfax, VA: George Mason University Press, 1991).

11. Wherry Report, 13; *Washington Times-Herald*, March 25, 1950; David Lawrence, *Washington Evening Star*, May 8, 1950, A-7.

12. Max Lerner, *New York Post*, July 18, 1950, 2; Blick remained with the vice squad until 1964 and stuck by his estimates. See *Washington Post*, September 29, 1963, E-2.

13. *Washington Daily News*, March 28, 1950, 5; see also *Washington Times-Herald*, April 1, 1950, 2.

14. "Memorandum of Conversation," March 29, 1950, "Sex Perversion" folder, Box 32, WHCF, HST Library.

15. Stahl to Harris, October 10, 1952, "P-508, Perversion from Health and Employee Relations Angle" folder, Box 51, Records of the Federal Personnel Council, Project Files 1943–53, Entry 22, RG 146, NARA; Bradlee quoted in Charles Kaiser, *The Gay Metropolis, 1940–1996* (New York: Houghton Mifflin, 1997), 71; Wherry Report, 5. Although I have no independent confirmation of this arrest, Washington newspapers reported similar large-scale arrests. See "Lafayette Park Cleanup Results in 41 Arrests," *Washington Star*, July 19, 1947.

16. *Washington Times-Herald*, March 28, 1950, 1; Fletcher to Nicholson, May 3, 1950, "Sex Perversion" folder, Box 32, WHCF, Confidential files, HST Library; U.S. Congress, Senate, *Report of Subcommittee of Subcommittee on Appropriations for the District of Columbia Made by the Chairman, the Senior Senator from the State of Alabama, Mr. Hill, with Reference to Testimony on Subversive Activity and Homosexuals in the Government Service*, S. Doc. 4178, 81st Cong., 2nd sess., May 1950, 6.

17. Karpman quoted in *Washington Star*, June 4, 1950; Biddle quoted in *Washington Star*, June 9, 1950, B-10; "Sexual 'Pervert' Probe," *Science News Letter*, July 1, 1950, 5; Kinsey quoted in *Washington Daily News*, June 22, 1950, 3.

18. U.S. Congress, Senate, *Report . . . on Subversive Activity and Homosexuals in the Government Service*, S. Doc. 4178, 81st Cong., 2nd sess., May 1950.

19. Peter Edson, "Government Kinsey Report?" *Washington Daily News*, March 17, 1950, 47; Wherry quoted in Max Lerner, "Scandal in the State Department," *New York Post*, July 17, 1950, 2; see also Wherry Report, 12.

20. Jack Lait and Lee Mortimer, *Washington Confidential* (New York: Crown, 1951), 116, and *U.S.A. Confidential*, 44; Arthur Guy Mathews, *Is Homosexuality a Menace?* (New York: Robert M. McBride, 1957), 138–39, 188–92.

21. Lait and Mortimer, *U.S.A. Confidential*, 351. On Greenwich village as a gay mecca in the early twentieth century, see George Chauncey, *Gay New York,: Gender, Urban Culture, and the Making of a Gay Male World, 1890-1940* (New York: Basic Books, 1994), 227–44.

22. Lait and Mortimer, *Washington Confidential*, 98–103, 117, and *U.S.A. Confidential*, 43.

23. Dixon and Mallon quoted in Liza Mundy, "Confidential Men," *Washington City Paper*, September 20, 1991, 26–27. On the history of *Confidential* magazine, published from 1952 to 1958, see Thomas K. Wolfe, "Public Lives: Confidential Magazine: Reflections in Tranquility by the Former Owner, Robert Harrison, Who Managed to Get Away with It," *Esquire*, April 1964, 87 f.

24. Ramspeck quoted in *Washington Star*, August 2, 1951. See also Donald R. Harvey, *The Civil Service Commission* (New York: Praeger, 1970), 110; Council Meeting Minutes, March 15, 1951, Box 51, Records of the Federal Personnel Council, Official Minutes 1939–50, Entry 19, RG 146, NARA.

25. Cindy Sondik Aron, *Ladies and Gentlemen of the Civil Service: Middle-Class Workers in Victorian America* (New York: Oxford University Press, 1987), 5, 36–39, 104.

26. Observer quoted in Paul P. Van Riper, *History of the United States Civil Service* (Evanston, IL: Row, Peterson, 1958), 325; Bromfield quoted in *The Freeman*, December 1, 1952, 158; congressman quoted in Richard Hofstadter, *Anti-Intellectualism in American Life* (New York: Random House, 1962), 36.

27. Hofstadter, *Anti-Intellectualism in American Life*, 35; Edward A. Shils, *The Torment of Secrecy: The Background and Consequences of American Security Policies*, with an introduction by Daniel P. Moynihan (Glencoe, IL: Free Press, 1956; reprint, Chicago: Ivan R. Dee, 1996), 18, 113–19; David Brinkley, *Washington Goes to War* (New York: Ballantine Books, 1988), 197.

28. Shils, *Torment of Secrecy*, 112; Edna Lonigan, "The Presidency," *Human Events*, December 26, 1951, 1; Reinhard Bendix, *Higher Civil Servants in American Society* (Boulder: University of Colorado Press, 1949); Norton Lang, *The Polity* (Chicago: Rand McNally, 1962); "The New Princes of Privilege Are the Bureaucrats," *Saturday Evening Post*, October 6, 1951, 10.

29. Taft quoted in *Washington Times-Herald*, May 2, 1950, 2; minister quoted in *Chicago Tribune*, May 15, 1950, 10; Senator Gore quoted in Gore Vidal, *Palimpsest: A Memoir* (New York: Random House, 1995), 64.

30. Jennifer Terry, "'Momism' and the Making of Treasonous Homosexuals," in Molly Ladd-Taylor and Lauri Umansky, eds., *"Bad Mothers": The Politics of Blame in Twentieth-Century America* (New York: New York University Press, 1998), 169–90; Philip Wylie, *Generation of Vipers* (New York: Rinehart, 1942; reprint, New York: Pocket Books, 1960), 184–205; K. A. Cuordileone, "'Politics in an Age of Anxiety': Cold War Political Culture and the Crisis in American Masculinity, 1949–1960," *Journal of American History* (September 2000): 515–45.

31. Goodwin Watson, "Problems of Bureaucracy—Introduction," *Journal of Social Issues* 1, no. 4 (December 1945): 1.

32. "Bureaucratic nightmare" from Arthur Herman, *Joseph McCarthy: Reexamining the Life and Legacy of America's Most Hated Senator* (New York: Free Press, 2000), 37; advertisement quoted in David M. Oshinsky, *A Conspiracy So Immense:*

The World of Joe McCarthy (New York: Free Press, 1983), 52; flyer quoted in Richard Rovere, *Senator Joe McCarthy* (New York: Meridian Books, 1959), 103; Michael O'Brien, *McCarthy and McCarthyism in Wisconsin* (Columbia: University of Missouri Press, 1980), 79–80.

33. William White, "Portrait of a 'Fundamentalist,'" *New York Times Magazine*, January 15, 1950, 14; *New York Times*, November 30, 1951, 1; Paul F. Healy, "Big Noise from Nebraska," *Saturday Evening Post*, August 5, 1950, 22; "confusion" quotation from *Current Biography 1946* (New York: Wilson, 1946), 637. See also Marvin E. Stromer, *The Making of a Political Leader: Kenneth S. Wherry and the United States Senate* (Lincoln: University of Nebraska Press, 1969). This hagiographic biography is silent on Wherry's role in the lavender purges. Wherry died suddenly in 1951.

34. Westbrook Pegler, *Washington Times-Herald*, June 3, 1950; John Gerassi, *The Boys of Boise: Furor, Vice, and Folly in an American City* (New York: Macmillan, 1966), 23, 38.

35. Blick quoted in Wherry Report, 13; *Washington Daily News*, May 8, 1950, 2; see also *Washington Times-Herald*, April 28, 1950, 9. On the FBI's new reporting procedures for sex crimes, see U.S. Congress, House, Hearings before the Subcommittee of the Committee on Appropriations, *Department of Justice Appropriations for 1952*, 82nd Cong., 1st sess., February 1951, 319; *Washington Star*, April 27, 1951, B-1.

36. Ferguson quoted in *Congressional Record*, May 19, 1950, 7329; McCarthy quoted in "Probe of Perversion in Capital Demanded," no provenance, "Homosexuals in Civil Service" vertical files, Kinsey Institute; Elmer Davis, May 19, 1950 Radio Transcript, Box 20, Elmer Davis Collection, LC. See also Senate Resolution no. 280, 81st Cong., 2nd sess., June 7, 1950; *New York Times*, May 20, 1950, 8, and May 22, 1950, 8; *Washington Star*, May 20, 1950, B-12; *Washington Daily News*, June 7, 1950, 6; *Newsweek*, May 29, 1950, 18.

Chapter Five: The Hoey Investigation

1. Interview with Francis Flanagan, April 11, 1996; Susan Tucker Hatcher, "The Senatorial Career of Clyde R. Hoey" (Ph.D. diss., Duke University, 1983), 148–64; *Memorial Services for Clyde Roark Hoey* (Washington, DC: GPO, 1954); "witch hunt" from *Congressional Record*, December 15, 1950, 16587.

2. Interview with Francis Flanagan, April 11, 1996; Hoey's opinion of McCarthy quoted in Hatcher, "The Senatorial Career of Clyde R. Hoey," 148–50. On McCarthy's role, see *New York Times*, June 15, 1960, 6; *Washington Star*, June 15, 1950, C-7. On the need for closed hearings, see Steven J. Spingarn, Memorandum for the Hoey Subcommittee Sex Pervert Investigation File, June 29, 1950, Box 32, WHCF, HST Library; *Washington Daily News*, May 22, 1950, 3.

3. Interview with Francis Flanagan, April 11, 1996; on Smith's participation, see *Washington Daily News*, June 15, 1950, 6.

4. Interview with Francis Flanagan, April 11, 1996; Roy Cohn and Sidney Zion, *The Autobiography of Roy Cohn* (Secaucus, NJ: Lyle Stuart, 1988), 87; Athan Theoharis, ed., *From the Secret Files of J. Edgar Hoover* (Chicago: Ivan R. Dee, 1991), 260–63; David M. Oshinsky, *A Conspiracy So Immense: The World of Joe McCarthy* (New York: Free Press, 1983), 318.

5. David D. Lloyd to Mr. Spingarn, July 3, 1950, and Stephen Spingarn, "Memorandum for the Hoey Subcommittee Sex Pervert Investigation File," June 29, 1950, both in "Sex Perversion" folder, Box 32, WHCF, HST Library; James E. Webb, "Meeting with the President, Thursday, June 22, 1950," Box 9, Entry 53D444, Secretary's Memoranda, 1949–1951, Records of the Executive Secretariat, RG 59, NARA.

6. Philleo Nash to Stephen Spingarn, July 7, 1950, and Elsey to S. J. S., June 30, 1950, "Sex Perversion" folder, Box 32, WHCF, HST Library; U.S. Congress, Senate, Committee on Expenditures in Executive Departments, Investigations Subcommittee, Hearings Pursuant to S. Res. 280, Executive Session, 81st Cong., 2nd sess., July 14–September 8, 1950, 2082–2793, RG 46, NARA [hereafter, Hoey Committee Hearings]. Transcripts of the executive session testimony were not released to the public until 1996. For a discussion of one scholar's unsuccessful attempt to access them in the 1980s, see Allan Bérubé, *Coming Out under Fire: The History of Gay Men and Women in World War II* (New York: Free Press, 1990), 284–85.

7. "Investigation of Homosexuals in Government Service," Case File 40-1-12, and June 27, 1950, Memorandum RE: Files Desired by Investigations Subcommittee, Case File 40-1-9, Permanent Subcommittee on Investigations, Committee on Government Operations, RG 46, NARA; Walter Goodman, *The Committee: The Extraordinary Career of the House Committee on Un-American Activities* (Baltimore: Penguin Books, 1968). J. Edgar Hoover also set up a "Sex Deviate program" within the FBI. Its three hundred thousand pages of files were destroyed with the permission of the National Archives in 1977. See Theoharis, *J. Edgar Hoover, Sex, and Crime*, 103–5.

8. Francis Flanagan to Charles Sawyer, June 15, 1950; Francis Flanagan, "Files Desired by Investigations Subcommittee in Conduct of Investigation," June 27, 1950; L. D. to Murphy, June 30, 1950; Stephen Spingarn, "Memorandum for the Hoey Subcommittee Sex Pervert Investigation File," July 10, 1950, all in "Sex Perversion" folder, Box 32, WHCF, HST Library; *Washington Daily News*, June 20, 1950, 2.

9. R. E. N. to Spingarn, July 5, 1950, and Spingarn, "Memorandum for the Hoey Subcommittee Sex Pervert Investigation File," July 10, 1950, Box 32, WHCF, HST Library.

10. *Washington Post*, June 25, 1950; *Washington Times-Herald*, June 24, 1950, 4; Robert H. Felix, "Prevention and Curing Mental Casualties," May 5, 1948, Box 1, Talks and Misc. Publications, Robert H. Felix Papers, National Library of Medi-

cine; Adler to Flanagan, June 22, 1950, Case File 40-17-7, Permanent Subcommittee on Investigations, Committee on Government Operations, RG 46, NARA. Records of the Federal Personnel Council contain notice of two of these sessions and a list of attendees, but no information on the substance of the talk; see "P-508, Perversion from Health and Employee Relations Angle" folder, Box 51, Project Files, March 1943–July 1953, Federal Personnel Council, Entry 22, RG 146, NARA. See also Testimony of Robert H. Felix, Hoey Committee Hearings, July 26, 1950, 2257–70; Margaret C. Rung, *Servants of the State: Managing Diversity and Democracy in the Federal Workforce, 1933–1953* (Athens: University of Georgia Press, 2002), 151–52.

11. *New York Post*, July 10–20, 1950. Some of Max Lerner's columns are reprinted in Max Lerner, *The Unfinished Country* (New York: Simon & Schuster, 1959), and in Jonathan Katz, *Gay American History* (New York: Thomas Y. Crowell, 1976); Joseph and Stewart Alsop, "Why Has Washington Gone Crazy?" *Saturday Evening Post*, July 29, 1950, 20. The text of Sevareid's broadcast appears in the *Congressional Record*, July 7, 1950, A4960. Herblock cartoon in *New York Post*, July 10, 1950, 4.

12. Steven J. Spingarn, "Memorandum for the Hoey Subcommittee Sex Pervert Investigation File," July 10, 1950, Box 32, WHCF, HST Library; interview with Francis Flanagan, April 11, 1996.

13. Stephen J. Spingarn, "Memorandum for the Hoey Subcommittee Sex Pervert Investigation File," July 10, 1950, and Arch K. Jean to Peurifoy, Report of Meeting with Mr. Flanagan, June 20, 1950, in Box 32, WHCF, HST Library; oral history interview with Stephen J. Spingarn, March 24, 1967, HST Library.

14. Hoey Committee Hearings, July 14, 1950, 2090–94. Hillenkoetter's source for the Redl story may have been Allen Dulles, a CIA deputy who went on to become CIA director under President Eisenhower. Dulles's first diplomatic post was Vienna, when Redl's suicide was still the talk of Viennese society, and he frequently cited the story in intelligence circles. See Peter Grose, *Gentleman Spy: The Life of Allen Dulles* (New York: Houghton Mifflin, 1994), 320; Allen Dulles, *The Craft of Intelligence* (New York: Harper & Row, 1963) 123–24.

15. "Sybaritic homosexual life" quoted from Vincent and Nan Buranelli, *Spy/Counterspy: An Encyclopedia of Espionage* (New York: McGraw-Hill, 1982), 261; "employers" from W. Nicolai, *The German Secret Service*, trans. George Renwick (London: Stanley Paul, 1924), 270–99; Edmond Taylor, *The Fall of the Dynasties: The Collapse of the Old Order, 1905–1922* (Garden City, NY: Doubleday, 1963), 176; Georg Markus, *Der Fall Redl* (Wien: Amalthea, 1984), 70–75. See also "Object Lesson," *Time*, December 25, 1950, 10; Robert B. Asprey, *The Panther's Feast* (New York: G. P. Putnam's Sons, 1959); Ian D. Armour, "Colonel Redl: Fact and Fantasy," *Intelligence and National Security* 2, no. 1 (Jan. 1987): 170–83.

16. Army and Air Force representatives quoted in Hoey Committee Hearings, July 14, 1950, 2124–29, 2154–57; ONI representatives quoted in James Sheridan to

Francis Flanagan, June 19, 1950, and James Sheridan to Francis Flanagan, September 11, 1950, Case File 40-5, Permanent Subcommittee on Investigations, Committee on Government Operations, RG 46, NARA. For rumors about a German list of English homosexuals during World War I, see Angus McLaren, *Twentieth Century Sexuality: A History* (Oxford: Blackwell, 1999), 9–10. On the history of gays and lesbians in the U.S. military, see Bérubé, *Coming Out under Fire*, 266–70; Randy Shilts, *Conduct Unbecoming: Gays and Lesbians in the U.S. Military* (New York: St. Martin's Press, 1993); Marc Wolinsky and Kenneth Sherrill, eds., *Gays and the Military: Joseph Stefan versus the United States* (Princeton, NJ: Princeton University Press, 1993).

17. Hoey Committee Hearings, July 19, 1950, 2158–69.

18. *Washington Times-Herald*, March 29, 1950, 1; Gore Vidal, *Washington, D.C.* (Boston: Little, Brown, 1967), 281–87; Sheridan to Flanagan, July 8, 1950, Case File 40-20-10, Permanent Subcommittee on Investigations, Committee on Government Operations, RG 46, NARA; W. E. Headley, "Beware of the Homo Frame-Up!" *Confidential*, April 1958, 16–17; Lloyd Wendt, "The Vilest of Rackets," *Esquire*, April 1950. See also "You Can Be Framed on a Perversion Rap," *True Crime*, March 1956; "How You Can Be Framed on a Sex Charge," *Suppressed*, June 1957.

19. Hoey Committee Hearings, July 14, 1950, 2123.

20. Ibid., 2093–2100.

21. Ibid., July 26, 1950, 2294 and prepared statement by Director of Central Intelligence, 24. On FBI use of homosexuals, see Curt Gentry, *J. Edgar Hoover: The Man and the Secrets* (New York: W. W. Norton, 1991), 412–13. For an example of a homosexual who resisted a Soviet blackmail attempt, see Edwin Yoder Jr., *Joe Alsop's Cold War: A Study of Journalistic Influence and Intrigue* (Chapel Hill: University of North Carolina Press, 1995), 153–58.

22. Hoey Committee Hearings, July 26, 1950, 2245–50.

23. Ibid., 2281–2301.

24. Ibid., 2256, 2300.

25. Hoey Committee Report. For the report's use by State Department security officers, see Draft of proposed manual for Special Agents, February 1952, "SY-General 1952" folder, Box 1, Entry 1508, Office of Security and Consular Affairs, Lot File 53-D-233, Subject Files of the Security Division, 1946–1953, RG 59, NARA. For the report's influence on Canadian government policy, see Daniel J. Robinson and David Kimmel, "The Queer Career of Homosexual Security Vetting in Cold War Canada," *Canadian Historical Review* 75 (September 1994): 331–32; Philip Girard, "From Subversion to Liberation: Homosexuals and the Immigration Act 1952–1977," *Canadian Journal of Law and Society* 2 (1987), 6–9. Excerpts from the report were reprinted in the appendix to Donald Webster Cory, *The Homosexual in America: A Subjective Approach* (New York: Greenberg, 1951).

26. S. Crittenden, *Report of the Board Appointed to Prepare and Submit Recommen-*

dations to the Secretary of the Navy for the Revision of Policies, Procedures, and Directives Dealing with Homosexuals (1957); Defense Personnel Security Research and Education Center (PERSEREC), *Homosexuality and Personnel Security* (prepared by Theodore R. Sarbin, 1991), 29; Lynn F. Fischer, "Espionage: Why Does It Happen?" *Security Awareness Bulletin 4-94*, DOD Security Institute; U.S. Congress, Senate, Committee on Governmental Affairs, Permanent Subcommittee on Investigations, *Federal Government Security Clearance Programs*, 99th Cong., 1st sess., 1985. On the Pentagon's suppression of the Crittenden Report, see Shilts, *Conduct Unbecoming*, 281–83.

27. "John Wayne Williams," 123-Personnel File 1950–54, RG 59, NARA; Carlisle H. Humelsine, *Executive Sessions of the Senate Foreign Relations Committee, Historical Series*, vol. 5, 83rd Cong., 1st sess., February 5, 1953, 70–71; *New York Times*, March 28, 1951, 1, and June 2, 1951, 36. Williams pled guilty to three counts of accepting bribes and was sentenced to six years in Federal prison.

28. Hoey Committee Report, 4.

29. *Washington Star*, August 19, 1950, B-6, and August 23, 1950, A-10; Hoey Committee Report, 10, 15–19.

30. Martin Bauml Duberman, *About Time: Exploring the Gay Past* (New York: Gay Presses of New York), 152.

31. "Perverts in Government," *Washington Post*, December 18, 1950.

Chapter Six: "Let's Clean House"

1. *Washington Post*, March 13, 1953, 1; *Washington Star*, March 13, 1953, A-2; Ford to McLeod, April 13, 1953, and Ambrose to Dulin, April 20, 1953, unfoldered material, Box 12, Lot File 62-D-146, Decimal Files 1953–1960, BSCA, RG 59, NARA. These materials were marked "P" for privacy and, according to NARA policy, should have been removed before the box was given to researchers. I have therefore not used the individuals' full names.

2. Republican rhetoric quoted from political pamphlets and 1952 Republican Platform, Political Collection (non-Becker), Museum of American History, Smithsonian Institution, Washington, D.C.; "wickedness in government" quoted in Richard H. Rovere, *Affairs of State: The Eisenhower Years* (New York: Farrar, Straus, & Cudahy, 1956), 35; on joint appearances, see Charles E. Bohlen, *Witness to History, 1929–1969* (New York: W. W. Norton, 1973), 335. See also David McCullough, *Truman* (New York: Simon & Schuster, 1992), 906; Stephen E. Ambrose, *Eisenhower: Soldier and President* (New York: Simon & Schuster, 1990), 285.

3. Athan Theoharis, "How the FBI Gaybaited Stevenson," *Nation*, May 7, 1990, 1; Athan Theoharis, ed., *From the Secret Files of J. Edgar Hoover* (Chicago: Ivan R. Dee, 1991), 282–91; Curt J. Gentry, *J. Edgar Hoover: The Man and the Secrets* (New York: W. W. Norton, 1991), 402–3; Jeff Broadwater, *Adlai Stevenson and American Politics: The Odyssey of a Cold War Liberal* (New York: Twayne Publishers, 1994),

121; John Bartlow Martin, *Adlai Stevenson of Illinois* (Garden City, NY: Anchor Press, 1977), 646–48.

4. Joseph M. Porter, "How That Stevenson Rumor Started," *Confidential*, August 1953, 41 ff.; "The Whispers Adlai Stevenson Couldn't Stop!" *Uncensored*, December 1956; Neal Gabler, *Winchell: Gossip, Power, and the Culture of Celebrity* (New York: Knopf, 1994), 499; Gentry, *J. Edgar Hoover*, 445. On Jorgensen, see David Harley Serlin, "Christine Jorgensen and the Cold War Closet," *Radical History Review* 62 (spring 1995), 136–65.

5. Charles Boultenhouse, "The Fifties," in *The Christopher Street Reader*, ed. Michael Denneny et al. (New York: Putnam, 1983), 291–92; Martin, *Adlai Stevenson*, 6.

6. Executive Order 10450, "Security Requirements for Government Employment," *Federal Register*, April 27, 1953, 2489; Eleanor Bontecou, "President Eisenhower's 'Security' Program," *Bulletin of Atomic Scientists*, June 1953, 217. Though it was the first presidential executive order to explicitly address the issue of "sexual perversion," E.O. 10450 was the culmination of a process begun under the Truman administration. Truman's National Security Council had also recommended adding "sexual perversion" to the security criteria. See *A Report to the National Security Council by the Interdepartmental Committee on Internal Security on Government Employee Security Program*, May 2, 1952, NSC 113/1, Box 15, NSC Policy Papers, RG 273, NARA; *Washington Star*, August 9, 1952, A-5.

7. "Televised Report to the American People by the President and Members of the Cabinet," June 3, 1953, and "The President's News Conference of December 16, 1953," both in *Public Papers of the Presidents of the United States: Dwight D. Eisenhower, 1953*, 374–75; Dwight D. Eisenhower, *Mandate for Change, 1953–1956* (Garden City, NY: Doubleday, 1963), 309.

8. *Washington Star*, August 17, 1952, A-23, and April 29, 1953; *Washington Post*, April 30, 1953, 8; *U.S. News & World Report*, February 12, 1954, 70; "Statement Concerning Information about Employee Security Program That Will Be Furnished to National Security Council," Box 7, Records of Gerald Morgan, DDE Library.

9. Transcript of Fulton Lewis broadcast, July 30, 1953, "Publicity—General, 1955" folder, Box 25, Decimal Files 1953–60, BSCA, RG 59, NARA; columnist quoted from Herbert Elliston, *Washington Post*, January 24, 1954; reporter quoted from William Harlan Hale, "'Big Brother' in Foggy Bottom," *Reporter*, August 17, 1954, 10; Stewart Alsop, *International Herald Tribune*, August 7, 1953. See also Townsend Hoopes, *The Devil and John Foster Dulles* (Boston: Little, Brown, 1973), 151–58.

10. McLeod quoted in *U.S. News & World Report*, February 12, 1954, 62; Hale, "'Big Brother' in Foggy Bottom," 10–17; Joseph and Stewart Alsop, "From the Horse's Mouth," *Washington Post*, February 10, 1954.

11. U.S. Congress, House, Committee on Appropriations, *Departments of State,*

Justice, and Commerce Appropriations for 1954, 83rd Cong., 1st sess., March 20, 1953, 102–3; *Washington Post*, March 13, 1953, 1; *Washington Star*, March 13, 1953, A-2; *New York Times*, March 14, 1953, 32; interview with John Haines, Dulles Oral History Collection, Princeton, quoted in David M. Oshinsky, *A Conspiracy So Immense: The World of Joe McCarthy* (New York: Free Press, 1983), 260–63.

12. Anthony Lewis, "State Spells Out Security Program," *Washington Daily News*, May 22, 1953; Scott McLeod, address before the American Legion Convention, Topeka, Kansas, August 8, 1953, Box 26, Lot File 62-D-146, Decimal Files 1953–60, BSCA, RG 59, NARA; "Press Relations—Scott McLeod," Box 25, Decimal Files 1953–1960, BSCA, RG 59, NARA.

13. Hoover quoted in Theoharis, ed. *From the Secret Files of J. Edgar Hoover*, 259; Dulles quoted in Bohlen, *Witness to History*, 335. Robert Dean, *Imperial Brotherhood: Gender and the Making of Cold War Foreign Policy* (Amherst: University of Massachusetts Press, 2001) provides a detailed analysis of the Bohlen nomination within the context of the Lavender Scare. Many previous historical treatments of the Bohlen nomination treat it as a matter solely of association with Communists; see Griffith, *Politics of Fear*, 200–202.

14. Flinn to McLeod, March 30, 1954, "Statistical Report—Miscellaneous M Unit," in "Checks on Security Risks (including Moral & Sex Deviates)" folder, Box 12, Decimal Files 1953–1960, BSCA, RG 59, NARA.

15. Clare to Flinn, December 15, 1953, and Flinn to McLeod, December 15, 1953, in "Security Clearance Procedures" folder, and Conference Report of Regional Security Supervisors, April 1953, all in Box 16, Decimal Files 1953–1960, BSCA, RG 59, NARA; *New York Times*, December 20, 1951, 1; "Polygraph," in "Operation of the Security Program" folder, Box 12, Decimal Files 1953–1960, BSCA, RG 59, NARA. The CIA was also using lie detectors in homosexual cases by 1950; *Washington Times-Herald*, May 21, 1950, 2.

16. O'Connor to McLeod, August 25, 1954, E.O. 10450 Security Requirements, Box 13, Decimal Files 1953–1960, BSCA, RG 59, NARA ["P" material]. On the coercive nature of the lie detector, see Ken Alder, "To Tell the Truth: The Polygraph Exam and the Marketing of American Expertise," *Historical Reflections* 24, no. 3 (1998): 487–525.

17. Conference Report of Regional Security Supervisors, April 1953, Box 16, Decimal Files 1953–1960, BSCA, RG 59, NARA; Szluk quoted in Griffin Fariello, *Red Scare: Memories of the American Inquisition, An Oral History* (New York: W. W. Norton, 1995), 124.

18. McLeod to Donegan, November 26, 1956, and McLeod to Cartwright, July 13, 1956, both in "Checks on Security Risks" folder, Box 12, Decimal Files 1953–1960, BSCA, RG 59, NARA.

19. Flinn to McLeod, January 26, 1955, in "Statistics-Security" folder, and Ford to McLeod, April 2, 1953, "Moral Deviation cases—statistics," in "Checks on Se-

curity Risks (Including Moral & Sex Deviates)" folder, both in Box 12, Decimal Files 1953–1960, BSCA, RG 59, NARA; *Washington Post*, January 24, 1954.

20. John W. Ford, "Role of the Administrative Officer in Security," May 30, 1953, "SY-General 1953" folder, Box 2, Lot 56-D-313, Deputy Undersecretary for Admin., Misc. Subject File 1951–1955, BSCA, RG 59, NARA. No such letters were found.

21. Anonymous to Scott McLeod, April 20, 1953, and John Ford to Scott McLeod, June 17, 1953, unfoldered materials, Box 12, Lot File 62-D-146, Decimal Files 1953–1960, BSCA, State, RG 59, NARA; *Washington Daily News*, June 29, 1953, 17.

22. *New York Times*, January 27, 1953, 1; *Washington Star*, June 3, 1953, A-2, and December 20, 1954; David Caute, *The Great Fear* (New York: Simon & Schuster, 1978), 325–38; USUN-New York to DOS-Washington, May 27, 1954, and U.S. Consulate General, Geneva, to DOS-Washington, June 8, 1954, both in "Suitability" folder, Box 12, Lot 88D3, Records Relating to E.O. 10422, 1946–1975, RG 59, NARA.

23. Fletcher to Flinn, "Employment of Homosexuals in International Agencies," September 22, 1954, and McLeod to Phillips, December 30, 1954, both in "Suitability" folder, Box 12, Lot 88D3, Records Relating to E.O. 10422, 1946–1975, RG 59, NARA; *Congressional Record*, July 24, 1950, 10843.

24. Key to Lodge, January 4, 1955, Babcock to Key, January 18, 1955, Phillips to McLeod, January 26, 1955, McLeod to Phillips, December 30, 1954, and Carroll to Buffum, June 21, 1974, all in "Suitability" folder, Box 12, Lot 88D3, Records Relating to E.O. 10422, 1946–1975, RG 59, NARA.

25. Robert MacKenzie to Sam Boykin, August 9, 1951, and Sam Boykin to Robert Mackenzie, August 23, 1951, "SY-General 1947–1951" folder, Box 1, Subject Files, Security Division, Lot 53-D-233, BSCA, RG 59, NARA; Scott McLeod to the Secretary of State, "Department of State's Personnel Security Position," June 27, 1956, unfoldered "P" material, Box 13, Decimal Files 1953–1960, BSCA, RG 59, NARA.

26. Andrew Hodges, *Alan Turing: The Enigma* (New York: Simon & Schuster, 1983), 507; Canadian official quoted in John Sawatsky, *Men in the Shadows: The RCMP Security Service* (Toronto: Doubleday Canada, 1980) 124–27. See also Daniel J. Robinson, and David Kimmel. "The Queer Career of Homosexual Security Vetting in Cold War Canada," *Canadian Historical Review* 75 (September 1994): 319–45; Gary Kinsman, "'Character Weakness' and 'Fruit Machines': Toward an Analysis of the Anti-Homosexual Security Campaign in the Canadian Civil Service," *Labour/Le Travail* 35 (1995), 133–61; Garry Wotherspoon, "'The Greatest Menace Facing Australia': Homosexuality and the State in NSW During the Cold War," *Labour History* [Australia] 56 (1989): 15–28.

27. Dewey and Nixon quoted in *New York Times*, July 30, 1956; McCarthy quoted in *U.S. News & World Report*, December 4, 1953, 109; James Hagerty, Tran-

script of October 23, 1953, press conference, "Statistics-Security" folder, Box 12, Lot 62-D-146, Decimal Files 1953–60, BSCA, RG 59; John Cramer, *Washington Daily News*, January 15, 1954, 2. See also *Washington Star*, February 7, 1954, A-25. Conservatives continue to characterize the thousands of dismissals under the Eisenhower security program as vindication of McCarthy. See William F. Buckley Jr., *The Redhunter: A Novel Based on the Life of Senator Joe McCarthy* (Boston: Little, Brown, 1999), 281, 340.

28. Young quoted in *Washington Daily News*, January 15, 1954, 2; McLeod quoted in *Washington Star*, February 11, 1954; Bender quoted in *Appendix to the Congressional Record*, February 19, 1954, A1387.

29. Murrey Marder, *Washington Post*, January 1, 1954, 9. On Marder's coverage of McCarthy, see Edwin R. Bayley, *Joe McCarthy and the Press* (New York: Pantheon, 1981), 148–51; Joseph and Stewart Alsop, *Washington Post*, January 20, 1954, and *The Reporter's Trade* (New York: Reynal, 1958), 222–25.

30. *Washington Daily News*, December 21, 1953–January 6, 1954. The series was the basis for the film "Three Brave Men," (Twentieth Century-Fox, 1957); *New York Post*, June 10, 1953, 4; *Washington Daily News*, January 4, 1954.

31. Fern Marja, "Peephole Probe," *New York Post*, June 8–12, 1953; Marcelle Henry, Box 8, Lot 56-D-352, Name Files, BSCA, RG 59, NARA; see also Caute, *Great Fear*, 323–24.

32. Ralph S. Brown, *Loyalty and Security: Employment Tests in the United States* (New Haven, CT: Yale University Press, 1958); HEW warnings quoted in Richard and Gladys Harkness, "Hunt for Reds in U.S. Employ," *U.S. News and World Report*, November 25, 1955, 82. A 1964 study estimated that 1 in 6 Americans had jobs tied to the federal service; see Franklin P. Kilpatrick, Milton C. Cummings Jr., M. Kent Jennings, *The Image of the Federal Service* (Washington, DC: Brookings Institution, 1964), 39–40.

33. *Washington Post*, February 19, 1954. For a detailed chronology of the press coverage concerning the security figures, see Report by the Democratic Senatorial Campaign Committee, February 9, 1954, "General Correspondence—Security Risks" folder, Box 32, Charles Murphy Papers, HST Library.

34. *Washington Post*, February 18, 1954, February 20, 1954, and March 2, 1954.

35. In the first year, the State Department dismissed 149 employees under E.O. 10450, of which 75 were dismissed for sex perversion; by 1956 it had dismissed 367, of which 213 were dismissed for sex perversion. See unnamed, undated, loose-leaf binder, "Employees Terminated for Cause" folder, Box 15, Decimal Files 1953–1960, BSCA, RG 59, NARA; U.S. Congress, Senate, Committee on Foreign Relations, *Nomination of Scott McLeod to be Ambassador to Ireland*, 81st Cong., 1st sess., 1957, 50. For Commerce statistics, see *Washington Post*, February 19, 1954; for CIA statistics, see *New York Times*, March 2, 1954.

36. U.S. Congress, Senate, *Administration of the Federal Employees Security Program*, Hearings before a Subcommittee of the Committee on Post Office and Civil Service, 84th Cong., 1st sess., 1954, 732.

37. Guenter Lewy, *The Federal Loyalty-Security Program: The Need for Reform* (Washington, DC: American Enterprise Institute, 1983), 28; The most famous case of a civil servant accused of homosexuality but officially dismissed for falsifying a federal form was that of Franklin Kameny.

38. Discussions at the 228th Meeting of the NSC, December 9, 1954, Box 6, NSC, Ann Whitman File, DDE Library. In January, 1955, the NSC formally agreed that transfers of security risks not accused of subversive activities to nonsensitive positions was consistent with E.O. 10450. Such transfers, however, were not available to homosexuals. See Discussions at 231st Meeting of the NSC, January 13, 1955, Box 6, NSC, Ann Whitman File, DDE Library.

39. Shilts, *Conduct Unbecoming*, 107–8; Howard Snyder to Eli Ginsberg December 21, 1951, Snyder Folder, Box 2, Eli Ginsberg Papers, DDE Library. Snyder would become known for misdiagnosing Eisenhower's 1955 heart attack; see Clarence G. Lasby. *Eisenhower's Heart Attack: How Ike Beat Heart Disease and Held on to the Presidency* (Lawrence: University Press of Kansas, 1997).

40. "Campaign for public understanding" quoted from Minutes of Cabinet Meeting, November 19, 1954, Box 4, Cabinet Series, Ann Whitman File, DDE Library; Nixon quoted from Discussions at the 228th Meeting of the NSC, December 9, 1954, Box 6, NSC, Ann Whitman File, DDE Library; Richard and Gladys Harkness, "How About Those Security Cases?" pts. 1 and 2, *Reader's Digest*, September and November, 1955; For a less sensationalistic explanation of the Joseph Petersen spy case, see James Bamford, *The Puzzle Palace: A Report on America's Most Secret Agency* (New York: Penguin, 1982), 173–77.

41. Rick Ewig, "McCarthy Era Politics: The Ordeal of Senator Lester Hunt," *Annals of Wyoming* 55 (spring 1983): 9–21; Interview no. 7 with Leonard H. Ballard, October 20, 1983, Senate Historical Office, U.S. Senate, 217–19; Tyler Abell, ed., *Drew Pearson Diaries, 1949–1959* (New York: Holt, Rinehart, & Winston, 1974), 319–23; *New York Post*, October 19, 1964; Von Hoffman, *Citizen Cohn*, 231; James J. Kiepper, *Styles Bridges: Yankee Senator* (Sugar Hill, N.H.: Phoenix, 2001), 145–47.

42. Ken Ringle, "Allen Drury, Father of the D.C. Drama," *Washington Post*, September 4, 1998, D-1.

43. Allen Drury, *Advise and Consent* (New York: Doubleday, 1959; reprint, New York: Pocket Books, 1961), 338, 523–29, 545. Columnist Peter Edson claimed in 1953 that Congress included several homosexual members, including one "notorious" senator. *Washington Daily News*, June 29, 1953. Since members of Congress were immune from prosecution on misdemeanor charges while attending Congress, they were not subject to the same enforcement mechanisms as civil servants. For rumors about the dropping of homosexual charges against one Con-

gressmen, see *Washington Newsletter*, Mattachine Society, December 16, 1956, Folder 19, Box 1961, ACLU Papers, Princeton University.

44. Administration officials quoted in Maxwell Robb to Sherman Adams, February 10, 1955, and agency head quoted in Halbert Dunn, M.D., Memorandum on the Existing Security Program, January 12, 1955, both in "Security #4" folder, Box 66, Subject Series, Confidential Files, WHCF, DDE Library. The Rockefeller Foundation funded a series of studies of the loyalty/security program, including one by Eleanor Bontecou, *The Federal Loyalty-Security Program* (Ithaca, NY: Cornell University Press, 1953). The Fund for the Republic funded Adam Yarmolinsky, *Case Studies in Personnel Security* (Washington, DC: Bureau of National Affairs, 1955). See also *Annals of the American Academy of Political and Social Science*, July 1955; *Bulletin of Atomic Scientists*, April 1955.

45. Committee on Cooperation with Governmental (Federal) Agencies of the Group for the Advancement of Psychiatry, "Report on Homosexuality with Particular Emphasis on This Problem in Governmental Agencies," Report no. 30, Topeka, Kansas, January 1955.

46. Karl M. Bowman and Bernice Engle, "A Psychiatric Evaluation of the Laws of Homosexuality," *American Journal of Psychiatry* 112, no. 6 (February 1956): 577–83; "A Noted Psychiatrist Asks Why So Much Hysteria?" *Mattachine Review*, July–August, 1955, 14–15.

47. Hubert Humphrey, "Wanted: An Efficient and Just Government Security Program," Address before the American Society of Public Administrators and the American Political Science Association, n.d., in "Federal Government Loyalty-Security Program" folder, Box 13, Decimal Files 1953–1960, Lot 62-D-146, BSCA, RG 59, NARA; Humphrey and Douglas Aircraft official quoted in *Washington Daily News*, March 14, 1955, 5. See also U.S. Congress, Senate, *Commission on Government Security*, Hearings of Subcommittee on Reorganization, Government Operations Committee, 84th Cong., 1st sess., March 1955; *Report of the Commission on Government Security*, June 21, 1957; *Washington Post*, June 23, 1957, B-10.

48. Bamford, *Puzzle Palace*, 177–96; Vincent and Nan Buranelli, *Spy/CounterSpy: An Encyclopedia of Espionage* (New York: McGraw-Hill, 1982), 204; *Newsweek*, September 19, 1960, 33–37.

49. *Los Angeles Times*, September 10, 1960, 2; R. G. Waldeck, "Homosexual International," *Human Events*, September 29, 1960, 453; *Los Angeles Examiner*, September 10, 1960, 2; George Sokolsky, *Los Angeles Express*, September 14, 1960; R. E. L. Masters, *The Homosexual Revolution* (New York: Julian Press, 1962), 139–43. See also James Shawcross, "How the Reds Blackmailed Homosexuals into Spying for Them!" *Top Secret*, February 1961, 14.

50. "Discussion at the 463rd Meeting of the National Security Council, October 13, 1960," Box 13, NSC Series, Papers of the President of the U.S., 1953–1961 (Ann Whitman Files), DDE Library.

51. U.S. Congress, House, *Security Practices in the National Security Agency,* Committee on Un-American Activities, 87th Cong., 2nd sess., August 13, 1962, 15; *New York Times,* July 29, 1961; interview with Joan Cassidy, February 13, 1997.

52. Eisenhower, *Mandate for Change, 1953-1956,* 331. For a similar critique of the Eisenhower security program, see Jeffrey Broadwater, *Eisenhower and the Anti-Communist Crusade* (Chapel Hill: University of North Carolina Press, 1992), 210–11.

53. Martin, *Adlai Stevenson,* 708.

Chapter Seven: Interrogations and Disappearances

1. Interview with Madeleine Tress, November 11, 1998; Len Evans interview with Madeleine Tress, April 16, 1983, GLHS OHP #00-07, GLHSNC; Madeleine Tress FBI file (given to the author by Tress). Quotations in the next two paragraphs are from these sources as well.

2. Interview with Ramon G., February 10, 1997; interview with Joan Cassidy, February 13, 1997; Bowling quoted in Keith Vacha, *Quiet Fire: Memoirs of Older Gay Men,* ed. Cassie Damewood (Trumansburg, NY: Crossing Press, 1985), 138. See also interview with Madeleine Tress, November 11, 1998; interview with Raymond Mailloux, March 12, 1997.

3. Interview with Madeleine Tress, November 11, 1998; Len Evans interview with Madeleine Tress, April 16, 1983, GLHS OHP #00-07, GLHSNC; Madeleine Tress FBI file.

4. Interview with J. R., Len Evans Papers, GLHSNC; interview with B. F., August 27, 2001; Collins quoted in Israel J. Gerber, *Man on a Pendulum: A Case History of an Invert* (New York: American Press, 1955), 255–63. See also interview with Bruce Scott, 1978, Gregory Sprague Collection, CHS.

5. Interview with Raymond Mailloux, March 12, 1997; Paul Clark quoted in the film *Before Stonewall* (dir. Greta Schiller, 1984); interview with Edward Keller, June 20, 2000; Len Evans interview with Madeleine Tress, April 16, 1983, GLHS OHP #00-07, GLHSNC.

6. Interview with Phil Hannema, July 24, 2001; Marcel Martin, "The Homosexual on the Job," *Tangents* 1, no. 4 (January 1966): 4–8; Fowler quoted in Esther Newton, *Cherry Grove, Fire Island: Sixty Years in America's First Gay and Lesbian Town* (Boston: Beacon Press, 1993), 101; "his own kind" from Hoey Committee Report, 4.

7. Interview with Joan Cassidy, February 13, 1997; Donald Webster Cory, *The Homosexual in America* (New York: Greenberg, 1951), 92–93.

8. Interview with P. A. and L. D., February 4, 1997; interview with Joan Cassidy, February 13, 1997.

9. Interview with P. A. and L. D., January 15, 1997, 4; U.S. Congress, House, Committee on D.C., *Crime and Law Enforcement in the District of Columbia,* 81st

Cong., 2nd sess., February 27, 1950, 631; "Pervert Elimination Campaign—Monthly Reports," Box 24, Entry 768, Office Files of Secretary Oscar Chapman, 1933–1953, RG 48, NARA; interview with Jack Frey and Peter Morris, January 20, 1997; vigilante violence noted in *Washington Evening Star*, October 31, 1950, B-1.

10. *Washington Star*, July 1, 1953.

11. Gruenberger and Kersey quoted in John Loughery, *The Other Side of Silence: Men's Lives and Gay Identities: A Twentieth-Century History* (New York: Henry Holt, 1998), 208; anonymous letter to the editor, *Drum* no. 23 (1967), 40; interview with Edward Kellar, June 20, 2000.

12. Frank S. Caprio, M.D., *Female Homosexuality: A Psychodynamic Study of Lesbianism* (New York: Citadel Press, 1954), 70–71; Hoey Committee Hearings, 2288; Leila J. Rupp and Verta Taylor, *Survival in the Doldrums: The American Women's Rights Movement, 1945 to the 1960s* (New York: Oxford University Press, 1987), 107; Betty Deran interview, May, 7, 1983, Len Evans Papers, GLHSNC. On lesbian communities in other cities, see Elizabeth Lapovsky Kennedy and Madeline Davis, *Boots of Leather, Slippers of Gold: The History of a Lesbian Community* (New York: Routledge, 1993); Lillian Faderman, *Odd Girls and Twilight Lovers: A History of Lesbian Life in Twentieth-Century America* (New York: Penguin, 1991).

13. Interview with Barbara Kraft, September 10, 1994; Jack Anderson and Fred Blumenthal, "Washington Tempo," *Tempo*, May 24, 1954, 34.

14. Interview with Bruce Scott, 1978, Gregory Sprague Collection, CHS; Bruce Scott's civil service file, author's possession. See also Bruce Scott, "Joint Appendix to the Appeal from the United States District Court," April 23, 1963, *Scott v. Macy et al.*, Civil Action No. 1050-63, Kinsey Institute.

15. Interview with Ted Richards, October 30, 1996; Brett Beemyn, "A Queer Capital: Lesbian, Gay, and Bisexual Life in Washington, D.C., 1890–1955" (Ph.D. diss., University of Iowa, 1997), 225.

16. John Logan, "You're Fired!" *Mattachine Review*, June 1956, 27–29; scientist quoted in Kay Tobin and Randy Wicker, *The Gay Crusaders* (New York: Paperback Library, 1972), 89–97, and interview with Frank Kameny, October 10, 1991; "three or four years" from B. D. H. of Washington, D.C., Letters to the Editor, *The Ladder*, May 1957, 22; Georgetown graduate quoted in interview with P. A. and L. D., February 4, 1997. On gay men discharged from the military becoming hair dressers, see interview with Henry Yaffe, March 1997 and interview with Bob Contillion, January 21, 1997.

17. Interview with Madeleine Tress, November 11, 1998; interview with Bruce Scott, 1978, Gregory Sprague Collection, CHS; Bruce Scott, "Joint Appendix to the Appeal from the United States District Court"; Bruce Scott to David Carliner, October 29, 1962, "Scott v. Macy" folder, Box 29, Gregory Sprague Collection, CHS. In *Scott v. Macy et al.*, 349 F. 2d 182 (D.C., 1965), the U.S. Court of Appeals found that Scott's dismissal "not only disqualified him from the vast field of all employ-

ment dominated by the Government but also jeopardized his ability to find employment elsewhere."

18. Szluk quoted in Griffin Fariello, *Red Scare: Memories of the American Inquisition: An Oral History* (New York: W. W. Norton, 1995), 123–24; GSA official quoted in James Thomas to Francis Flanagan, June 29, 1950, Case File 40-20, Permanent Subcommittee on Investigations, Committee on Government Operations, RG 46, NARA; U.S. Congress, House, Committee on Government Operations, *Security and Personnel Practices and Procedures of the Department of State*, House Report no. 1334, 83rd Cong., 2nd sess., March 9, 1954, 2, 10. On the Braverman suicide, see also Nicholas Von Hoffman, *Citizen Cohn: The Life and Times of Roy Cohn* (New York: Bantam Books, 1988), 128; *Washington Times-Herald*, April 30, 1953.

19. "Andrew Ferrence," Box 29, Name Files 1954–56, BSCA, RG 59, NARA; interview with B. F., August 27, 2001.

20. Conference Report of Regional Security Supervisors, April 1953, Box 16, Decimal Files 1953–1960, BSCA, RG 59, NARA; U.S. Congress, Senate, *Executive Sessions of the Senate Foreign Relations Committee, Historical Series*, vol. 5, 83rd Cong., 1st sess., February 5, 1953, 87.

21. *Washington Evening Star*, July 13, 1948; *Washington Post*, April 21, 1953, 22. Research into these cases is warranted, but the response time for FOIA requests can exceed one year.

22. Gregory Hayes, "Caught in Act, Pervert Quits State Dept. Post," *Washington Times-Herald*, August 4, 1950, 3; Beemyn, "Queer Capital" (Ph.D. diss.), 196–97; Sylvia Nasar, *A Beautiful Mind* (New York: Touchstone Books, 2001), 184–89.

23. Victor S. Navasky, *Naming Names* (New York: Penguin, 1980), ix. John Ford to W. Scott McLeod, "Informant Development among Dismissed Homosexuals," May 26, 1953, unfoldered material, Box 12, Decimal Files 1953–1960, BSCA, RG 59, NARA; Hoey Committee Hearings, July 26, 1950, 2302; Thomas H. Tattersall FBI File #11509. The Tattersall documents were obtained by Robert J. Richards, one of the civil servants on whom Tattersall informed. Richards also acted as a government informant against suspected homosexuals; see Lou Chibbaro Jr., "Ex-employee Suing over 1955 Resignation," *Washington Blade*, November 26, 1982, 1. I thank John D'Emilio for sharing these documents with me. For a parallel case of an ex-Communist informant with a history of mental illness, see discussion of Matt Cvetic, protagonist in the film *I Was a Communist*, in Michael Paul Rogin, *Ronald Reagan, the Movie and Other Episodes in Political Demonology* (Berkeley and Los Angeles: University of California Press, 1987), 247.

24. Interview with P. A. and L. D., January 15, 1997, and February 4, 1997.

25. Interview with P. A. and L. D., February 4, 1997.

26. E. M., "To Be Accused Is to Be Guilty," *One*, April 1953, 3–4; many gay men discovered the gay subculture by indirect contacts with the Lavender Scare, such as reading the proscriptive literature it generated. For accounts of gay men who

first learned of gay venues by reading *Washington Confidential*, see Jack Nichols, unpublished memoirs; interview with Jack Frey and Peter Morris, January 20, 1997.

27. Chibbaro, *Washington Blade*, November 26, 1982, 1. On the complex transition from a gender identity to a sexual identity and how it varied by class and ethnicity, see George Chauncey, *Gay New York: Gender, Urban Culture, and the Making of a Gay Male World, 1890–1940* (New York: Basic Books, 1994), 47–63.

28. Interview with Jack Frey and Peter Morris by Brett Beemyn, March 22, 1994; interview with Bruce Scott, August 26, 1985, Gregory Sprague Collection, CHS; interview with Frank Kameny, October 19, 1991; interview with Chuck Bradshaw, March 13, 1997; "one man" quoted in Gerber, *Man on a Pendulum*, 244; see also Beemyn, "A Queer Capital: Race, Class, Gender and the Changing Social Landscape of Washington's Gay Communities, 1940–1955," in *Creating a Place for Ourselves: Lesbian, Gay and Bisexual Community Histories*, ed. Brett Beemyn (New York: Routledge, 1997), 185–86.

29. Jack Nichols, unpublished memoir; interview with Jack Nichols, July 15, 1994; interview with Jack Frey and Peter Morris by Brett Beemyn, March 22, 1994; Jack Lait and Lee Mortimer, *Washington Confidential* (New York: Crown, 1951), 120; Beemyn, "Queer Capital," in *Creating a Place for Ourselves*, 186. Sometime in the late 1950s or early 1960s another Copper Skillet opened on Eighteenth and Pennsylvania.

30. Interview with Raymond Mailloux, March 12, 1997.

31. Interview with Henry Yaffe, March 1997; interview with Ramon G., February 10, 1997; interview with Ted Richards, October 30, 1996. While nearly everyone I have interviewed refers to the bars being watched or raided, I have no concrete evidence or even recollection of a specific raid in the 1950s. This suggests a police or security presence at times, but few if any actual raids. Yaffe remembers vice officers Blick and Fochett coming into the bars to observe people, but does not recall any raids.

32. Beemyn, "Queer Capital," in *Creating a Place for Ourselves*, 187; interview with Frank Kameny, October 19, 1991, 35; interview with Jack Frey and Peter Morris by Brett Beemyn, March 22, 1994. On "The Whiffenpoof Song," see www.whiffenpoofs.com/history.html.

33. In 1973, plaintiffs in a lawsuit against the Civil Service Commission requested statistics on the number of homosexuals separated each year. The CSC denied the request, claiming it was "burdensome and oppressive." See *Society for Individual Rights v. Hampton*, 63 FRD 399 (1973).

34. Figures for 1947–1950 quoted in Hoey Committee Report, 25; figures for 1953–1955 quoted in U.S. Congress, Senate, *Administration of the Federal Employees Security Program*, Hearings before a Subcommittee of the Committee on Post Office and Civil Service, 84th Cong., 1st sess., 1954, 732; Lourie quoted in *Washington*

Post, April 21, 1953. During House and Senate appropriation hearings each year, the State Department reported on the number of homosexuals separated during the previous year. The total reported at such hearings between 1947 and 1967 was approximately 950. This is consistent with the estimation of department security officer Paul H. Clarke, who estimated in 1984 that 900–1,000 homosexuals had been separated. See the documentary film *Before Stonewall*, (dir. Greta Schiller, 1984).

35. Newton, *Cherry Grove, Fire Island*, 100–102.

36. Poe quoted in Roy Wampler to David Johnson, February 7, 1997 (see also George Poe's obituary in *Washington Blade*, September 8, 1995, 33); Chicagoan quoted from interview with Charles B., September 1980, Gregory Sprague Collection, CHS; applicant statistics from Hoey Committee Report, 9. I have intentionally excluded dismissals from the military for homosexuality because such dismissals came under different jurisdiction, had a different rationale, and have been covered more extensively by scholars. See Allan Bérubé, *Coming Out under Fire: The History of Gay Men and Women in World War II* (New York: Free Press, 1990); and Randy Shilts, *Conduct Unbecoming: Gays and Lesbians in the U.S. Military* (New York: St. Martin's Press, 1993).

37. Fitzsimmons quoted in *Washington Daily News*, March 14, 1955, 5, and U.S. Congress, Senate, Committee on Government Operations, Subcommittee on Reorganization, *Commission on Government Security*, 84th Cong., 1st sess., March 14, 1955; Adams quoted in Newton, *Cherry Grove, Fire Island*, 100–102; Mattachine materials quoted in John Logan, "You're Fired!" *Mattachine Review*, June 1956, 27–29.

38. On private security consulting firms, see Robert Kirk, "Fair Employment Practices and the Homosexual," *Mattachine Review*, April 1956, 41–42; and Logan, "You're Fired!" 27–29; on the experience of one West Coast company with such security firms, see "Are You Now or Have You Ever Been a Homosexual?" *One*, April 1953, 6–13; psychiatrist quoted in Karl M. Bowman, M.D., and Bernice Engle, M.A., "A Psychiatric Evaluation of Laws of Homosexuality," *American Journal of Psychiatry* 112 (February 1956): 580.

39. Robert Bellah, "Veritas at Harvard: An Exchange," *New York Review of Books* 24, no. 12 (July 14, 1977): 38, cited in John McCumber, *Time in the Ditch: American Philosophy and the McCarthy Era* (Evanston, IL: Northwestern University Press, 2001), 20–21. On anticommunism in the academy, see Ellen W. Schrecker, *No Ivory Tower: McCarthyism and the Universities* (New York: Oxford University Press, 1986).

40. Interview with Ramon G. and "Patrick W.," February 10, 1997; interview with Joan Cassidy, February 13, 1997.

41. Harry Hay to David Johnson, February 25, 1997, author's files. A similar but less detailed account of Hay's first learning of the State Department firings is

provided in Stuart Timmons, *The Trouble with Harry Hay: Founder of the Modern Gay Movement* (Boston: Alyson Publications, 1990), 132.

42. Harry Hay interview with Jonathan Katz, March 31, 1974, quoted in Jonathan Ned Katz, *Gay American History: Lesbians and Gay Men in the U.S.A.* (New York: Thomas Y. Crowell, 1976), 408. Hay also points to the antigay purges as the reason for founding the Mattachine Society in an interview published in Nancy Adair and Casey Adair, *Word Is Out: Stories of Some of Our Lives* (San Francisco: New Glide Publications, 1978) 240–41. Hay's July 1950 "Preliminary Concepts" quoted in Harry Hay, *Radically Gay: Gay Liberation in the Words of Its Founder*, ed. Will Roscoe (Boston: Beacon Press, 1996), 63–64; on Hay's own encounter with government security policies, see Timmons, *Trouble with Harry Hay*, 118; "second U.S. capital" from *Washington Star*, October 4, 1953; on California's dependence on government workers and contracts, see Stephen J. Whitfield, *The Culture of the Cold War* (Baltimore: Johns Hopkins University Press, 1991), 75; and U.S. Civil Service Commission, *72nd Annual Report*, June 30, 1955, 171.

43. Hay quoted in Katz, *Gay American History*, 408–11; Hay also discusses his canvassing of gay beaches with a controversial antiwar petition and a comparatively modest gay proposal in Anne-Marie Cusac, "The Progressive Interview: Harry Hay," *Progressive*, September 1998. In his groundbreaking history of Hay's Mattachine Society, John D'Emilio stresses Hay's participation in the Communist and Progressive parties in his decision to found Mattachine but downplays the role of the Lavender Scare. See D'Emilio, *Sexual Politics, Sexual Communities: The Making of the Homosexual Minority, 1940–1970* (Chicago: University of Chicago Press, 1983), 57–62. In a recent critique of D'Emilio, Martin Meeker questions the notion of a "retreat to respectability" but also ignores the role the purges played in the group's founding. See Martin Meeker, "Behind the Mask of Respectability: Reconsidering the Mattachine Society and Male Homophile Practice, 1950s and 1960s," *Journal of the History of Sexuality* 10, no. 1 (2001): 78–116. Literary critic Robert Corber argues that the concern with gay security risks was a reaction to the founding of Mattachine and the beginnings of gay political organizing. But the purges began before Mattachine was founded, and none of the records that I have examined suggest that the politicians and security agents behind the purges were aware of Mattachine. See Robert J. Corber, *In the Name of National Security: Hitchcock, Homophobia, and the Political Construction of Gender in Postwar America* (Durham, NC: Duke University Press, 1993), 6–8, 65–68.

44. Harry Johnson, "And a Red Too . . ." *One*, September 1953, 2; "Open Letter to Sen. Dirksen," *Mattachine Review*, January–February, 1955, 12–14; D'Emilio, *Sexual Politics, Sexual Communities*, 114. On the history of *Mattachine Review, One*, and other publications, see Rodger Streitmatter, *Unspeakable: The Rise of the Gay and Lesbian Press in America* (Boston: Faber & Faber, 1995), 17–50.

45. The Mattachine Society, Inc., *Washington Newsletter* 1, no. 2 (August 16, 1956), Folder 19, Box 1961, ACLU Papers, Princeton University.

46. Huggins quoted in B. D. H. of Washington, D.C., Letters to the Editor, *The Ladder*, May 1957, 22. I pieced together Huggins story from a variety of different sources, including many that only refer to him by his initials. Huggins described his background and trouble at the University of Illinois in a letter he wrote to the ACLU complaining of FBI harassment after he left the civil service. See B. D. Huggins to ACLU, "Personal and Confidential," September 18, 1964, Box 1063, ACLU Papers, Princeton University. D'Emilio cites his case, but was unaware that he was the founder of a Mattachine chapter; see D'Emilio, *Sexual Politics, Sexual Communities*, 47.

47. Letter from Gonzalo Segura Jr., to Dwight Huggins, September 4, 1956, quoted in Toby Marotta, *The Politics of Homosexuality* (Boston: Houghton Mifflin, 1981), 14.

48. I have located six issues of the *Washington Newsletter* of the Mattachine Society. Four are preserved at the ACLU archives at Princeton University and two at the New York Public Library. The earliest is dated Aug 16, 1956 (vol. 1., no. 2), while the latest is dated August, 1958 (vol. 3, no. 7). See Mattachine Society, Inc., *Washington Newsletter*, August 16, 1956, December 16, 1956, January 1957, and February 1958, all located in Folder 19, Box 1961, ACLU Papers, Princeton University; issues January 1958 and August 1958 in Folder 6, Box 8, IGIC, New York Public Library. An FBI report estimated the chapter had 40 members; see Document 664, June 19, 1958, Mattachine Society FBI File #100-33796; the *Mattachine Review* of September, 1957, lists membership of the various chapters as follows: New York (31 "active members"), Los Angeles (25–30), D.C. (25), Chicago (4). Total membership in all homophile organizations in 1960 numbered about 350; see D'Emilio, *Sexual Politics, Sexual Communities*, 115. For one of the gay legal cases where Edward Kehoe served as counsel, see *McDermett v. United States*, 98 A. 2d 287 (D.C. Mun. App., 1953).

49. Mattachine Society, Inc., *Washington Newsletter*, January 1958 and August 1958; Document 649, April 1, 1957, and Document 664, June 19, 1958, Mattachine Society FBI File #100-33796. Gay Washingtonians who knew of this early Mattachine chapter in the late 1950s remember it being headed by Bill Frye, who had a reputation for "playing fast and loose with things" and being "out to make an easy buck," which may have contributed to its decline and disappearance. Interview with Frank Kameny, October 19, 1991; see also interview with Jack Nichols, July 15, 1994.

50. Robert L. Thomas to One, Inc., February 17, 1955, "Washington, D.C." clippings file, One Institute and Archives; beating reported in *Washington Daily News*, February 11, 1955.

51. Brief of Appellee, Docket 901, *Kelly v. U.S.*, Records of the Municipal Court

of Appeals for the District of Columbia; *Kelly v. U.S.*, 73 A. 2d 232 (D.C. Mun. App., 1950).

52. *Washington Times-Herald*, November 10, 1948, 21; see also *Washington Times-Herald*, November 11, 1948; *Washington Star*, September 19, 1948, A-2, and October 27, 1949.

53. *Kelly v. United States*, 194 F. 2d 150 (U.S. App. D.C., 1952); *Washington Star*, May 5, 1950, B-19, January 10, 1952.

54. Guard's new trial reported in *Washington Star*, January 11, 1952; conviction rate quoted in *Washington Star*, April 2, 1954; other retrials resulting from *Kelly* reported in *Washington Star*, January 13, and February 11, 1952. For appeals brought in the wake of the Kelly counsels, see *Bicksler v. United States*, 90 A. 2d 233 (D.C. Mun. App., 1952); *King v. United States*, 90 A. 2d 229 (D.C. Mun. App., 1952); and *Reed v. United States*, 93 A. 2d 568 (D.C. Mun. App., 1953). On the effect of the Kelly counsels, see Harold Jacobs, "Decoy Enforcement of Homosexual Laws," *University of Pennsylvania Law Review* 112 (1963): 259–84.

55. "Hotbed of perversion" from *Washington Star*, April 24, 1952; on the controversial meeting between the U.S. Attorney and the D.C. judges, see *Washington Star*, March 31, April 2, 3, 5, 6, 1952; conviction statistics quoted in *Washington Star*, May 7, 1954.

56. *Guarro v. United States*, 237 F. 2d 578 (U.S. App. D.C., 1956); *Washington Evening Star*, September 27, 1956; *Washington Post*, September 28, 1956.

57. *Mattachine Review*, December 1956, 10–11; Mattachine Society, Inc., *Washington Newsletter*, December 16, 1956. On the use of homosexual slang, see *Bicksler v. United States*, 90 A. 2d 233 (D.C. Mun. App., 1952); "one prosecutor" quoted in *Dyson v. United States*, 97 A. 2d 135 (D.C. Mun. App., 1953).

Chapter Eight: "Homosexual Citizens"

1. Interview with Frank Kameny, October 19, 1991; *Kameny v. Brucker*, Petition for Writ of Certiorari, no. 676, U.S. Supreme Court, October 1960; B. D. Hull to Franklin Kameny, October 15, 1957, FEK Papers. On Kameny's role in the U.S. Army Map Service project, see *Chico Enterprise Record*, October 4, 1957.

2. Robert A. Divine, *The Sputnik Challenge* (New York: Oxford University Press, 1993); Kay Tobin and Randy Wicker, *The Gay Crusaders* (New York: Paperback Library, 1972), 89–95; interview with Rae Beck Kameny, 1992.

3. On the federal government as the primary employer of scientists, see *Science*, April 2, 1965, 51; Edward Shils, "Security and Science Sacrificed to Loyalty," *Bulletin of the Atomic Scientists*, April 1955, 106; Kameny to the Mattachine Society (New York), May 5, 1960, FEK Papers. On the relationship of scientists to the security system, see also Shils, *Torment of Secrecy*, 176–91; Walter Gellhorn, *Security, Loyalty, and Science* (Ithaca, NY: Cornell University Press, 1950).

4. *Kameny v. Brucker et al.*, 282 F. 2d 823 (1960); *Kameny v. Brucker*, Petition for

Writ of Certiorari, no. 676, U.S. Supreme Court, October 1960 term; see also Tobin and Wicker, *Gay Crusaders*, 89–95.

5. Donald Webster Cory, *The Homosexual In America: A Subjective Approach* (New York: Greenberg, 1951); on the Supreme Court denial, see *Kameny v. Brucker et al.*, 365 U.S. 843 (1961); and *Washington Star*, March 21, 1961. On the importance of Kameny's legal brief from the perspective of a legal scholar, see William N. Eskridge Jr., *Gaylaw: Challenging the Apartheid of the Closet* (Cambridge, MA: Harvard University Press, 1999), 96–97 and "January 27, 1961: The Birth of Gaylegal Equality Arguments," *NYU Annual Survey of American Law* 57, no. 2 (2000): 39–48.

6. Memo to FBI Director, August 8, 1961, Document 122, FBI File #HQ 100-403320; interview with Frank Kameny, October 19, 1991, 77–78; *New York Mattachine Newsletter*, November 1961.

7. Franklin Kameny to Robert Kennedy, June 28, 1962, Document 125, FBI File #100-403320, interview with Frank Kameny, October 19, 1991, 40–41.

8. Mattachine Society of Washington, "Constitution" and "Application for Membership," both in FEK Papers; officer quoted in interview with John Swanson, July 1992; on the MSW reunion, see *Washington Blade*, November 21, 1986, 1. See also interview with Bruce Scott, October 24, 1992.

9. Frank Kameny, "Civil Liberties: A Progress Report," *New York Mattachine Newsletter*, January 1965, 7–22; interview with Frank Kameny, October 19, 1991; John D'Emilio, *Sexual Politics, Sexual Communities: The Making of the Homosexual Minority, 1940–1970* (Chicago: University of Chicago Press, 1983), 150–54. The MSW's references to the Declaration of Independence and Constitution stood in stark contrast to the founding documents of the original Mattachine Society in California, which referenced the Atlantic Charter and the United Nations Charter. See Harry Hay, *Radically Gay: Gay Liberation in the Words of Its Founder*, ed. Will Roscoe (Boston: Beacon Press, 1996), 67.

10. Jack Nichols, unpublished memoir; see also Lige Clarke and Jack Nichols, *I Have More Fun with You Than Anybody* (New York: St. Martin's Press, 1972); James T. Sears, *Lonely Hunters: An Oral History of Lesbian and Gay Southern Life, 1948–1968* (Boulder, CO: Westview Press, 1997), 185–211.

11. Interview with Frank Kameny, October 19, 1991, 47; Public Law 85-87, 71 Stat. 278, 85th Congress, H.R. 3400, July 10, 1957; U.S. Congress, House, Committee on the District of Columbia, Subcommittee no. 4, *Amending District of Columbia Charitable Solicitation Act*, 88th Cong., 1st sess., August 8–9, 1963, and January 10, 1964, 91–92 [hereafter *Charitable Solicitation Act Hearings*].

12. *Washington Star*, September 16, 1962, A-22; *Charitable Solicitation Act Hearings*, 1–3. Because it singled out one organization for punishment, H.R. 5990 was an unconstitutional "bill of attainder." In 1971, Dowdy was convicted of accepting a $25,000 bribe from a Texas construction company official. See *New York Times*, December 31, 1971, 1.

13. *Washington Post*, August 8, 1963, A14; MSW to Homophile Organizations, September 4, 1963, "Recent Congressional Hearings on the bill H.R. 5990," FEK Papers. The *Washington Post* published a series of articles on homosexuality in February 1965 that received praise from the MSW. See Letters to the Editor, *Washington Post*, February 28, 1965.

14. *Charitable Solicitation Act Hearings*, 22–29, 58–71.

15. *Charitable Solicitation Act Hearings*, 7–8, 22, 28, 68. The hearings and subsequent controversy were widely covered by the Washington press. See *Washington Post*, August 9, 10, October 4, November 9, 1963; *Washington Star*, August 8, 9, 10, September 18, November 9, 1963; *Washington Daily News*, August 9, 1963. The conservative *Washington Times-Herald*, champion of the antigay purges in the early 1950s, ceased publication in 1954 after it was bought by the *Washington Post*. See Edwin R. Bayley, *Joe McCarthy and the Press* (New York: Pantheon, 1981), 151; Katharine Graham, *Personal History* (New York: Vintage Books, 1998), 216–24.

16. *Charitable Solicitation Act Hearings*, 28–38; Los Angeles television journalist Paul Coates had a similar reaction in 1962 when a member of the Daughters of Bilitis lesbian organization appeared on *Confidential Files* and estimated DOB membership to be between 125 and 150. "Don't you mean thousand?" he responded; see Edward Alwood, *Straight News: Gays, Lesbians, and the News Media* (New York: Columbia University Press, 1996), 42–43.

17. *Charitable Solicitation Act Hearings*, 12, 41–44, 76–79; *Washington Post*, August 10, 1963.

18. Dowdy quoted in *Congressional Record*, August 11, 1964, 18943–49; U.S. Congress, House, Committee on the District of Columbia, *Amending District of Columbia Charitable Solicitation Act*, Report no. 1222, 88th Cong., 2nd sess., March 6, 1964. See also *Washington Post*, October 4, 1963, and March 21, 1964; *Hollywood Citizen-News*, October 30, 1964.

19. *Indianapolis News*, October 28, 1964; *Binghamton (New York) Press*, October 28, 1964; on newspaper coverage, see *New York Mattachine Newsletter*, September 1963, 6, and October 1964, 3; "Roll Call," *Drum*, October 1964, 33; Frank Kameny, "A Message to the Members of the Mattachine Society of Washington from the President of the Society on the State of the Society," April 1964, FEK Papers. See also D'Emilio, *Sexual Politics, Sexual Communities*, 50–54. *Drum* magazine was a radical new gay publication that featured both news and erotic images of interest to gay men. See Marc Stein, *City of Sisterly and Brotherly Loves: Lesbian and Gay Philadelphia, 1945–1972* (Chicago: University of Chicago Press, 2000), 231–40.

20. Director of the national ACLU quoted in "Civil Liberties on the 'Upswing' Again," *Mattachine Review*, July–August 1955, 37; "ACLU Position on Homosexuality," January 7, 1957, Folder 7, Box 1127, ACLU Papers, Princeton; reprinted in *Mattachine Review*, March 1957, 7, and *Civil Liberties*, March 1957; Merle Miller, "What It Means to Be a Homosexual," *New York Times Magazine*,

January 17, 1971, 10; "Resolution of the NCACLU on Federal Employment of Homosexuals," August 7, 1964, and "ACLU Statement on Homosexuality," n.d., FEK Papers. The NCACLU's statement was reported in *Washington Post*, October 11, 1964. See also Vern Bullough, "Lesbianism, Homosexuality, and the American Civil Liberties Union," *Journal of Homosexuality* 13 (fall 1986): 23–33; Charles Markmann, *The Noblest Cry: A History of the American Civil Liberties Union* (New York: St. Martin's Press, 1965), 226, 387–88, 397; William A. Donohue, *The Politics of the American Civil Liberties Union* (New Brunswick, NJ: Transaction Books, 1985), 281–85.

21. James Ridgeway, "Snooping in the Park," *New Republic*, January 16, 1965, 9; *Norton v. Macy et al.*, 417 F. 2d 1161 (D.C. Cir., 1969); "Federal Employment of Homosexuals: Narrowing the Efficiency Standard," *Catholic University Law Review* 19 (1969): 267.

22. Pamphlets reprinted in *Homosexual Citizen*, January 1967.

23. Scott arguments quoted from "Joint Appendix," *Scott v. Macy et al.*, Civil Action no. 1050-63, (D.C.), Kinsey Institute; Scott as symbol quoted in *Washington Star*, April 24, 1963; Scott's attorney quoted in "Cross-Currents," *The Ladder*, August 1963; gay press reaction quoted from *New York Mattachine Newsletter*, November and December 1964; Judge Hart quoted in *Washington Post*, April 21, 1964, A-12. See also *Scott v. Macy et al.*, 349 F. 2d 182 (D.C., 1965); *Chicago Evening American*, April 25, 1963; *Washington Post*, April 24, 1963.

24. Interview with John Swanson, July 1992; interview with Lilli Vincenz, July 15, 1992; Jack Nichols, unpublished memoirs; Constitution of the Mattachine Society of Washington, Article II, Section 2, FEK Papers; Mattachine Society of Washington *Gazette*, June 1963; President (Frank Kameny) to the Executive Board, April 16, 1964, "'Programs' at membership meetings," FEK Papers.

25. Interview with John Swanson, July 1992; interview with Lilli Vincenz, July 15, 1992. On the size of the MSW, see *Charitable Solicitation Act Hearings*, 29, 41; *Insider*, April 1965; *Washington Post*, March 24, 1966. On Kameny's racial attitudes, see Kameny to *Washington Post*, November 17, 1964, DOB folder, FEK Papers, and interview with Frank Kameny, January 26, 1992. Circulation of MSW's principal publication, *Homosexual Citizen*, never exceeded four hundred; see Rodger Streitmatter, *Unspeakable: The Rise of the Gay and Lesbian Press in America* (Boston: Faber & Faber, 1995), 60.

26. Robert and Ron to Fellow Members, January 10, 1963, FEK Papers.

27. Lilli Vincenz to Dick Leitsch, January 8, 1965, Vincenz Papers; "Elect Robert K. for President," n.d., FEK Papers.

28. On Kameny's speech to the Janus Society, see Stein, *City of Sisterly and Brotherly Loves*, 230; Kameny New York speech reprinted in *New York Mattachine Newsletter*, January 1965; Hodges to Kameny, December 14, 1965, Mattachine NY folder, FEK Papers.

29. Frank Kameny to Dick Leitsch, December 26, 1965, and Dick Leitsch to Lilli Vincenz, December 28, 1964, both in FEK Papers.

30. On the Kennedy presidential order, see Cynthia E. Harrison, "A 'New Frontier' for Women: The Public Policy of the Kennedy Administration," *Journal of American History* 67 (December 1980): 641–42; Macy and African American employment statistics quoted in *Washington Evening Star*, November 4, 1965, A-2; on Johnson administration programs and the effort to hire the handicapped, see Donald R. Harvey, *The Civil Service Commission* (New York: Praeger, 1970), 110–19, 171. See also Samuel Krislov, *The Negro in Federal Employment: The Quest for Equal Opportunity* (Minneapolis: University of Minnesota Press, 1967).

31. *Federal Personnel Manual, Supplement* (Int.) 731–71, Instruction 6, December 1964, 32–34. See also James Ridgeway, "The Snoops: Private Lives and Public Service," *New Republic*, December 19, 1964, 13–17; *New York Times*, June 4, 1965, and September 15, 1967; *Washington Post*, September 3, 1967, A-27.

32. Questioning of Cuban refugees reported in *New York Mattachine Newsletter*, May 1961, quoting *Time*, April 28, 1961; Job Corps exclusion reported in *New York Times*, November 21, 1964, 30; Fritz Fischer, *Making Them Like Us: Peace Corps Volunteers in the 1960s* (Washington, DC: Smithsonian Institution Press, 1998), 71–76, 96–100. The federal application form was not changed until January 1969; see William Parker, *Homosexuals and Employment*, Essays on Homosexuality, no. 4 (San Francisco: Corinthian Foundation, 1970), 11.

33. The State Department separated sixteen employees for homosexuality in 1960, twenty-four in 1961, twenty-four in 1962, and forty-five in 1963; see U.S. Congress, Senate, Committee on the Judiciary, Subcommittee to Investigate the Administration of the Internal Security Act and Other Internal Security Laws, *State Department Security—1963–1965, The Otepka Case—7*, 89th Cong., 1st sess., 1965, 534; 1965 State Department statistics quoted from U.S. Congress, House, Committee on Appropriations, *State Department Appropriations*, 89th Cong., 2nd sess., 1966; Crockett quoted in *Washington Post*, September 21 1966, A-7.

34. Johnson quoted in Conversation 5888 with Abe Fortas, October 15, 1964, LBJ White House Tapes; see also Michael Beschloss, *Taking Charge: The Johnson White House Tapes, 1963–1964* (New York: Touchstone Books, 1998), 526–38. Circumstances of previous arrest noted in *Los Angeles Times*, October 18, 1964. The Jenkins affair generated hundreds of newspaper stories and has been the subject of numerous historical essays. One of the best contemporary overviews is "The Senior Staff Man," *Time*, October 23, 1964, 19–25. One of the best historical treatments by a cultural theorist is Lee Edelmen, "Tearooms and Sympathy, or the Epistemology of the Water Closet," in *The Lesbian and Gay Studies Reader*, ed. Henry Abelove, Michele Aina Barale, and David Halperin, 553–74 (New York: Routledge, 1993); see also Al Weisel, "LBJ's Gay Sex Scandal," *Out*, December 1999, 76–83; Vance Musto, "LBJ'S Greatest Loss," *George*, May 1999, 92–104.

35. Goldwater quoted in *Los Angeles Times*, October 16, 1964; Republican committee chair quoted in *Washington Post*, October 18, 1964; Miller quoted in *Washington Star*, October 16 and 18, 1964; tabloid quoted is Glenn Kenmore, "Washington's Growing Homosexual Menace," *Lowdown*, March 19, 1965, 19; Johnson quoted from Conversation 5886 with Clark Clifford and Abe Fortas, October 14, 1964, LBJ White House Tapes; Max Lerner, "Cause Celebre," unnamed newspaper, October 26, 1964, "Homosexuals in Civil Service" vertical files, Kinsey Institute.

36. Gay man quoted in Beemyn, "Queer Capital," (Ph.D. diss., University of Iowa, 1997), 168. For right-wing interpretations, see Reginald Dunsany, "Final Solutions to the Assassination Question," *Realist*, April 1968, 1; Frederick Seelig, *Destroy the Accused*, with a foreword by Westbrook Pegler (Miami: Freedom Press, 1967), 5–22, 153–59. Seelig provides a sensationalist history of homosexual influence in Washington since the Franklin Roosevelt administration. The dust jacket features an endorsement by Congressman John Dowdy.

37. *New York Times*, April 16, 1965, 2.

38. Clarke and Nichols, *I Have More Fun with You Than Anybody*, 4; Jack Nichols, "The Calamus Chronicles," *Weekly News (Miami)*, November 4, 1992; interview with Frank Kameny, January 26, 1992; Frank Kameny, undated, untitled speech ("I am speaking to you on a controversial subject—picketing."), FEK Papers; *Insider*, April 1965; "10 Oppose Gov't on Homosexuals," *Washington Afro-American*, April 20, 1965. See also *Washington Afro-American*, June 15, 1963; on African American press coverage of gay issues, see George Chauncey, *Gay New York: Gender, Urban Culture, and the Making of a Gay Male World, 1890–1940* (New York: Basic Books, 1994), 7, 10.

39. Kameny and other picketer quoted in Kameny, undated, untitled speech, FEK Papers. The Franklin E. Kameny Papers contain press releases and after-action "information bulletins" on each 1965 picket after the first one in April: The White House (May 29), the Civil Service Commission (June 26), the Pentagon (July 31), the State Department (August 28), and the White House (October 23). On press coverage of the pickets, see *Washington Star*, May 30, 1965; *New York Times*, May 30, 1965; *Washington Post*, August 29, 1965; Oscar Marlowe, "The Day They Picketed the White House," *Confidential*, October 1965; Alwood, *Straight News*, 54. The MSW discussed picketing nongovernmental institutions, such as the *Washington Post*, which refused to print its advertisements, but did not because representatives of the *Post* agreed to a meeting. See Committee on Picketing and Other Lawful Demonstrations, Minutes, December 12, 1965, FEK Papers.

40. "Why Are Homosexuals Picketing the U.S. Civil Service Commission?" n.d., FEK Papers; see also Franklin E. Kameny, "On Picketing," *Eastern Mattachine Magazine*, July 1965, 20–21; Franklin E. Kameny "White House Picketed," *Homosexual Citizen*, January 1966, 12–13.

41. See, for example, MSW to the president, October 23, 1965, FEK Papers; the MSW began publishing *The Homosexual Citizen* in January 1966.

42. MSW, Committee on Picketing and Other Lawful Demonstrations, "Regulations for Picketing," FEK Papers; "Picketing: The Impact and the Issue," *The Ladder*, September 1965, 4. On the controversy in the homophile movement over picketing dress codes, see Martin Duberman, *Stonewall* (New York: Dutton, 1993), 111.

43. Franklin E. Kameny, "On Picketing," *Eastern Mattachine Magazine*, July 1965, 20–21; Stein, *City of Sisterly and Brotherly Loves*, 273, 291–95.

44. Alwood, *Straight News*, 12–13; interview with Ramon G. and "Patrick W.," February 10, 1997; interview with P. A. and L. D., February 4, 1997.

45. *Scott v. Macy et al.*, 349 F. 2d 182 (D.C., 1965); *Washington Post*, June 17, 1965, A-3; gay observer quoted in *Vector*, January, 1966, 4; gay activist quoted in Don Slater to Bruce Scott, June 17, 1965, "Scott v. Macy" folder, Box 29, Gregory Sprague Collection, CHS; "Federal Jericho" from "Scott vs. Macy," *Drum*, September 1965, 26. See also "The Charge of Immorality," *New Republic*, July 3, 1965, 6–7.

46. The *Scott v. Macy* decision is discussed in many law journal articles on federal employment policies and gay rights. See William N. Eskridge Jr., "Privacy Jurisprudence and the Apartheid of the Closet," *Florida State University Law Review* 24 (1997); Irving Kovarsky, "Fair Employment for the Homosexual," *Washington University Law Quarterly* (1971): 527–81; Elaine Davis, "Homosexuals in Government Employ: Boys in the Bureau," *Seaton Hall Law Review* 3 (1971): 89–107; "Government-Created Employment Disabilities of the Homosexual," *Harvard Law Review* 82 (1969): 1738-51; "Government Employment and the Homosexual," *St. John's Law Review* 45 (1970): 303–23.

47. Kameny to Scott, December 16, 1965, FEK Papers; Johnson quoted in interview with Frank Kameny, January 26, 1992, 101–3; interview with Lilli Vincenz, June 2, 1992; background on Johnson from "Chairman's Briefing Book," November 1968, Box 12, Murphy, Aides Files, LBJ Library.

48. John W. Macy Jr. to the Mattachine Society of Washington, February 25, 1966, reprinted in *Government Employees' Exchange*, April 20, 1966; Macy letter reported in *Washington Evening Star*, April 20, 1966, A-16; interview with Kimbell Johnson, January 23, 1969, quoted in "Government-Created Employment Disabilities of the Homosexual," *Harvard Law Review* 82 (1969): 1741. Johnson was also interviewed by Philip Shander, *Washington Star*, August 18, 1970. For an overview of Macy's career, see Frank Sherwood, "The Legacy of John W. Macy Jr.," *Public Administration Review* (May/June 1987): 221–26.

49. *Singer v. U.S. Civil Service Commission*, 530 F. 2d 247 (9th Cir., 1976); Rhonda R. Rivera, "Our Straight-Laced Judges: the Legal Position of Homosexual Persons in The United States," *Hastings Law Journal* 30 (March 1979): 1040–43; John E. B. Myers, "*Singer v. U.S. CSC*—Dismissal of Government Employee for Advocacy of

Homosexuality," *Utah Law Review* (1976): 172–85; "High Hypocrisy," *Advocate*, January 31, 1973.

50. *Scott v. Macy*, 402 F. 2d 644 (D.C., 1968); *Washington Post*, May 29, 1966.

51. Footage of the press conference appears in the documentary film *Before Stonewall* (dir. Greta Schiller, 1984). See also *Washington Post*, August 29, 1965, A-27; "Rusk Probed on Picketing," *The Ladder*, October 1965, 18; MSW News Release, "Homosexuals to Picket State Department," August 26, 1965, and MSW Information Bulletin, August 28, 1965, FEK Papers.

52. Reporter, Kameny, and Defense Department quoted in *Wall Street Journal*, July 17, 1968; "national hero" quoted in Franklin Kameny to Edward Sagarin, March 27, 1968, Cory folder, FEK collection. See also *New York Times*, November 26, 1967; Tom Wicker, "The Undeclared Witch-Hunt," *Harper's*, November 1969, 108–10; Kathleen Graham, "Security Clearances for Homosexuals," *Stanford Law Review* 25 (1973): 403–29. Bennington eventually won the right to retain his security clearance; see *Washington Post*, May 27, 1972; *New York Times*, June 27, 1972; *Gayer, Ulrich, and Wentworth v. Schlesinger*, 490 F. 2d 740 (1973).

53. "MSW Wins Civil Service Case," *Insider*, September 1968, FEK Collection.

54. U.S. Civil Service Commission, *1968 Annual Report*, 84–85; *New York Times*, January 7, 1967, 1.

55. *Norton v. Macy*, 417 F. 2d 1161 (D.C. Cir., 1969); see also *Washington Post*, July 2, 1969, A-10, and July 5, 1969, A-16; "Dismissal of Homosexuals from Government Employment," *Georgetown Law Journal* 58 (1970): 632–45; "Federal Employment of Homosexuals: Narrowing the Efficiency Standard," *Catholic University Law Review* 19 (1969): 267–75. Bazelon, a Truman appointee, served on the National Institute of Mental Health Task Force on Homosexuality. He resigned from the task force on June 3, 1969, one month before the *Norton* decision. See National Institute of Mental Health Task Force on Homosexuality, *Final Report and Background Papers* (Washington, DC: Department of Health, Education, and Welfare, 1969).

56. Frank Kameny, "Gay Cases 1: Employment by Government," June 28, 1974, FEK Papers; Jim Kepner, "Can't Fire Gay Just Because He's Gay, Court Tells CSC," *Advocate*, September 1969, 4.

Epilogue

1. *Schlegel v. United States*, 416 F. 2d 1372 (1969); "Statement of Kimbell Johnson before the Committee on Internal Security of the U.S. House of Representatives," September 30, 1970, CSC Library. For another decision favorable to the CSC, see *Anonymous v. Macy*, 398 F. 2d 317 (1968).

2. Guenter Lewy, *The Federal Loyalty-Security Program: The Need For Reform* (Washington, DC: American Enterprise Institute, 1983), 38–39; *Mindel v. Civil Service Commission*, 312 F. Supp. 485 (N.D. Calif., 1970).

3. *Society for Individual Rights et al. v. Hampton*, 528 F. 2d 905 (N.D. Calif., 1973). See also *San Francisco Examiner*, November 9, 1973, 60; George Mendenhall, "Federal Judge Orders U.S. to End Hiring Ban," *Advocate*, December 5, 1973, 3.

4. U.S. Civil Service Commission, Bulletin no. 731–32, December 3, 1973; U.S. Civil Service Commission, Press Release, December 3, 1973, and July 3, 1975; Kameny quoted in Kay Tobin and Randy Wicker, *The Gay Crusaders* (New York: Paperback Library, 1972), 106; *New York Times*, July 16, 1975. See also Gary R. Siniscalco, "Homosexual Discrimination in Employment," *Santa Clara Law Review* 16 (1976): 495; interview with Frank Kameny, January 1992. Also in 1975, the Department of Defense conceded defeat in a pivotal security clearance case, signaling an end to blanket exclusion of gays and lesbians from holding security clearances. In agencies such as the FBI, CIA, and NSA, the security clearance issue would linger. See Marion Halliday Lewis, "Unacceptable Risk or Unacceptable Rhetoric? An Argument for a Quasi-Suspect Classification for Gays Based on Current Government Security Clearance Procedures," *Journal of Law and Politics* 7 (1990): 133–76. For a personal account of one gay man ousted from the FBI in the 1980s, see Frank Buttino, with Lou Buttino, *A Special Agent: Gay and Inside the FBI* (New York: William Morrow, 1993).

5. Clark Polak, "What Organized Homosexuals Want," *Sexology* 33, no. 6 (January 1967): 378–80; *New York Mattachine Newsletter*, November 1968; Jim Foster quoted in Randy Shilts, *Conduct Unbecoming: Gays and Lesbians in the U.S. Military* (New York: St. Martin's Press, 1993), 169.

6. D'Emilio, *Sexual Politics, Sexual Communities*, 238; Marc Stein, "'Birthplace of the Nation': Imagining Lesbian and Gay Communities in Philadelphia, 1969–1970," in *Creating a Place for Ourselves: Lesbian, Gay and Bisexual Community Histories*, ed. Brett Beemyn (New York: Routledge, 1997), 264.

7. *Chicago Sun-Times Midwest Magazine*, December 14, 1969; "The Homosexual: Newly Visible, Newly Understood," *Time*, October 31, 1969, 56; "The Militant Homosexual," *Newsweek*, August 23, 1971, 45.

8. *New York Mattachine Newsletter*, November 1963, and January 1965.

9. Jim Marks, "Frank Kameny: Tribute to a Pioneer," *Pride Guide '81, Washington Blade*, June 19, 1981 15; see also Tobin and Wicker, *Gay Crusaders*, 205–24.

10. Dick Leitsch to Frank Kameny, May 27, 1966, FEK Papers; Steve Endean, *Into the Mainstream: A First Hand Account of Twenty Years' Progress on Lesbian/Gay Rights*, unpublished, unpaginated memoir, 1993; Dudley Clendinen and Adam Nagourney, *Out for Good: The Struggle to Build a Gay Rights Movement in America* (New York: Simon & Schuster, 1999), 114.

11. Interview with Frank Kameny, September 12, 1991; *Advocate*, March 17–30, 1971, 1; *Washington Post*, March 13, 1971; Lorena Dumas, "The Sexual Orientation Clause of the District of Columbia Human Rights Act," *Law and Sexuality* 1 (summer 1991): 267–83.

12. Larry Van Dyne, "Is Washington Becoming the Gay Capital of America?" *Washingtonian*, September 1980, 96–101; Donia Mills, "Washington Called the Gay Capital," *Washington Star*, October 30, 1977, A-1; Kameny quoted in Edmund White, *States of Desire: Travels in Gay America* (New York: E. P. Dutton, 1980), 329; see also Clendinen and Nagourney, *Out for Good*, 391–96.

Oral History Interviews

Note: All interviews were conducted by the author in Washington, D.C., unless otherwise noted.

"P. A.," January 15, 1997, and February 4, 1997
Chuck Bradshaw, March 13, 1997
Joan Cassidy, February 13 1997, Wheaton, MD
Bob Contillion, January 21, 1997
"L. D.," January 15, 1997, and February 4, 1997
"B. F.," August 27, 2001, telephone interview
Francis Flanagan, April 11, 1996, and February 21, 1997
Jack Frey, January 20, 1997
Ramon G., February 10, 1997
Phil Hannema, July 24, 2001, Chicago, IL
David Jenkins, August 5, 2001, Chicago, IL
Frank Kameny, October 10 and 19, 1991
Rae Beck Kameny, 1992, New York, NY
Edward Keller, June 20, 2000

Barbara S. Kraft, September 10, 1994

Raymond Mailloux, March 12, 1997

Murrey Marder, October 1996

Peter Morris, January 20, 1997

Jack Nichols, May 28, 1992, and July 15, 1994

Ted Richards, October 30, 1996

Jack Seymour, March 1997, Rockville, MD

Bruce Scott, April 21, 1994, and October 24, 1992, Chicago, IL

John Swanson, July 1992

Madeleine Tress, November 11, 1998, San Francisco, CA

Lilli Vincenz, July 15, 1992, Arlington, VA

"Patrick W.," February 10, 1997

Henry Yaffe, March 1997

Index